KOYOHARU GOTOUGE

I did it! I'm Gotouge. I got a positive review from Akimoto Sensei (author of *Kochikame*). My father also liked Akimoto Sensei, so I think he's pleased in his grave. I'm deeply moved. Thank you very much. For the most part, even if you work hard in life, it doesn't pay off. When it does pay off, I think a miracle is occurring. The current miracle is thanks to all of you. Thank you, everyone, thank you.

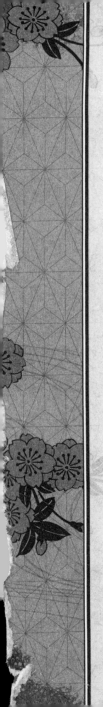

DEMON SLAYER: KIMETSU NO YAIBA VOLUME 5

Shonen Jump Edition

Story and Art by
KOYOHARU GOTOUGE

TRANSLATION John Werry
ENGLISH ADAPTATION Stan!
TOUCH-UP ART & LETTERING John Hunt
DESIGN Adam Grano
EDITOR Mike Montesa

Printed in Italy

Published by VIZ Media, LLC
P.O. Box 77010
San Francisco, CA 94107

10 9 8
First printing, March 2019
Eighth printing, May 2021

ratings.viz.com RATED T TEEN

PARENTAL ADVISORY
DEMON SLAYER: KIMETSU NO YAIBA is rated T for Teen and recommended for ages 13 and up. This volume contains realistic and fantasy violence.

VIZ MEDIA
viz.com

SHONEN JUMP

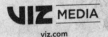

5

TO HELL

KIMETSU NO YAIBA

**KOYOHARU
GOTOUGE**

CHARACTERS

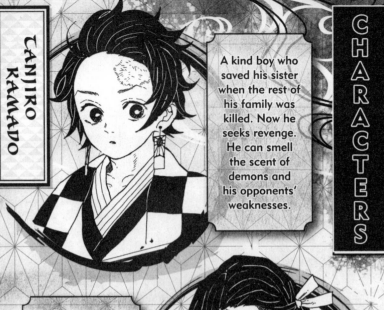

TANJIRO KAMADO

A kind boy who saved his sister when the rest of his family was killed. Now he seeks revenge. He can smell the scent of demons and his opponents' weaknesses.

NEZUKO KAMADO

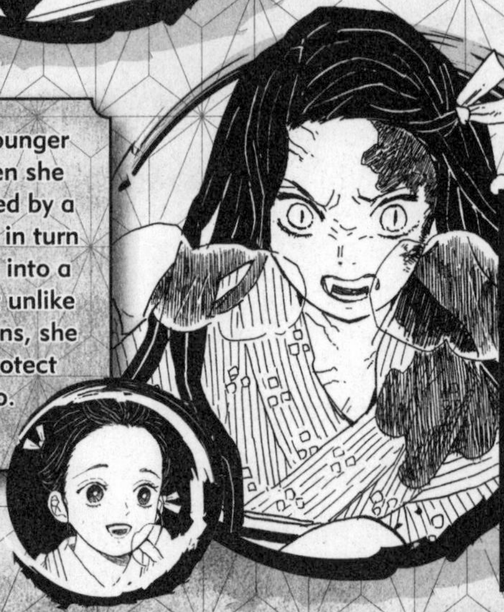

Tanjiro's younger sister. When she was attacked by a demon, she in turn was turned into a demon, but unlike other demons, she tries to protect Tanjiro.

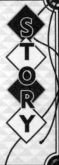

STORY

In Taisho-Era Japan, young Tanjiro makes a living selling charcoal. One day, demons kill his family and turn his younger sister Nezuko into a demon. Tanjiro and Nezuko set out to find a way to return Nezuko to human form and defeat Kibutsuji, the demon who killed their family!

Tanjiro reluctantly teams up with two other Demon Slayers—the cowardly Zenitsu Agama and the hotheaded Inosuke Hashibara—and they head for Mt. Natagumo to investigate the disappearance of many people in the area. After defeating a bizarre group of demons who call themselves a family, the monster they call Father attacks Tanjiro and Inosuke!

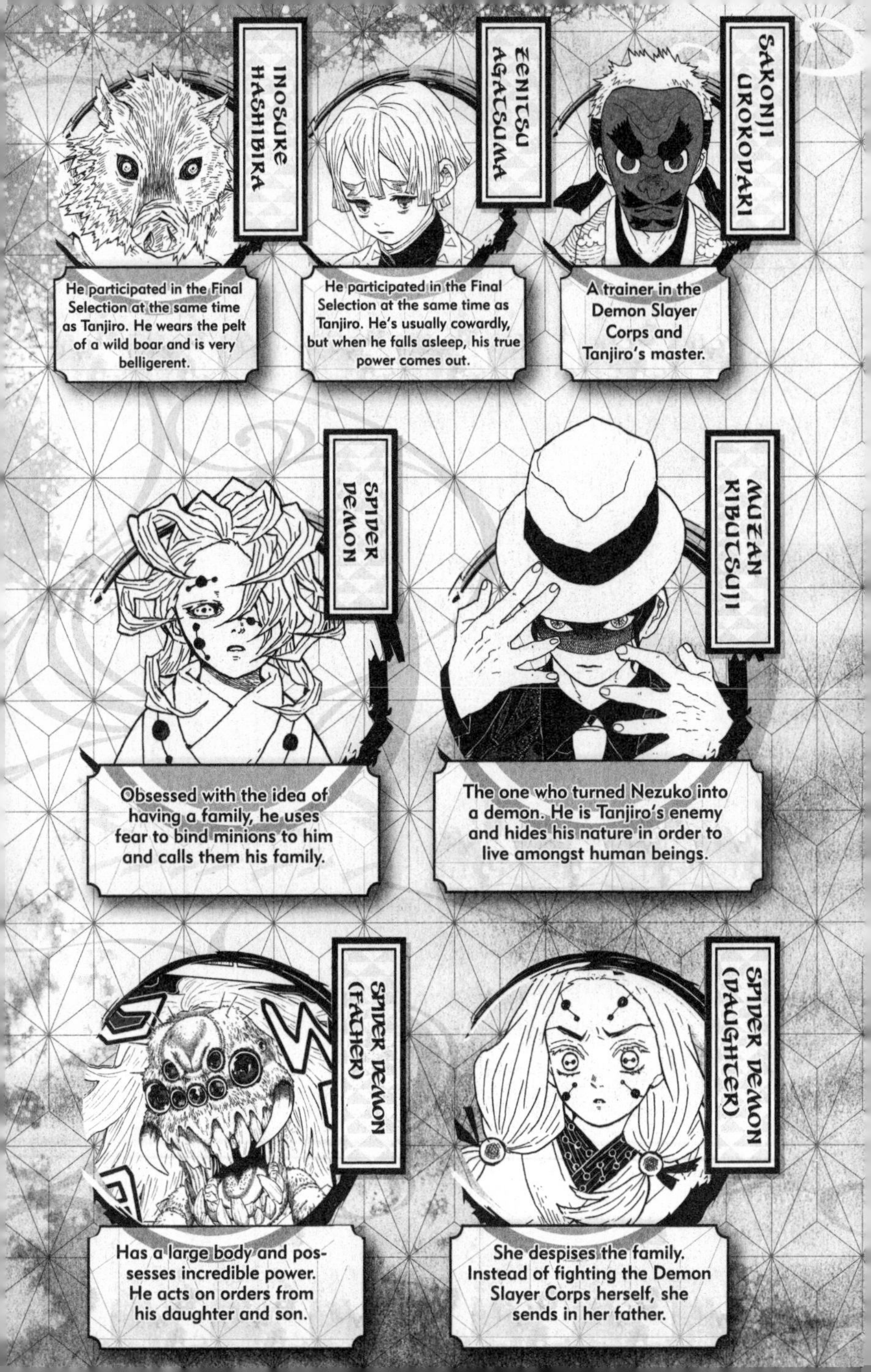
SAKONJI UROKODAKI
A trainer in the Demon Slayer Corps and Tanjiro's master.
ZENITSU AGATSUMA
He participated in the Final Selection at the same time as Tanjiro. He's usually cowardly, but when he falls asleep, his true power comes out.
INOSUKE HASHIBIRA
He participated in the Final Selection at the same time as Tanjiro. He wears the pelt of a wild boar and is very belligerent.
MUZAN KIBUTSUJI
The one who turned Nezuko into a demon. He is Tanjiro's enemy and hides his nature in order to live amongst human beings.
SPIDER DEMON
Obsessed with the idea of having a family, he uses fear to bind minions to him and calls them his family.
SPIDER DEMON (DAUGHTER)
She despises the family. Instead of fighting the Demon Slayer Corps herself, she sends in her father.
SPIDER DEMON (FATHER)
Has a large body and possesses incredible power. He acts on orders from his daughter and son.

CONTENTS

DEMON SLAYER

KIMETSU NO YAIBA

5

TO HELL

Chapter 35
SCATTERED
7

Chapter 36
THIS IS BAD!
27

Chapter 37
BROKEN BLADE
47

Chapter 38
REAL AND FAKE
67

Chapter 39
**LIFE PASSING
BEFORE ONE'S EYES**
87

Chapter 40
HINOKAMI
107

Chapter 41
SHINOBU KOCHO
127

Chapter 42
BEHIND
147

Chapter 43
TO HELL
169

CHAPTER 35: SCATTERED

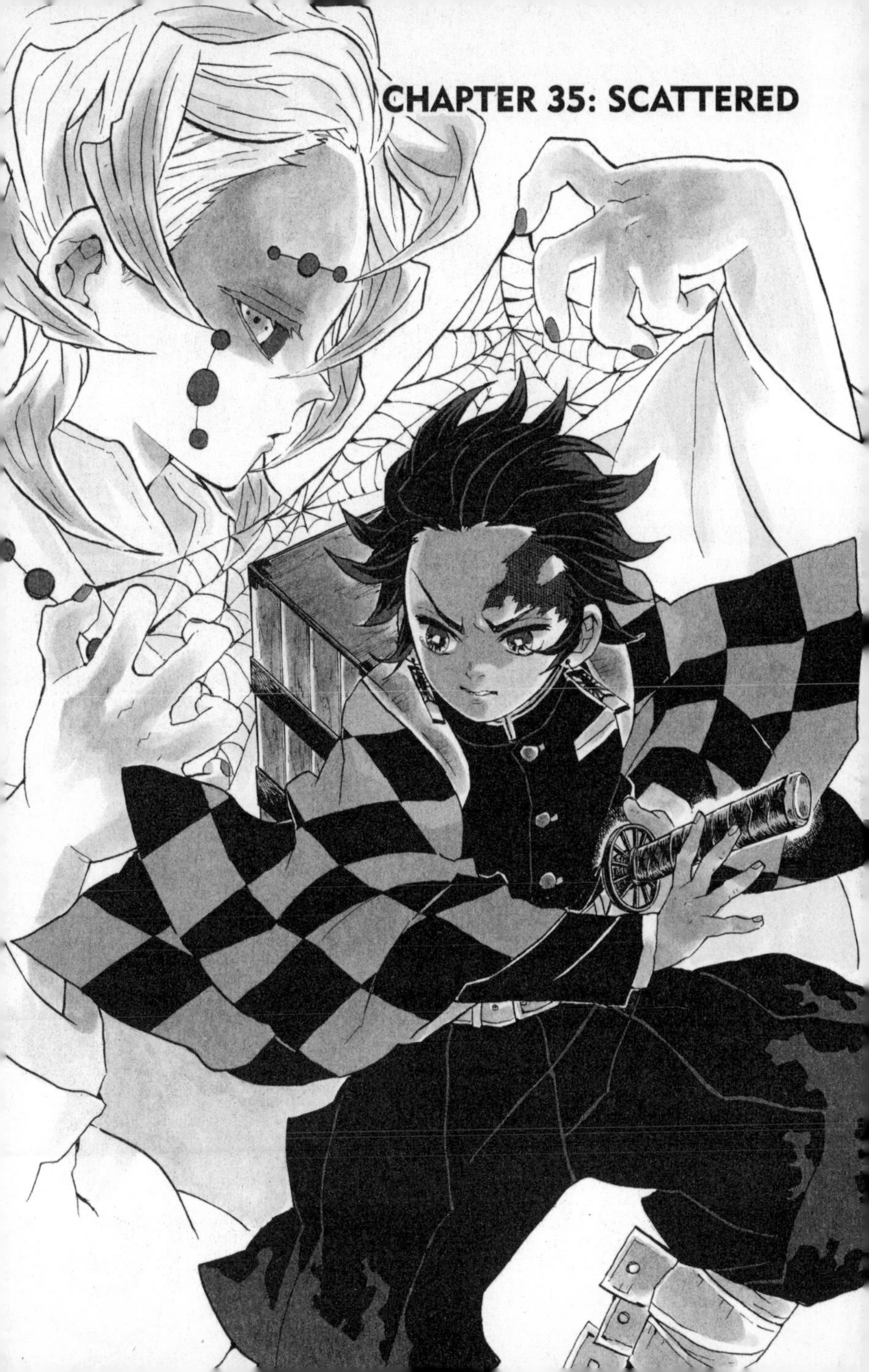

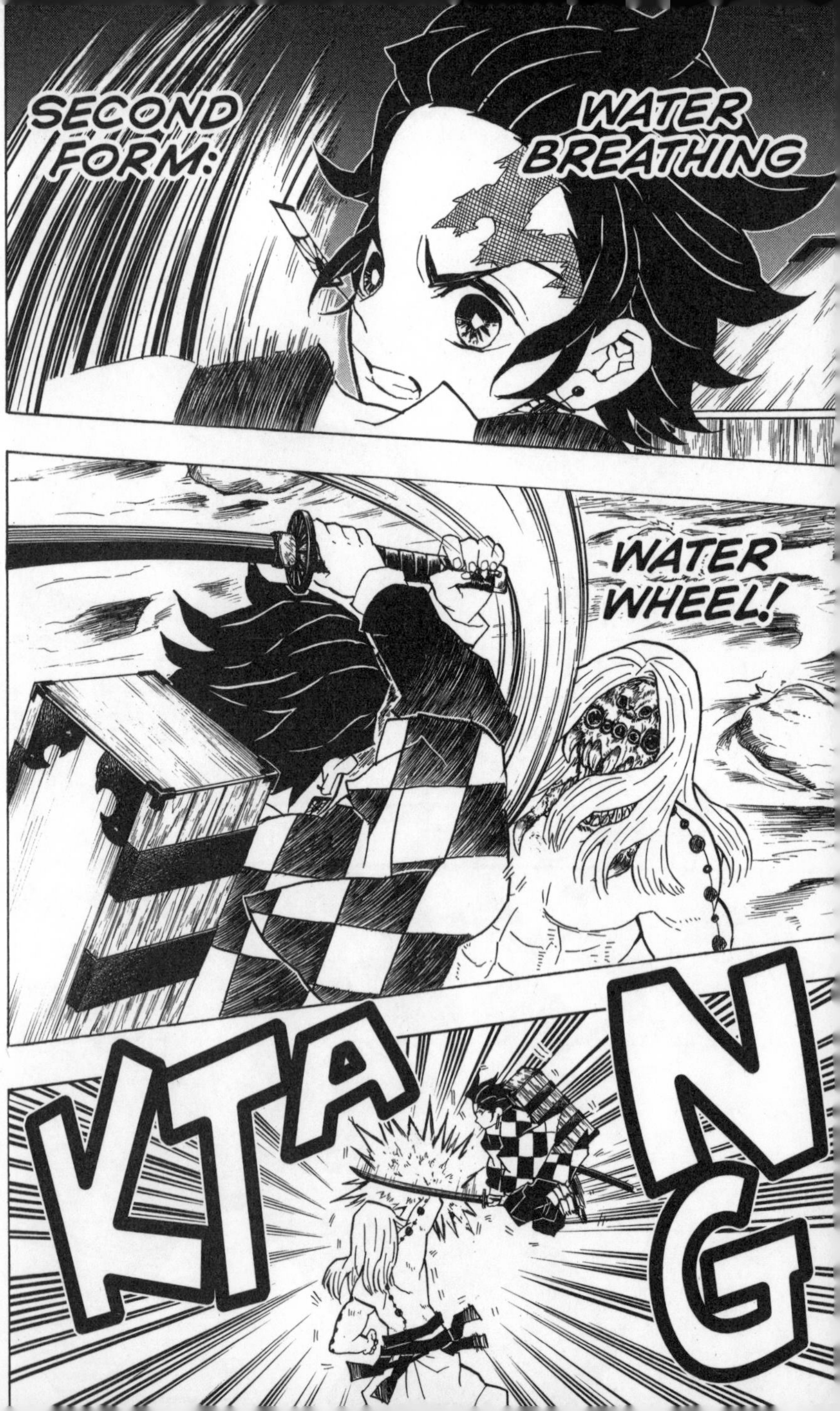
WATER BREATHING
SECOND FORM:
WATER WHEEL!
KTANG

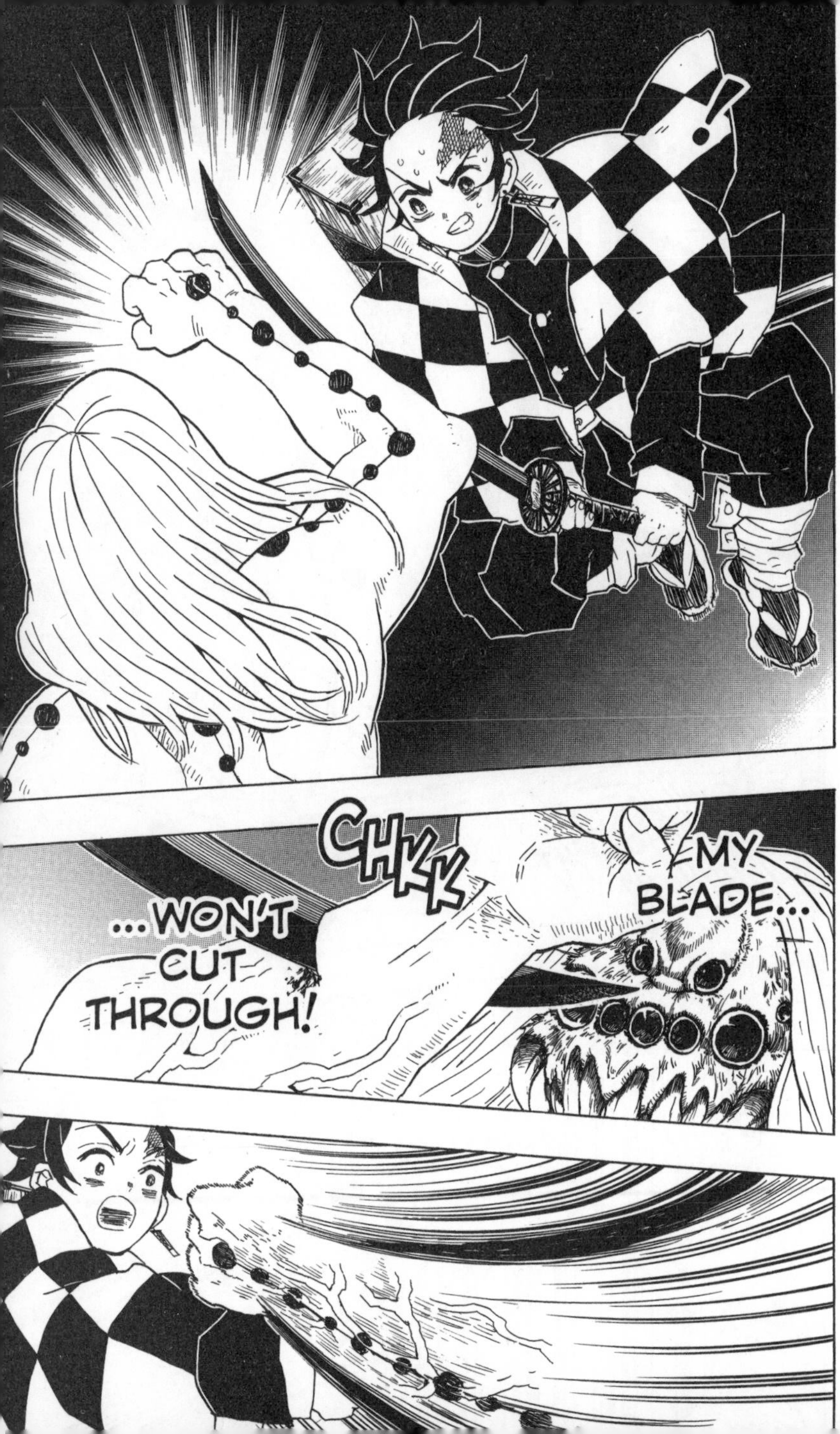
!
CHKK
MY BLADE...
...WON'T CUT THROUGH!

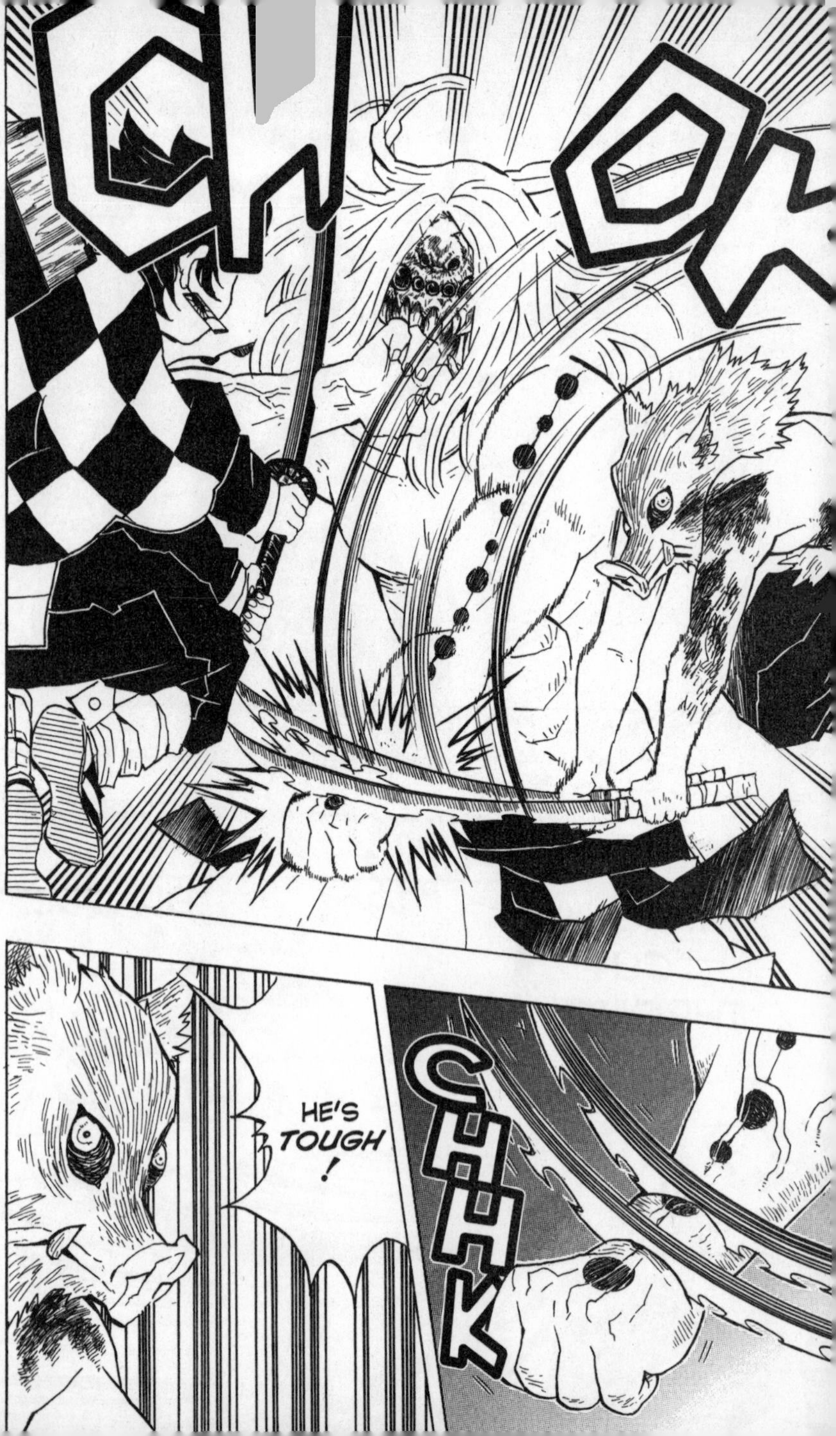
CHOK
CHHK
HE'S TOUGH!

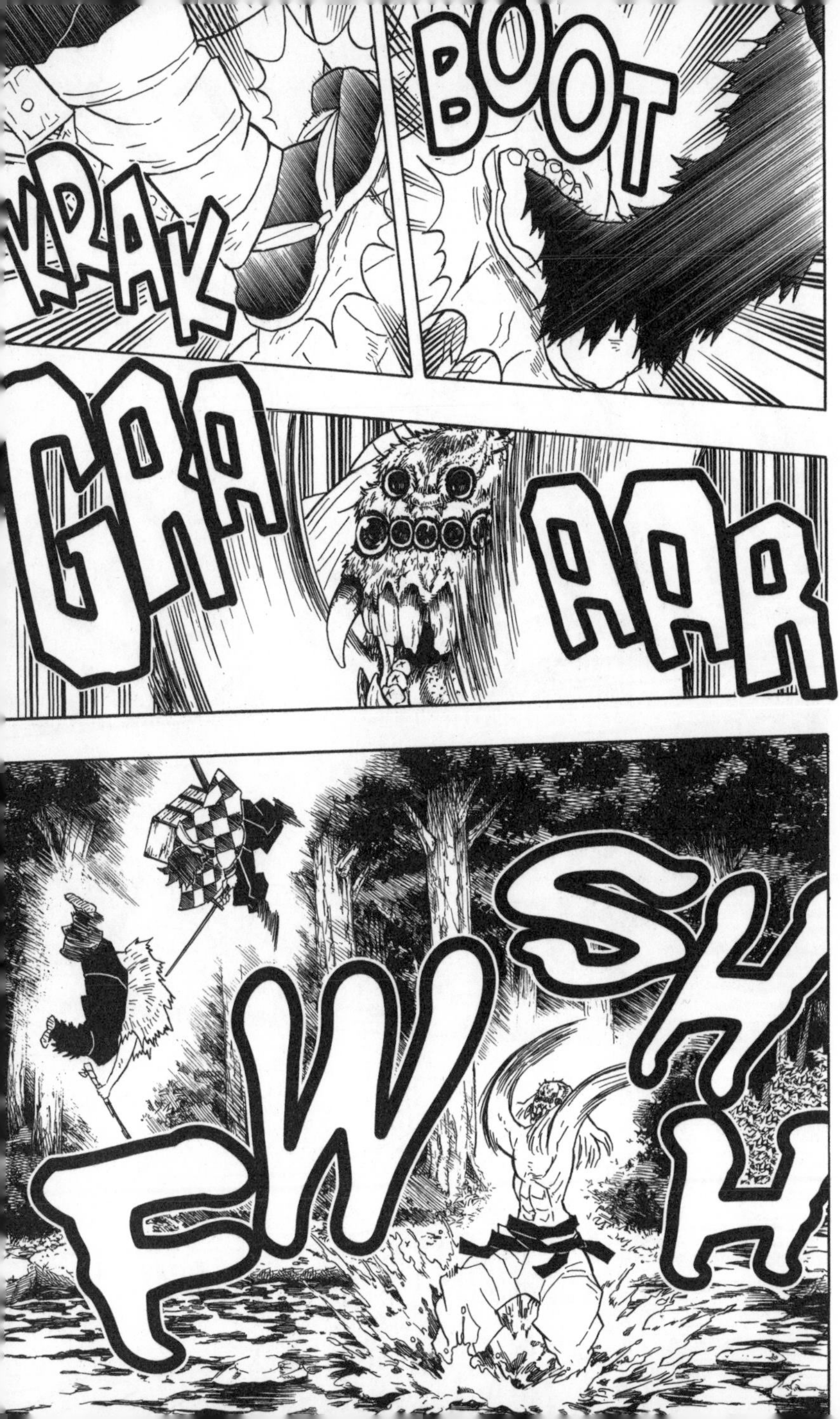
BOOT
KRAK
GRA
AAR
FW
SH
H

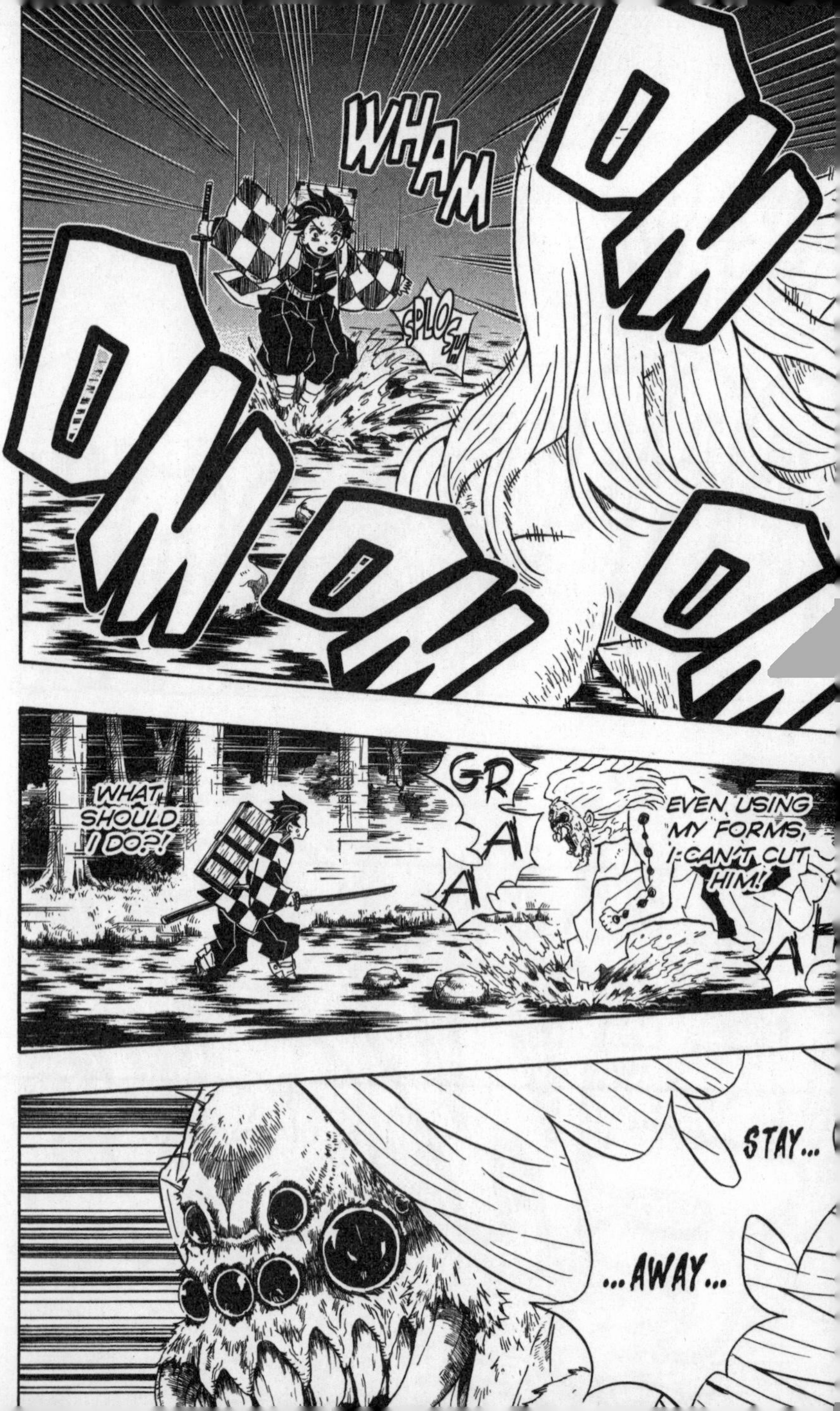
WHAM
SPLOSH
EVEN USING MY FORMS, I CAN'T CUT HIM!
GRAAA
WHAT SHOULD I DO?!
STAY...
...AWAY...

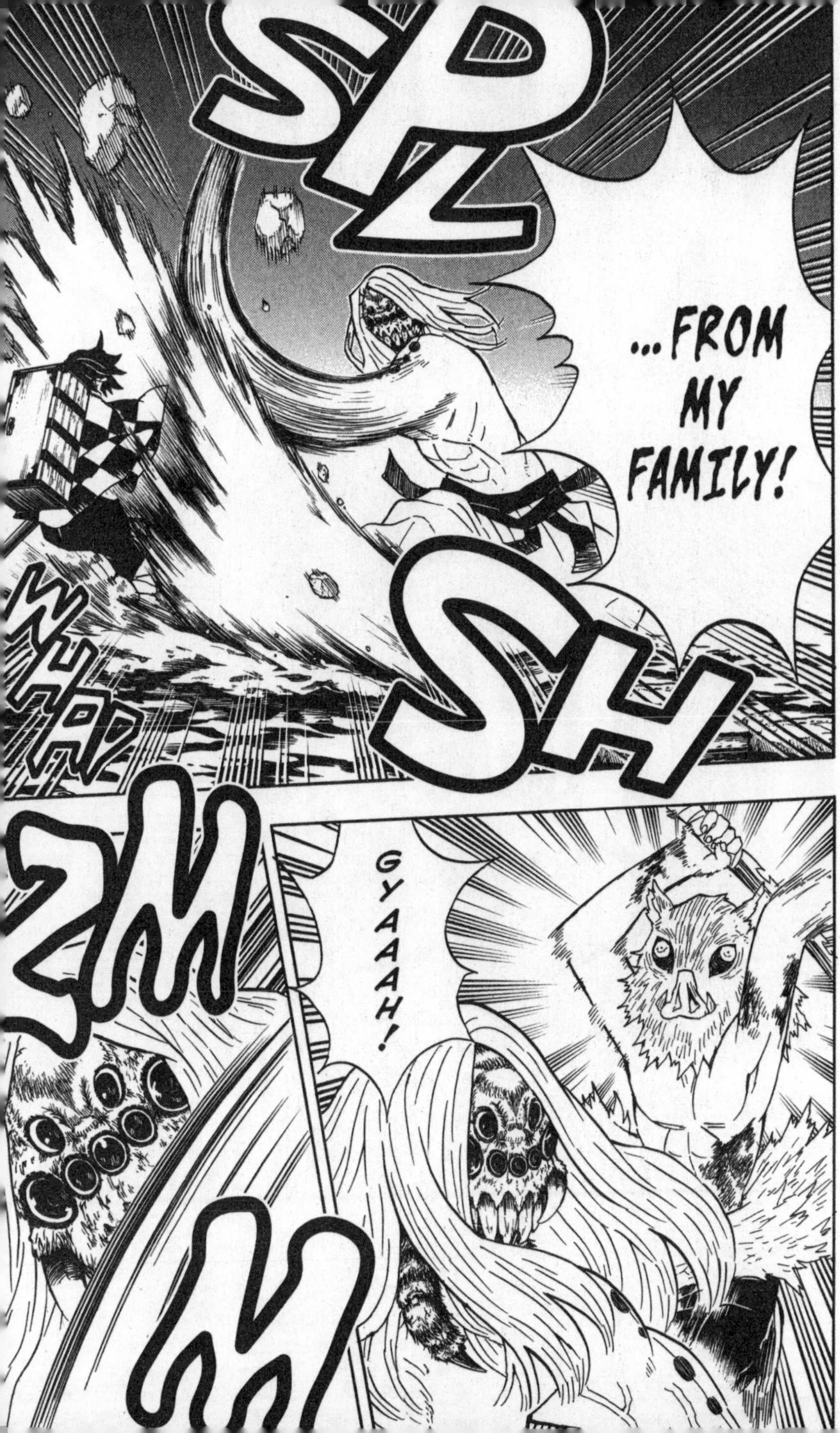
...FROM MY FAMILY!
SPL
SH
WHAP
GYAAAH!

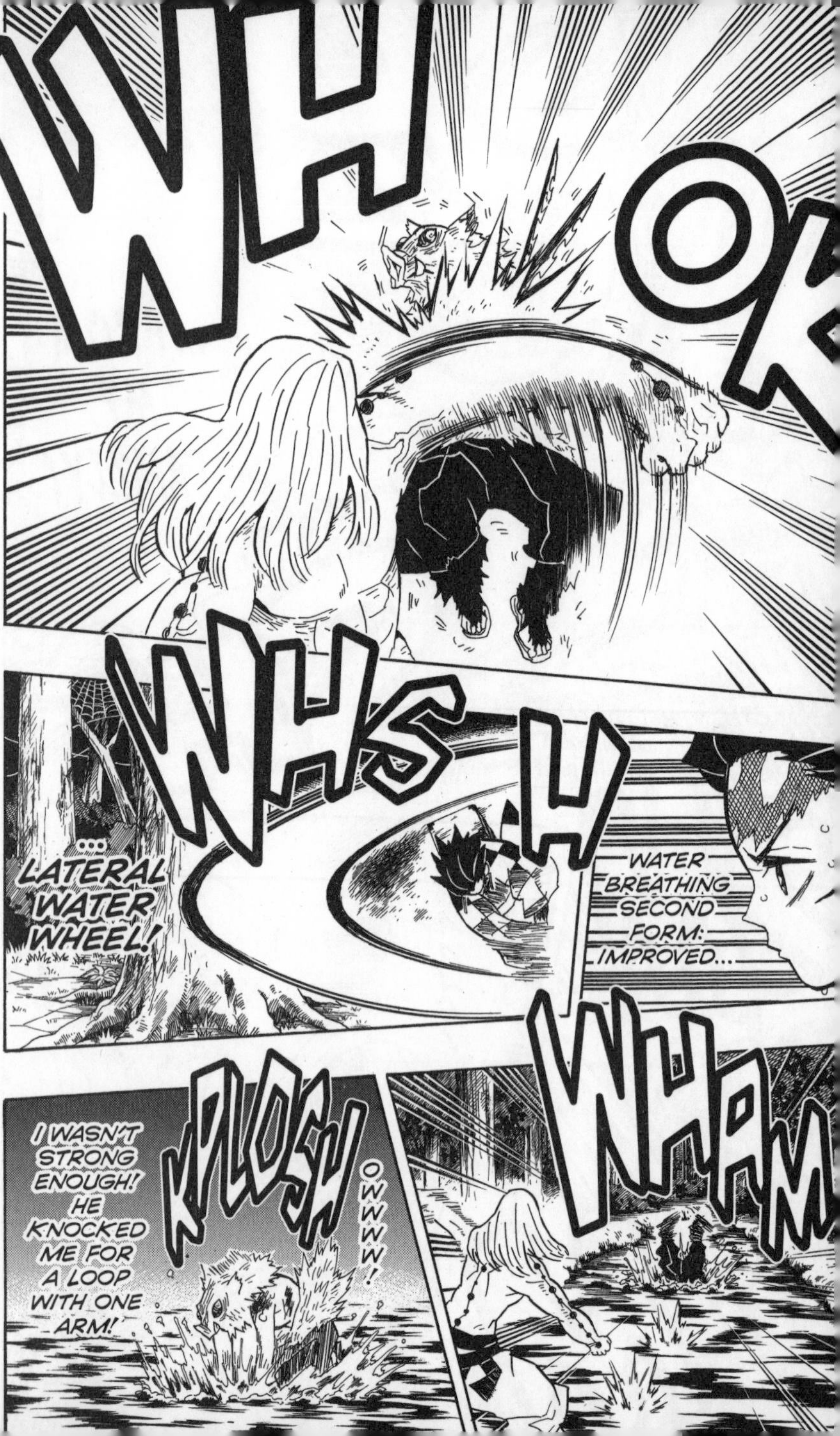
WHO
WHSH
WATER BREATHING SECOND FORM: IMPROVED...
...LATERAL WATER WHEEL!
WHAM
KPLOSH
OWWWW!
I WASN'T STRONG ENOUGH! HE KNOCKED ME FOR A LOOP WITH ONE ARM!

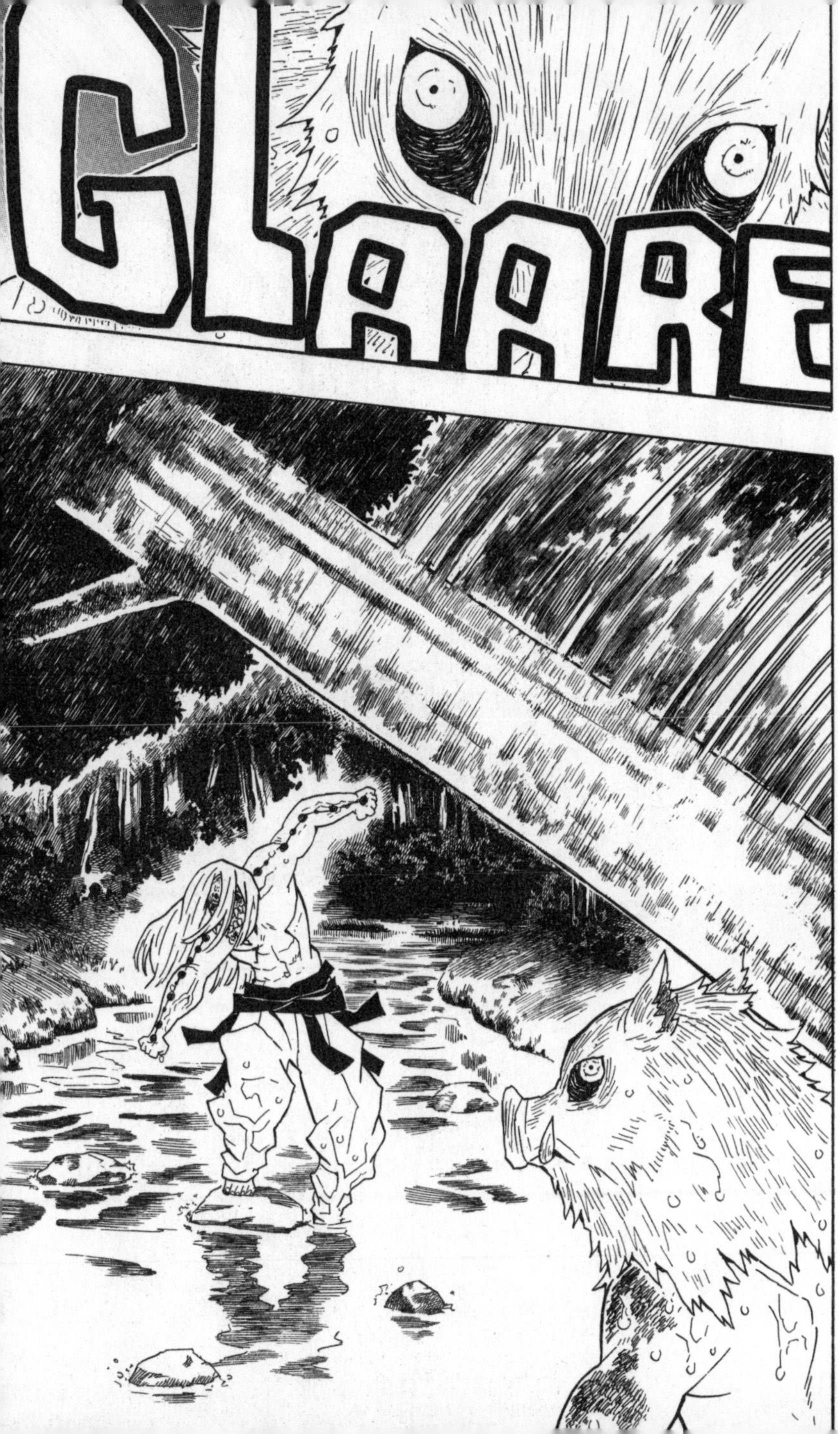
GLAARE

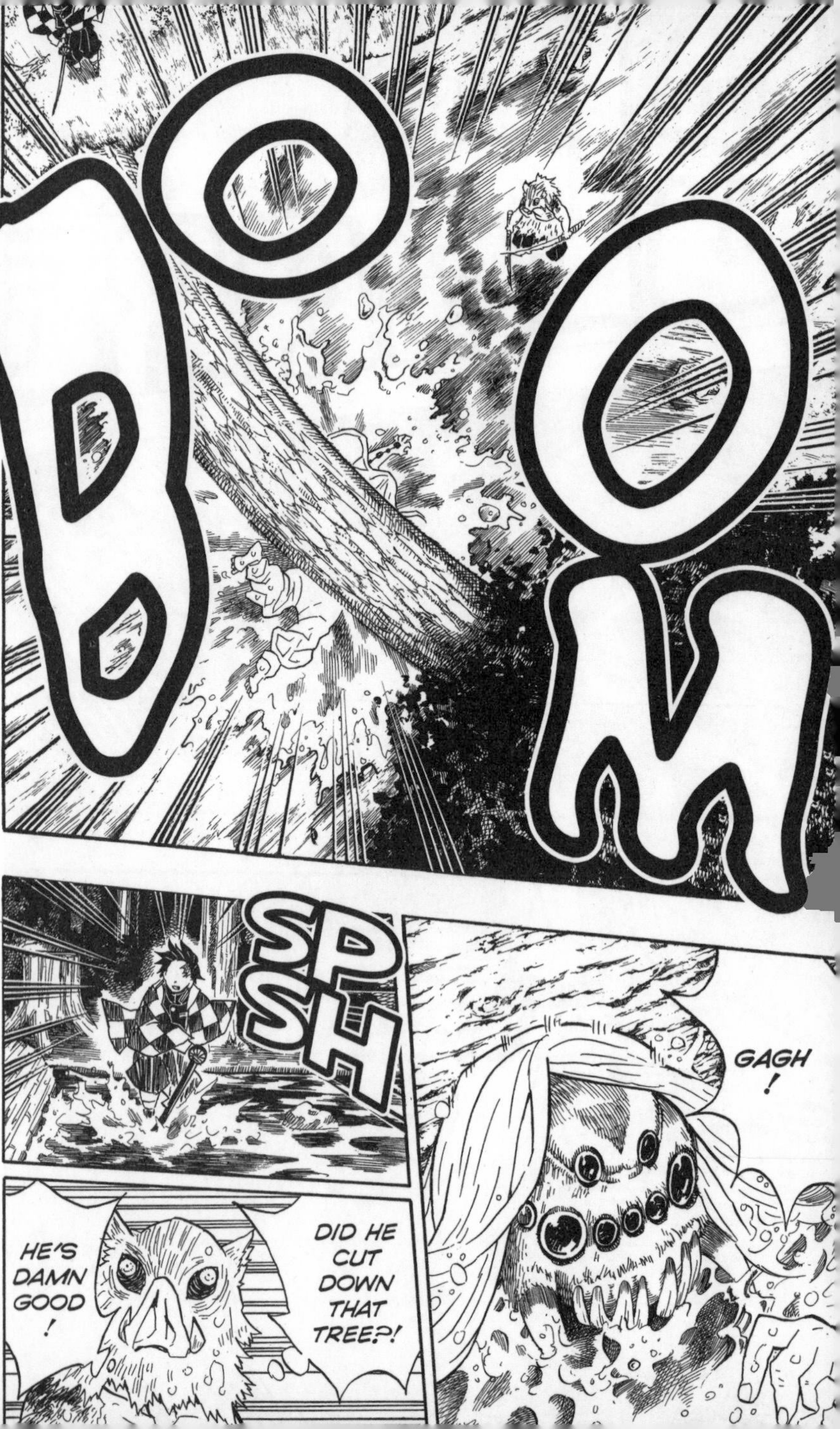
DOOM
GAGH!
SPSH
DID HE CUT DOWN THAT TREE?!
HE'S DAMN GOOD!

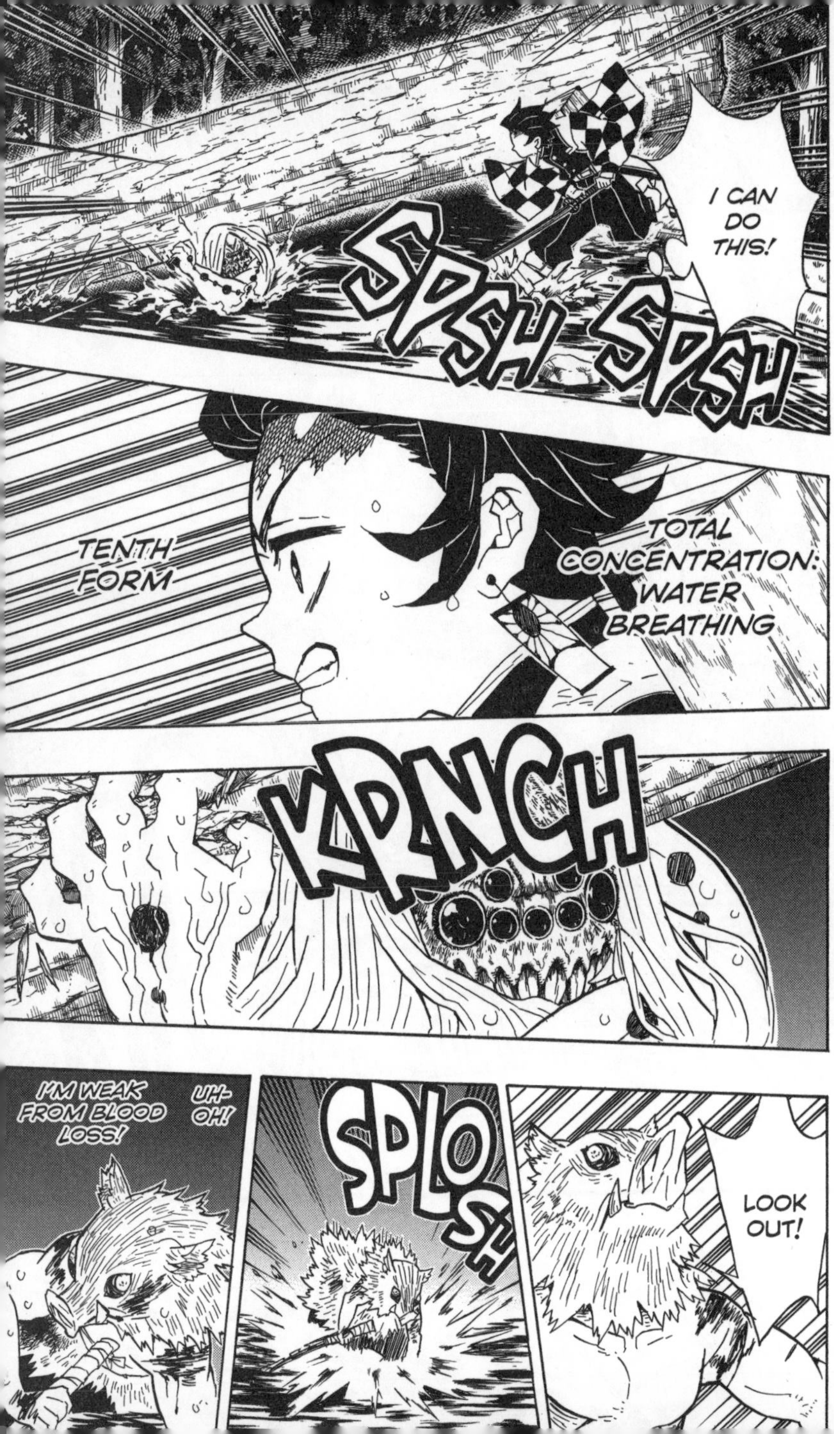
I CAN DO THIS!
SPSH SPSH
TOTAL CONCENTRATION: WATER BREATHING
TENTH FORM
KRNCH
LOOK OUT!
SPLOSH
UH-OH!
I'M WEAK FROM BLOOD LOSS!

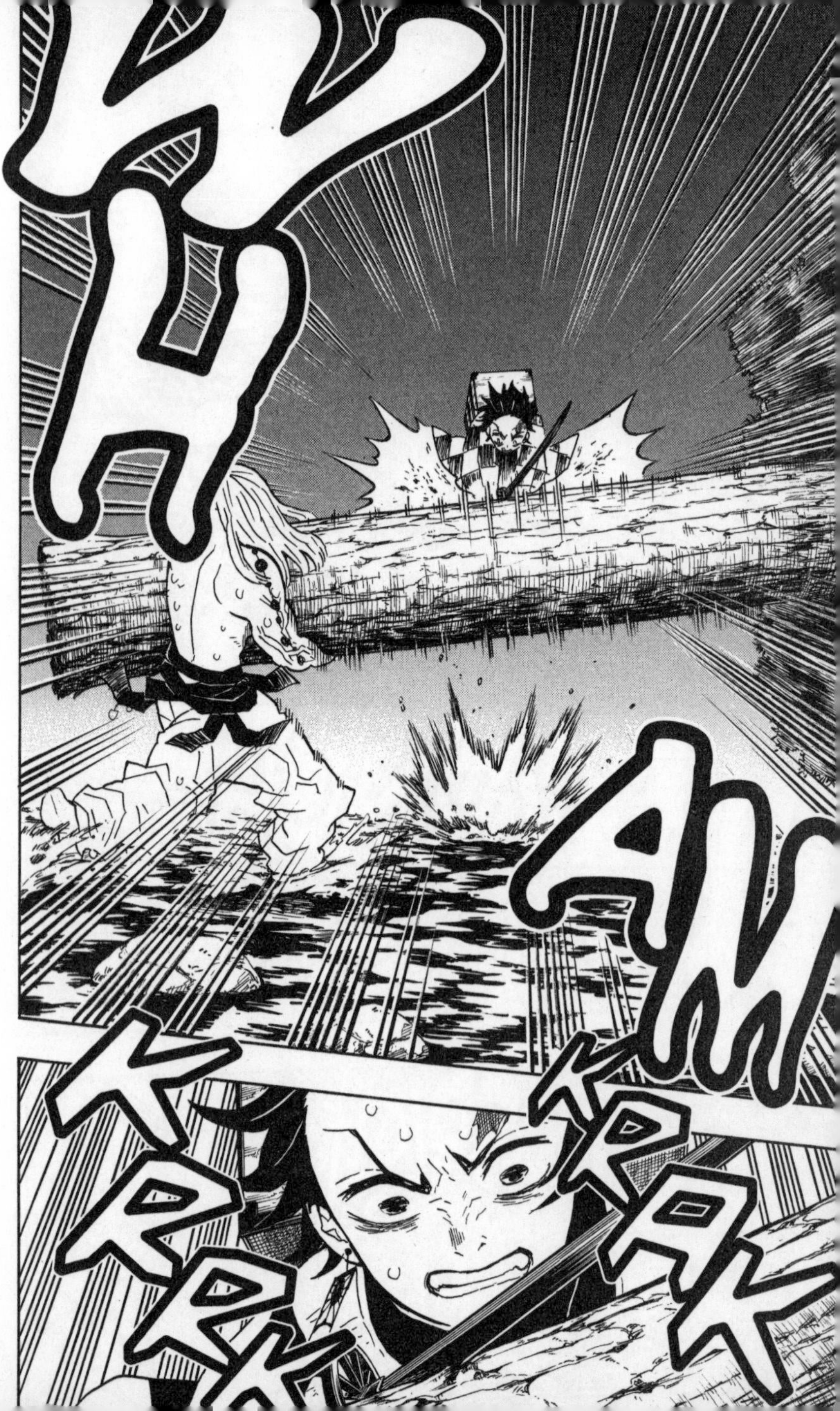
KRAK

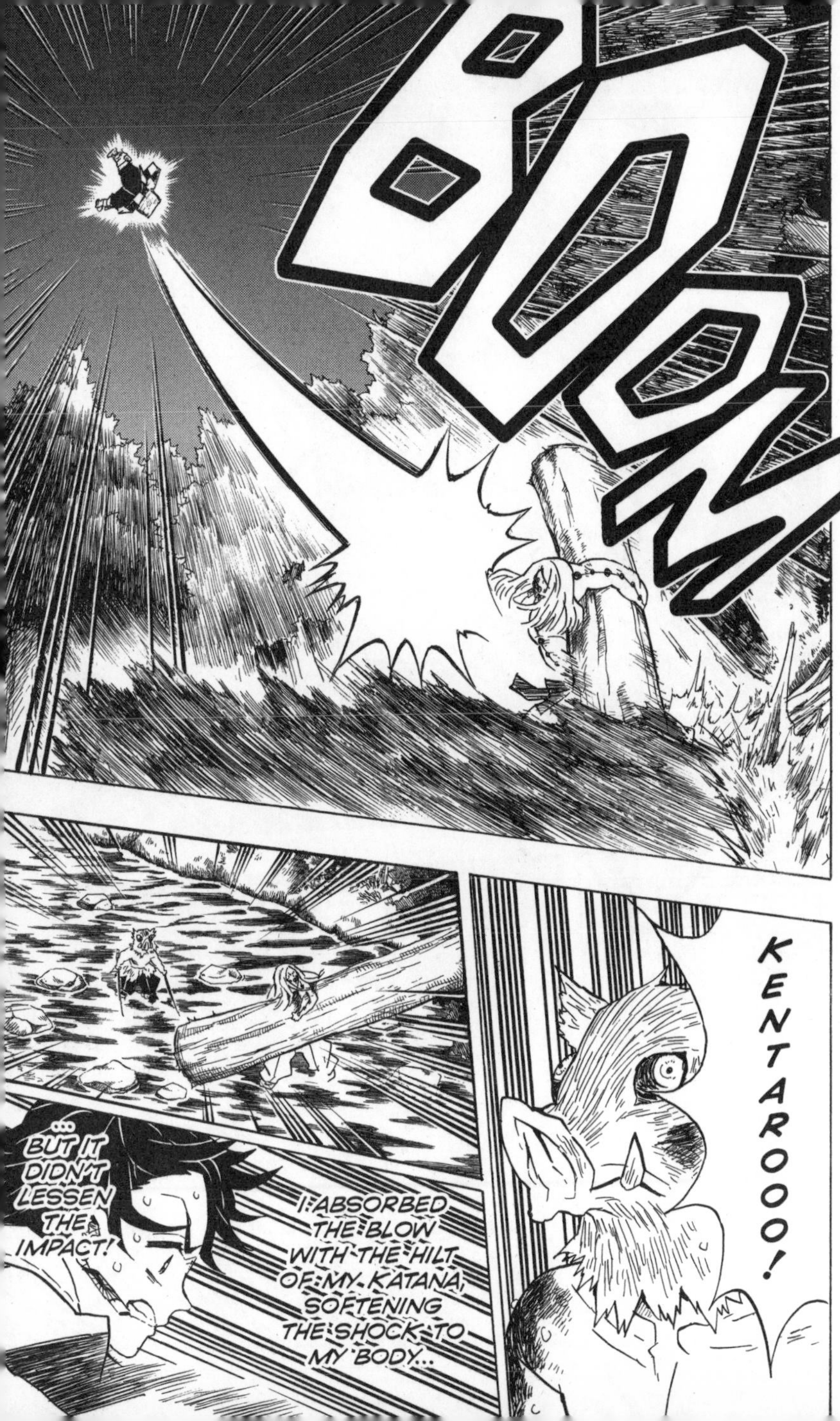
BOOM
KENTAROOOO!
I ABSORBED THE BLOW WITH THE HILT OF MY KATANA, SOFTENING THE SHOCK TO MY BODY...
...BUT IT DIDN'T LESSEN THE IMPACT!

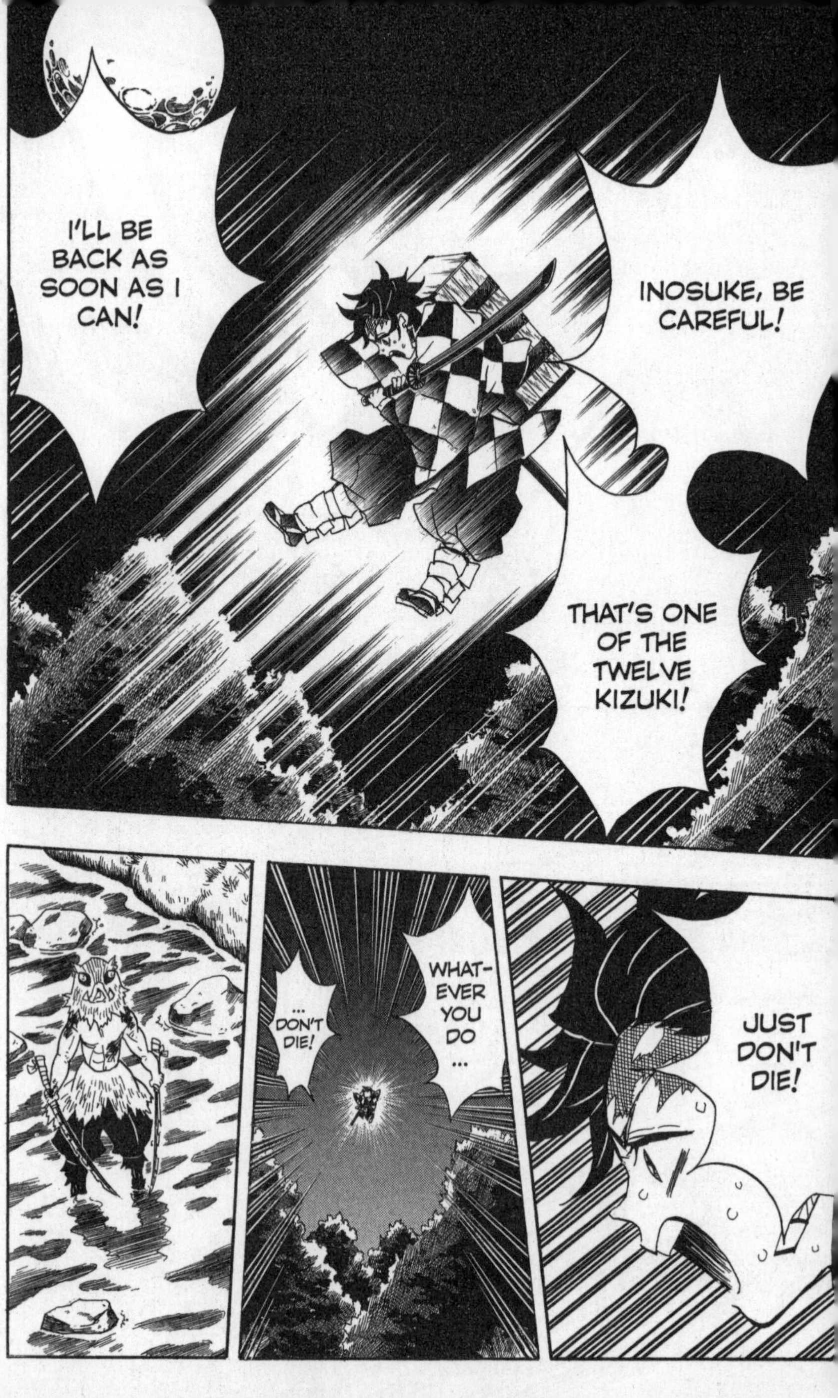
INOSUKE, BE CAREFUL!
THAT'S ONE OF THE TWELVE KIZUKI!
I'LL BE BACK AS SOON AS I CAN!
JUST DON'T DIE!
WHAT-EVER YOU DO ...
... DON'T DIE!

GETTING HARDER TO BREATHE...

...NEZUKO...

I'M SORRY...

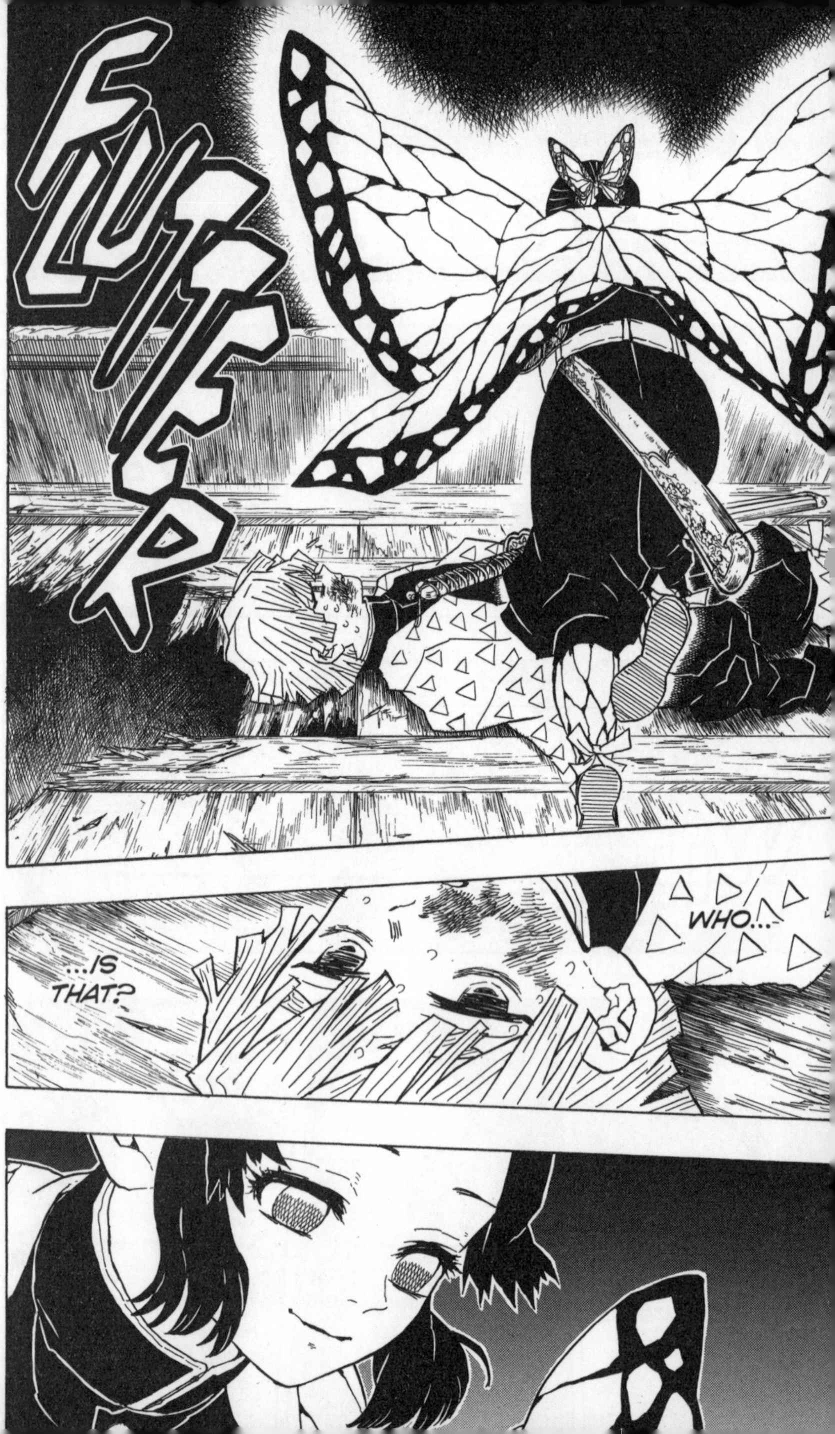
FLUTTER
WHO...
...IS THAT?

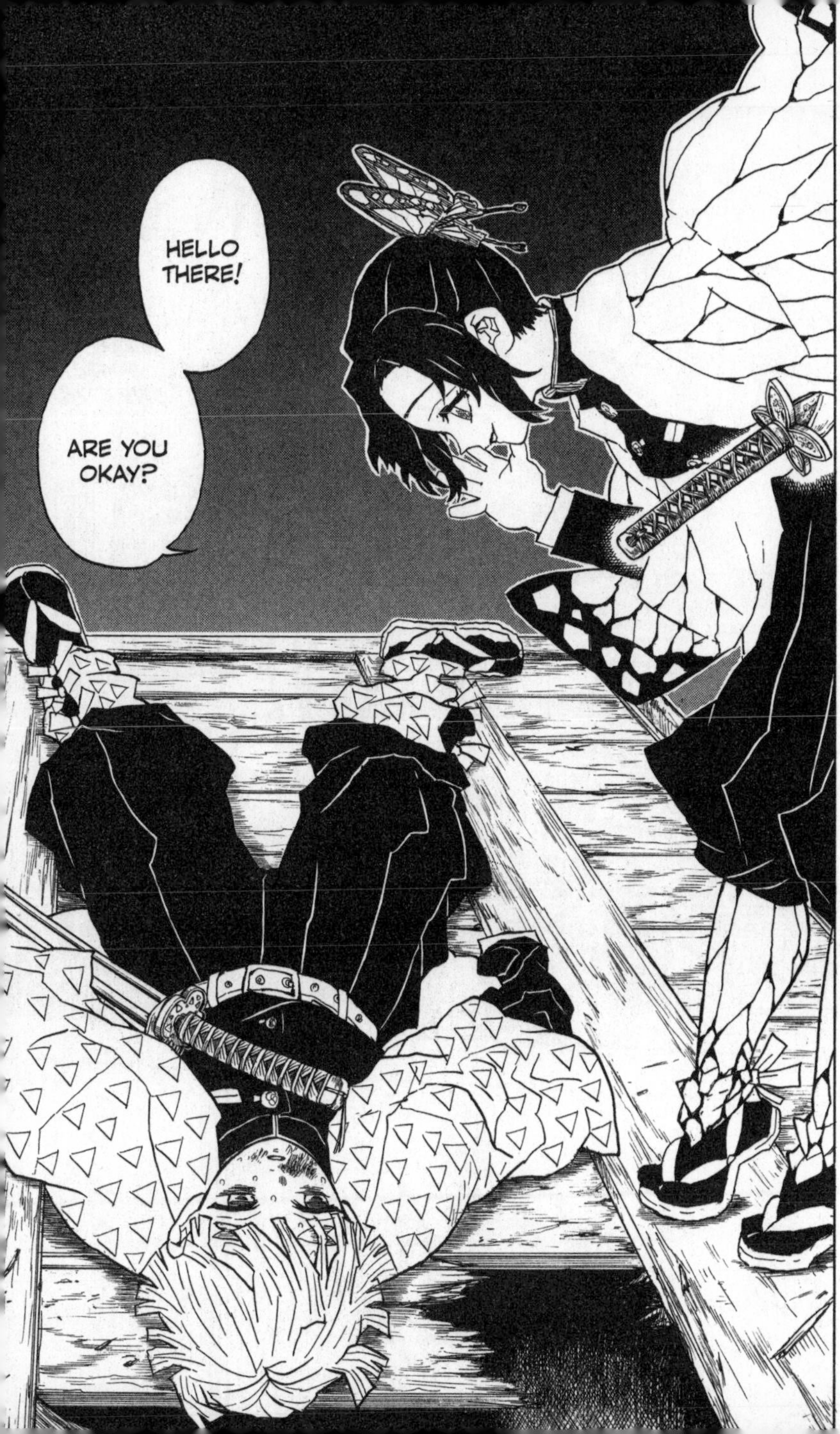
HELLO THERE!
ARE YOU OKAY?

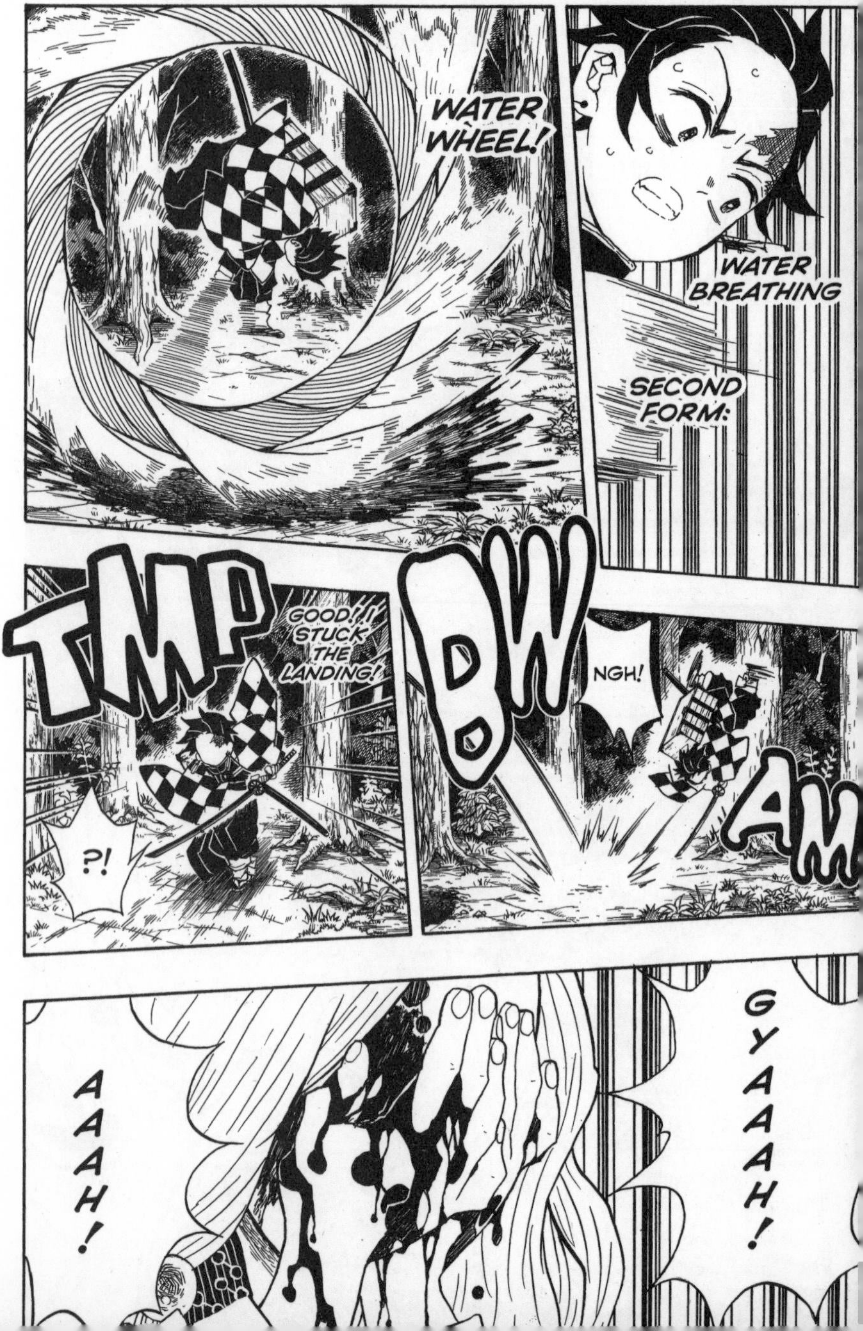
WATER BREATHING
SECOND FORM:
WATER WHEEL!
BW
NGH!
AM
TMP
GOOD! I STUCK THE LANDING!
?!
GYAAAAH!
AAAAH!

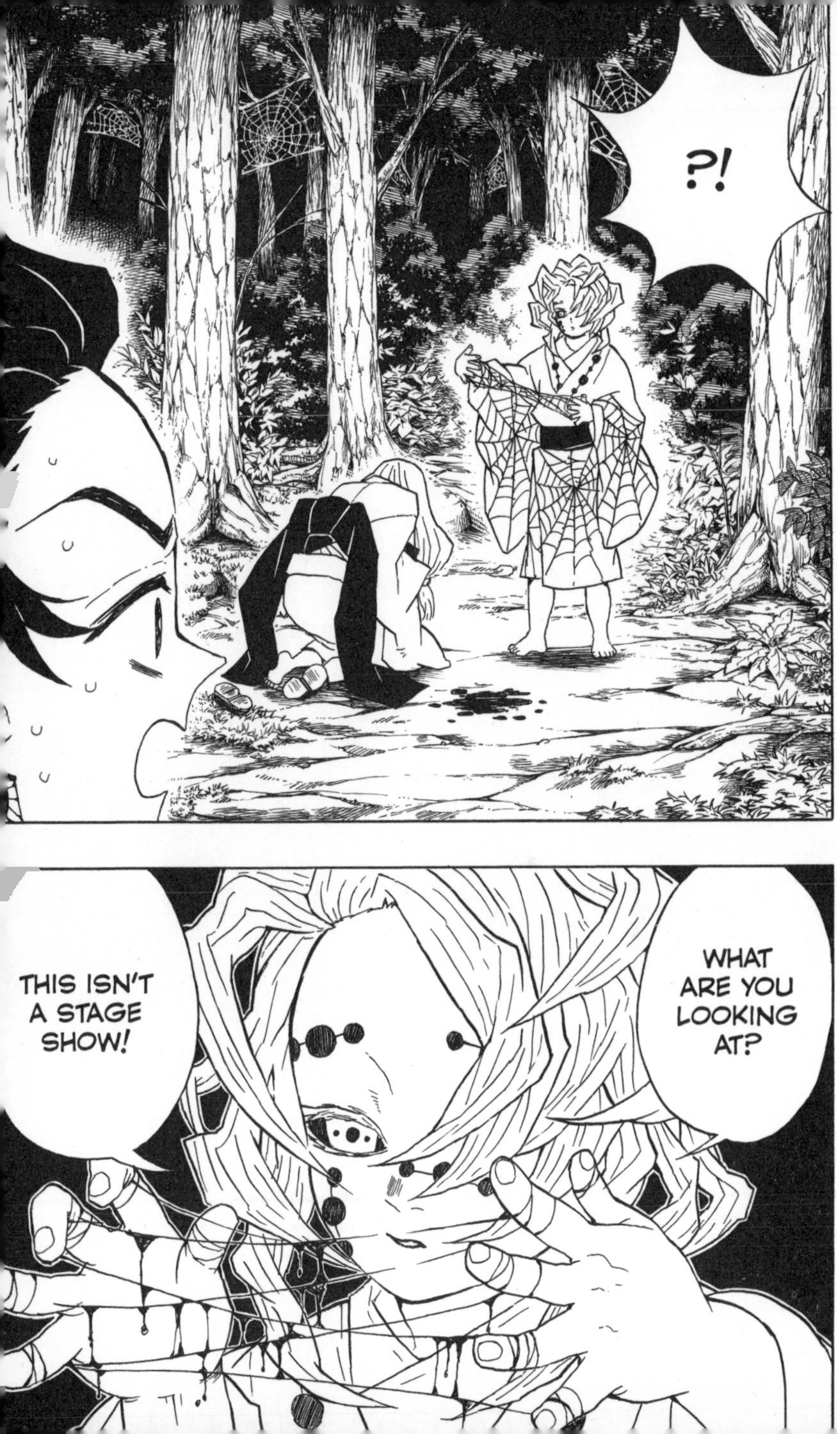
?!
WHAT ARE YOU LOOKING AT?
THIS ISN'T A STAGE SHOW!

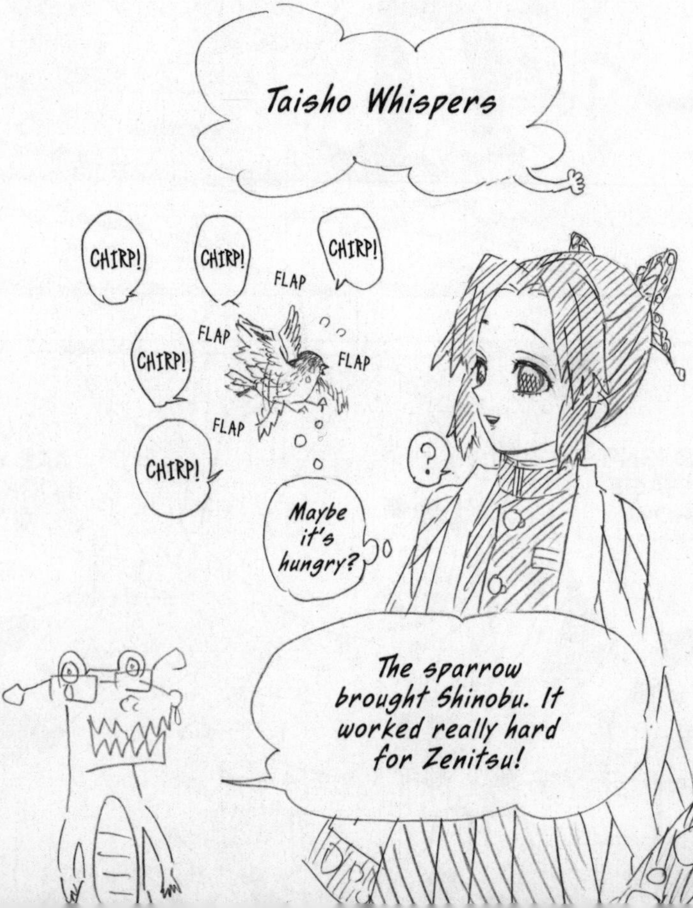
Taisho Whispers
CHIRP!
FLAP
CHIRP!
CHIRP!
FLAP
FLAP
CHIRP!
FLAP
CHIRP!
Maybe it's hungry?
The sparrow brought Shinobu. It worked really hard for Zenitsu!

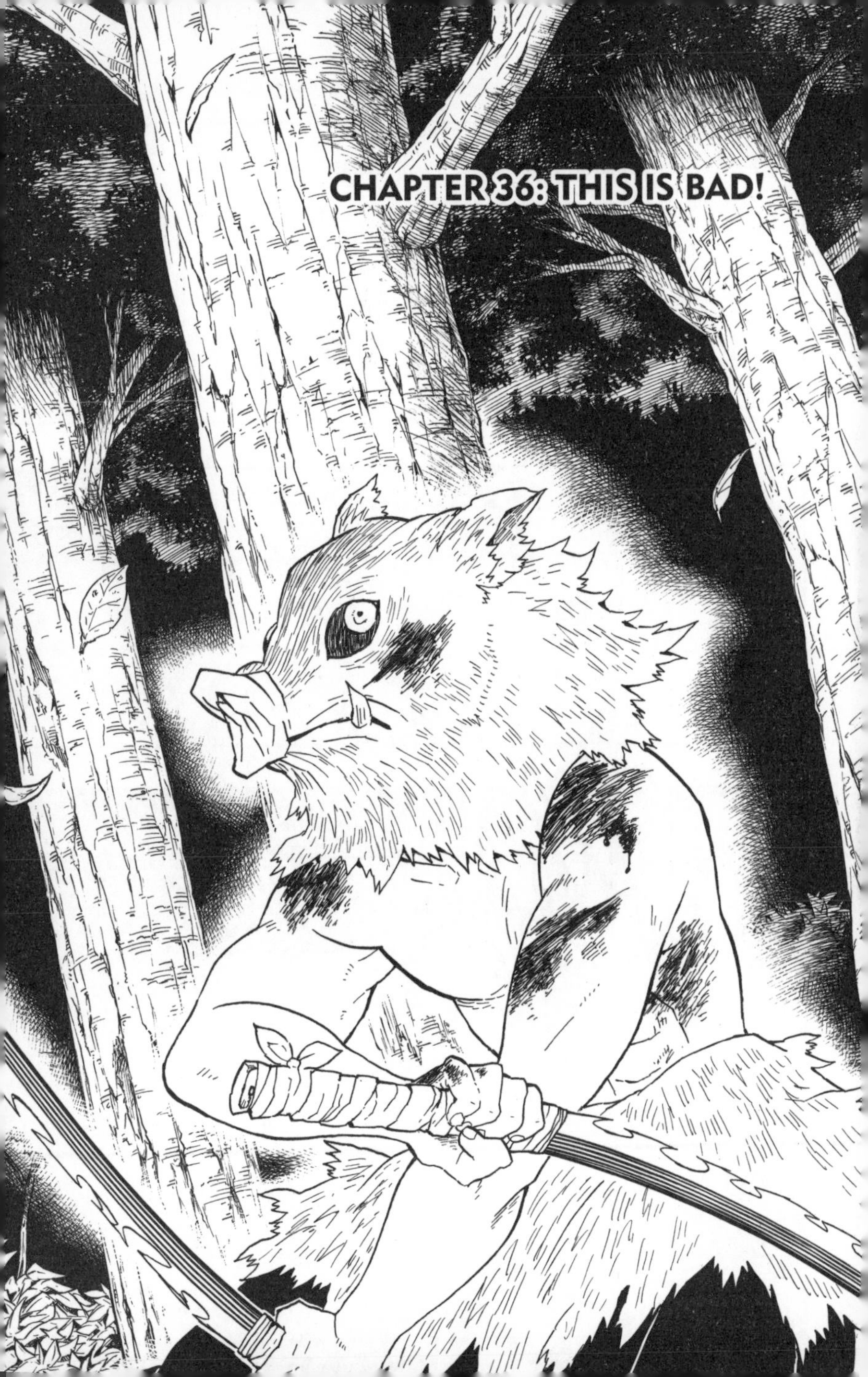
CHAPTER 36: THIS IS BAD!

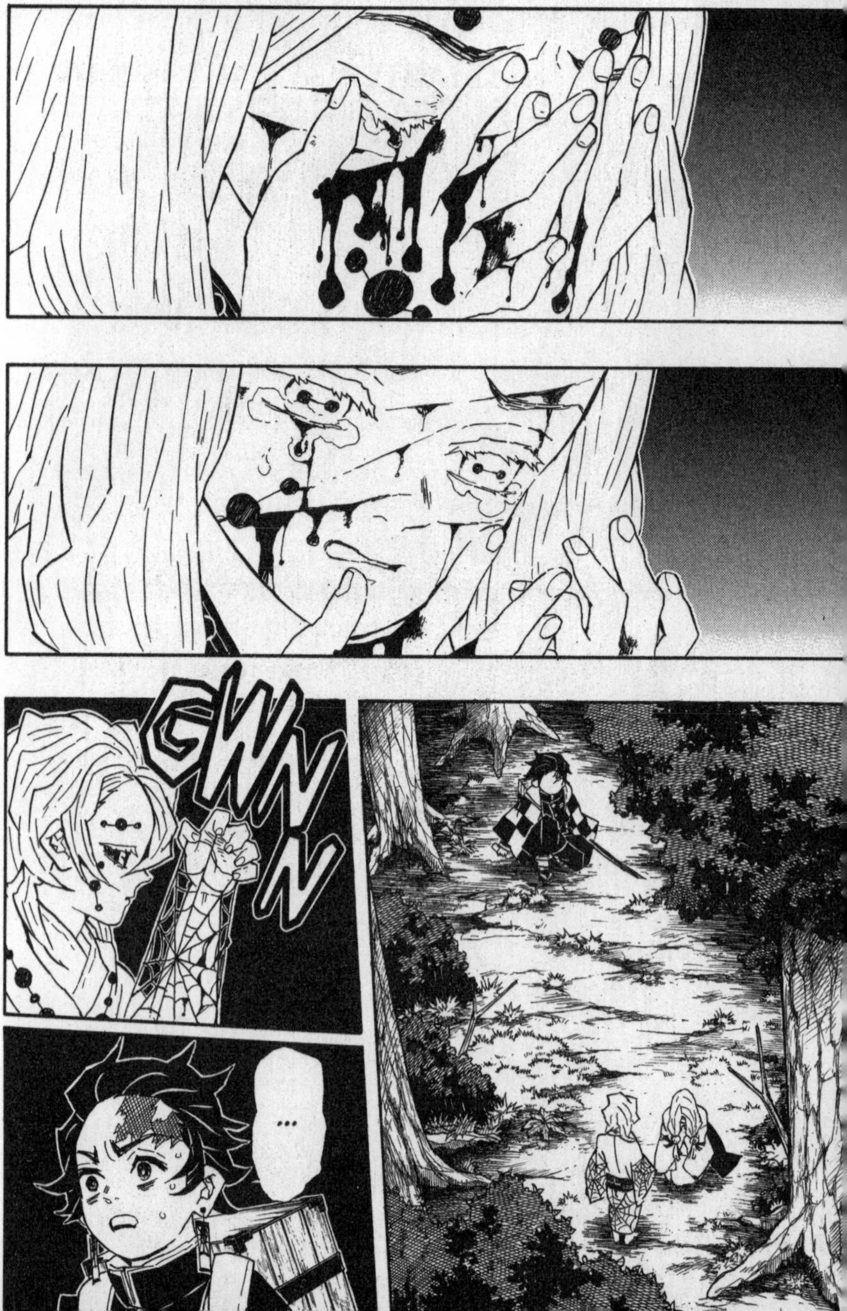
GWNNN
...

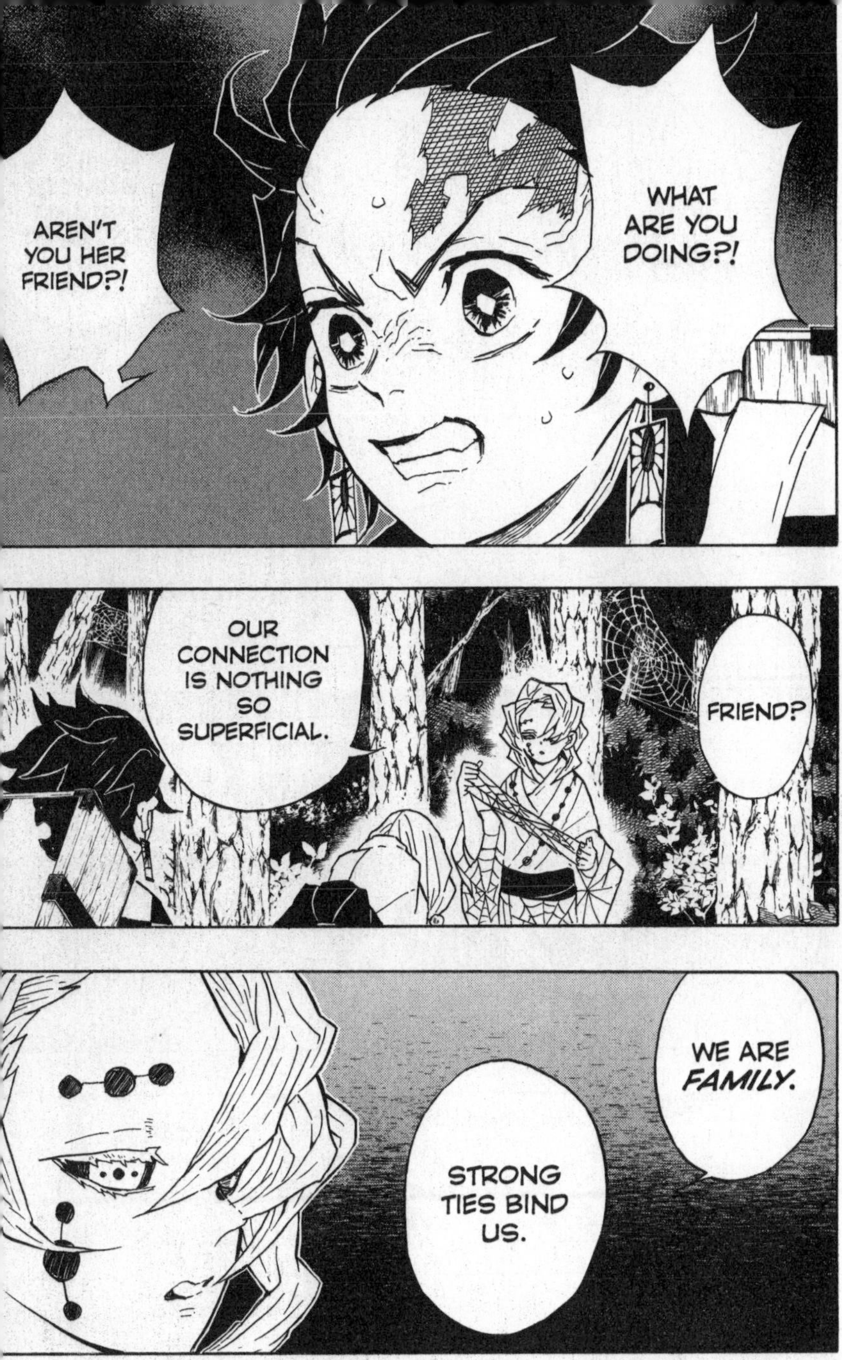
WHAT ARE YOU DOING?!
AREN'T YOU HER FRIEND?!
FRIEND?
OUR CONNECTION IS NOTHING SO SUPERFICIAL.
WE ARE *FAMILY.*
STRONG TIES BIND US.

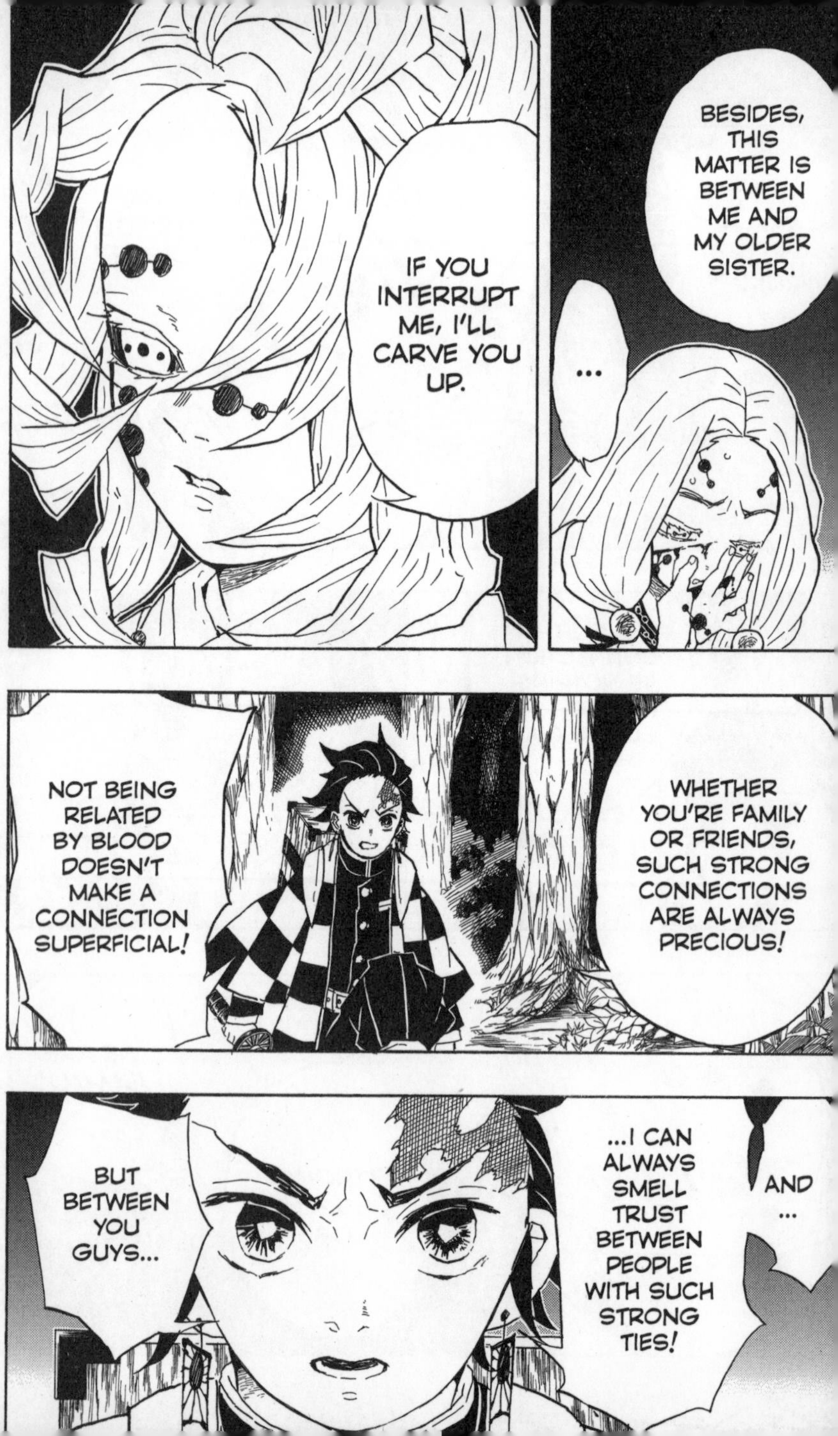
BESIDES, THIS MATTER IS BETWEEN ME AND MY OLDER SISTER.
...
IF YOU INTERRUPT ME, I'LL CARVE YOU UP.
WHETHER YOU'RE FAMILY OR FRIENDS, SUCH STRONG CONNECTIONS ARE ALWAYS PRECIOUS!
NOT BEING RELATED BY BLOOD DOESN'T MAKE A CONNECTION SUPERFICIAL!
AND ...
...I CAN ALWAYS SMELL TRUST BETWEEN PEOPLE WITH SUCH STRONG TIES!
BUT BETWEEN YOU GUYS...

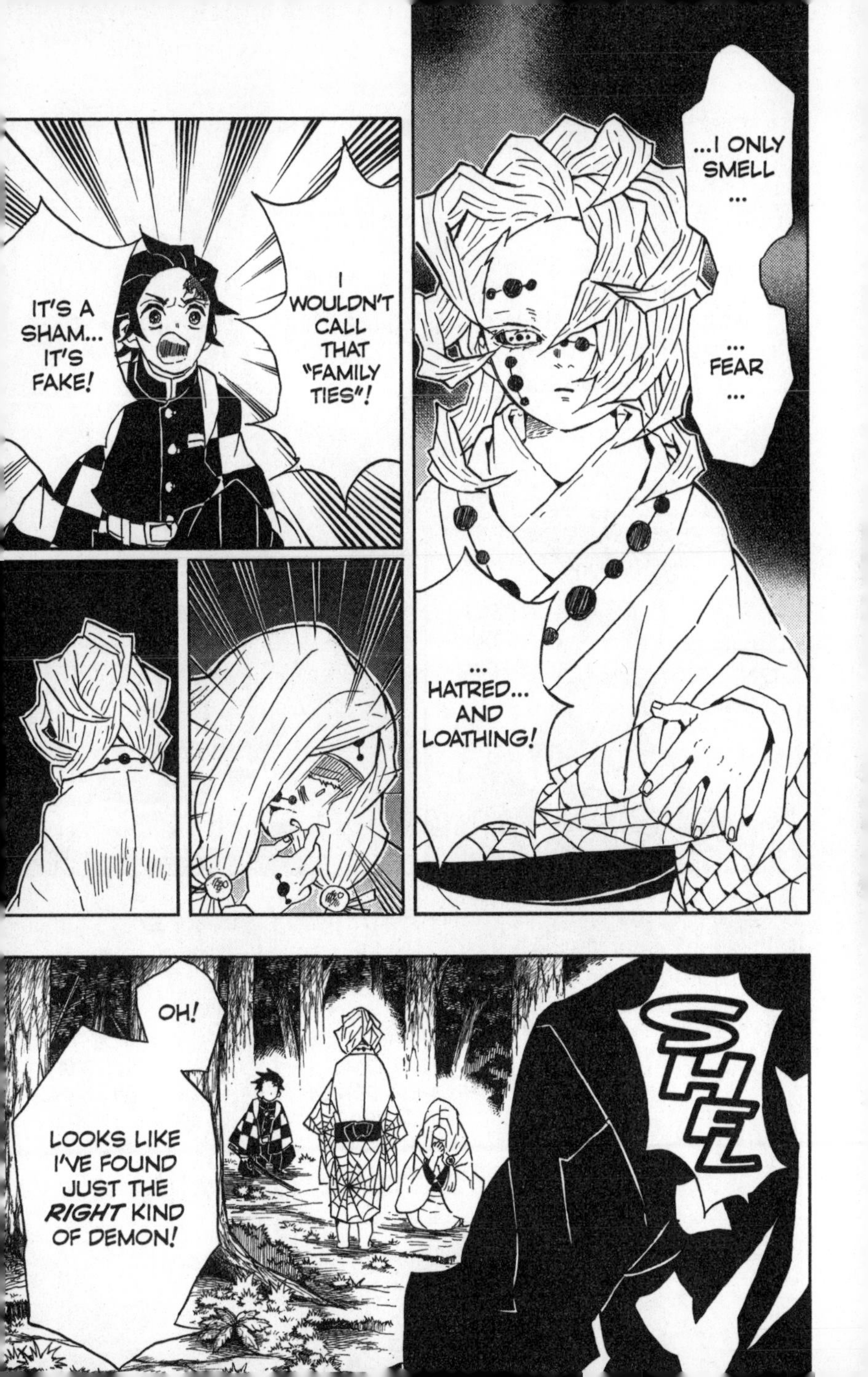
...I ONLY SMELL ...
... FEAR ...
... HATRED... AND LOATHING!
I WOULDN'T CALL THAT "FAMILY TIES"!
IT'S A SHAM... IT'S FAKE!
SHFL
OH!
LOOKS LIKE I'VE FOUND JUST THE *RIGHT* KIND OF DEMON!

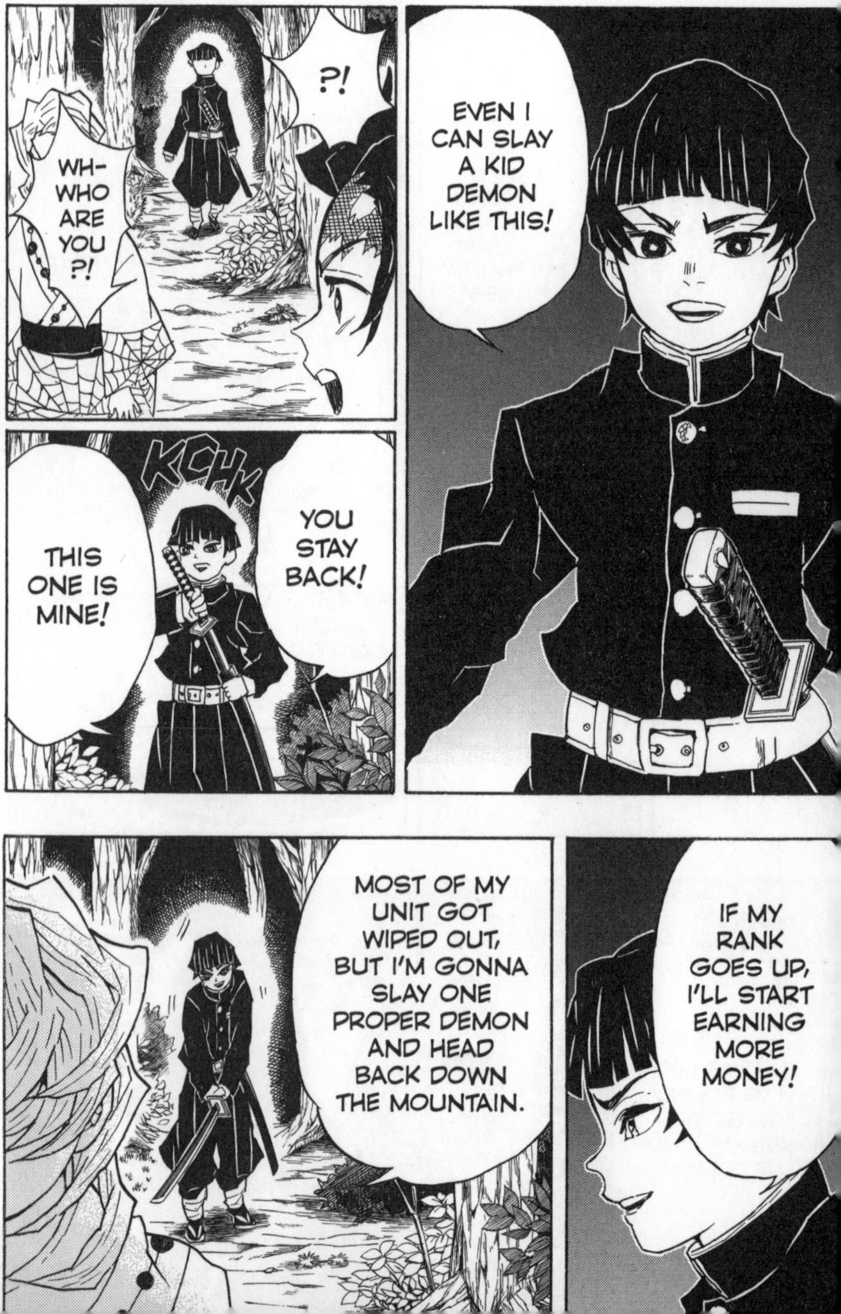
EVEN I CAN SLAY A KID DEMON LIKE THIS!
?!
WH- WHO ARE YOU ?!
KCHK
YOU STAY BACK!
THIS ONE IS MINE!
IF MY RANK GOES UP, I'LL START EARNING MORE MONEY!
MOST OF MY UNIT GOT WIPED OUT, BUT I'M GONNA SLAY ONE PROPER DEMON AND HEAD BACK DOWN THE MOUNTAIN.

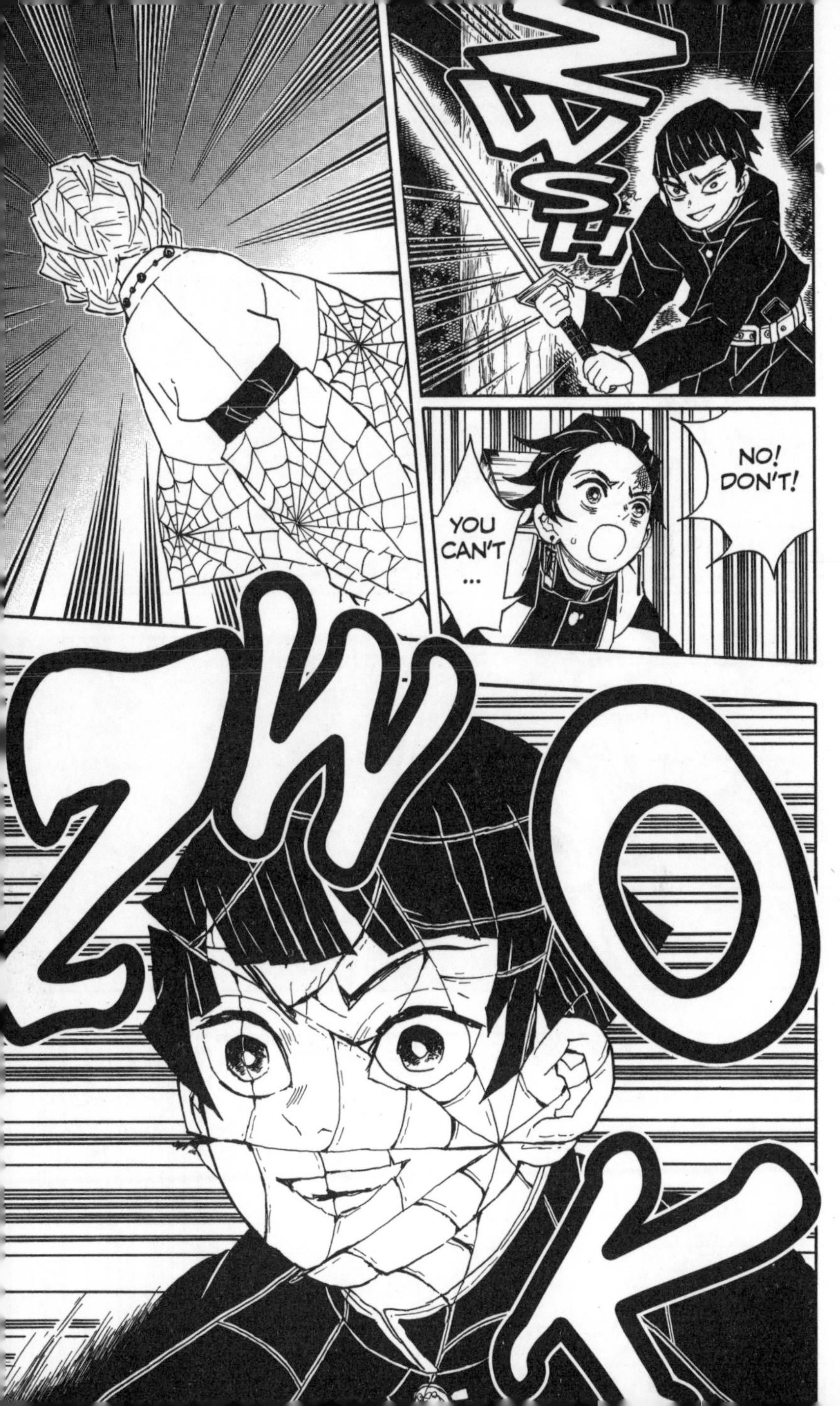
WASH
NO! DON'T!
YOU CAN'T ...
ZWOK

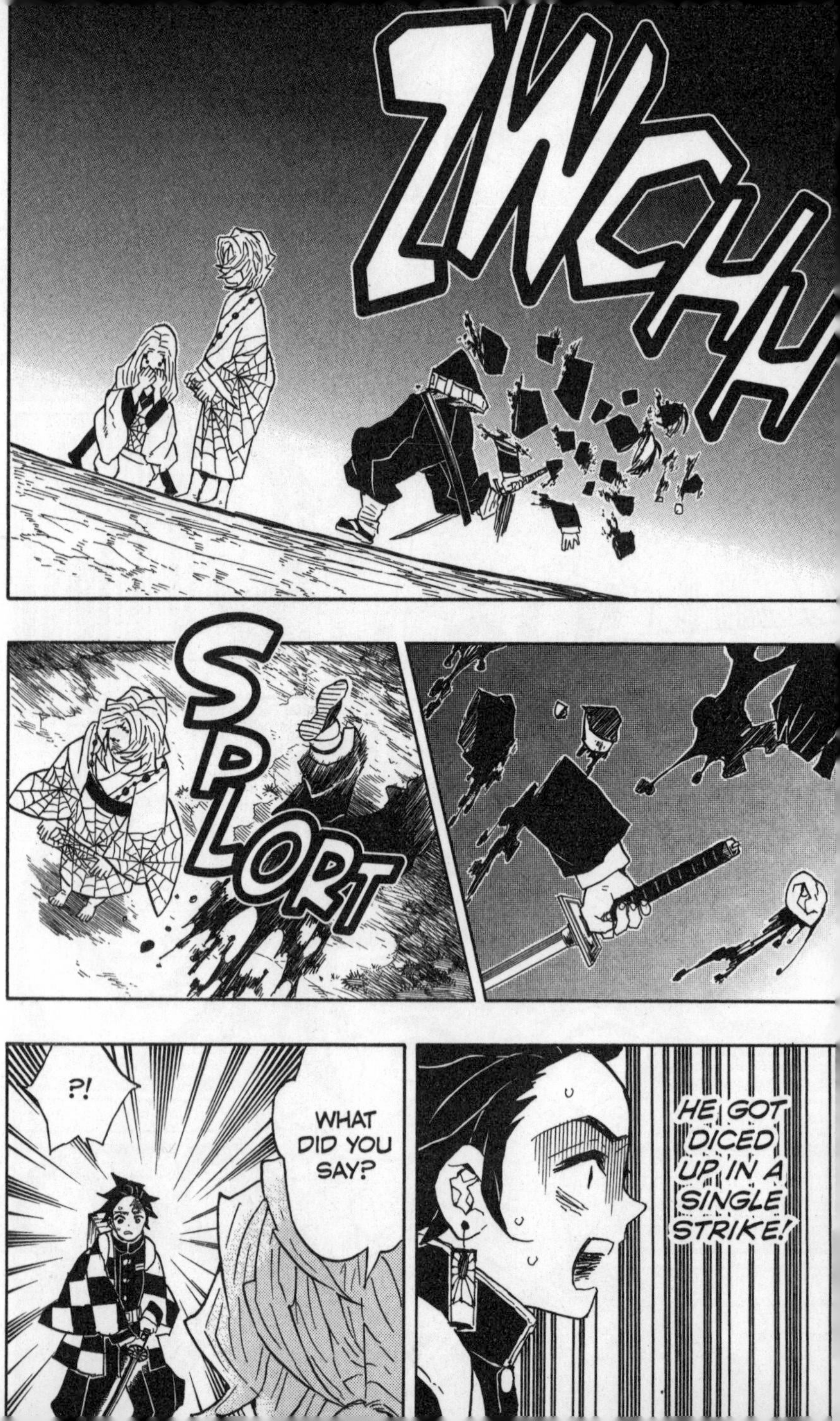
SPLORT
HE GOT DICED UP IN A SINGLE STRIKE!
WHAT DID YOU SAY?
?!

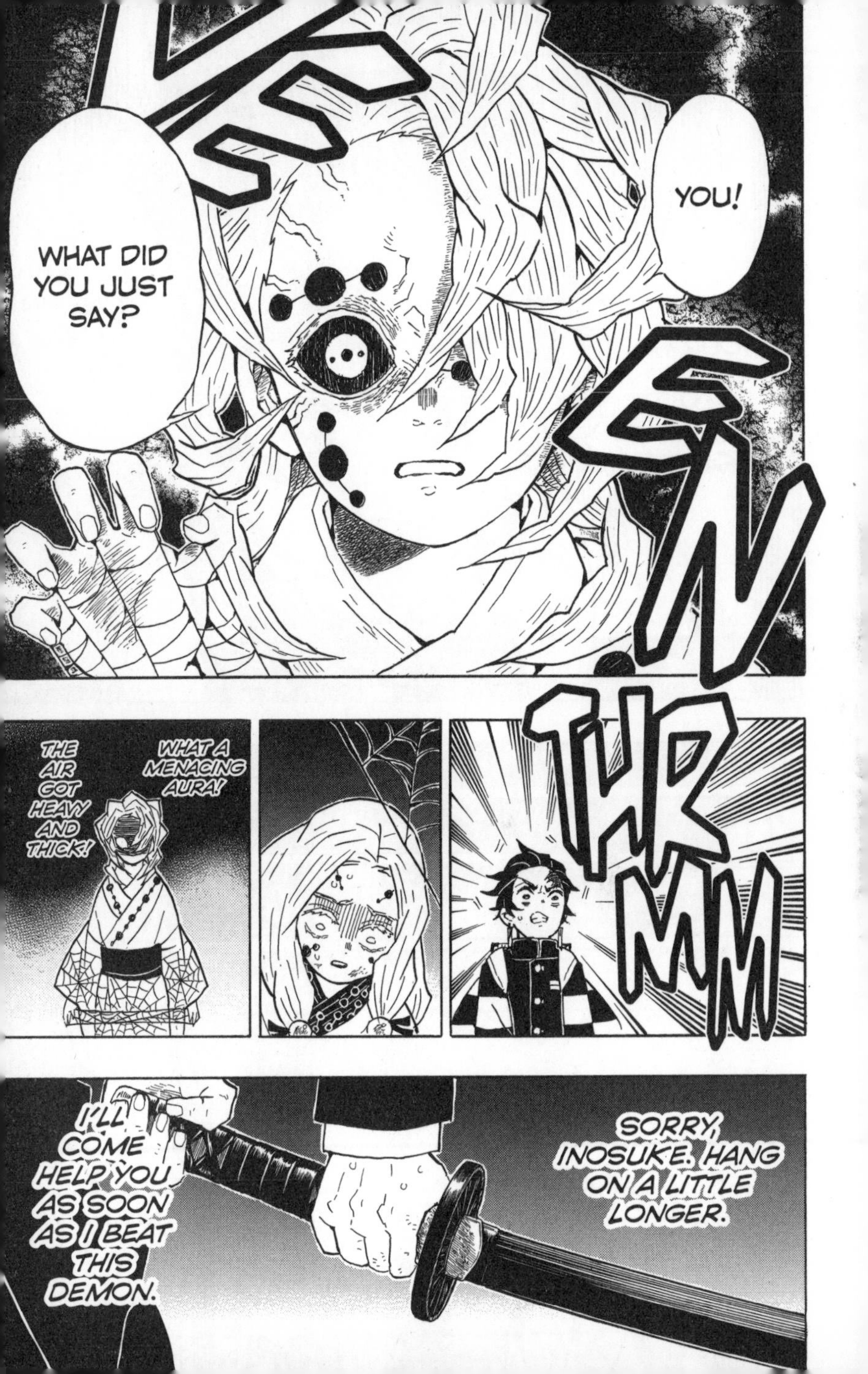
YOU!
WHAT DID YOU JUST SAY?
THRMM
WHAT A MENACING AURA!
THE AIR GOT HEAVY AND THICK!
SORRY, INOSUKE. HANG ON A LITTLE LONGER.
I'LL COME HELP YOU AS SOON AS I BEAT THIS DEMON.

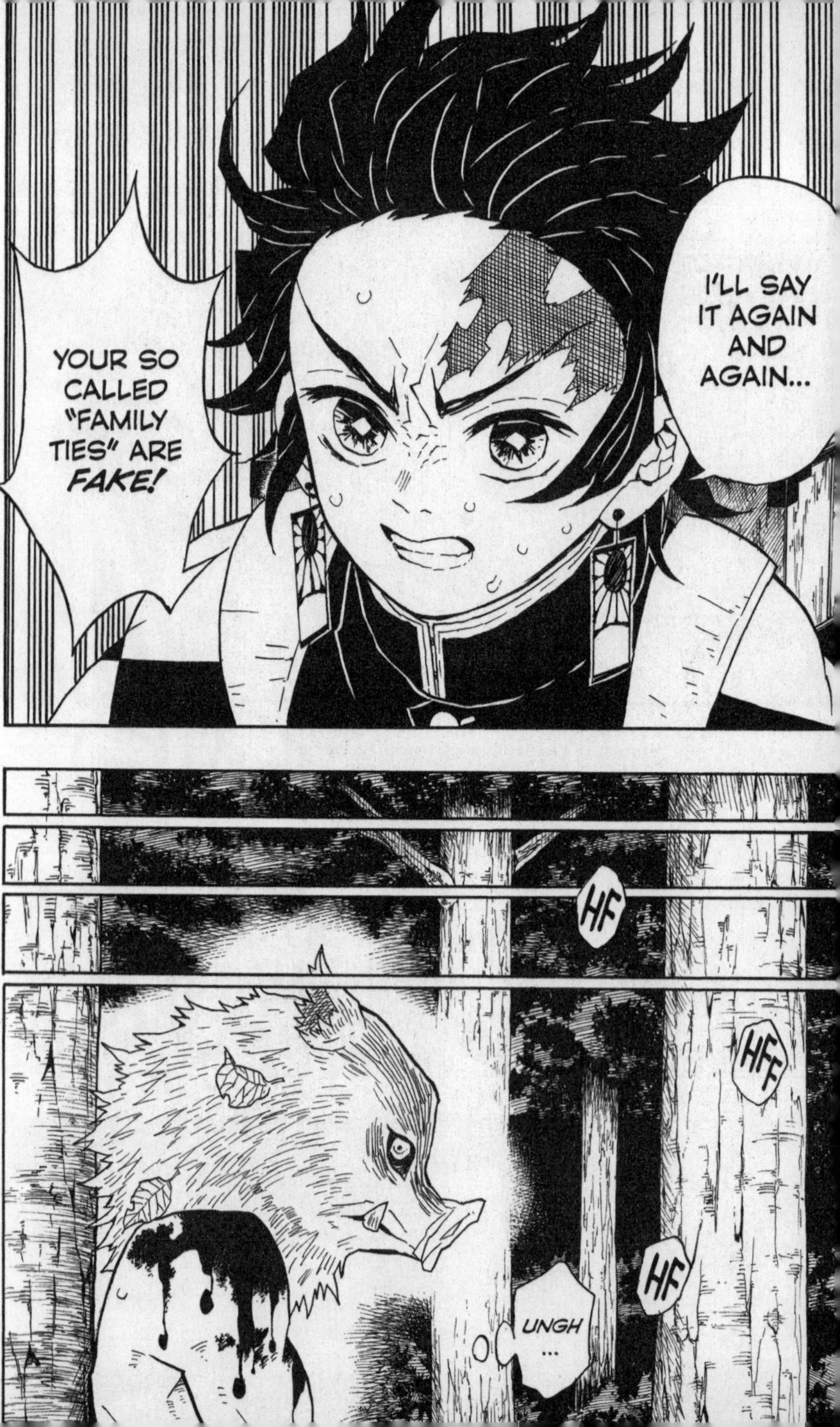
I'LL SAY IT AGAIN AND AGAIN...
YOUR SO CALLED "FAMILY TIES" ARE *FAKE!*
HF
HFF
HF
UNGH ...

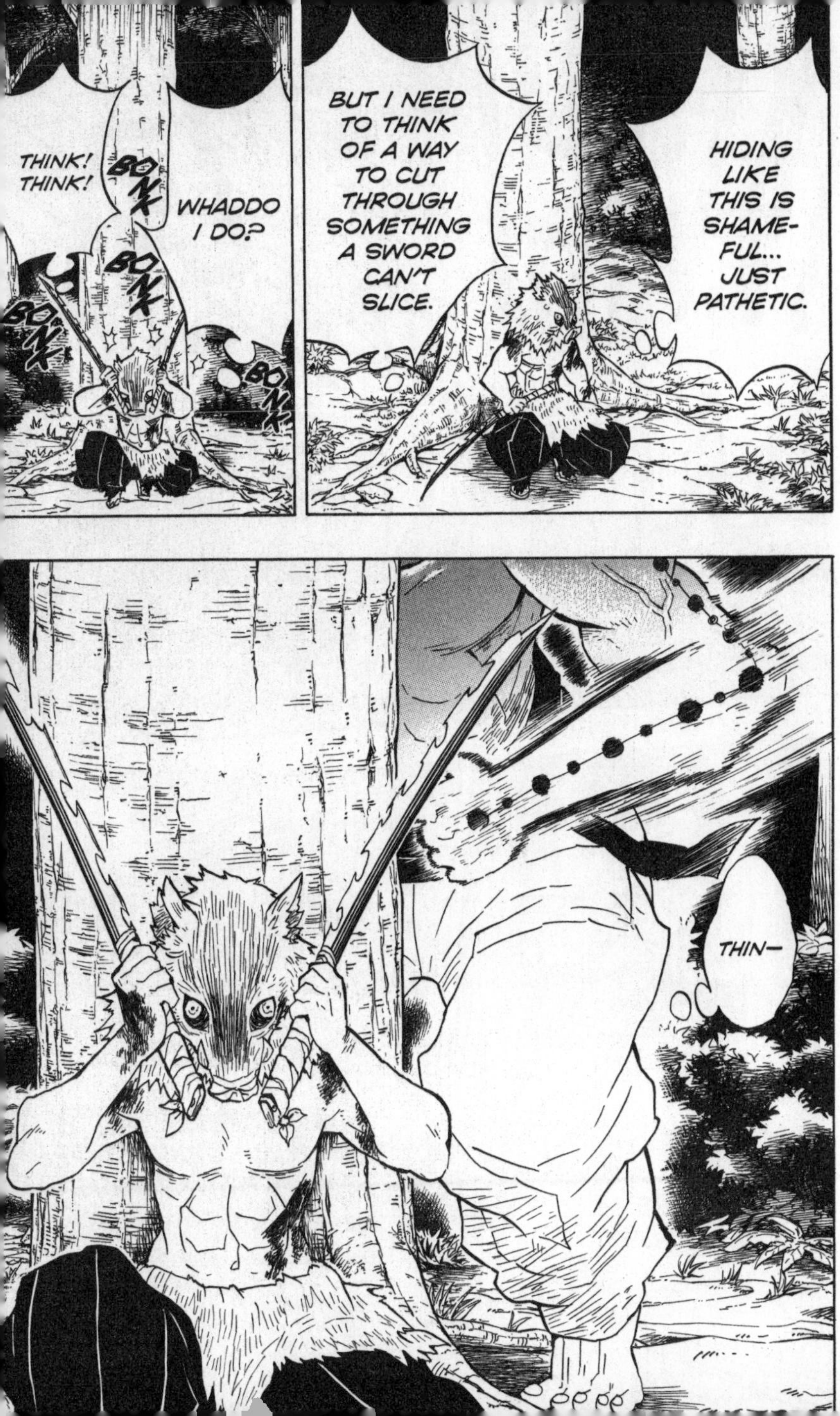
HIDING LIKE THIS IS SHAME-FUL... JUST PATHETIC.
BUT I NEED TO THINK OF A WAY TO CUT THROUGH SOMETHING A SWORD CAN'T SLICE.
WHADDO I DO?
THINK! THINK!
BONK
BONK
BONK
BONK
THIN—

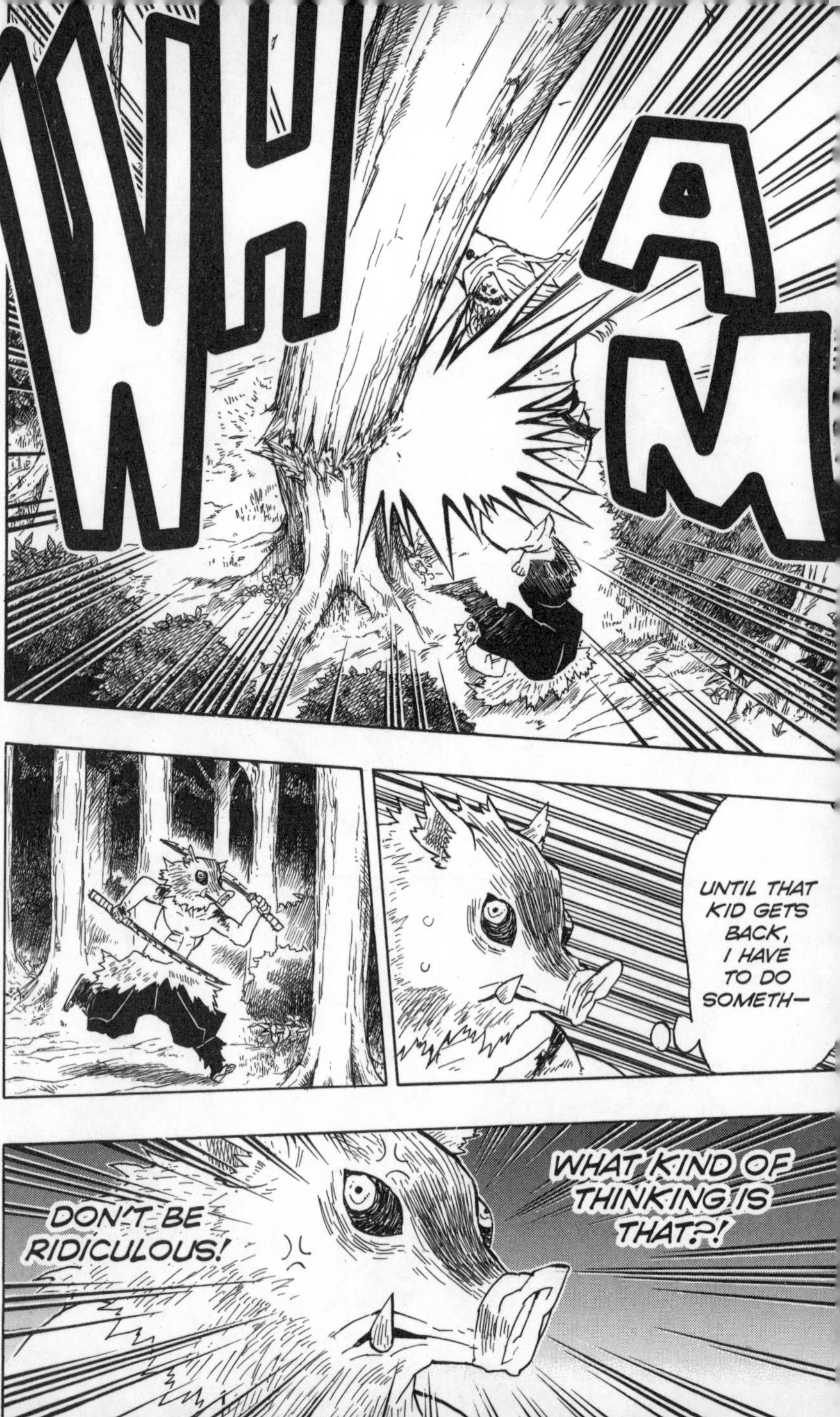
WHAM
UNTIL THAT KID GETS BACK, I HAVE TO DO SOMETH—
WHAT KIND OF THINKING IS THAT?!
DON'T BE RIDICULOUS!

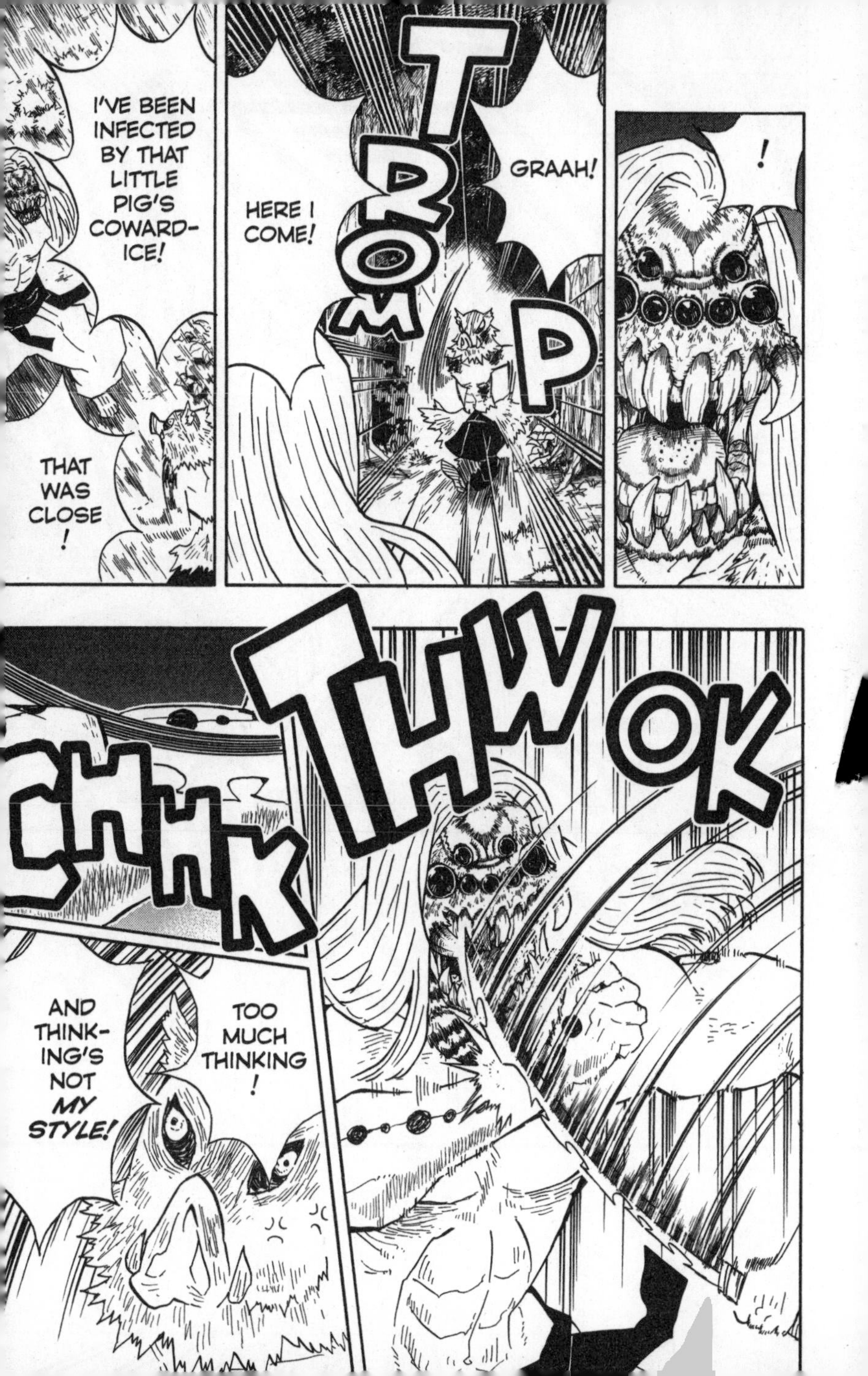
!
GRAAH!
HERE I COME!
TROMP
I'VE BEEN INFECTED BY THAT LITTLE PIG'S COWARD-ICE!
THAT WAS CLOSE!
THWOK
CHHK
TOO MUCH THINKING!
AND THINK-ING'S NOT *MY STYLE!*

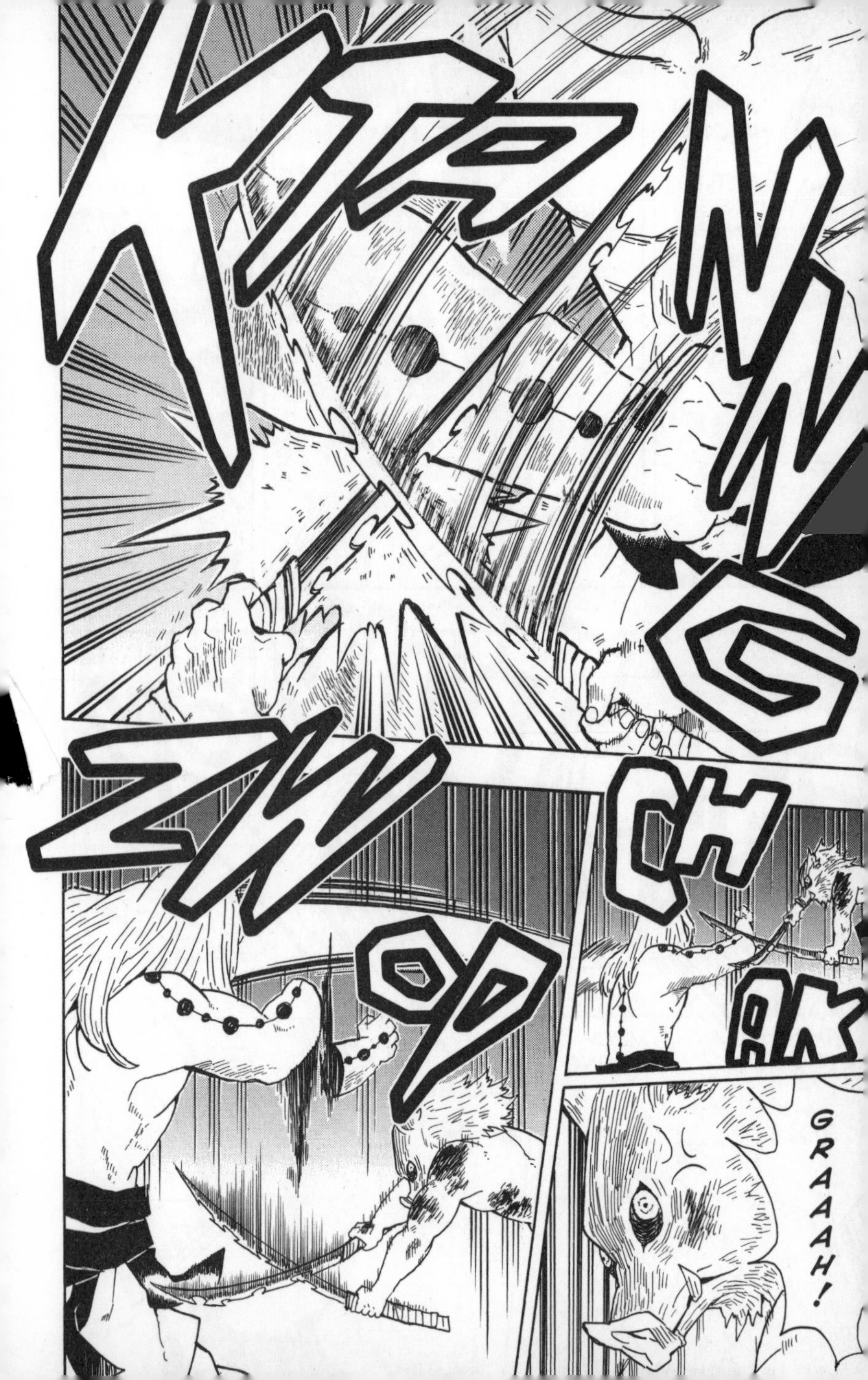
GRAAAH!

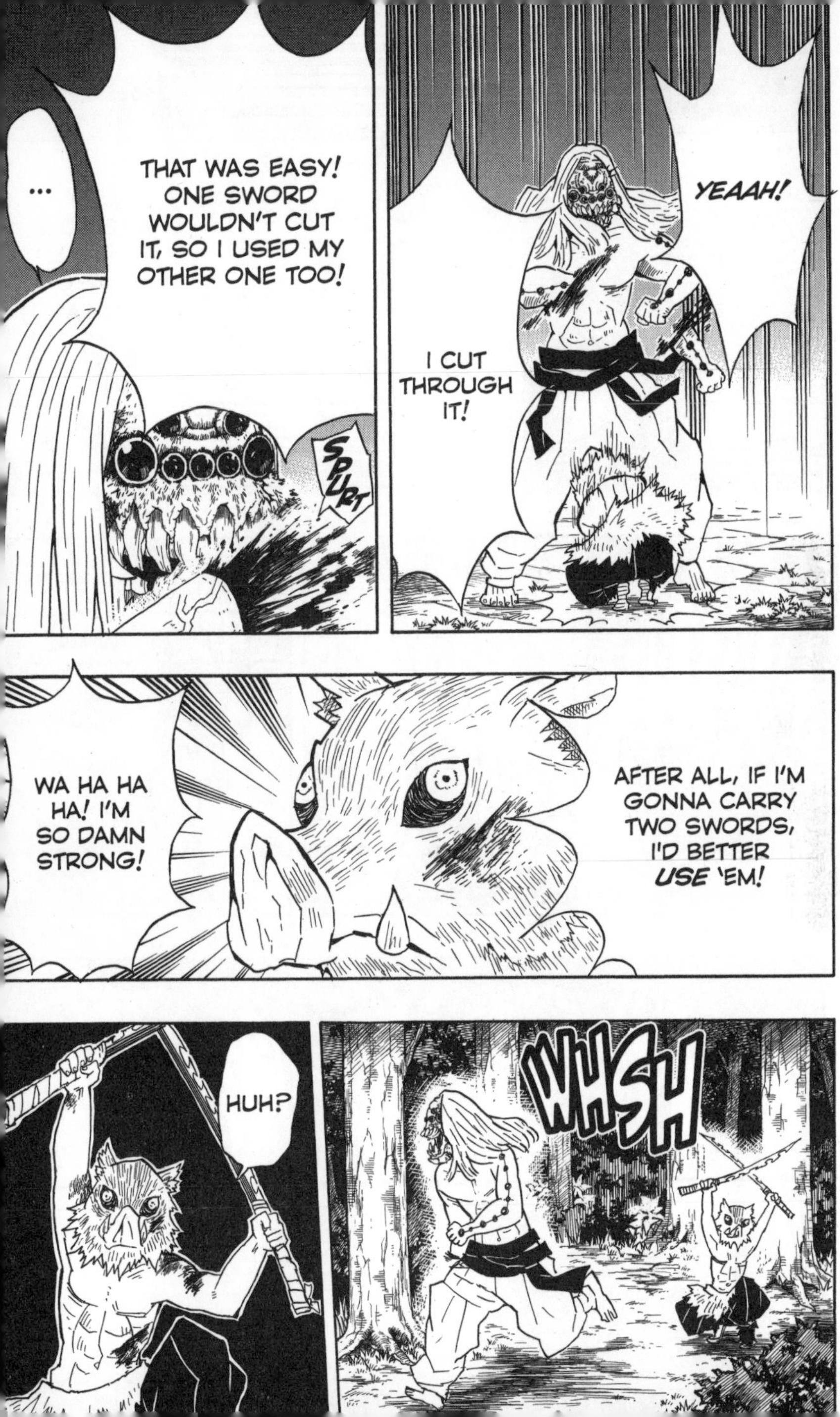
YEAAH!
I CUT THROUGH IT!
THAT WAS EASY! ONE SWORD WOULDN'T CUT IT, SO I USED MY OTHER ONE TOO!
...
SPURT
AFTER ALL, IF I'M GONNA CARRY TWO SWORDS, I'D BETTER *USE* 'EM!
WA HA HA HA! I'M SO DAMN STRONG!
WHSH
HUH?

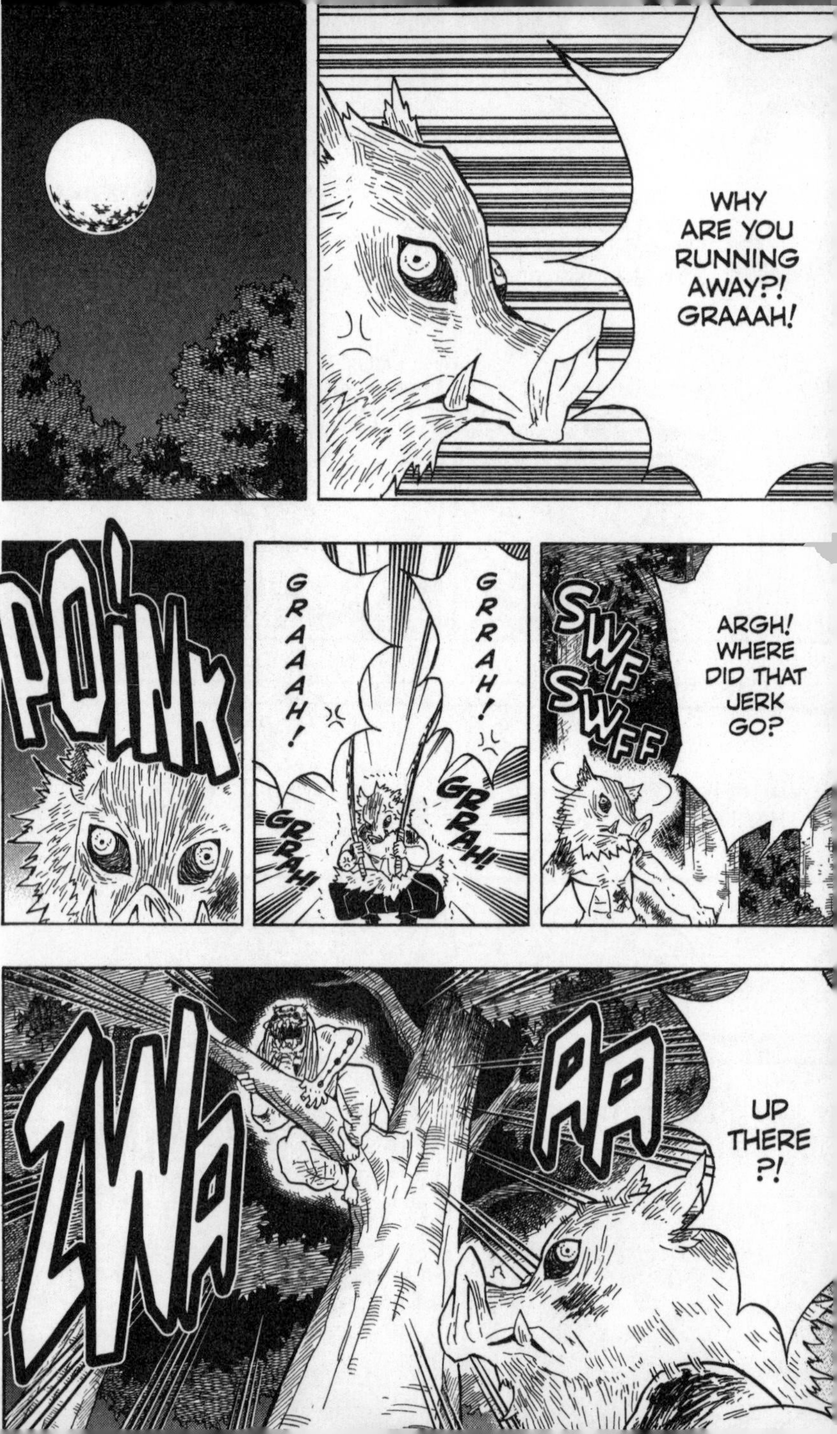
WHY ARE YOU RUNNING AWAY?! GRAAAH!
SWF SWFF
ARGH! WHERE DID THAT JERK GO?
GRRAH!
GRAAAAH!
GRRAH!
GRRAH!
POINK
UP THERE?!
ZWAA

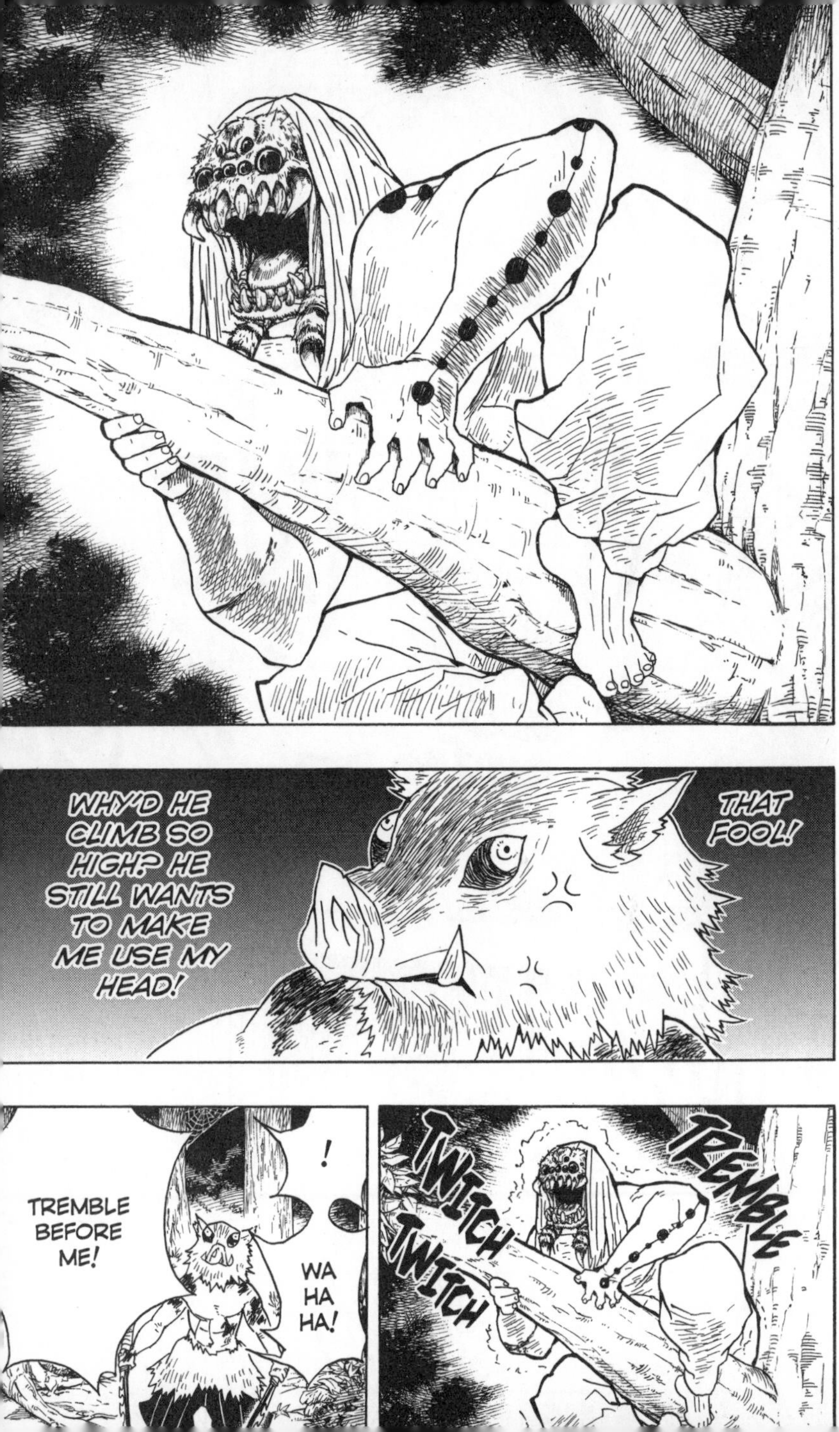
THAT FOOL!
WHY'D HE CLIMB SO HIGH? HE STILL WANTS TO MAKE ME USE MY HEAD!
TREMBLE
TWITCH
TWITCH
!
TREMBLE BEFORE ME!
WA HA HA!

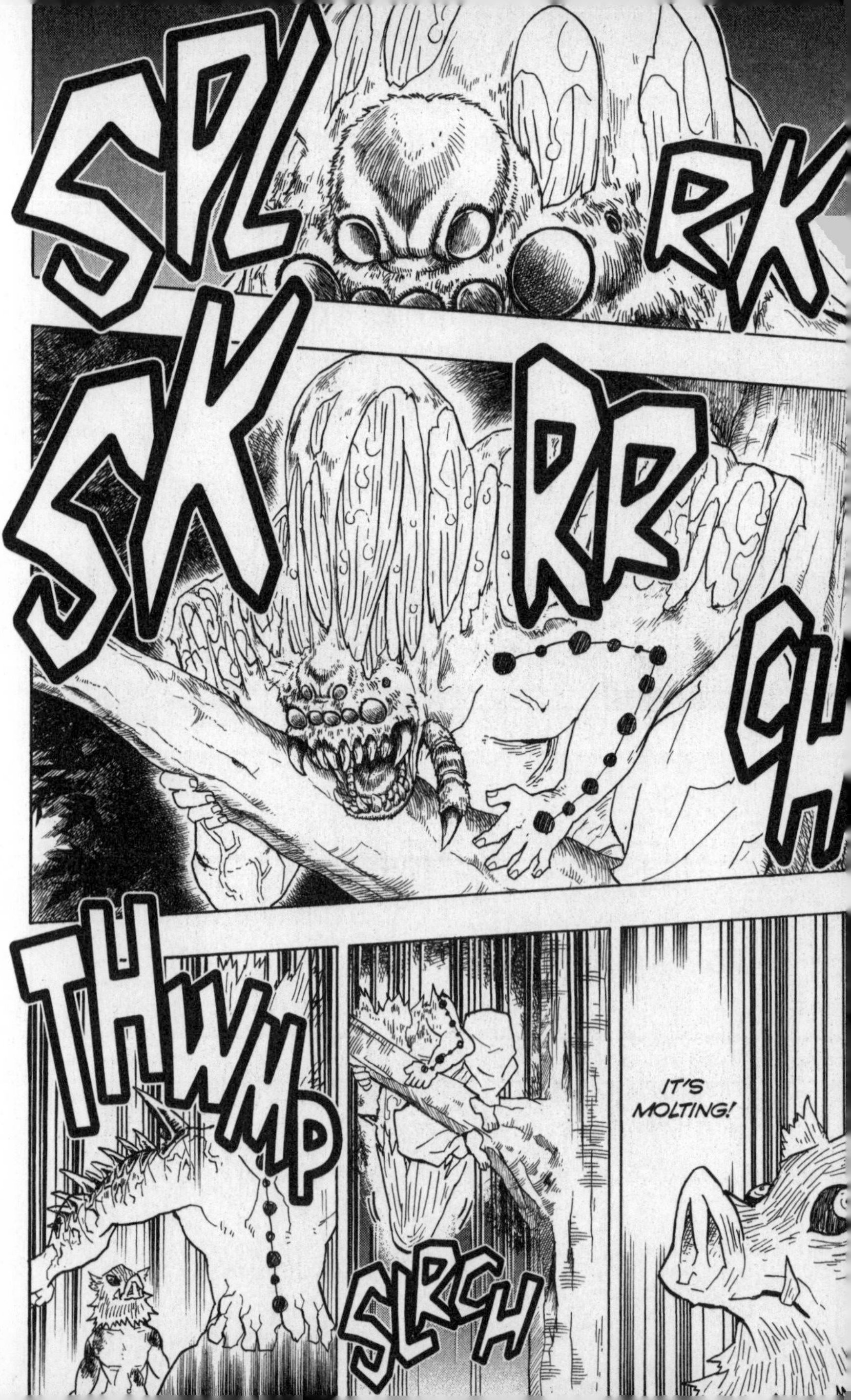
SPL
RK
SK
RR
QU
IT'S MOLTING!
SLRCH
THWMP

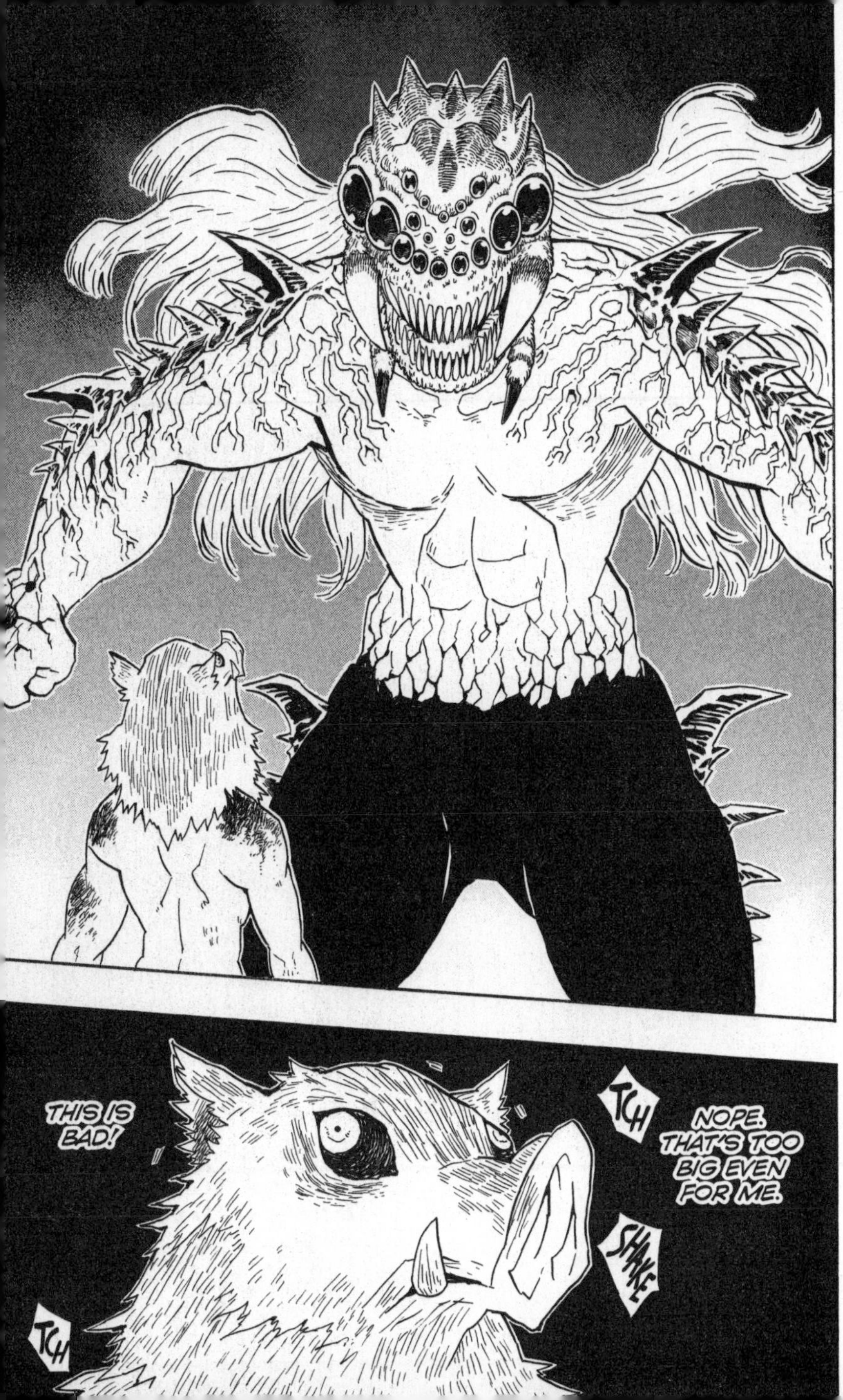
TCH
NOPE. THAT'S TOO BIG EVEN FOR ME.
SHAKE
THIS IS BAD!
TCH

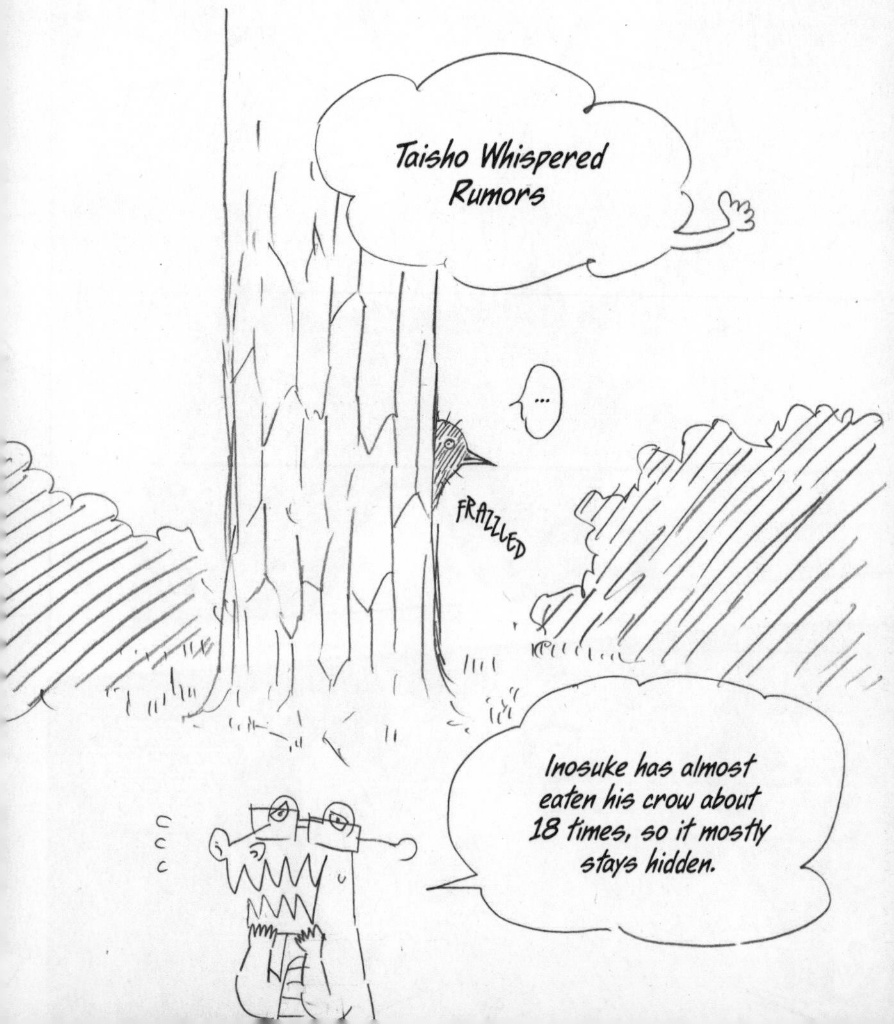
Taisho Whispered Rumors
...
FRAZZLED
Inosuke has almost eaten his crow about 18 times, so it mostly stays hidden.

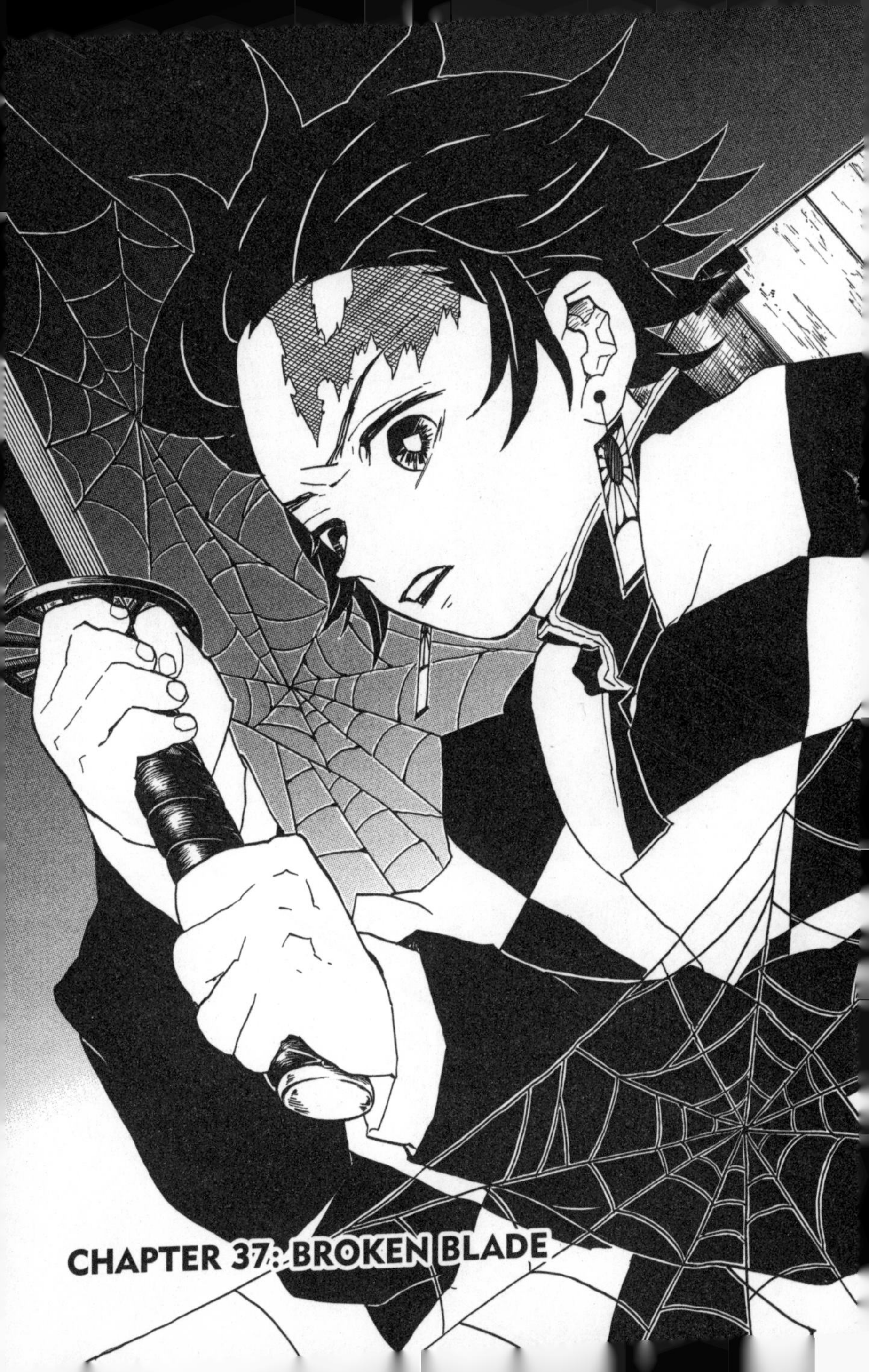
CHAPTER 37: BROKEN BLADE

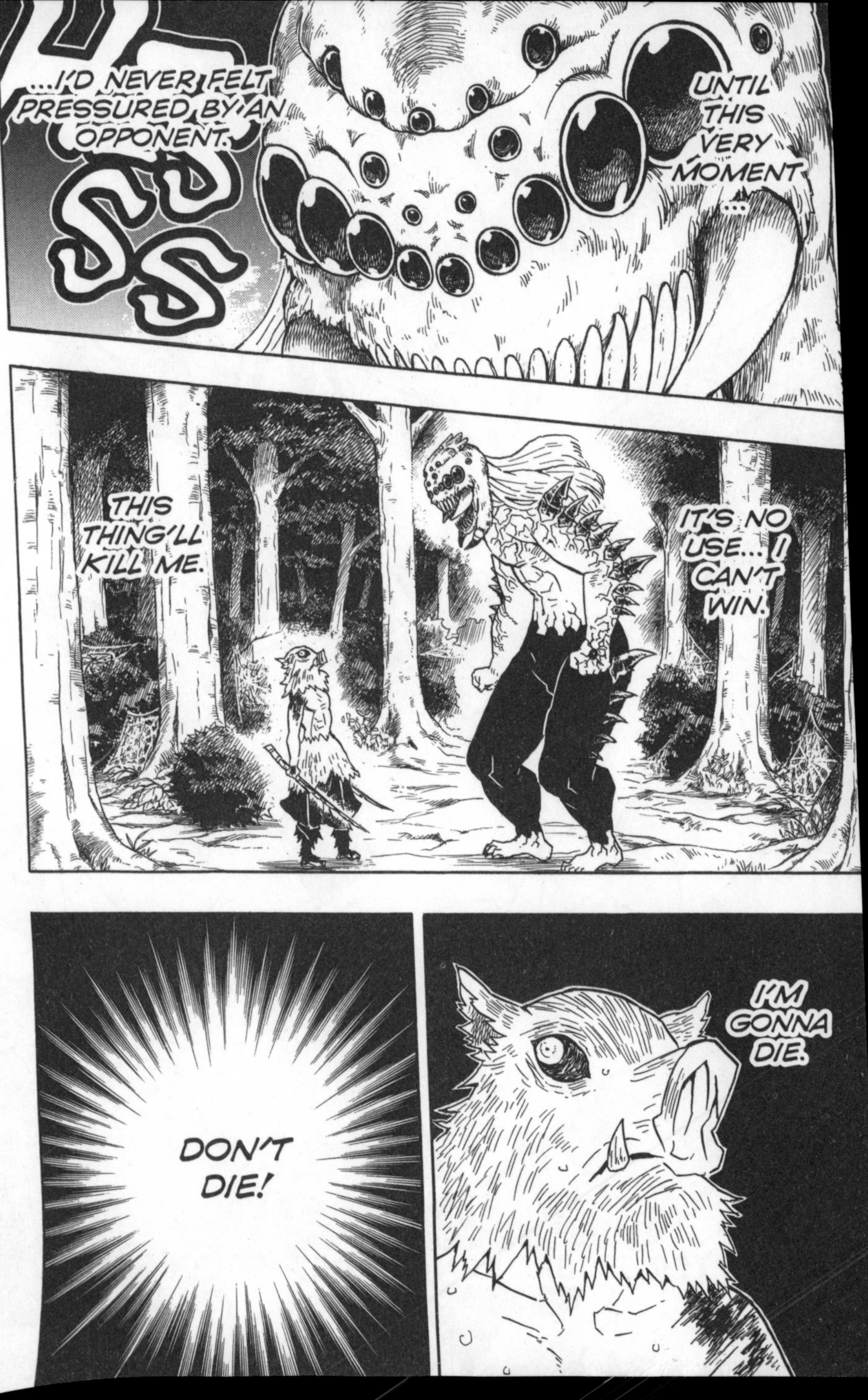
UNTIL THIS VERY MOMENT...
...I'D NEVER FELT PRESSURED BY AN OPPONENT.
IT'S NO USE... I CAN'T WIN.
THIS THING'LL KILL ME.
I'M GONNA DIE.
DON'T DIE!

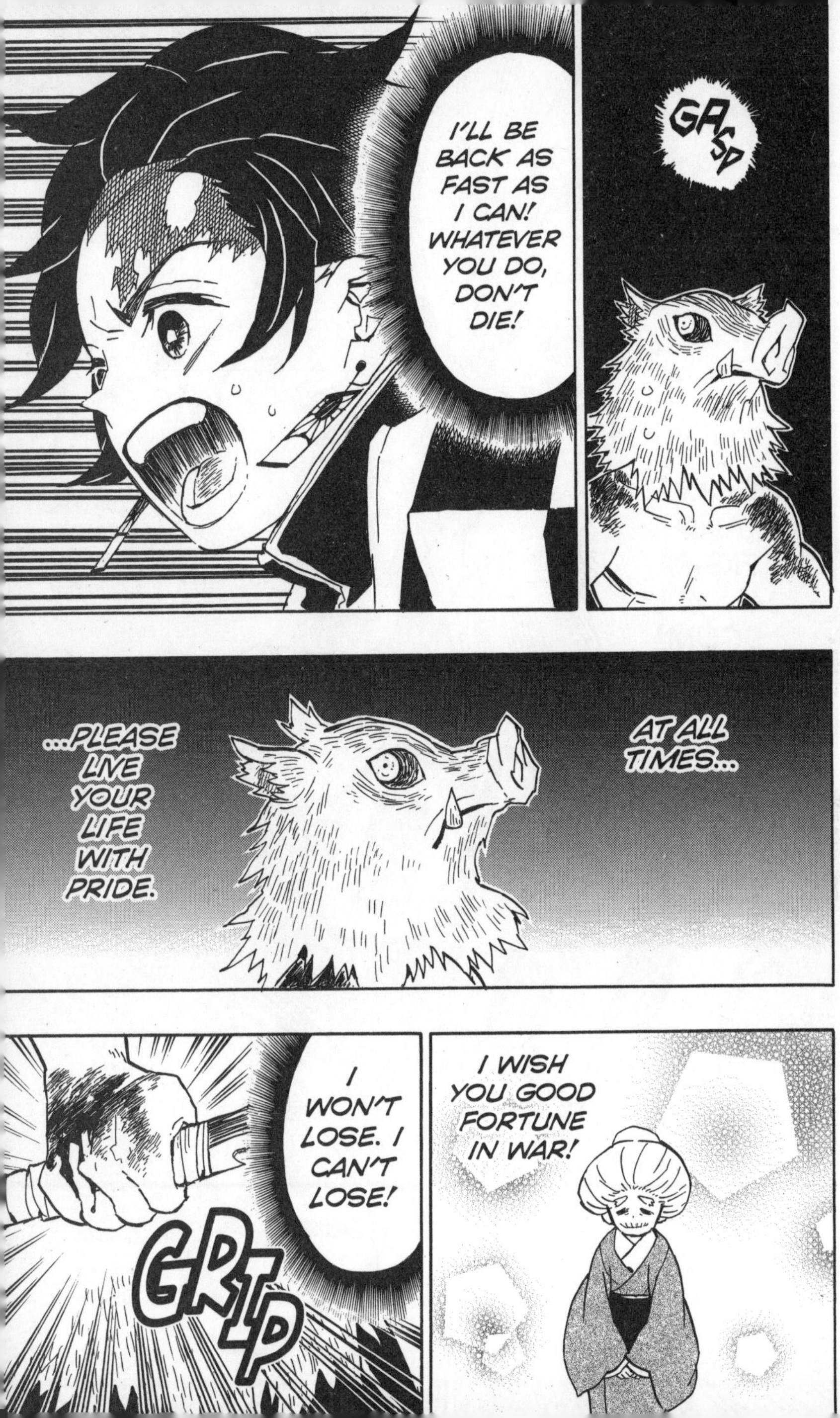
GASP
I'LL BE BACK AS FAST AS I CAN! WHATEVER YOU DO, DON'T DIE!
AT ALL TIMES...
...PLEASE LIVE YOUR LIFE WITH PRIDE.
I WISH YOU GOOD FORTUNE IN WAR!
I WON'T LOSE. I CAN'T LOSE!
GRIP

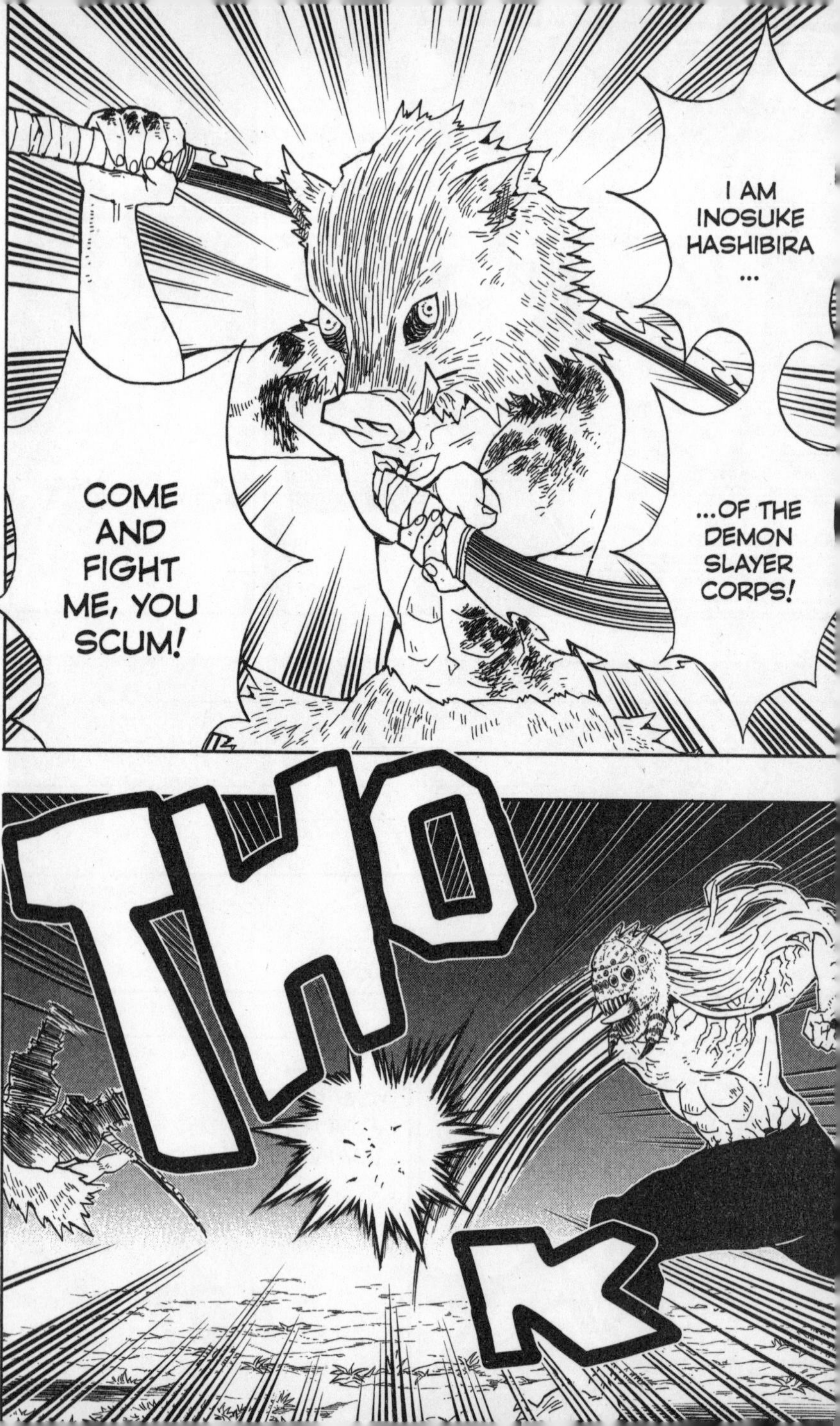
I AM INOSUKE HASHIBIRA ...
...OF THE DEMON SLAYER CORPS!
COME AND FIGHT ME, YOU SCUM!
THOK

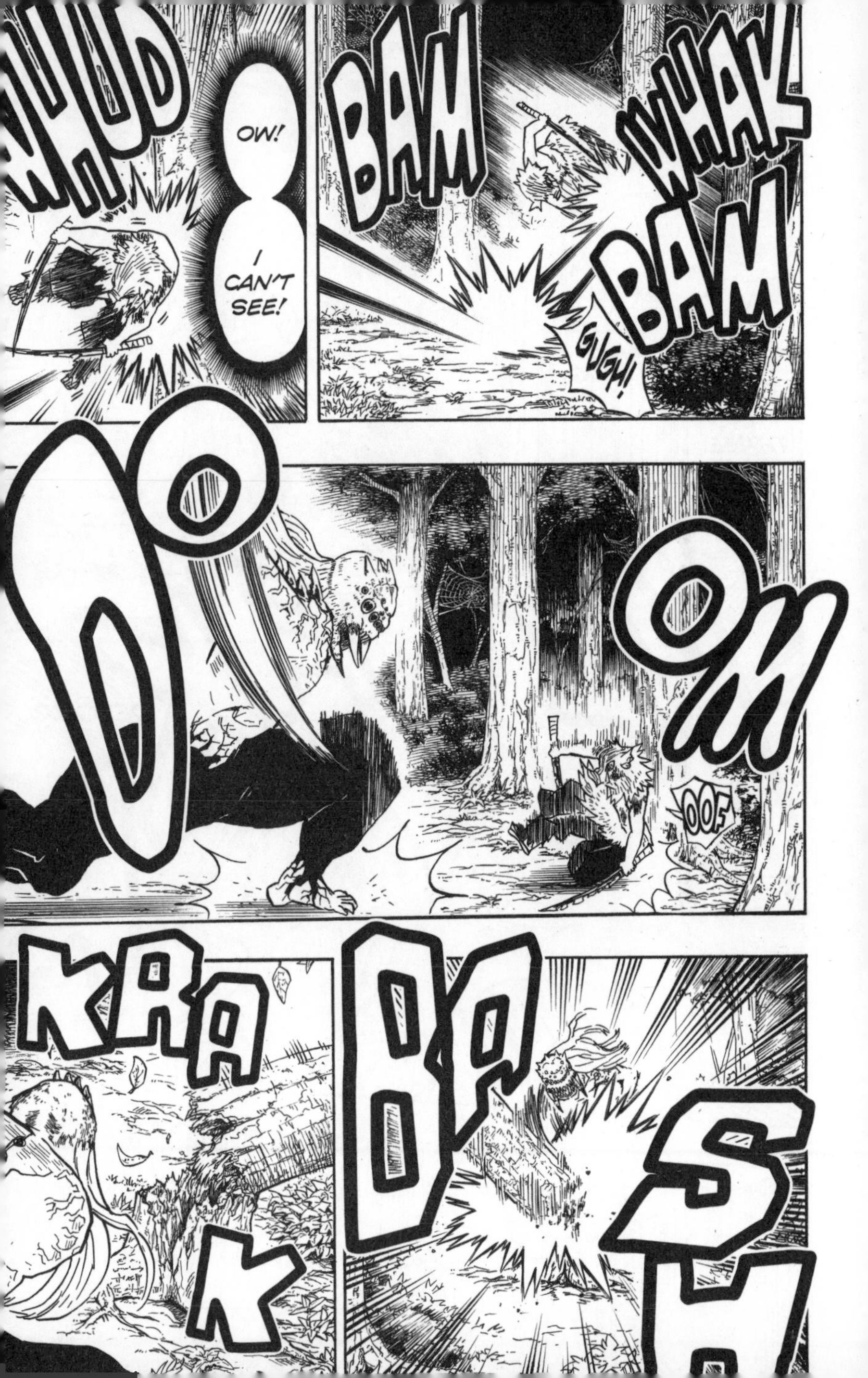
WHAK
BAM
BAM
GUGH!
OW!
I CAN'T SEE!
WHUD
OM
OOF
DO
BA
SH
KRA
K

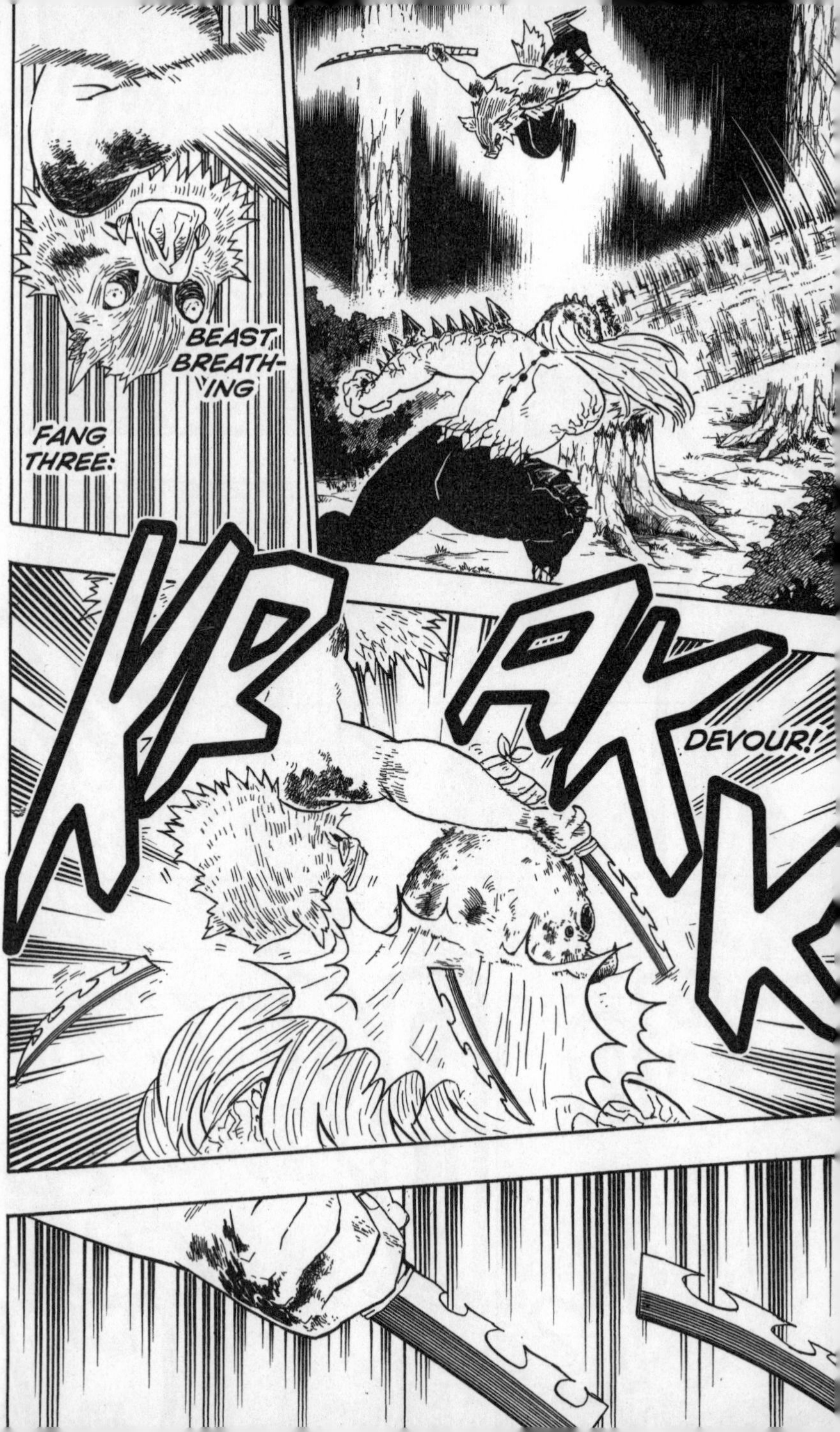
BEAST BREATH-ING
FANG THREE:
KRAK
DEVOUR!

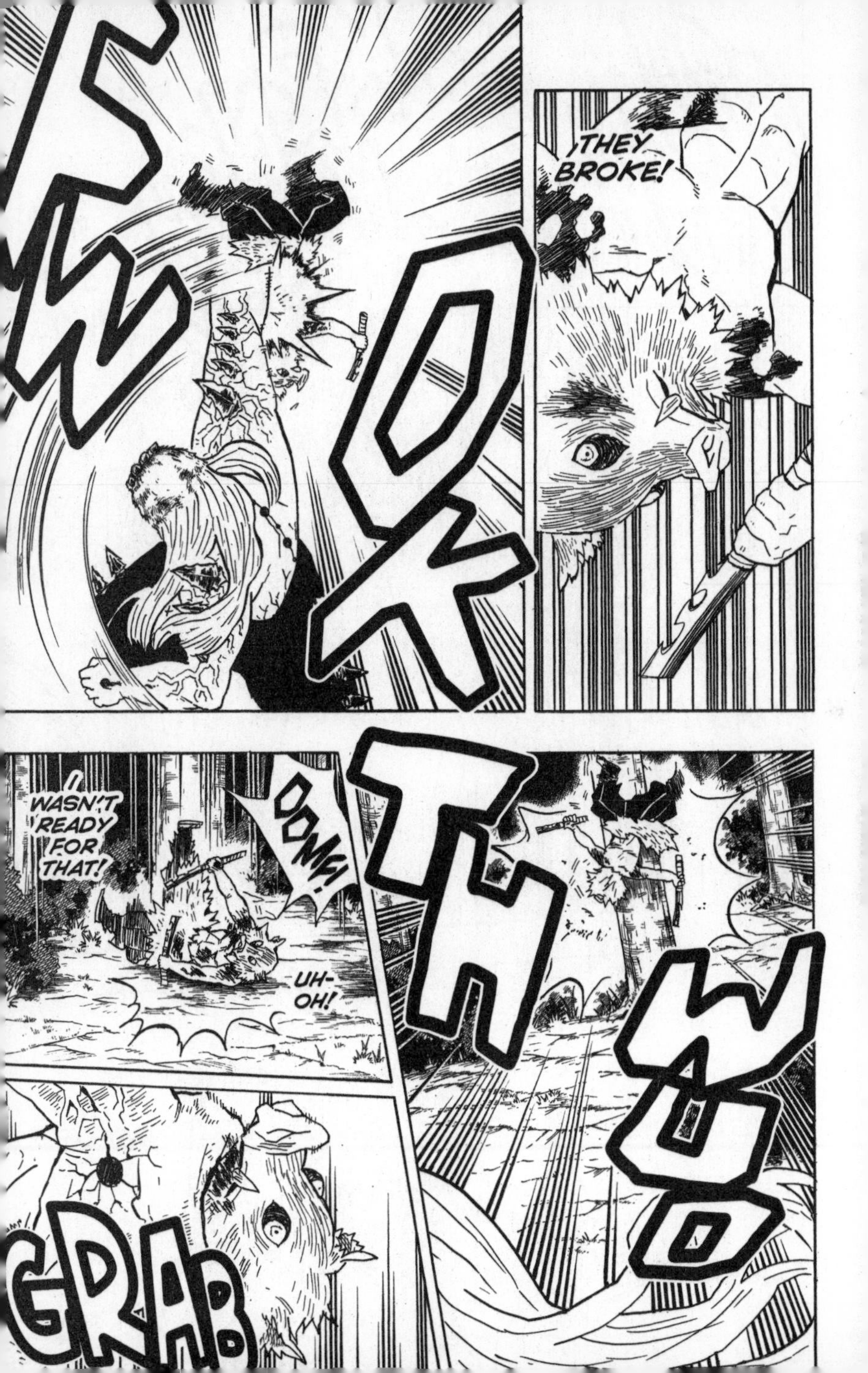
THEY BROKE!
THWUD
I WASN'T READY FOR THAT!
DOMF!
UH-OH!
GRAB

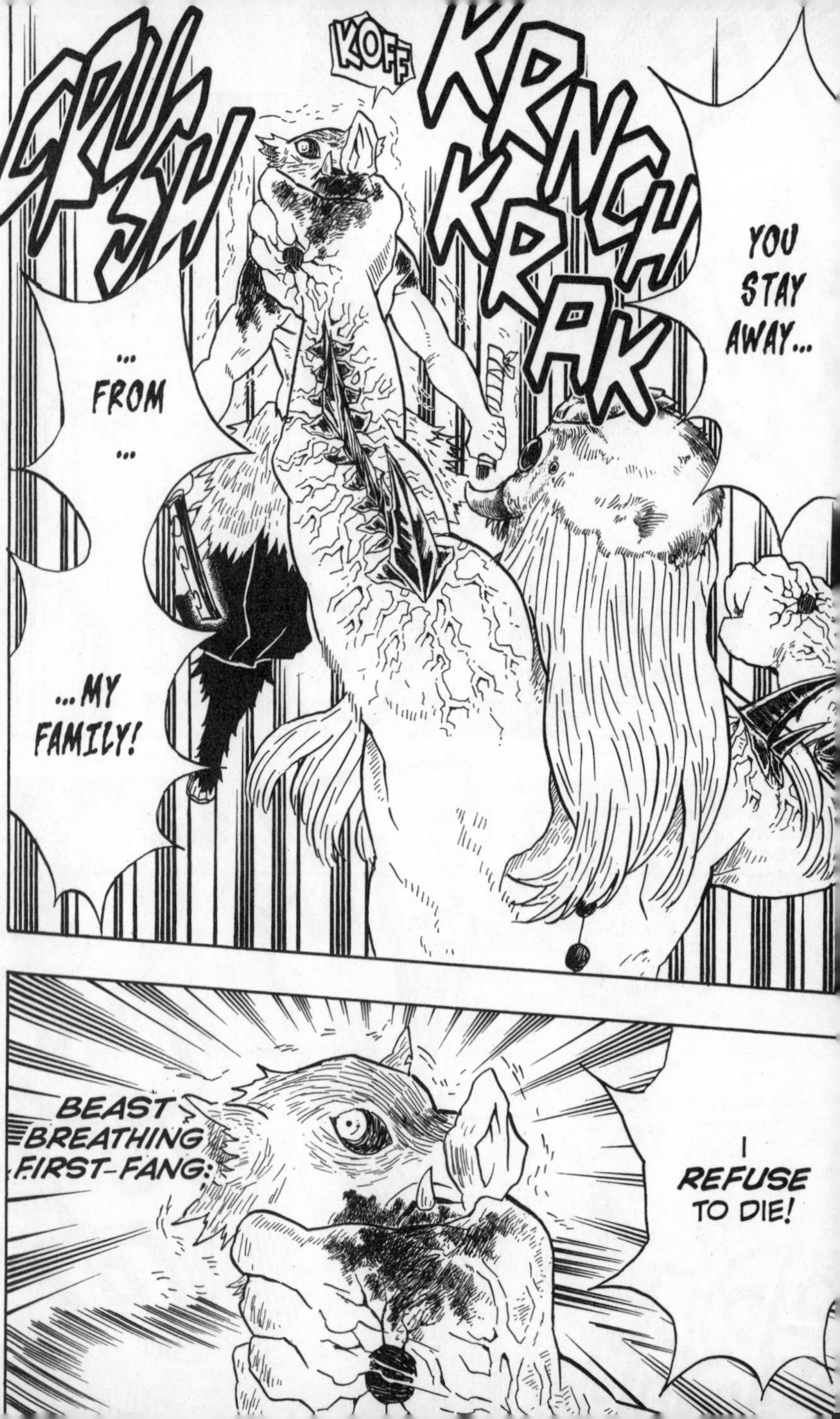
KRNCH
KRAK
KOFF
GRUSH
YOU STAY AWAY...
... FROM ...
...MY FAMILY!
I REFUSE TO DIE!
BEAST BREATHING FIRST-FANG:

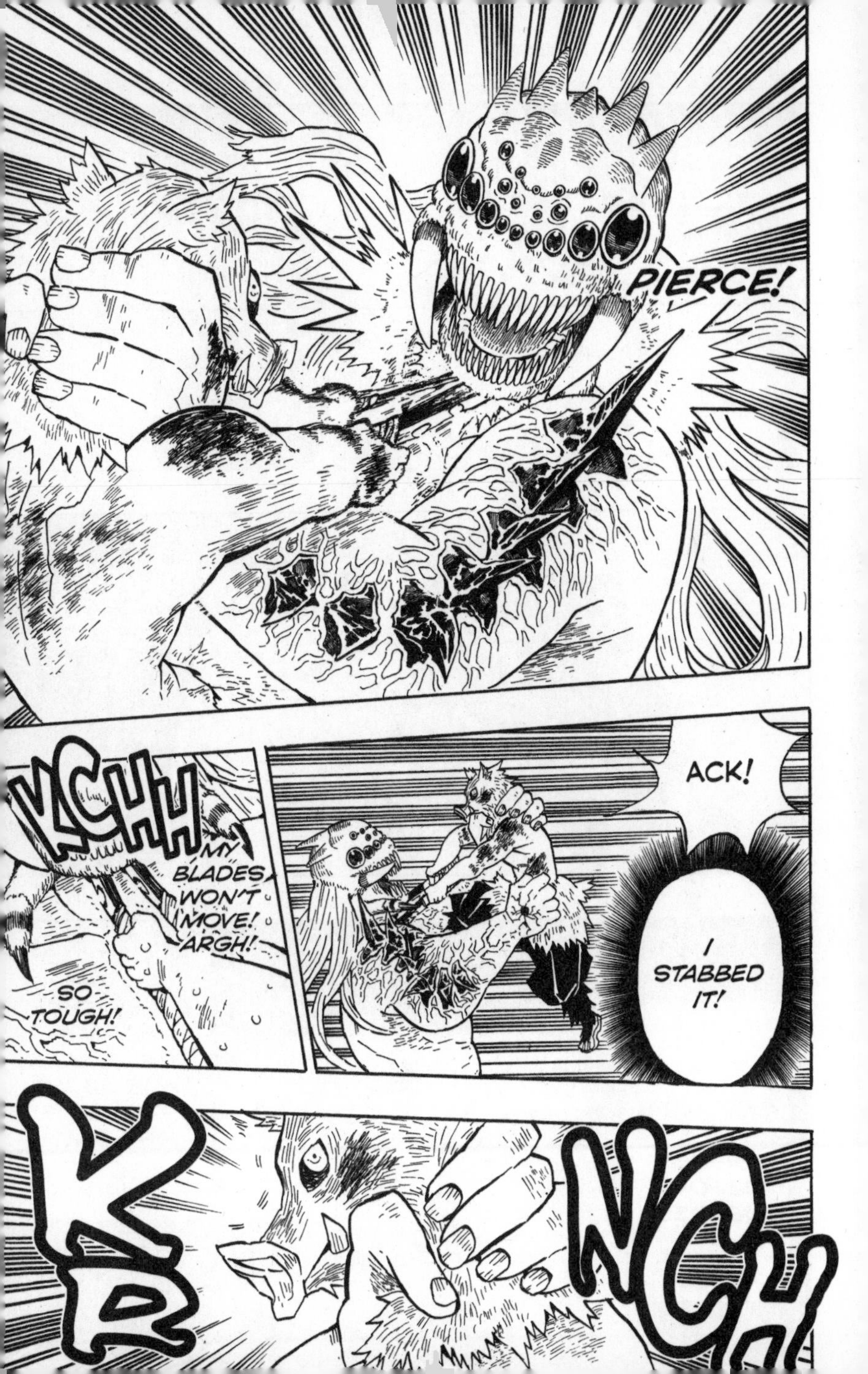
PIERCE!
ACK!
I STABBED IT!
KCHH
MY BLADES WON'T MOVE! ARGH!
SO TOUGH!
KR
NCH

FORGIVE ME!

I'M SORRY, INOSUKE.

...INOSUKE'S LIFE PASSED BEFORE HIS EYES.

IN THE MOMENT BEFORE THE DEMON WAS ABOUT TO CRUSH HIS NECK...

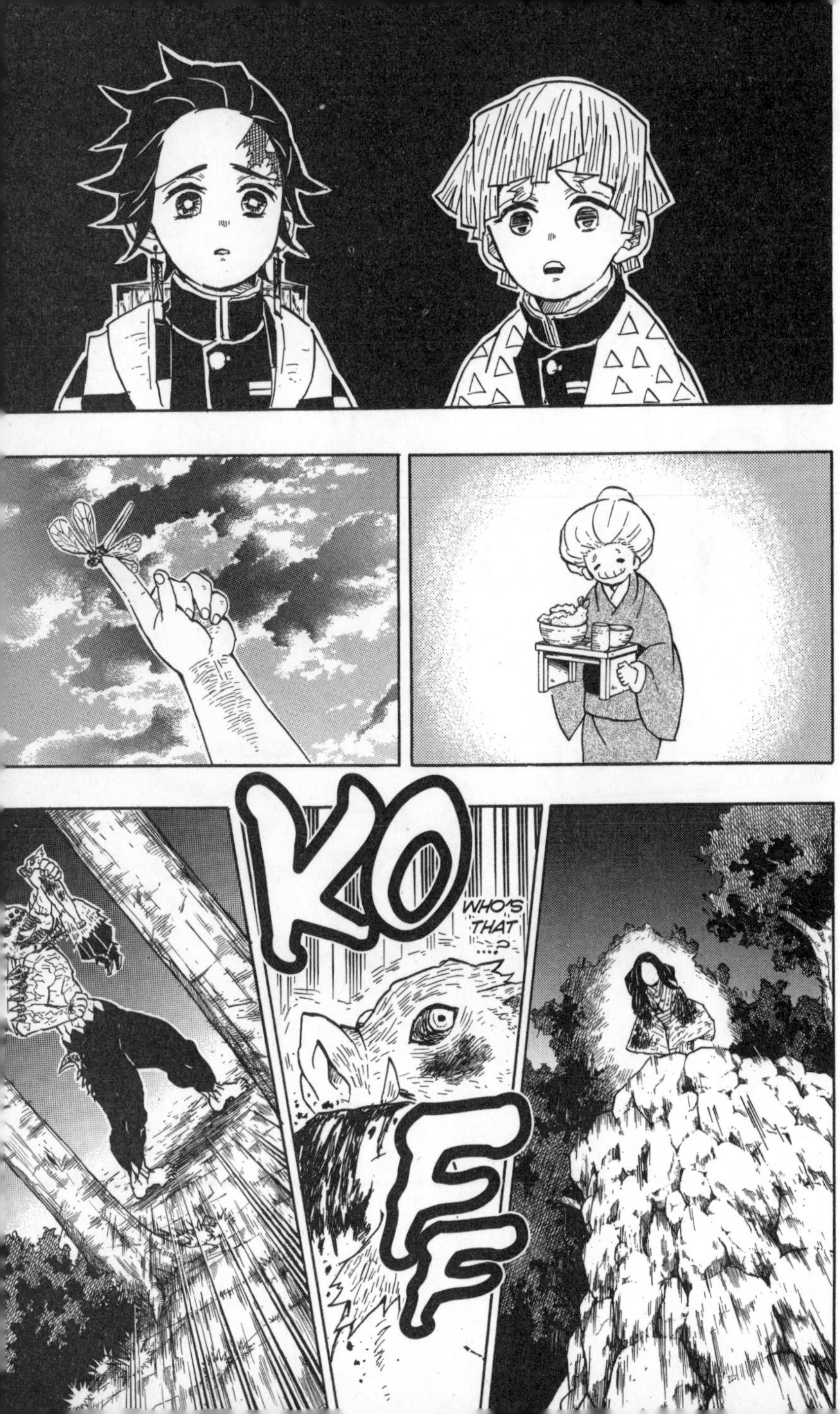
KO
WHO'S THAT ...?
F

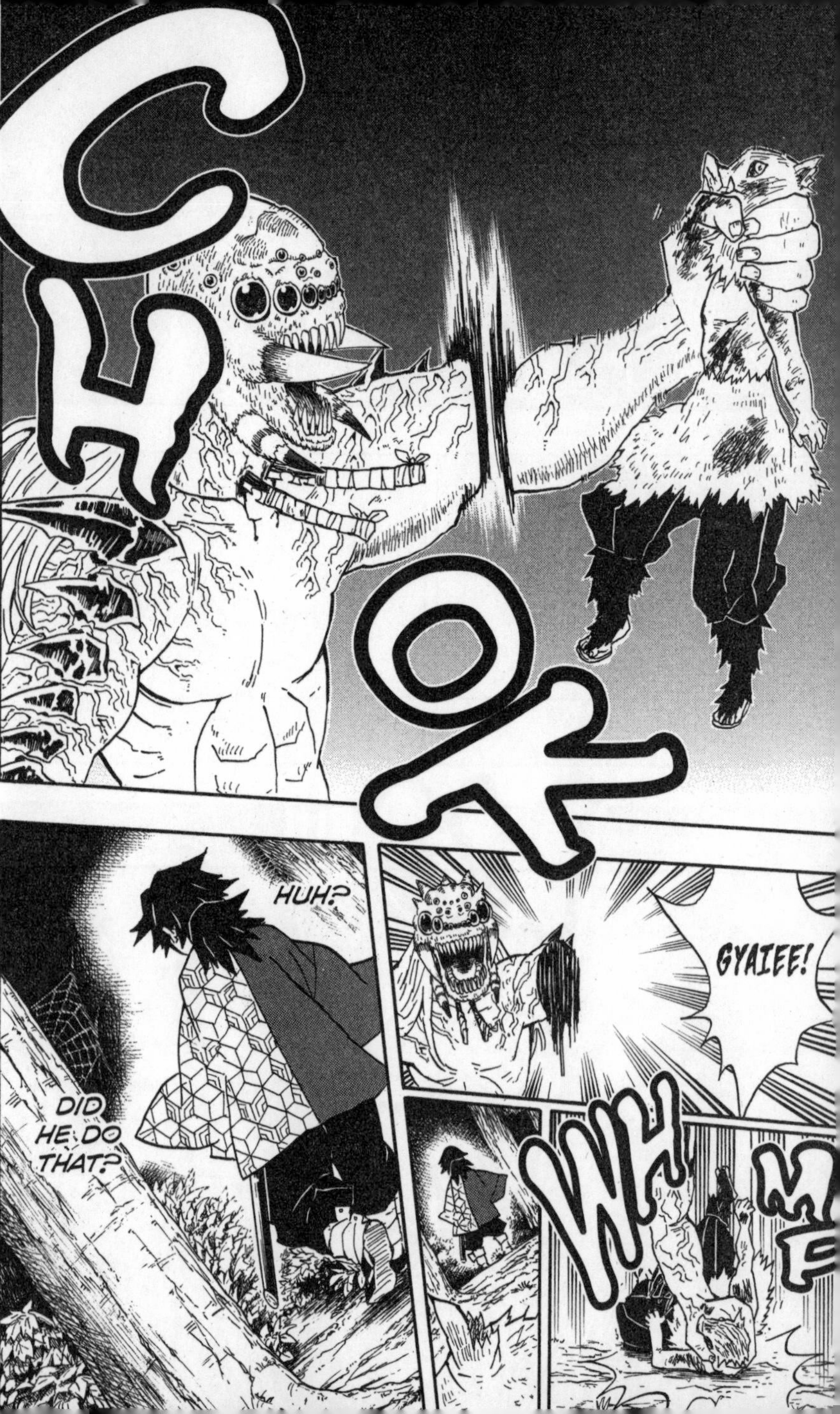
CHOK
GYAIEE!
WHM
HUH?
DID HE DO THAT?

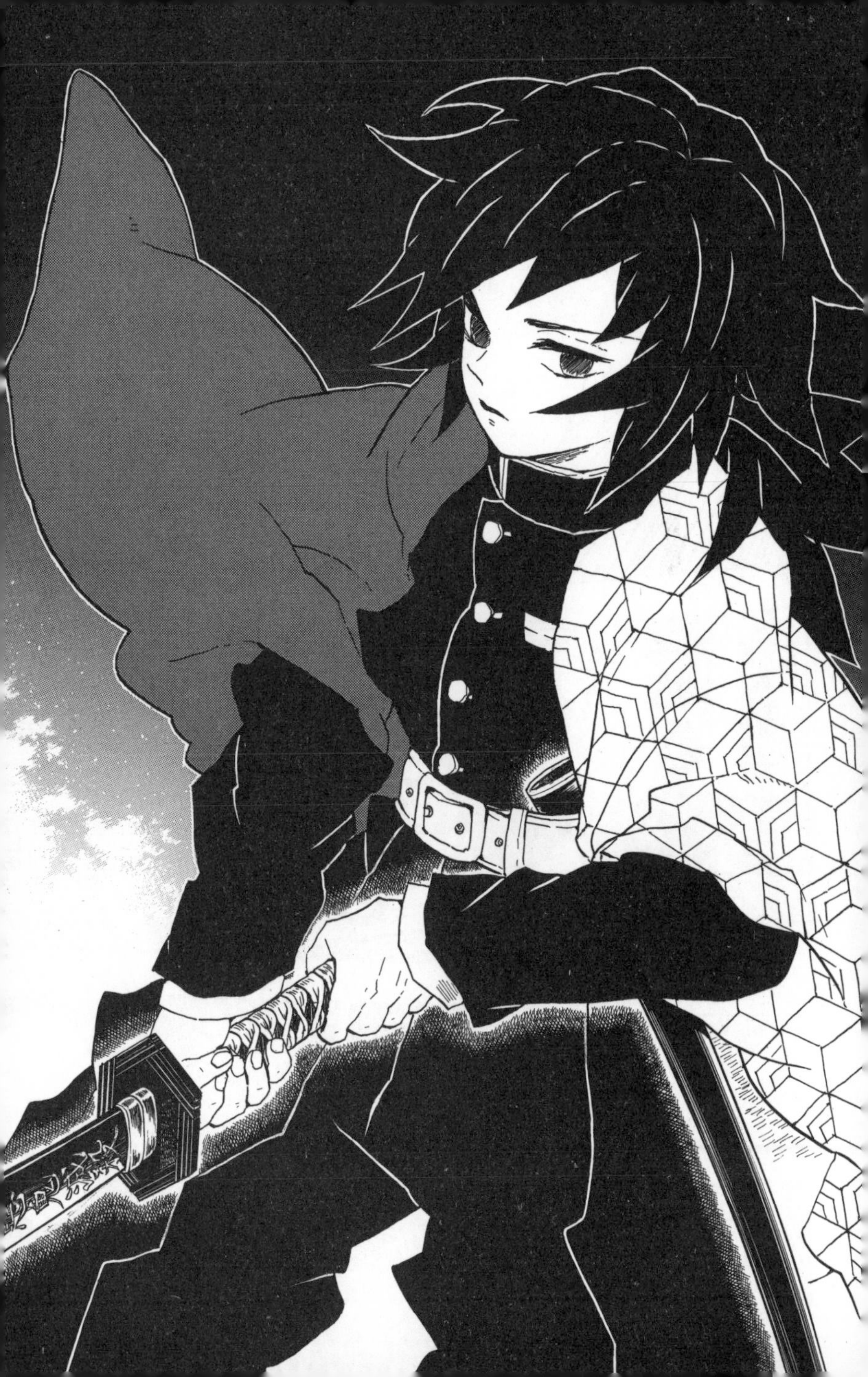

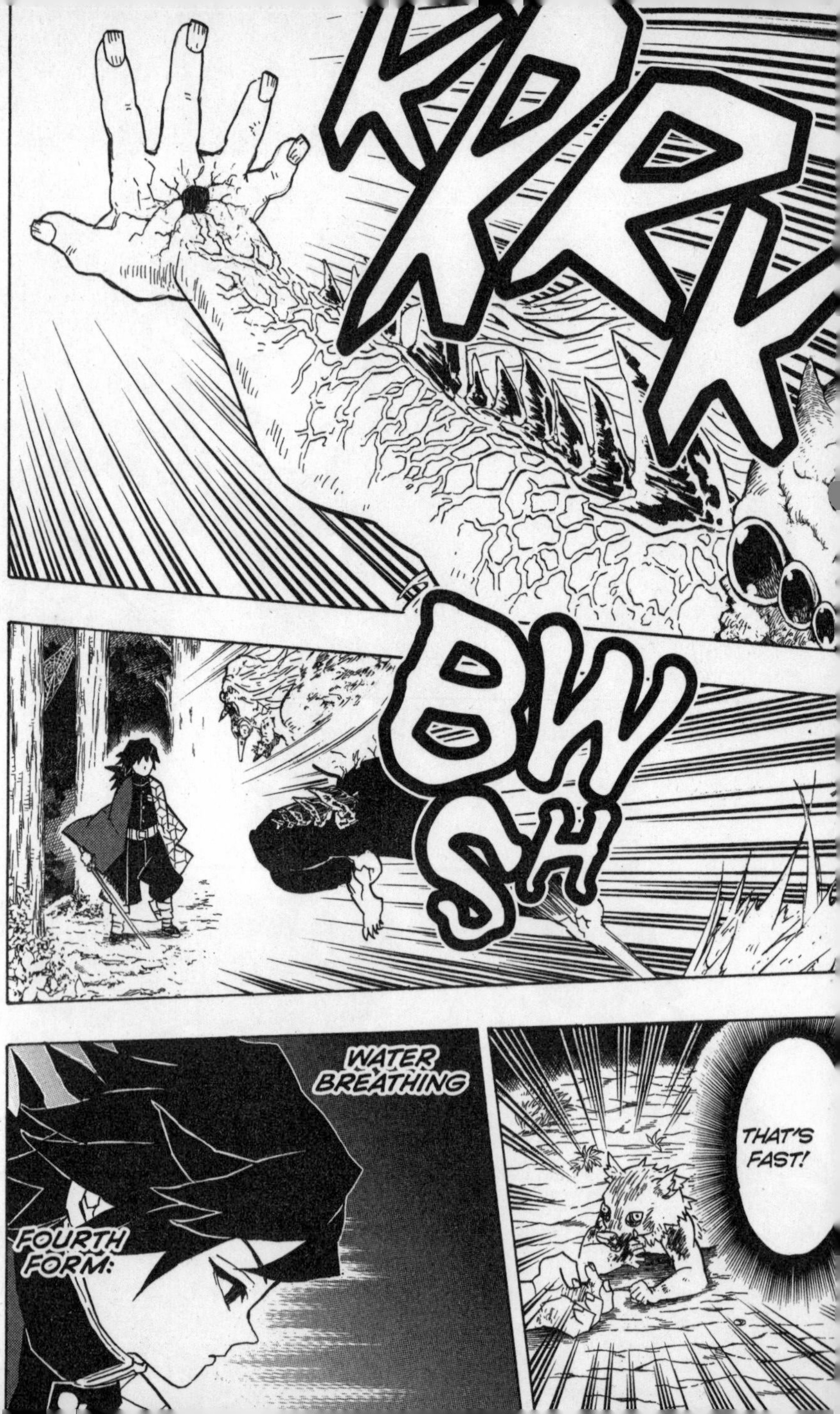
KRRK
BWSH
THAT'S FAST!
WATER BREATHING
FOURTH FORM:

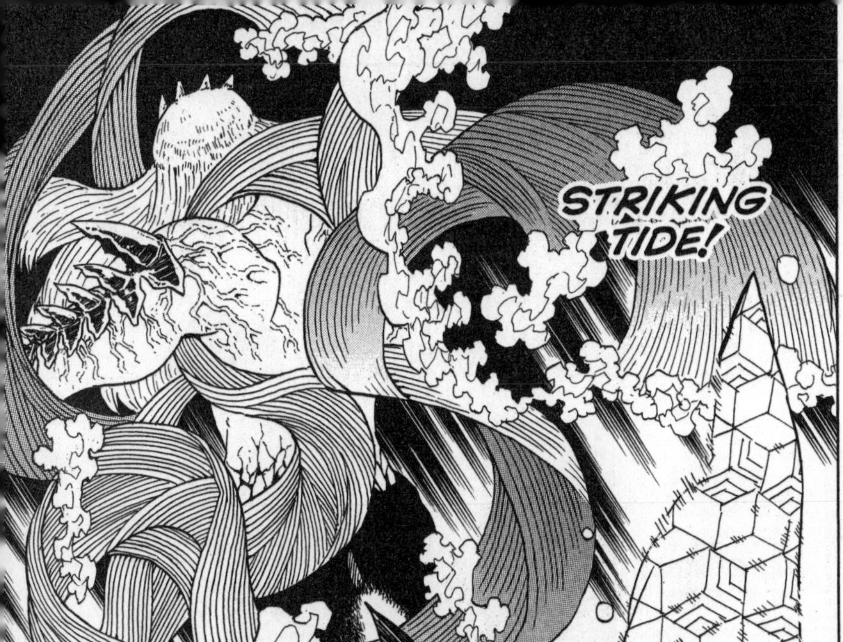
STRIKING TIDE!
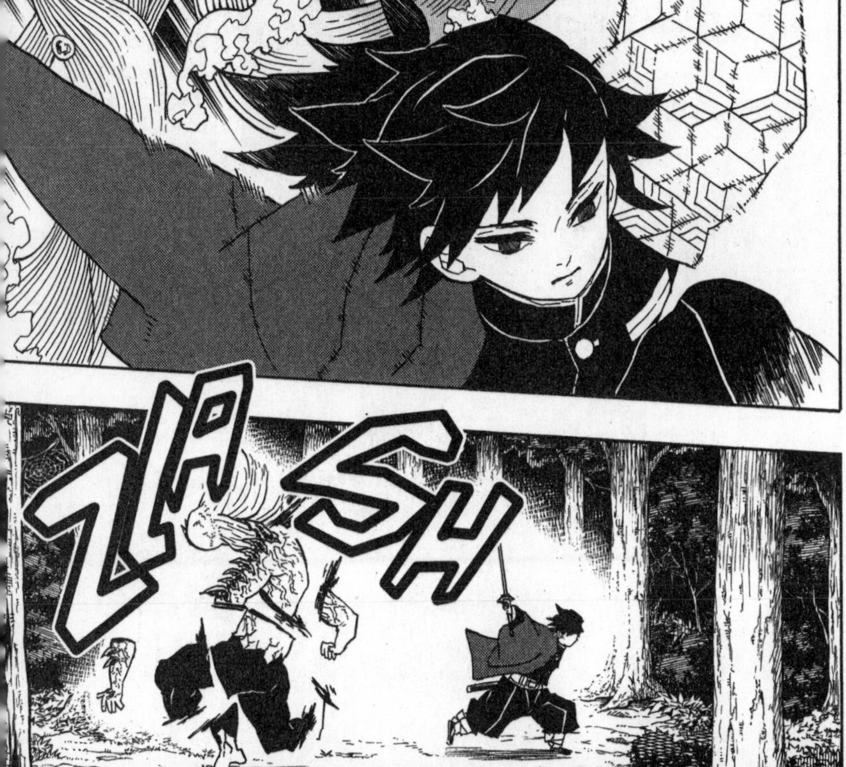
ZHSH

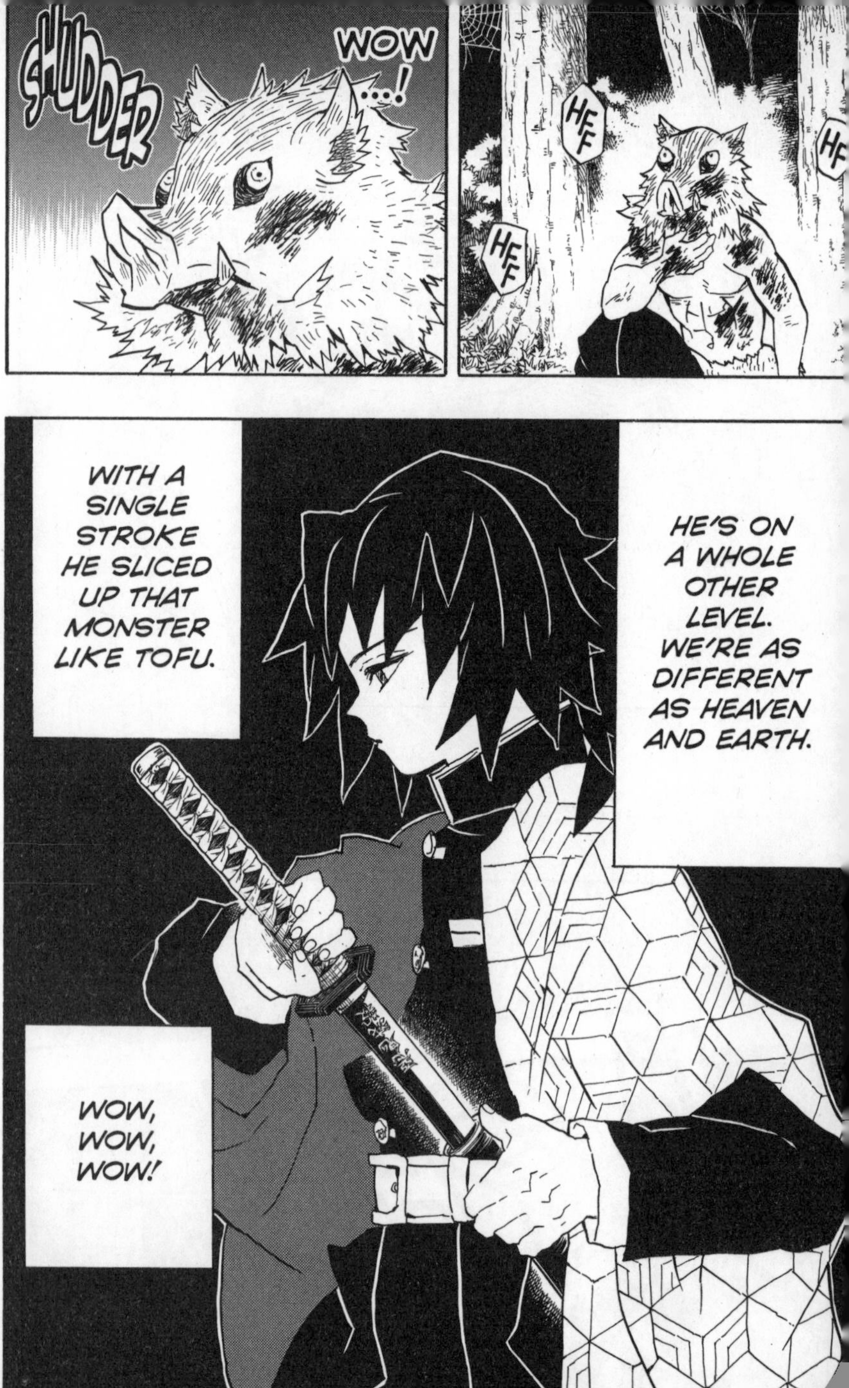
HEF
HF
HEF
SHUDDER
WOW...!
HE'S ON A WHOLE OTHER LEVEL. WE'RE AS DIFFERENT AS HEAVEN AND EARTH.
WITH A SINGLE STROKE HE SLICED UP THAT MONSTER LIKE TOFU.
WOW, WOW, WOW!

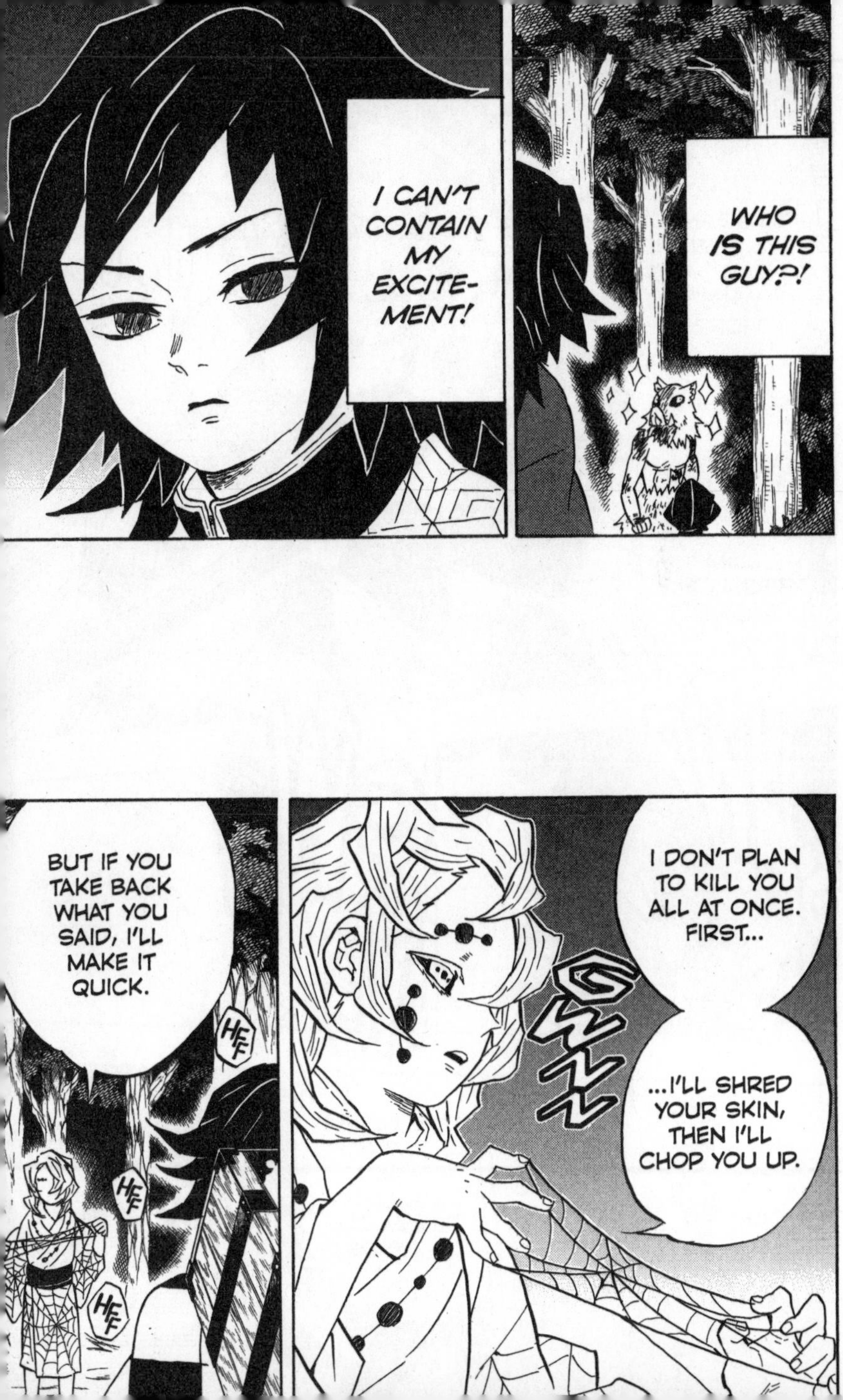
WHO IS THIS GUY?!
I CAN'T CONTAIN MY EXCITE-MENT!
I DON'T PLAN TO KILL YOU ALL AT ONCE. FIRST...
...I'LL SHRED YOUR SKIN, THEN I'LL CHOP YOU UP.
GWNN
BUT IF YOU TAKE BACK WHAT YOU SAID, I'LL MAKE IT QUICK.
HEF
HEF
HEF

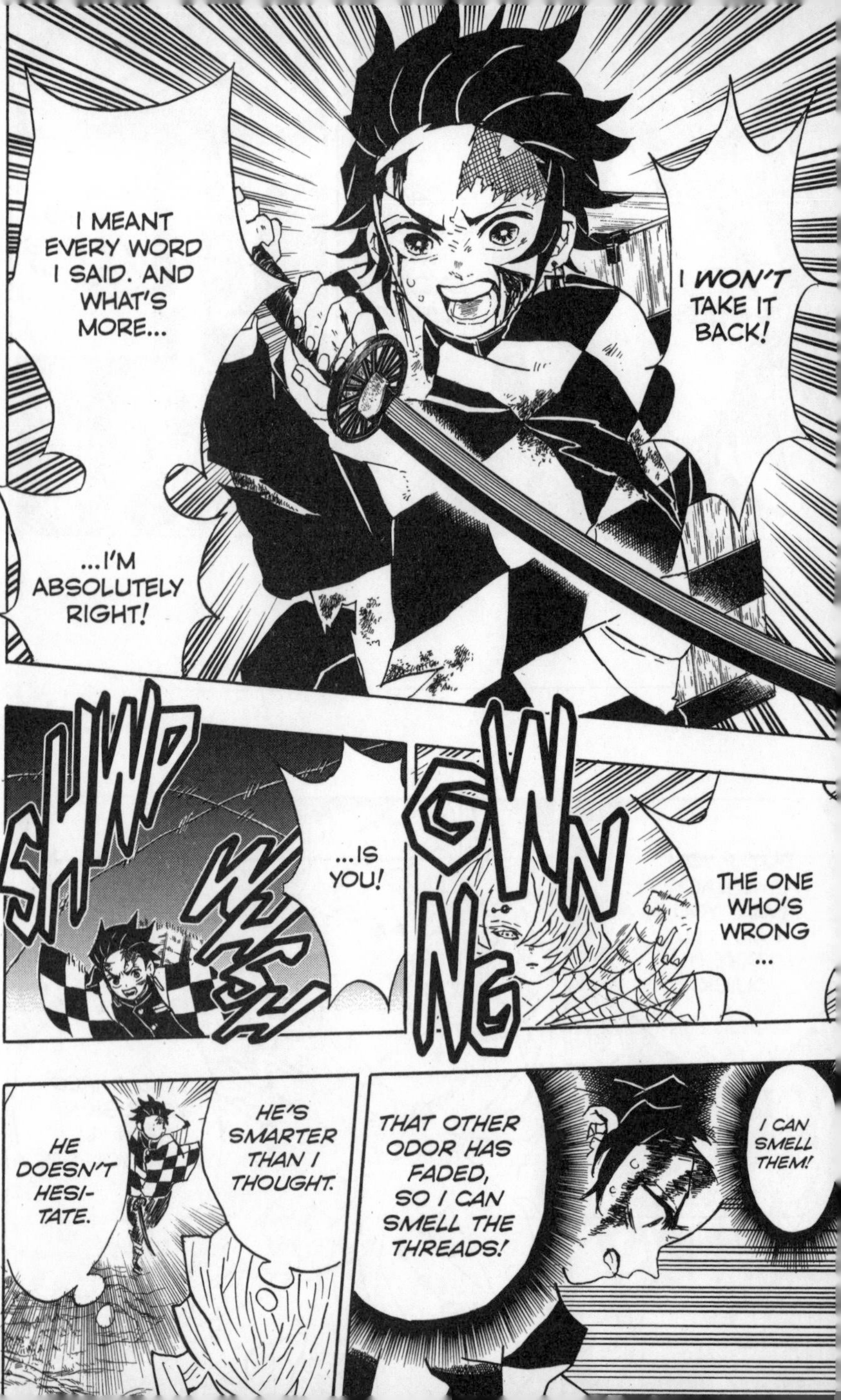
I WON'T TAKE IT BACK!
I MEANT EVERY WORD I SAID. AND WHAT'S MORE...
...I'M ABSOLUTELY RIGHT!
THE ONE WHO'S WRONG ...
GWNNG
...IS YOU!
SHWP
WHSH
I CAN SMELL THEM!
THAT OTHER ODOR HAS FADED, SO I CAN SMELL THE THREADS!
HE'S SMARTER THAN I THOUGHT.
HE DOESN'T HESI-TATE.

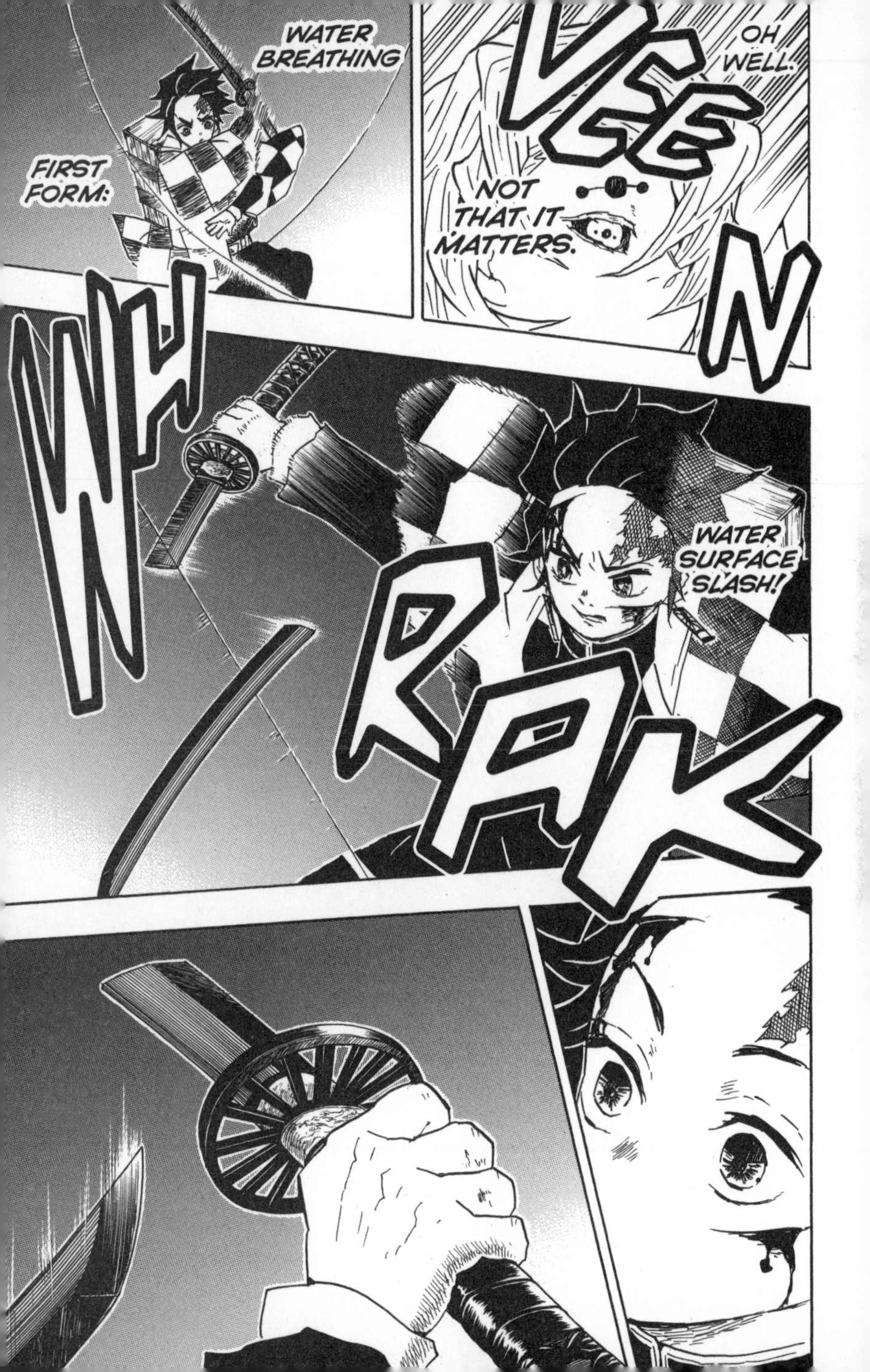
OH WELL.
VEEEN
NOT THAT IT MATTERS.
WATER BREATHING
FIRST FORM:
WH
RAK
WATER SURFACE SLASH!

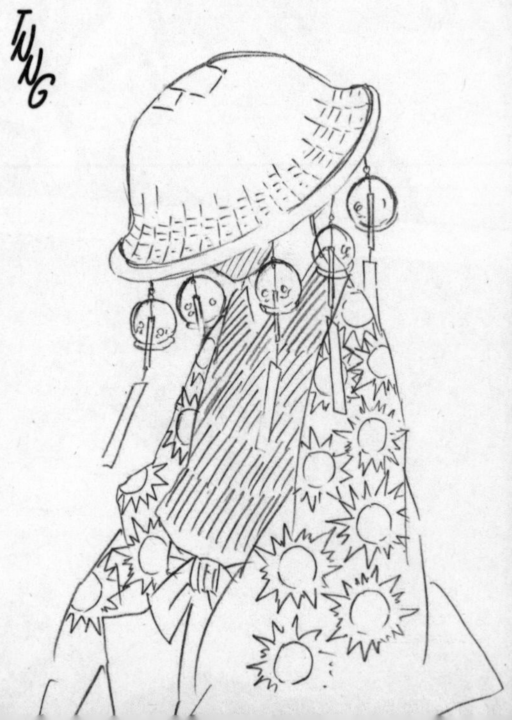
TWNG

CHAPTER 38: REAL AND FAKE

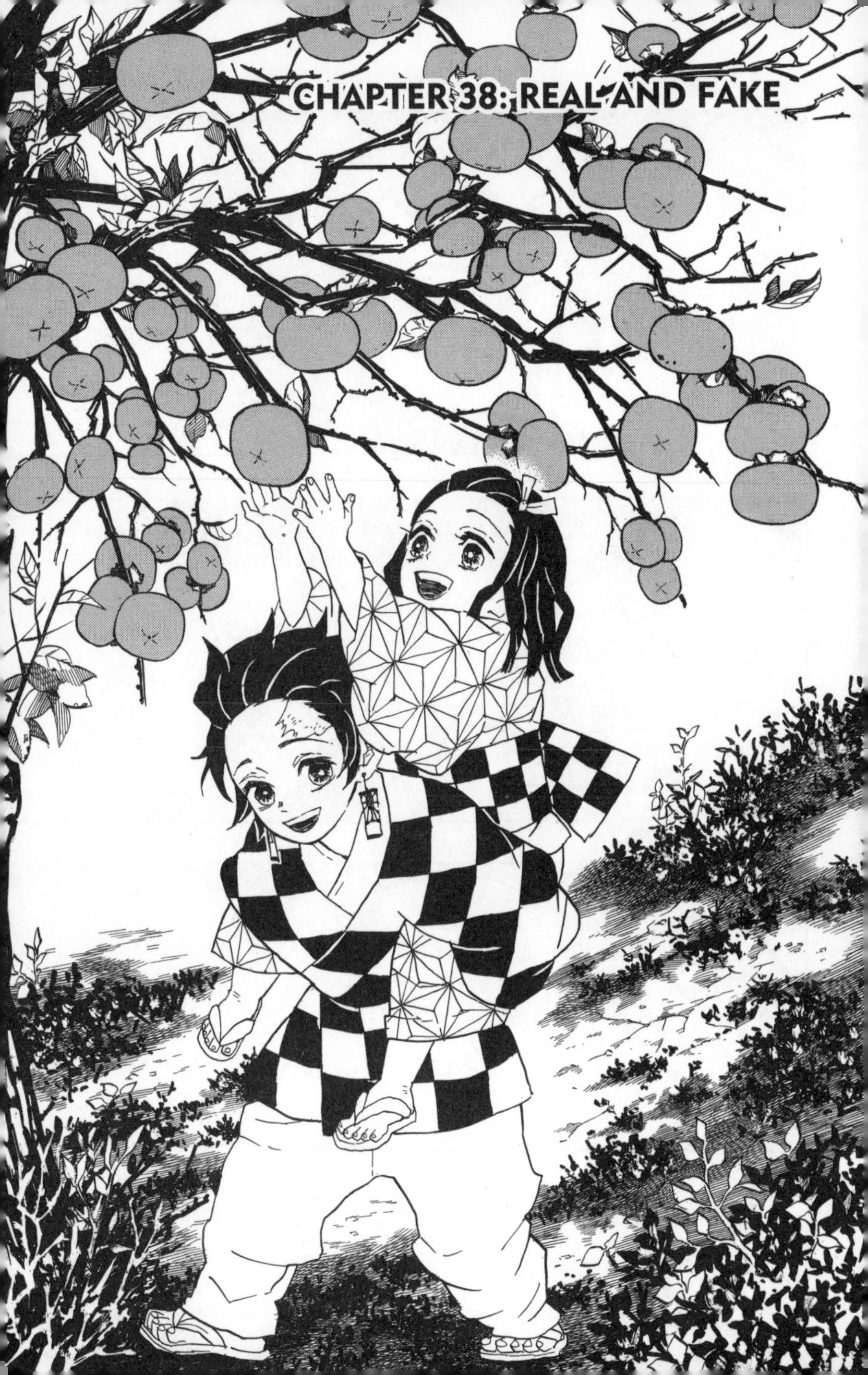

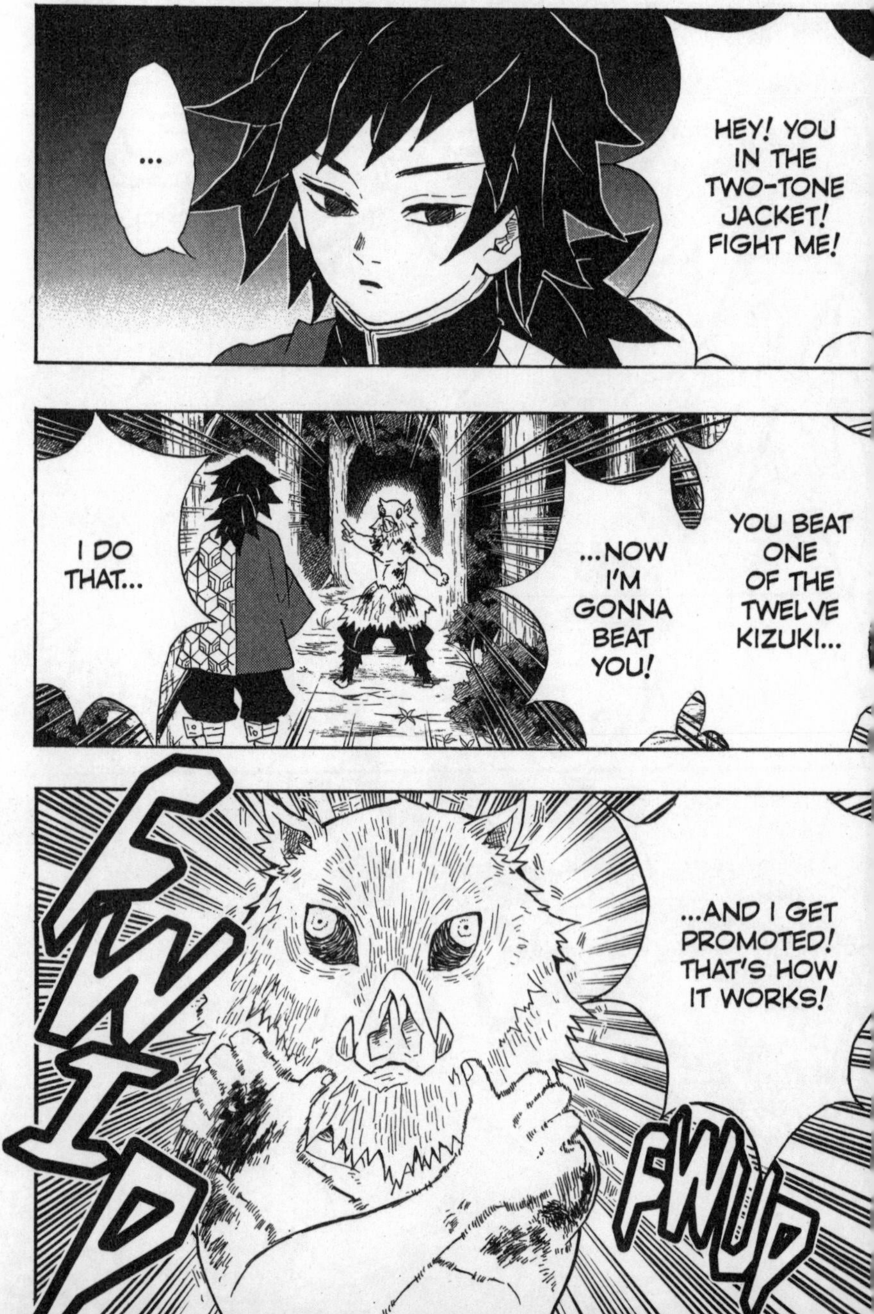
HEY! YOU IN THE TWO-TONE JACKET! FIGHT ME!
...
YOU BEAT ONE OF THE TWELVE KIZUKI...
...NOW I'M GONNA BEAT YOU!
I DO THAT...
...AND I GET PROMOTED! THAT'S HOW IT WORKS!
FWUP
FWIP

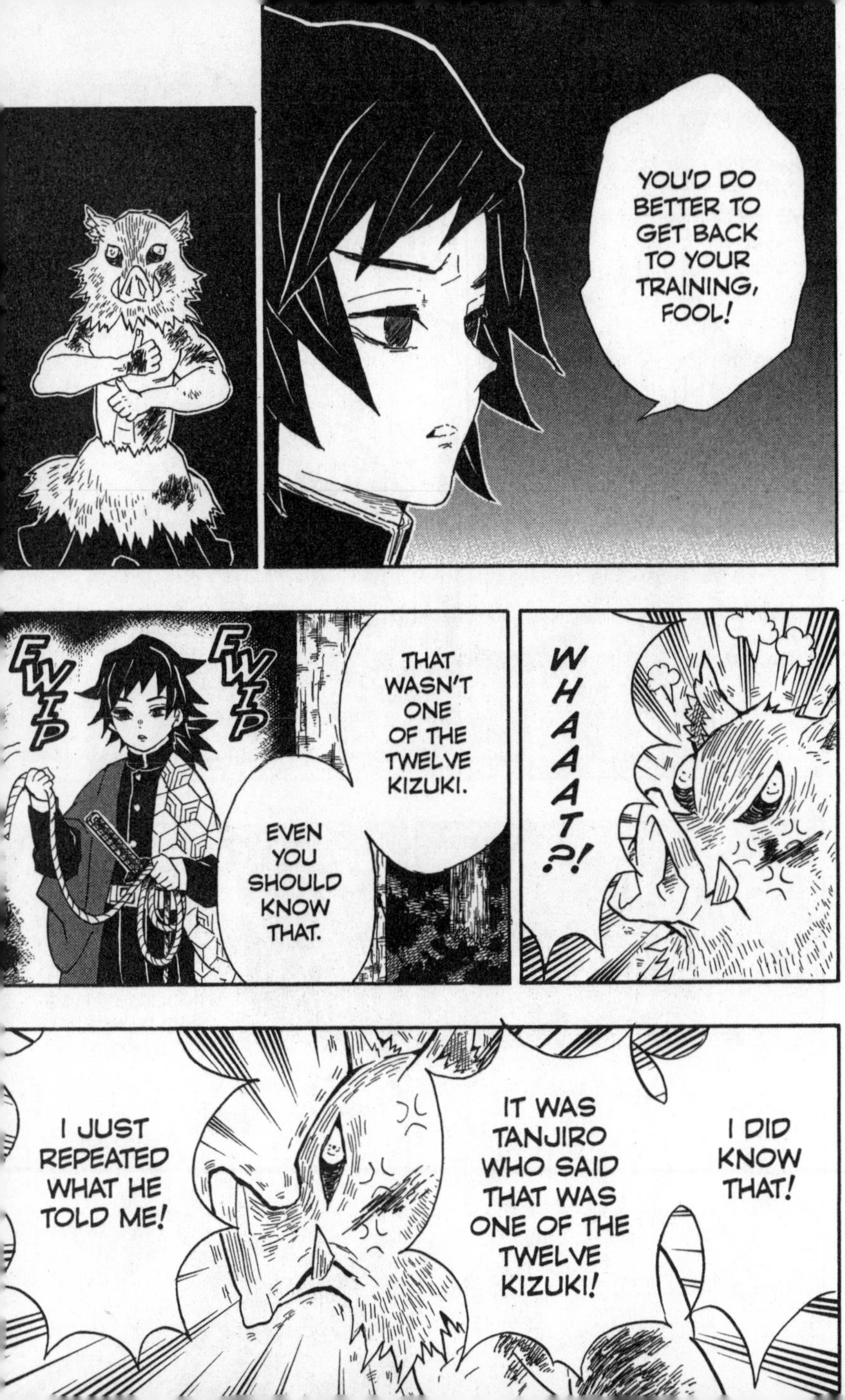
YOU'D DO BETTER TO GET BACK TO YOUR TRAINING, FOOL!
WHAAAAT?!
FWIP FWIP
THAT WASN'T ONE OF THE TWELVE KIZUKI.
EVEN YOU SHOULD KNOW THAT.
I DID KNOW THAT!
IT WAS TANJIRO WHO SAID THAT WAS ONE OF THE TWELVE KIZUKI!
I JUST REPEATED WHAT HE TOLD ME!

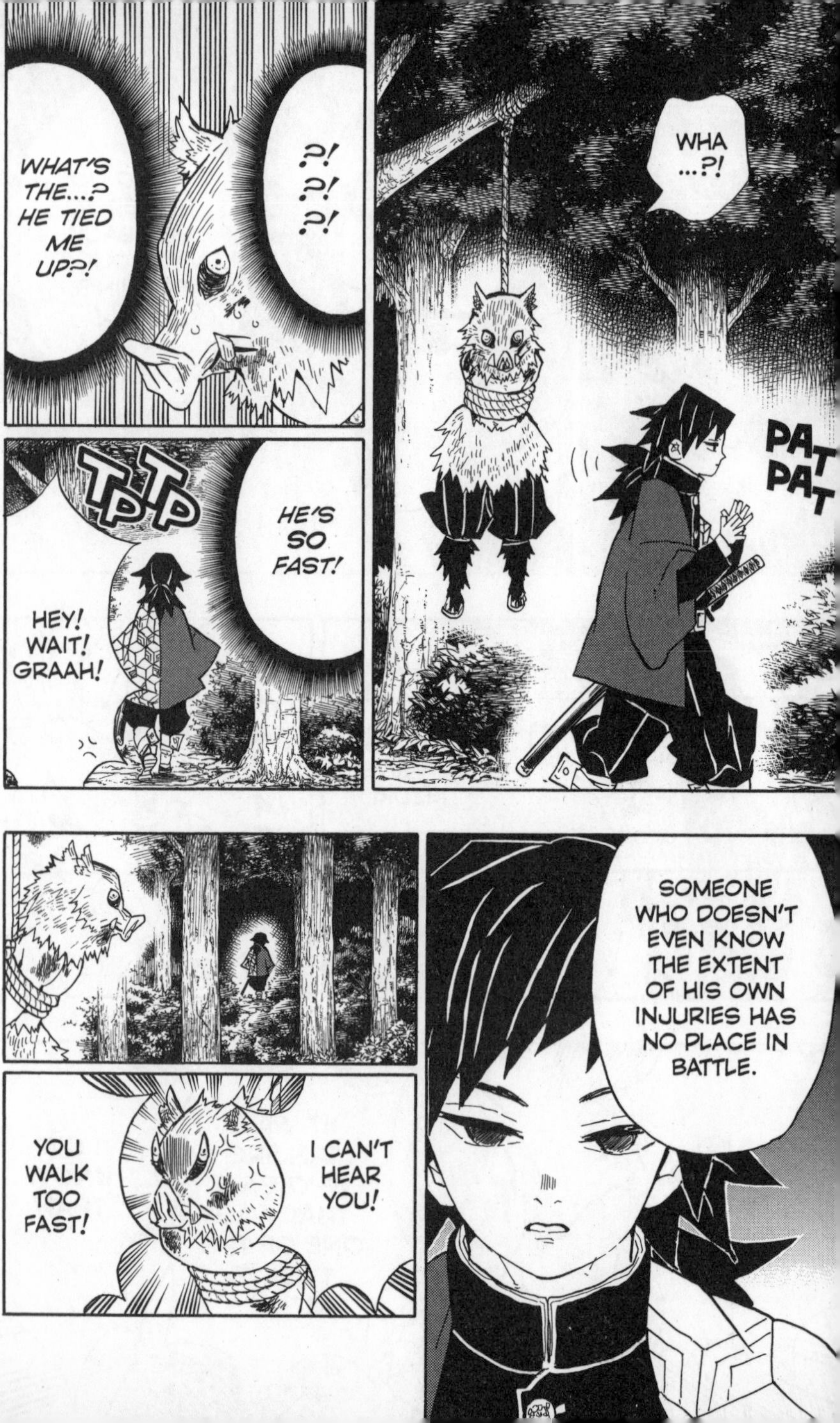
WHA ...?!
PAT PAT
?! ?! ?!
WHAT'S THE...? HE TIED ME UP?!
HE'S SO FAST!
TP TP
HEY! WAIT! GRAAH!
SOMEONE WHO DOESN'T EVEN KNOW THE EXTENT OF HIS OWN INJURIES HAS NO PLACE IN BATTLE.
I CAN'T HEAR YOU!
YOU WALK TOO FAST!

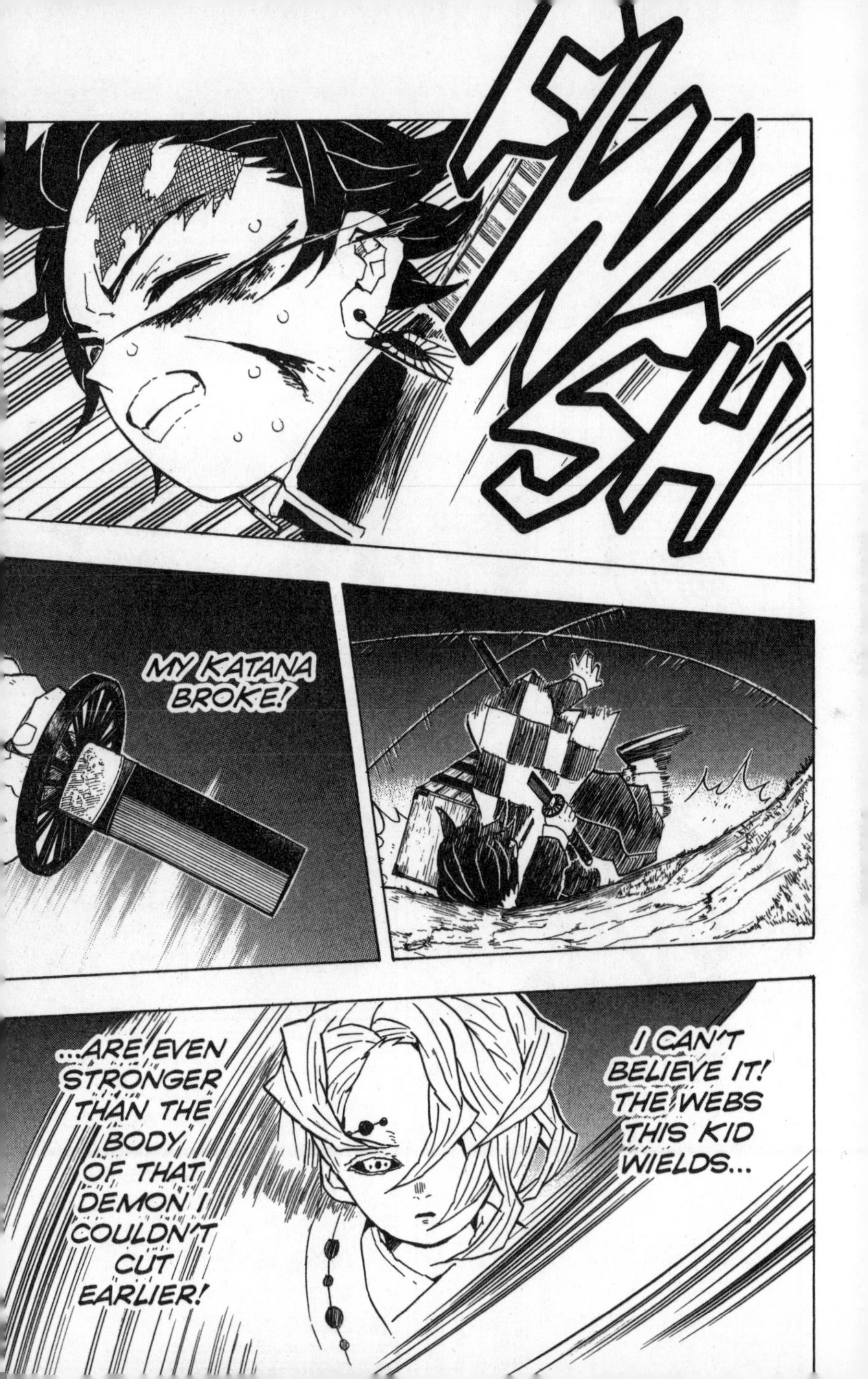
SNAP
MY KATANA BROKE!
I CAN'T BELIEVE IT! THE WEBS THIS KID WIELDS...
...ARE EVEN STRONGER THAN THE BODY OF THAT DEMON I COULDN'T CUT EARLIER!

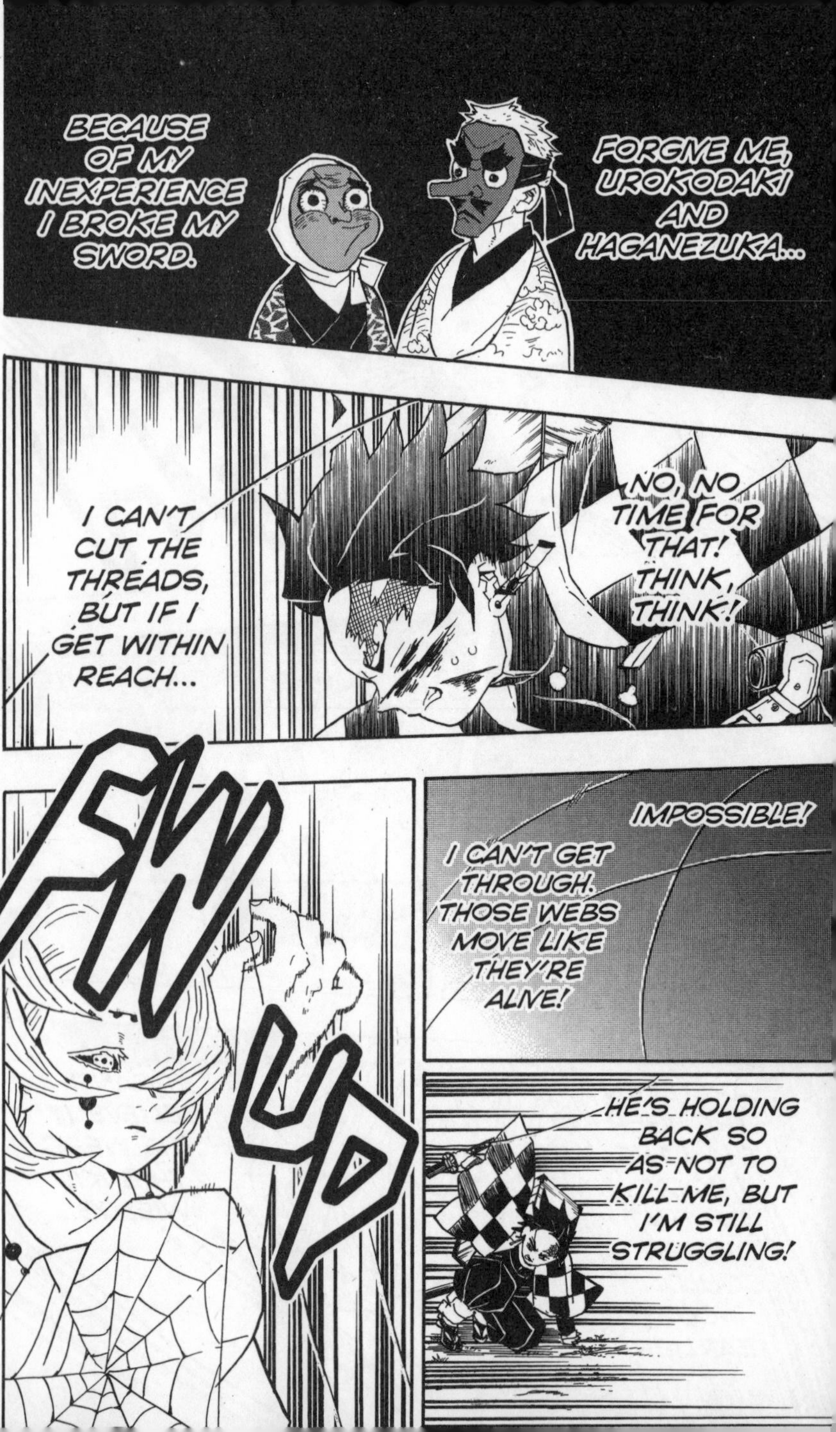
FORGIVE ME, UROKODAKI AND HAGANEZUKA...
BECAUSE OF MY INEXPERIENCE I BROKE MY SWORD.
NO, NO TIME FOR THAT! THINK, THINK!
I CAN'T CUT THE THREADS, BUT IF I GET WITHIN REACH...
IMPOSSIBLE!
I CAN'T GET THROUGH. THOSE WEBS MOVE LIKE THEY'RE ALIVE!
HE'S HOLDING BACK SO AS NOT TO KILL ME, BUT I'M STILL STRUGGLING!
FWUP

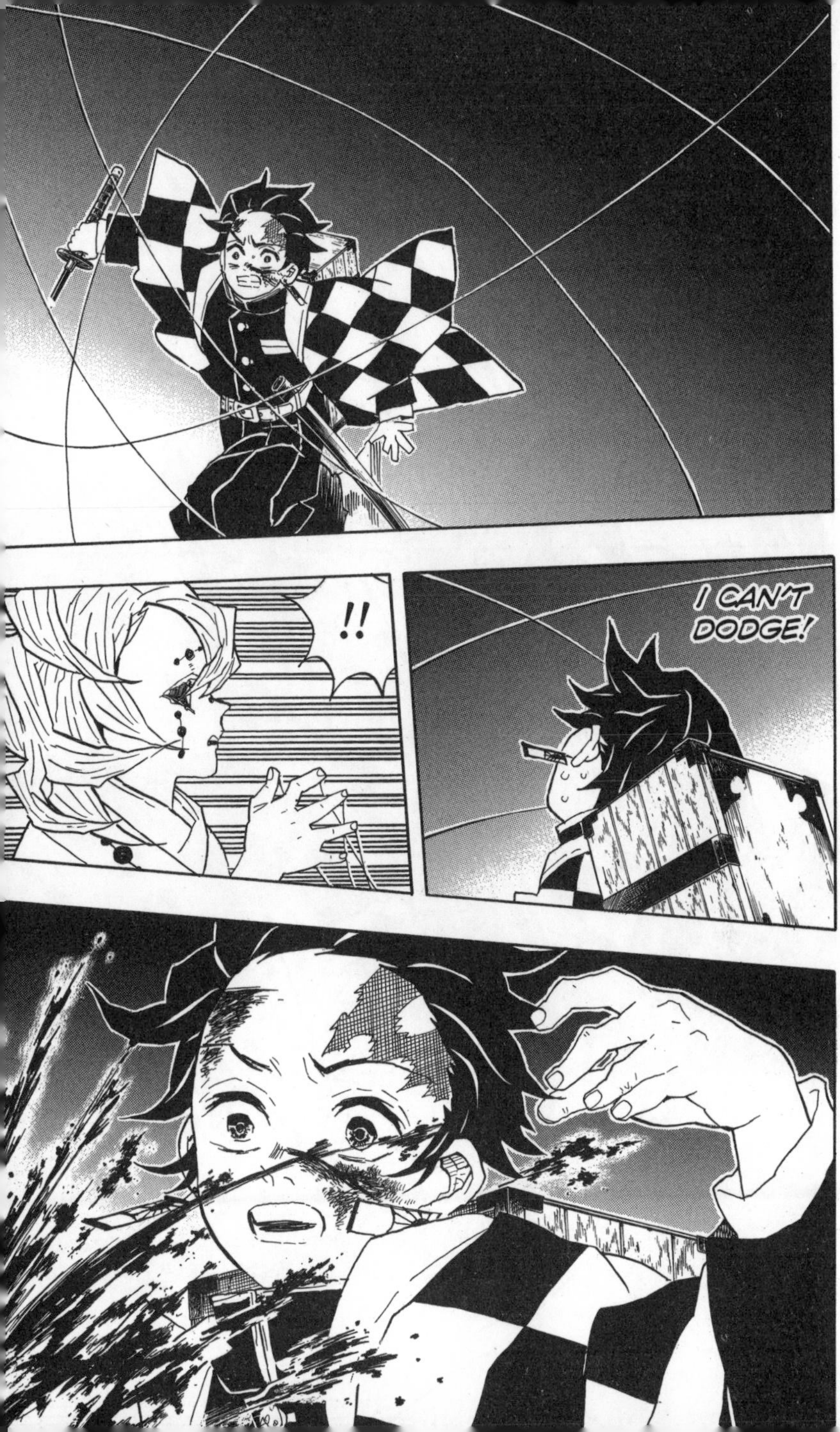
I CAN'T DODGE!
!!

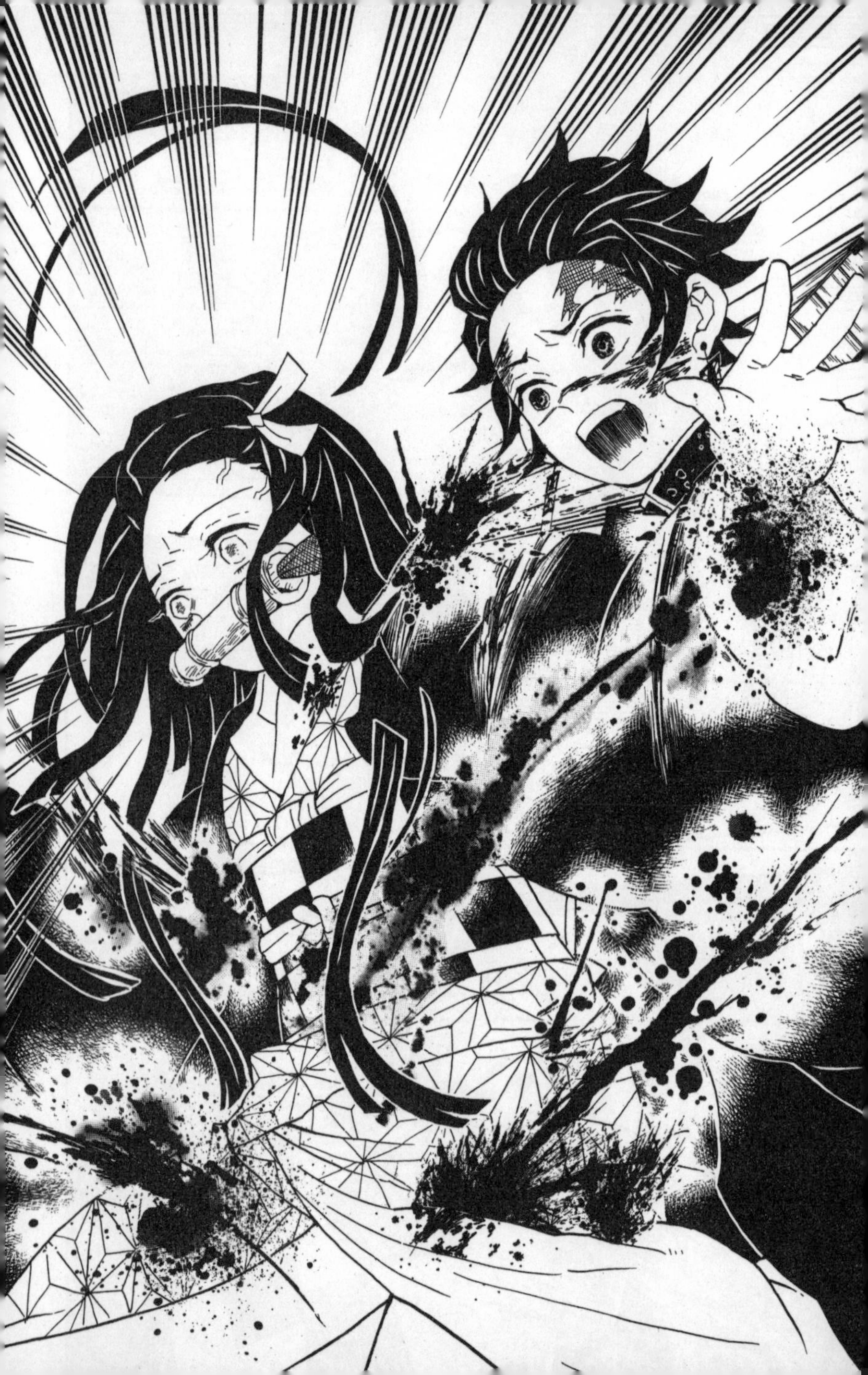

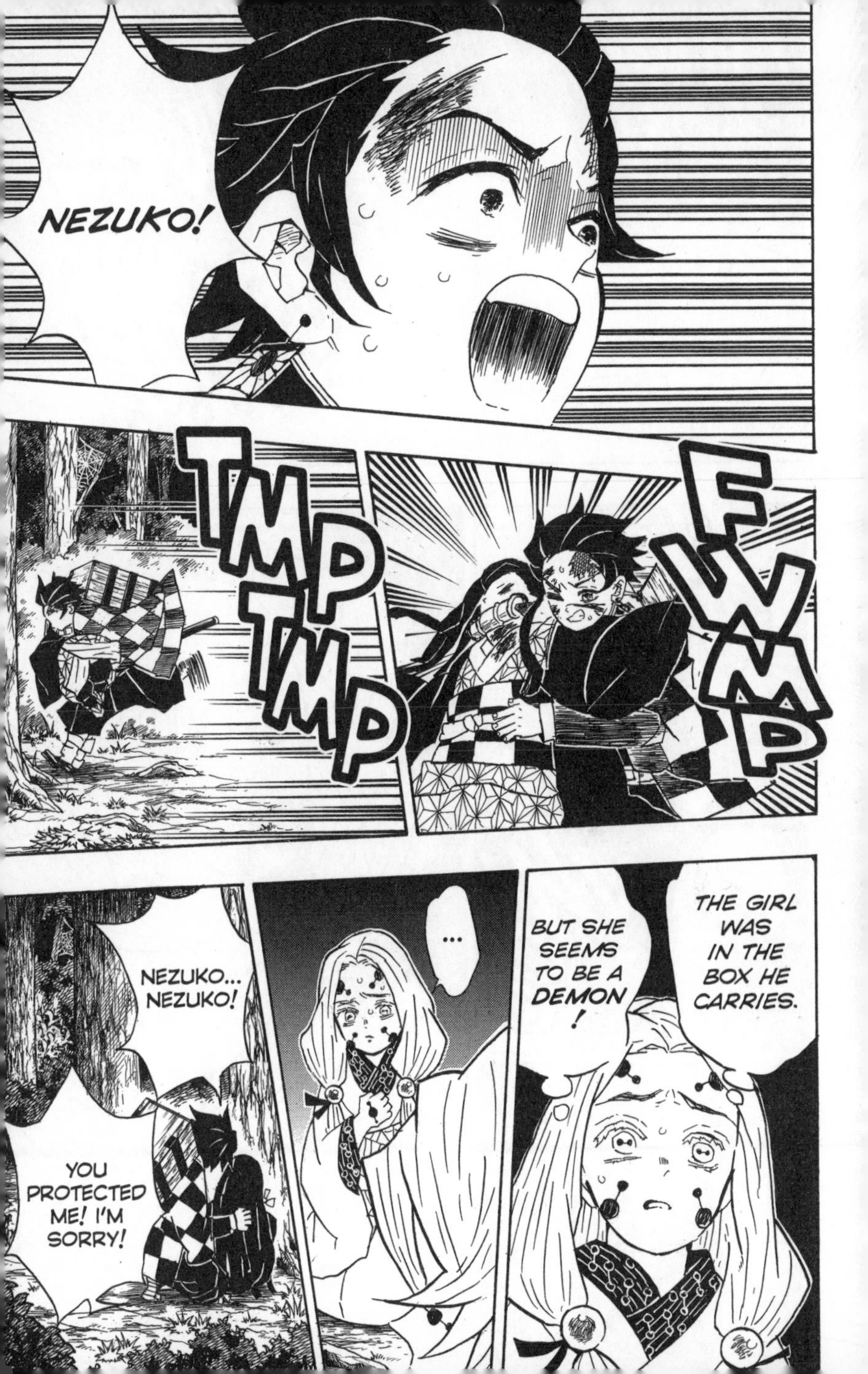
NEZUKO!
FWMP
TMP TMP
THE GIRL WAS IN THE BOX HE CARRIES.
BUT SHE SEEMS TO BE A DEMON!
...
NEZUKO... NEZUKO!
YOU PROTECTED ME! I'M SORRY!

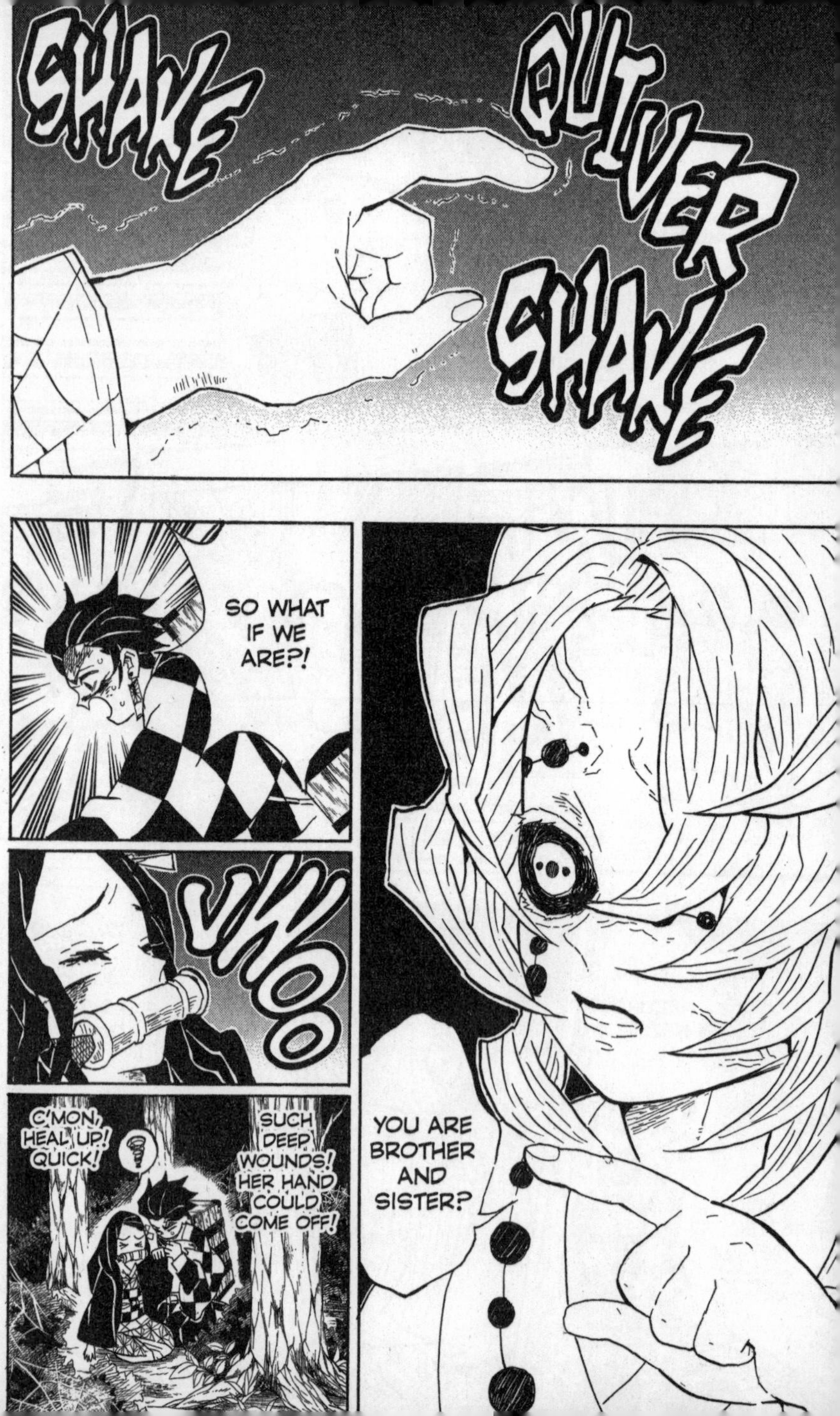
QUIVER
SHAKE
SHAKE
YOU ARE BROTHER AND SISTER?
SO WHAT IF WE ARE?!
WHOO
SUCH DEEP WOUNDS! HER HAND COULD COME OFF!
C'MON, HEAL UP! QUICK!

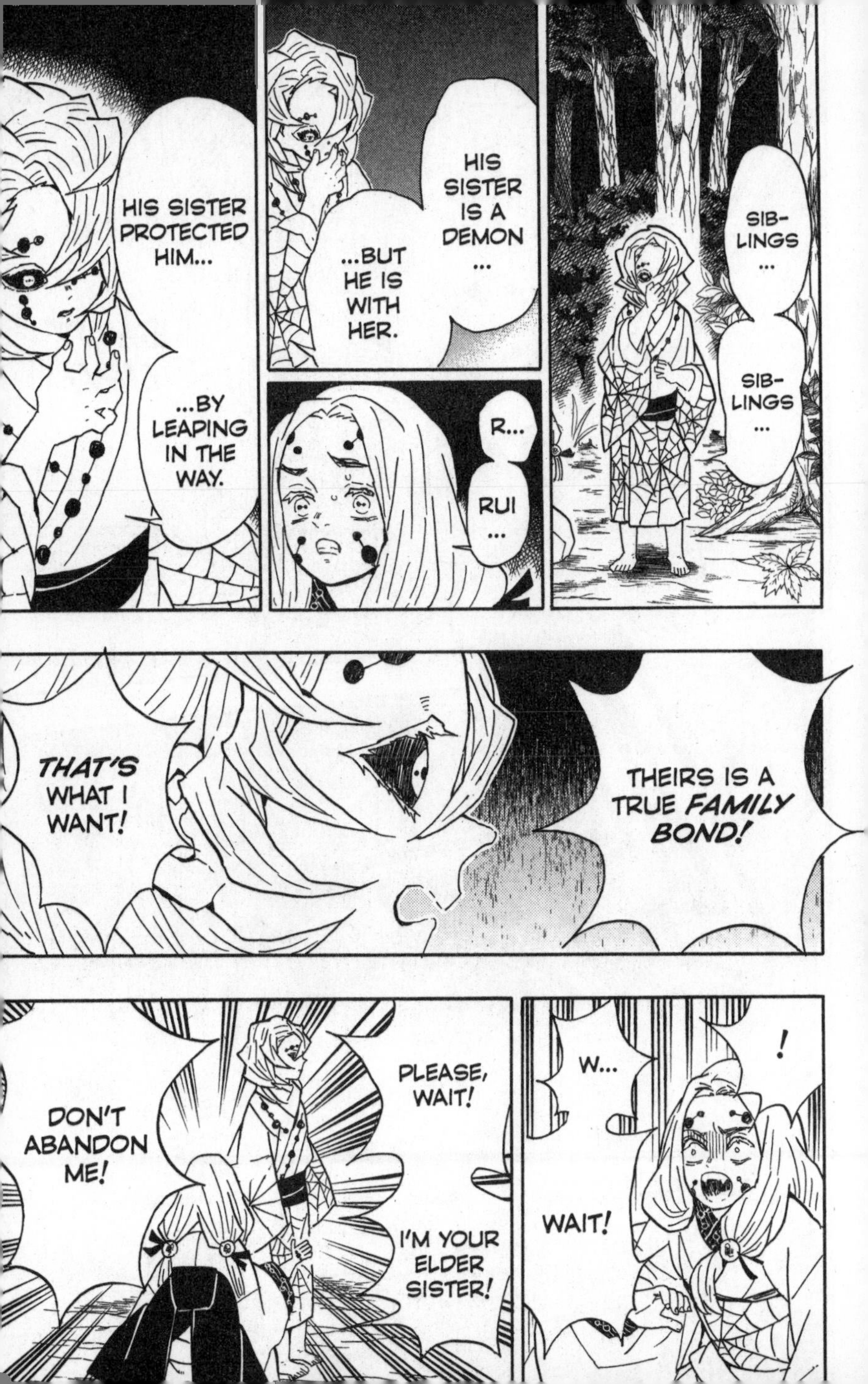
SIB-LINGS ...
SIB-LINGS ...
HIS SISTER IS A DEMON ...
...BUT HE IS WITH HER.
R...
RUI ...
HIS SISTER PROTECTED HIM...
...BY LEAPING IN THE WAY.
THEIRS IS A TRUE *FAMILY BOND!*
THAT'S WHAT I WANT!
!
W...
WAIT!
PLEASE, WAIT!
I'M YOUR ELDER SISTER!
DON'T ABANDON ME!

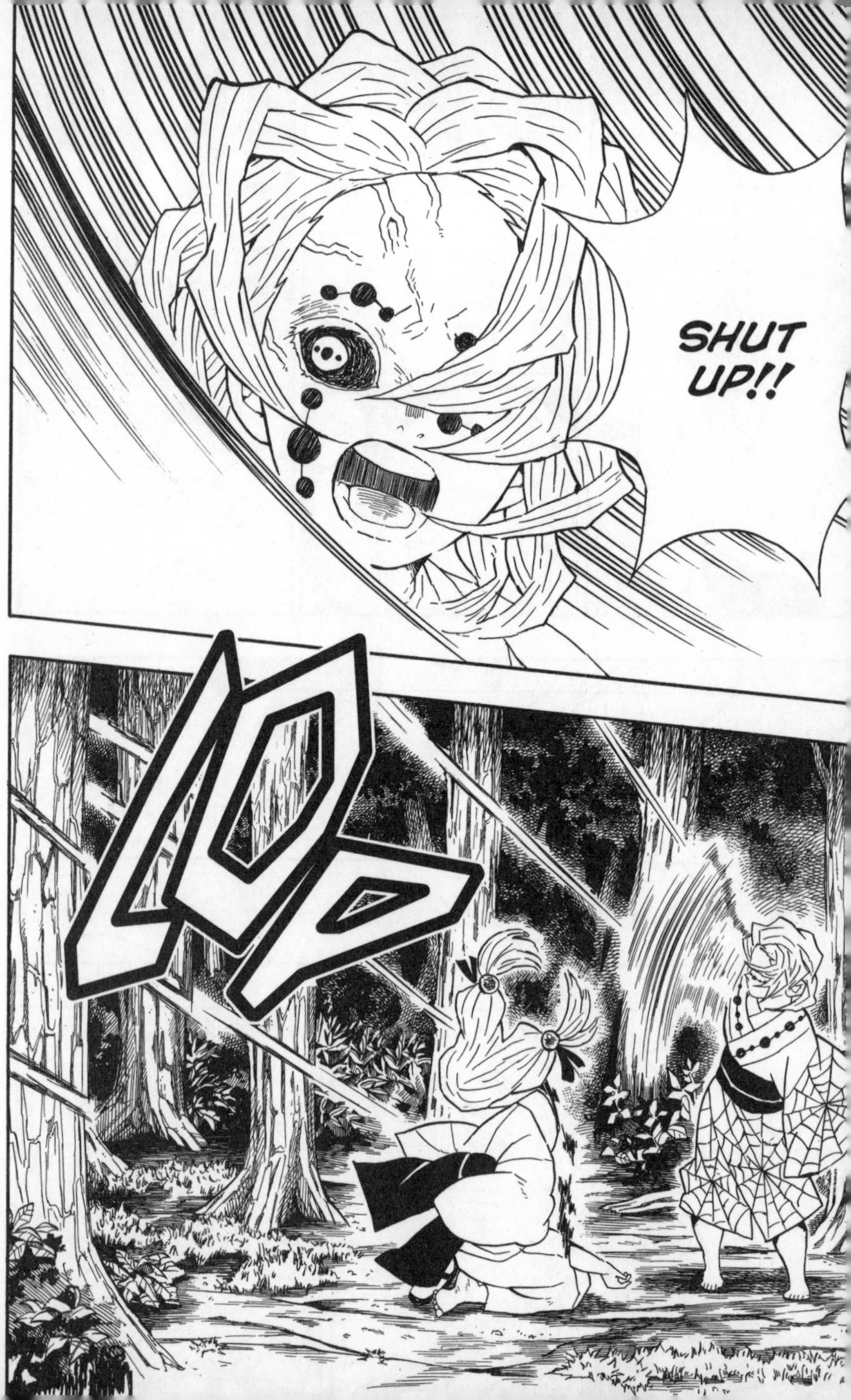
SHUT UP!!

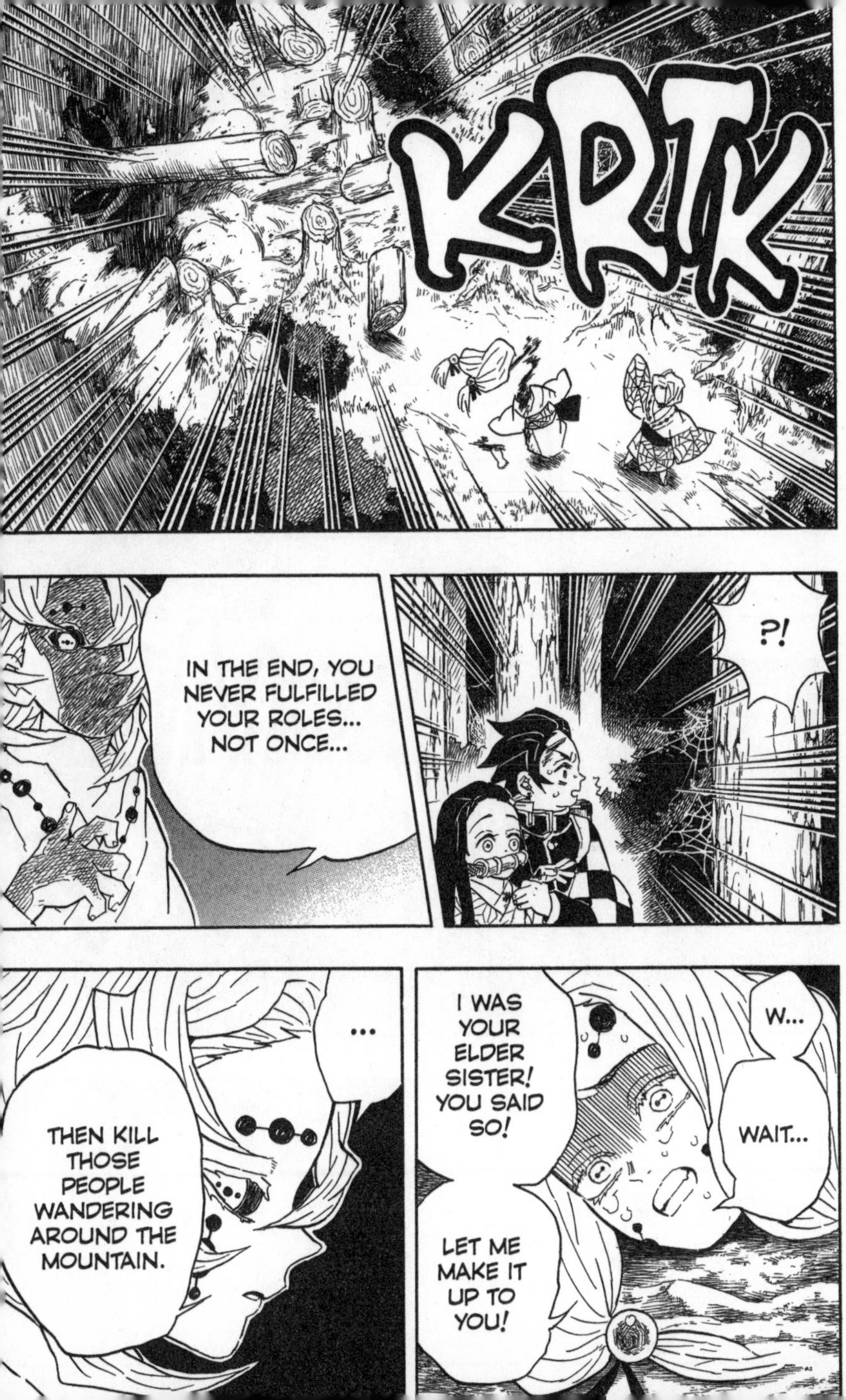
KRTK
?!
IN THE END, YOU NEVER FULFILLED YOUR ROLES... NOT ONCE...
W...
WAIT...
I WAS YOUR ELDER SISTER! YOU SAID SO!
LET ME MAKE IT UP TO YOU!
...
THEN KILL THOSE PEOPLE WANDERING AROUND THE MOUNTAIN.

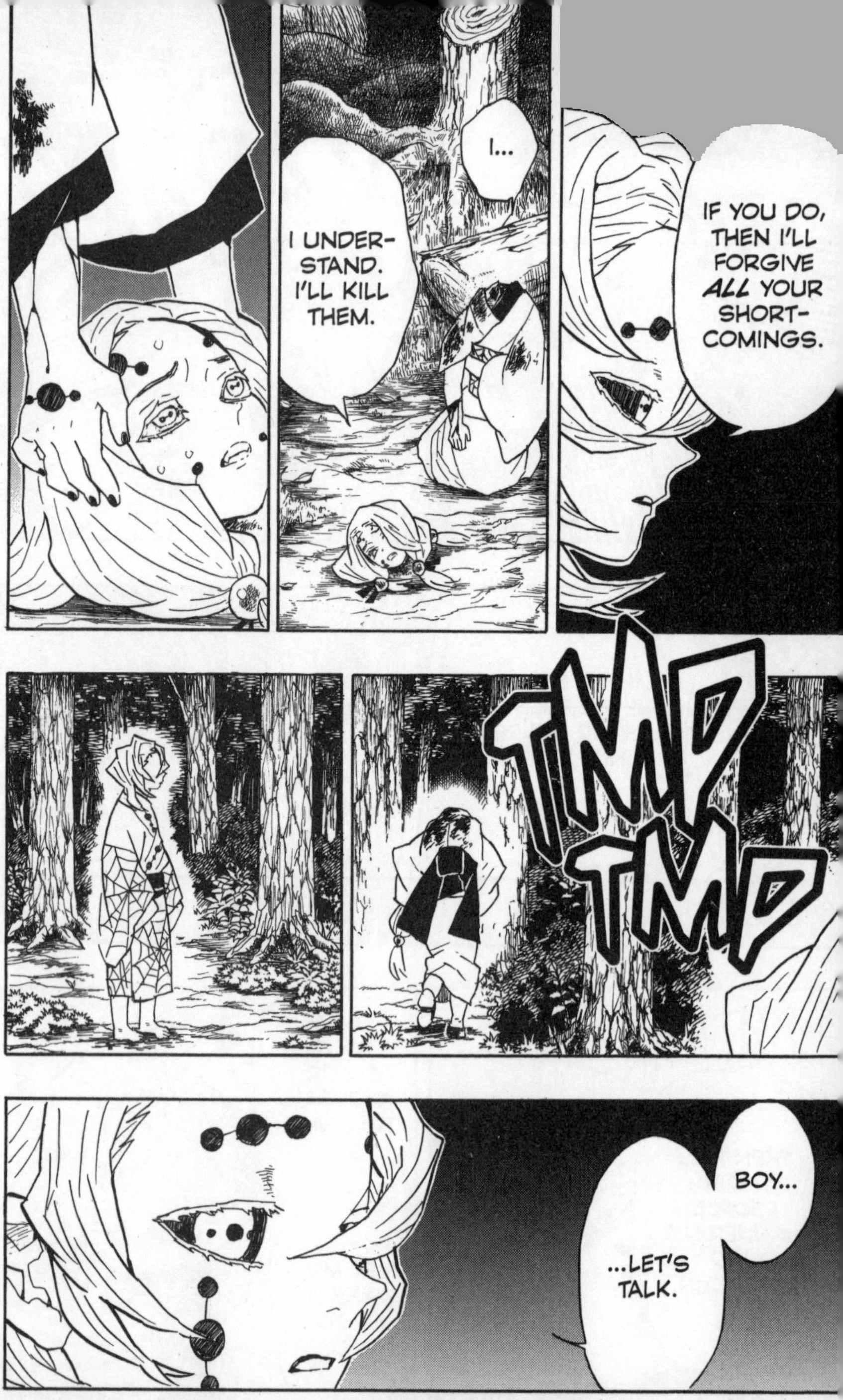
IF YOU DO, THEN I'LL FORGIVE ALL YOUR SHORT-COMINGS.
I...
I UNDER-STAND. I'LL KILL THEM.
TMP TMP
BOY...
...LET'S TALK.

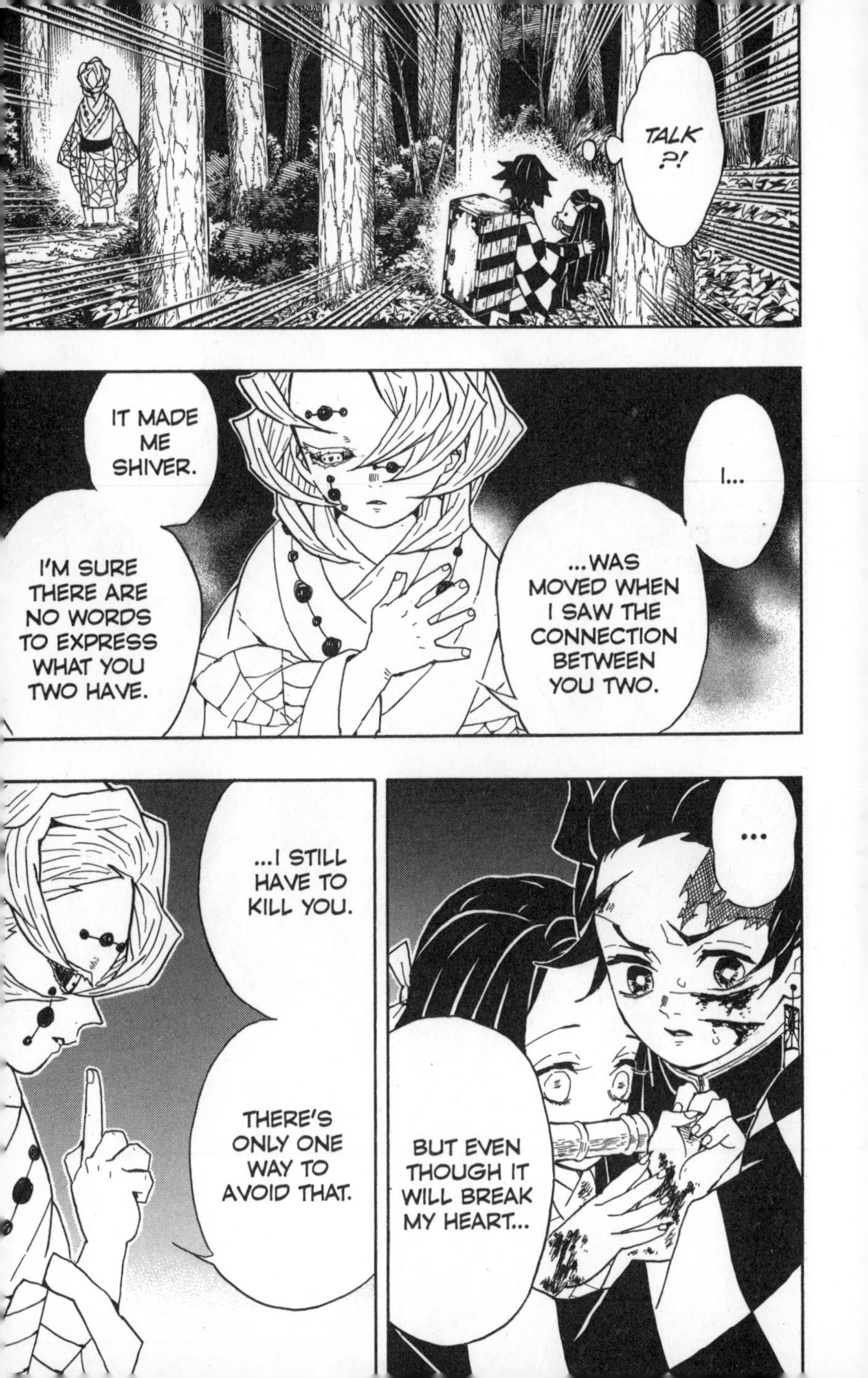
TALK ?!
I...
...WAS MOVED WHEN I SAW THE CONNECTION BETWEEN YOU TWO.
IT MADE ME SHIVER.
I'M SURE THERE ARE NO WORDS TO EXPRESS WHAT YOU TWO HAVE.
...
BUT EVEN THOUGH IT WILL BREAK MY HEART...
...I STILL HAVE TO KILL YOU.
THERE'S ONLY ONE WAY TO AVOID THAT.

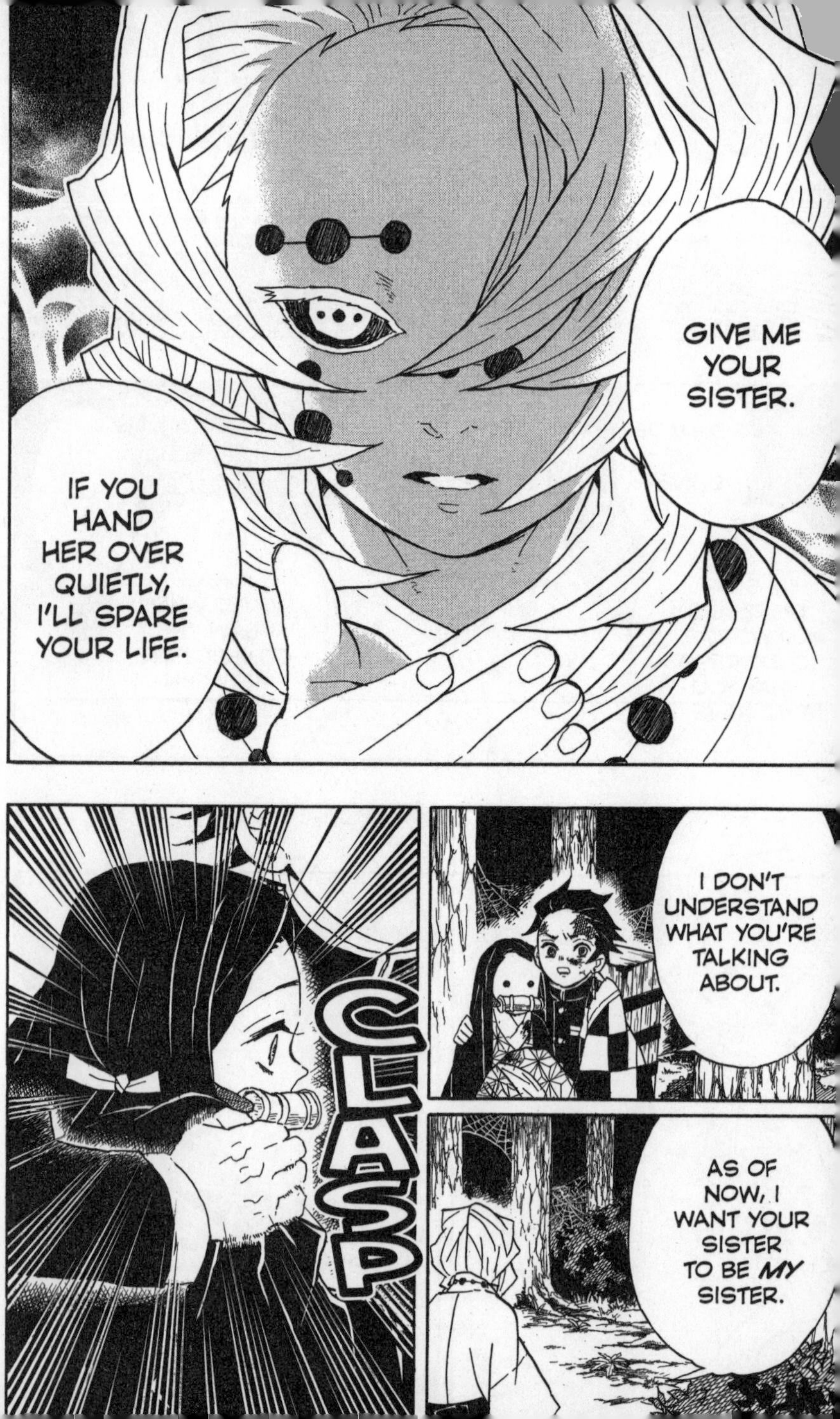
GIVE ME YOUR SISTER.
IF YOU HAND HER OVER QUIETLY, I'LL SPARE YOUR LIFE.
I DON'T UNDERSTAND WHAT YOU'RE TALKING ABOUT.
AS OF NOW, I WANT YOUR SISTER TO BE *MY* SISTER.
CLASP

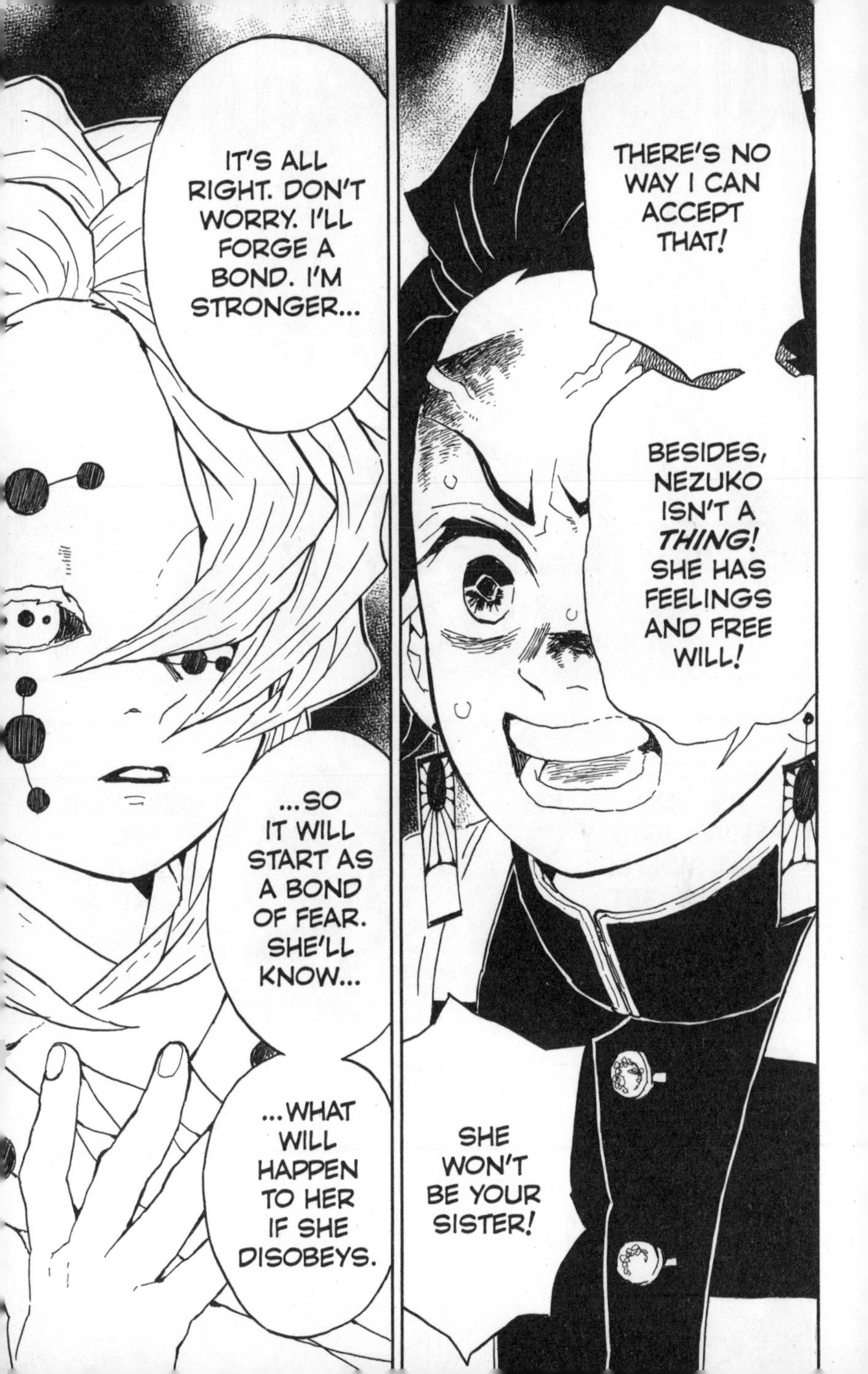
THERE'S NO WAY I CAN ACCEPT THAT!
BESIDES, NEZUKO ISN'T A *THING*! SHE HAS FEELINGS AND FREE WILL!
SHE WON'T BE YOUR SISTER!
IT'S ALL RIGHT. DON'T WORRY. I'LL FORGE A BOND. I'M STRONGER...
...SO IT WILL START AS A BOND OF FEAR. SHE'LL KNOW...
...WHAT WILL HAPPEN TO HER IF SHE DISOBEYS.

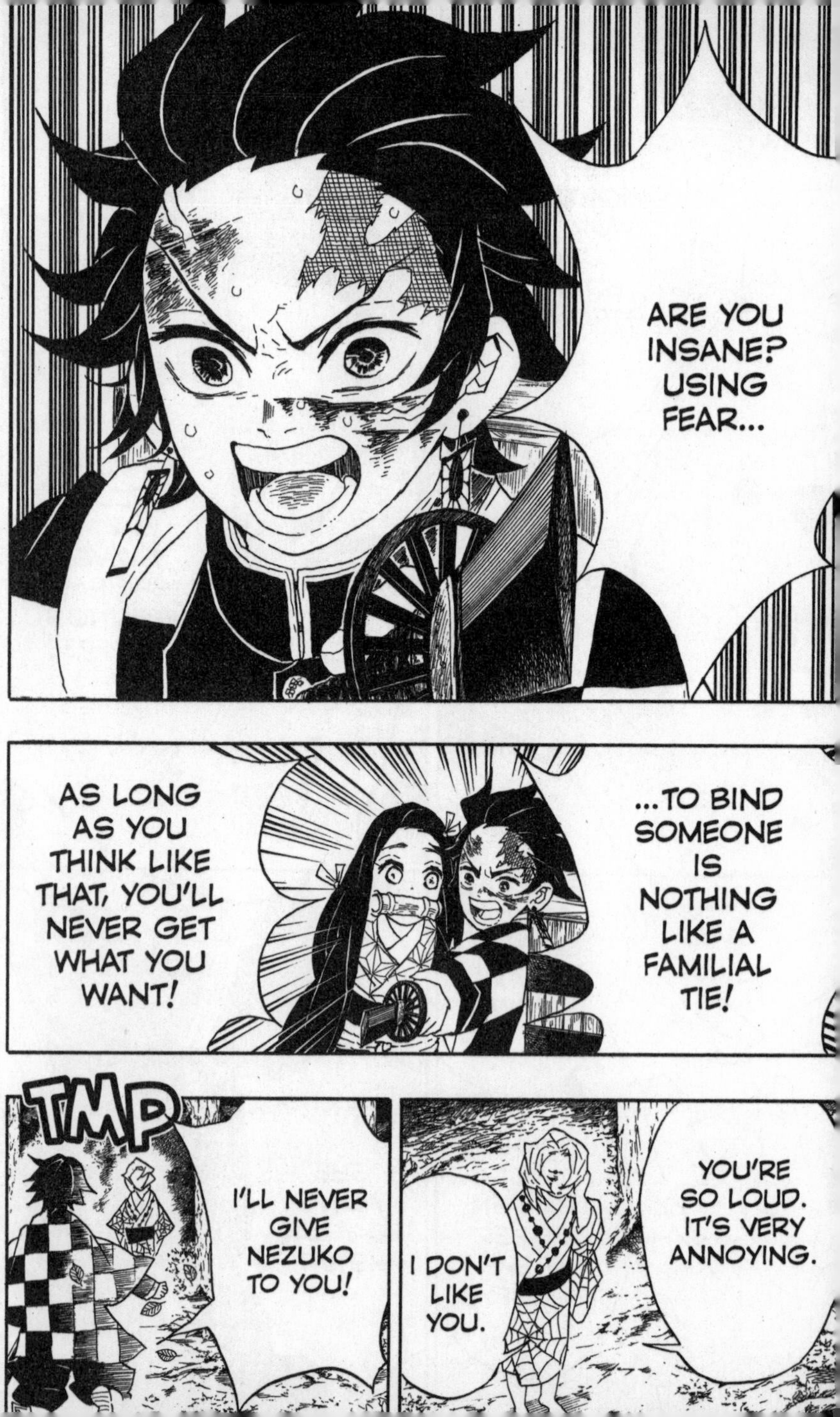
ARE YOU INSANE? USING FEAR...
...TO BIND SOMEONE IS NOTHING LIKE A FAMILIAL TIE!
AS LONG AS YOU THINK LIKE THAT, YOU'LL NEVER GET WHAT YOU WANT!
YOU'RE SO LOUD. IT'S VERY ANNOYING.
I DON'T LIKE YOU.
TMP
I'LL NEVER GIVE NEZUKO TO YOU!

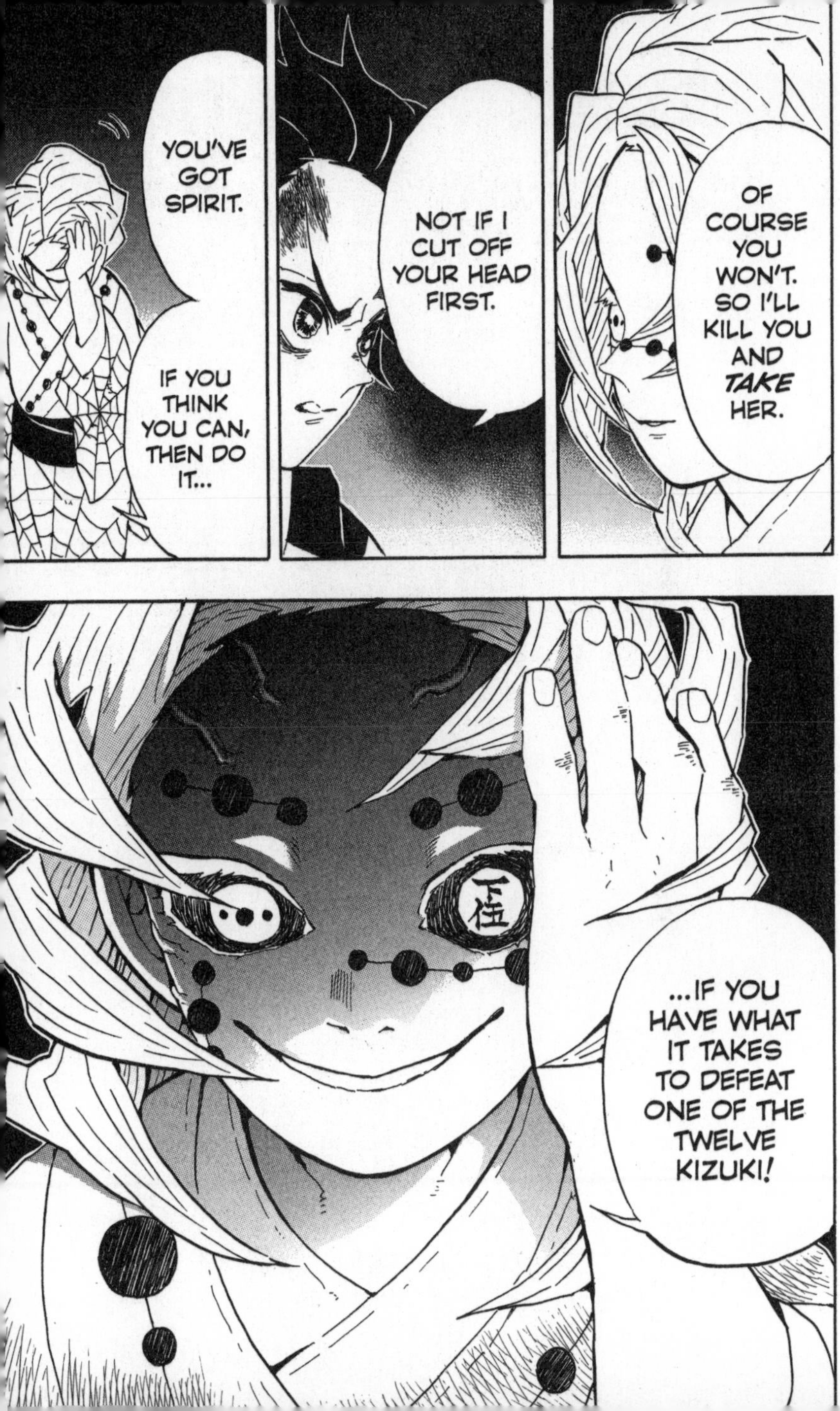
OF COURSE YOU WON'T. SO I'LL KILL YOU AND *TAKE* HER.
NOT IF I CUT OFF YOUR HEAD FIRST.
YOU'VE GOT SPIRIT.
IF YOU THINK YOU CAN, THEN DO IT...
下伍
...IF YOU HAVE WHAT IT TAKES TO DEFEAT ONE OF THE TWELVE KIZUKI!

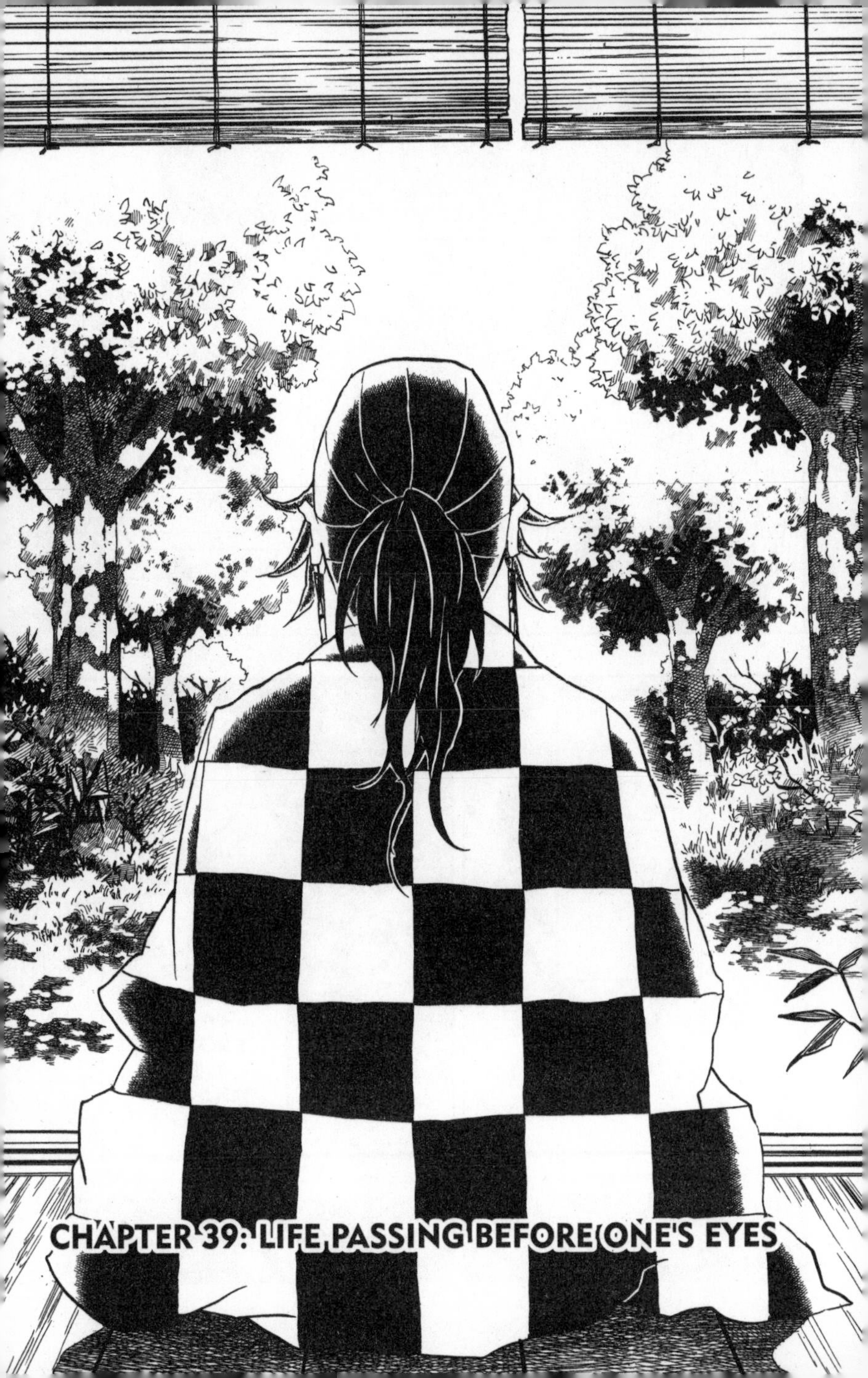
CHAPTER 39: LIFE PASSING BEFORE ONE'S EYES

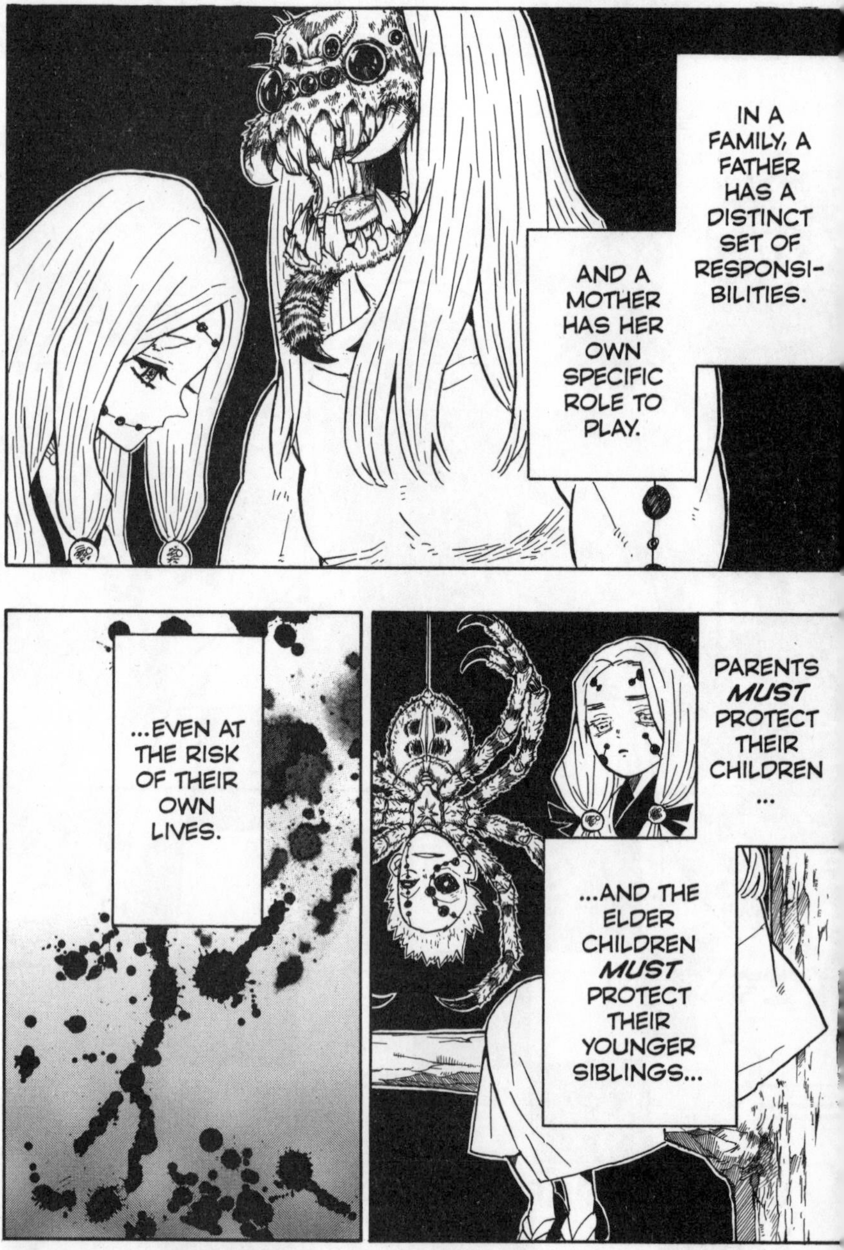
IN A FAMILY, A FATHER HAS A DISTINCT SET OF RESPONSI-BILITIES.
AND A MOTHER HAS HER OWN SPECIFIC ROLE TO PLAY.
PARENTS *MUST* PROTECT THEIR CHILDREN ...
...AND THE ELDER CHILDREN *MUST* PROTECT THEIR YOUNGER SIBLINGS...
...EVEN AT THE RISK OF THEIR OWN LIVES.

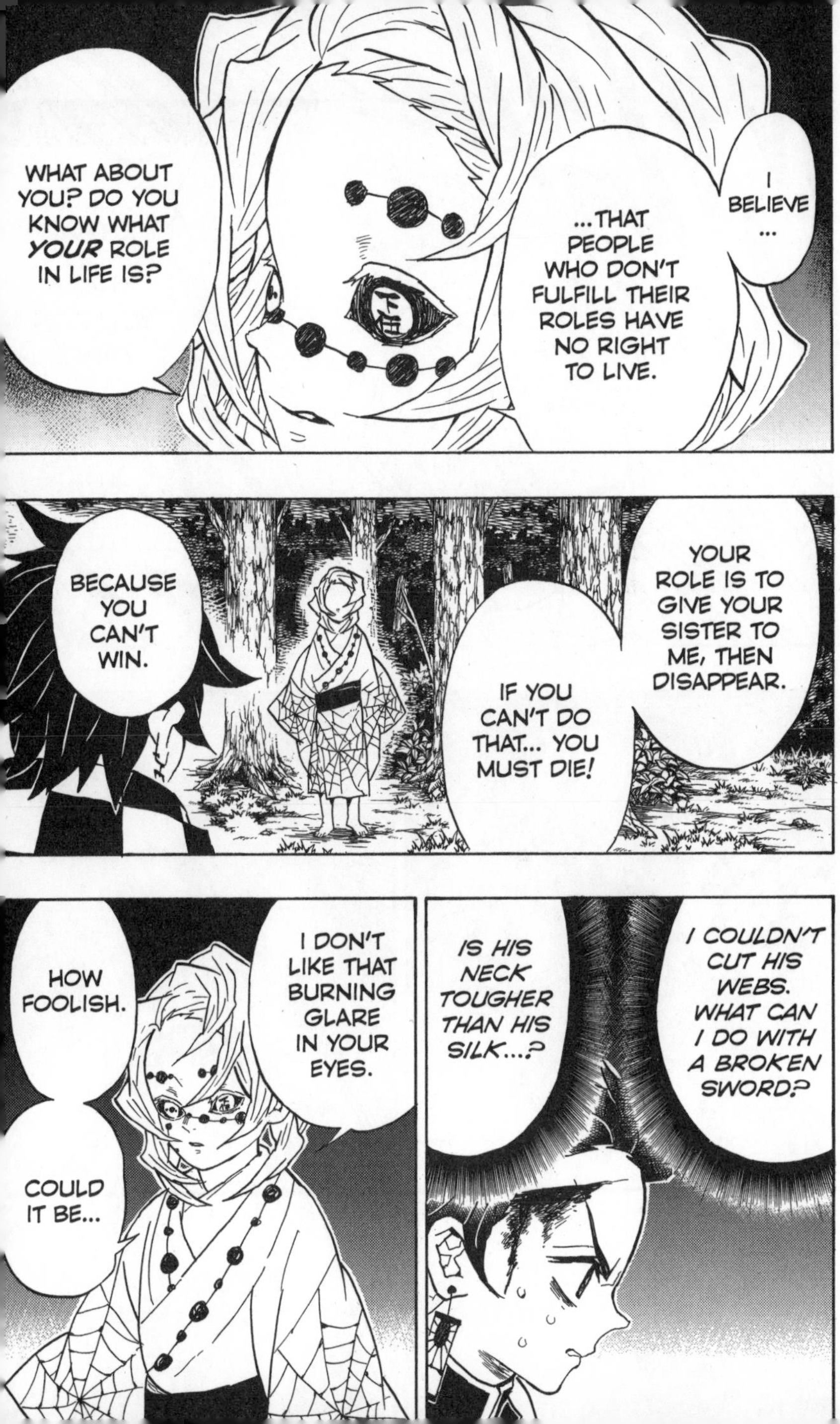
I BELIEVE ...
...THAT PEOPLE WHO DON'T FULFILL THEIR ROLES HAVE NO RIGHT TO LIVE.
WHAT ABOUT YOU? DO YOU KNOW WHAT *YOUR* ROLE IN LIFE IS?
YOUR ROLE IS TO GIVE YOUR SISTER TO ME, THEN DISAPPEAR.
IF YOU CAN'T DO THAT... YOU MUST DIE!
BECAUSE YOU CAN'T WIN.
I COULDN'T CUT HIS WEBS. WHAT CAN I DO WITH A BROKEN SWORD?
IS HIS NECK TOUGHER THAN HIS SILK...?
I DON'T LIKE THAT BURNING GLARE IN YOUR EYES.
HOW FOOLISH.
COULD IT BE...

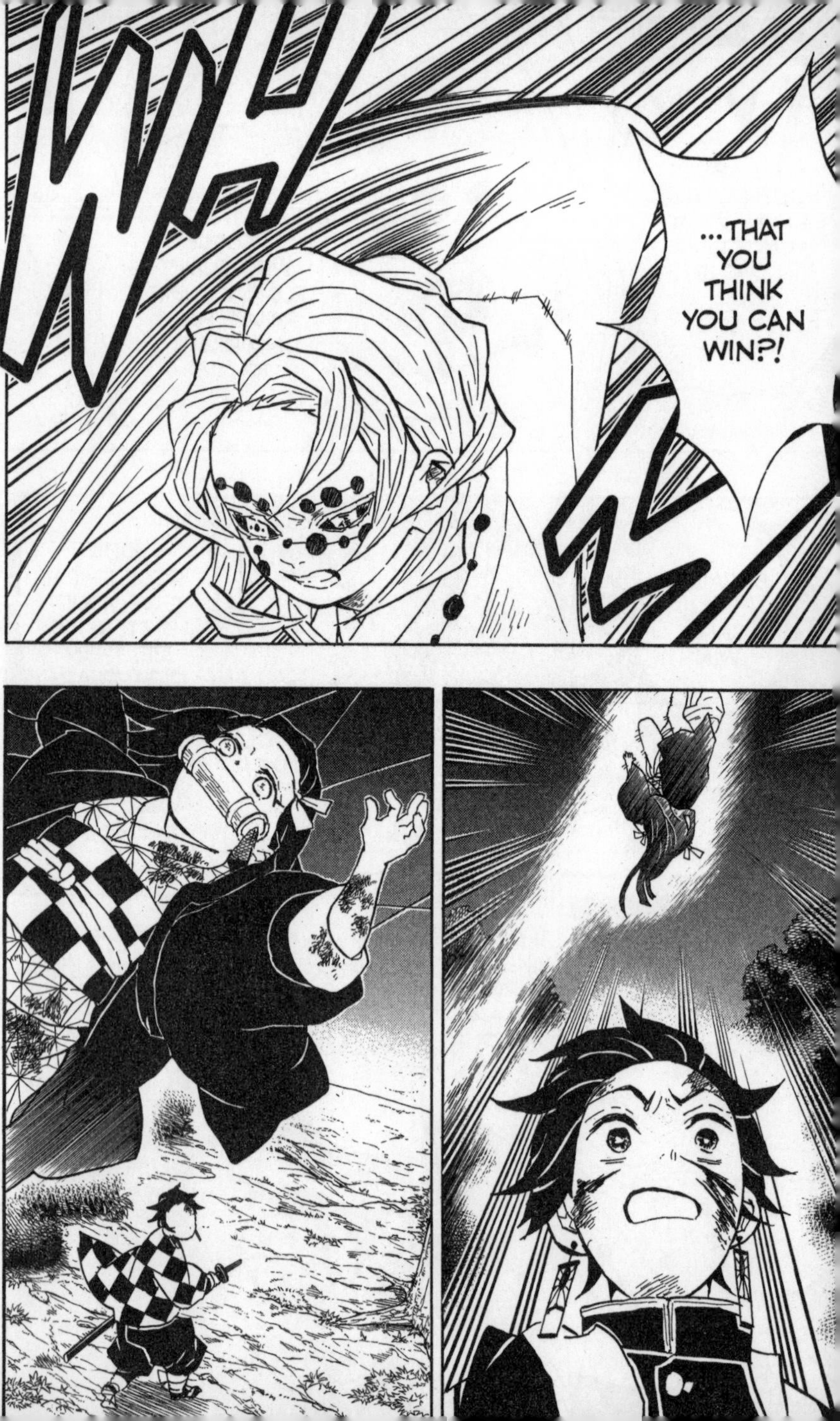
...THAT YOU THINK YOU CAN WIN?!

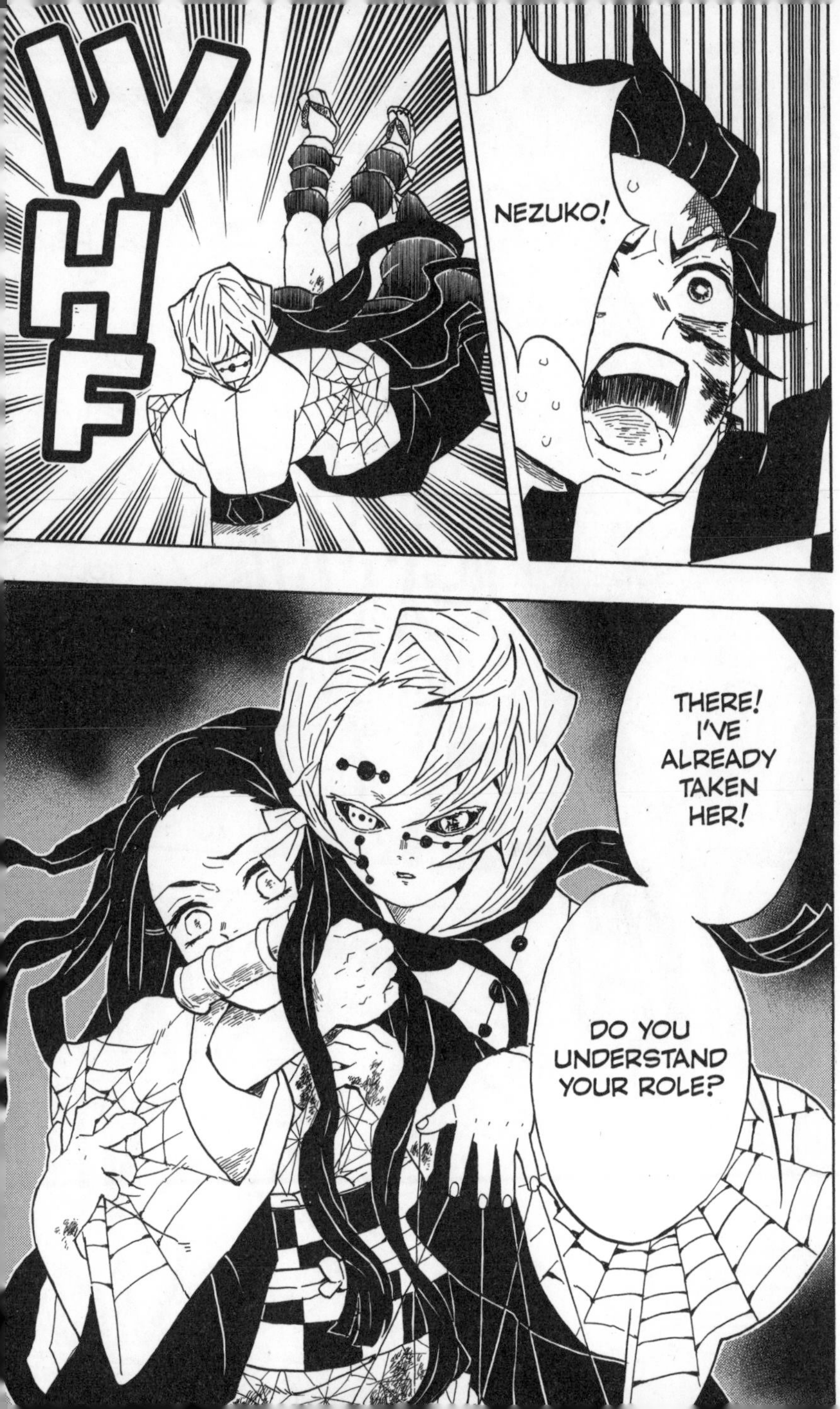
NEZUKO!
WHF
THERE! I'VE ALREADY TAKEN HER!
DO YOU UNDERSTAND YOUR ROLE?

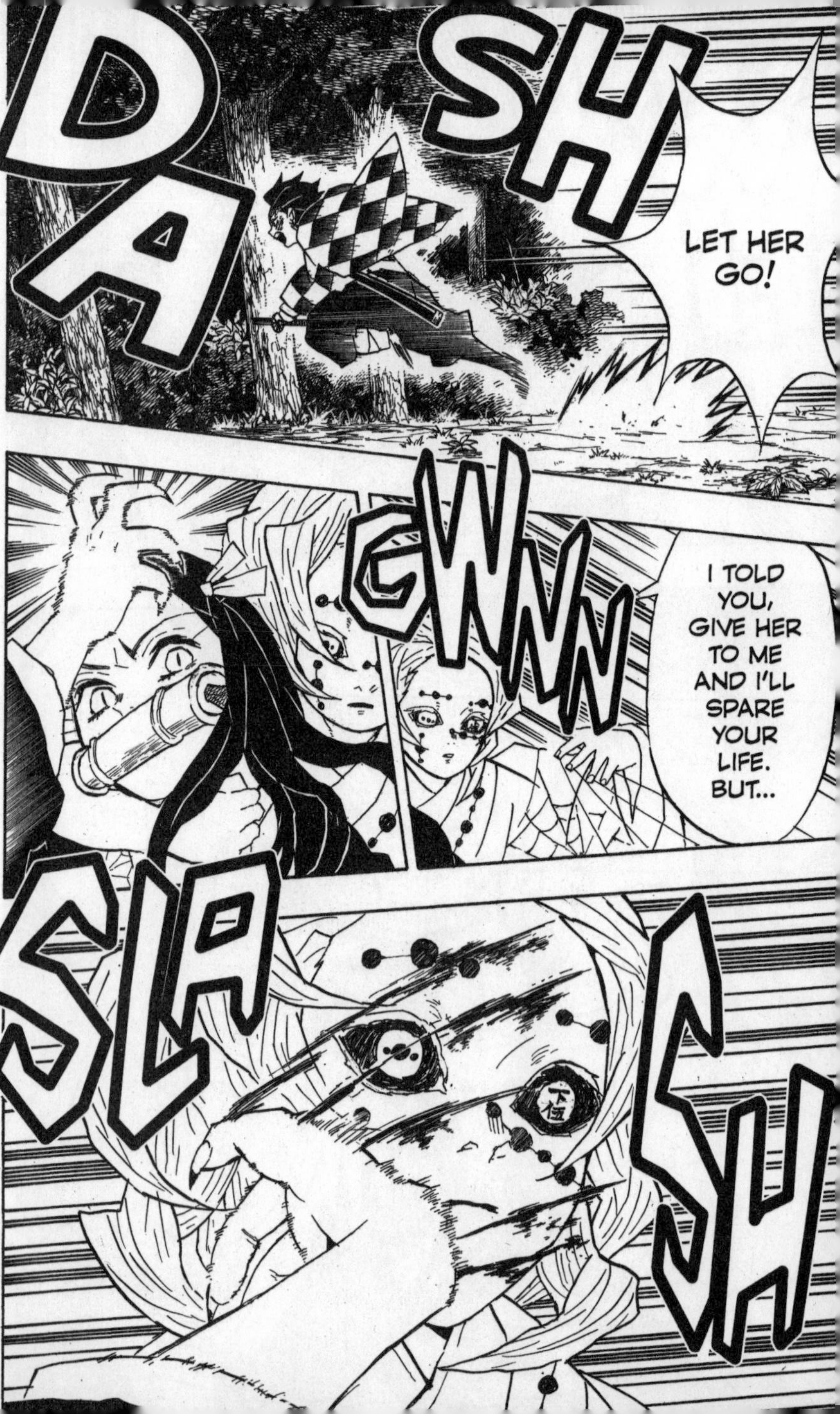
LET HER GO!
DASH
I TOLD YOU, GIVE HER TO ME AND I'LL SPARE YOUR LIFE. BUT...
GWNN
SLASH

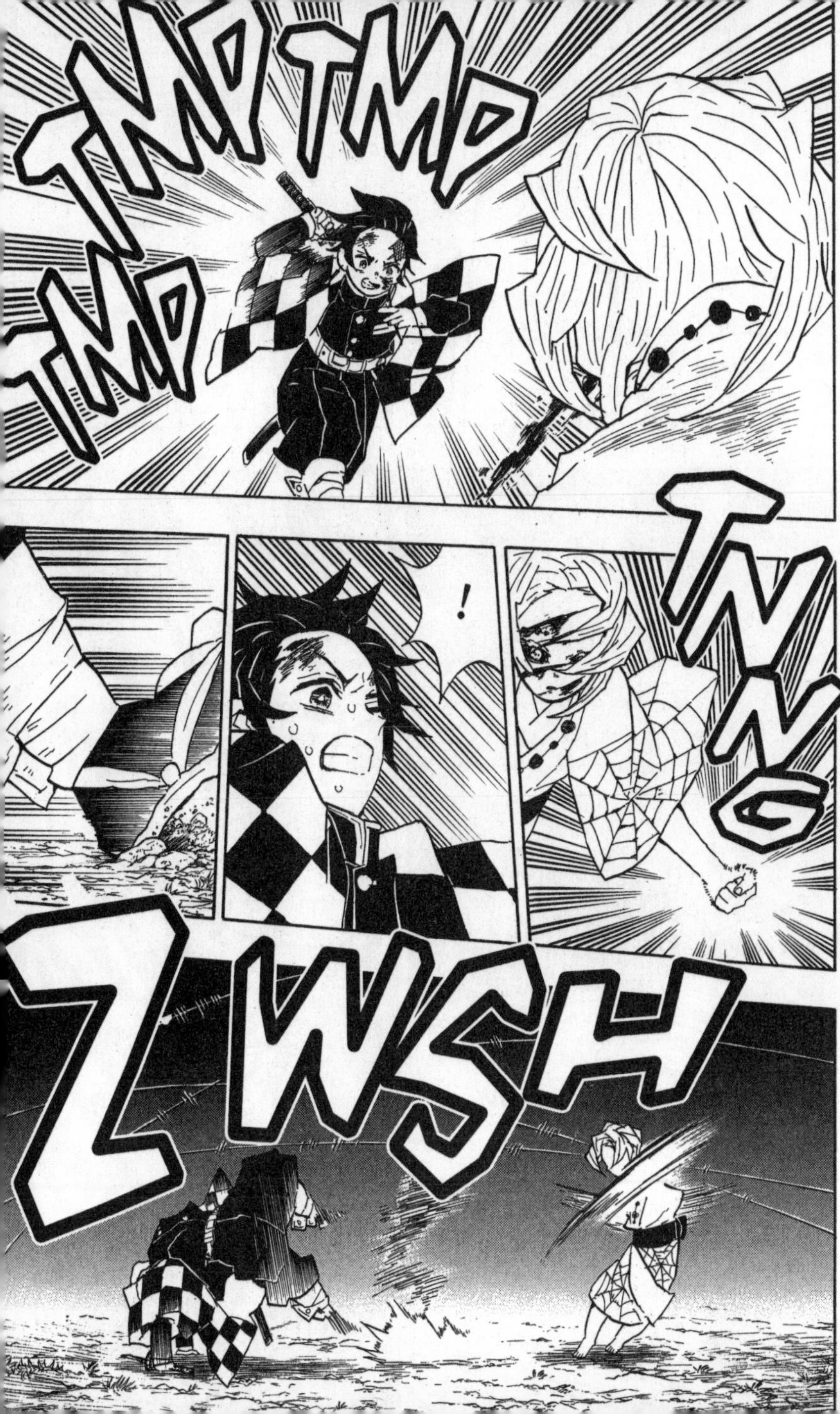
TMP TMP
TMP
TNNG
!
ZWSH

?!

WHERE'S NEZUKO?

FWMP

NE—

PLIP
PLIP
PLIP

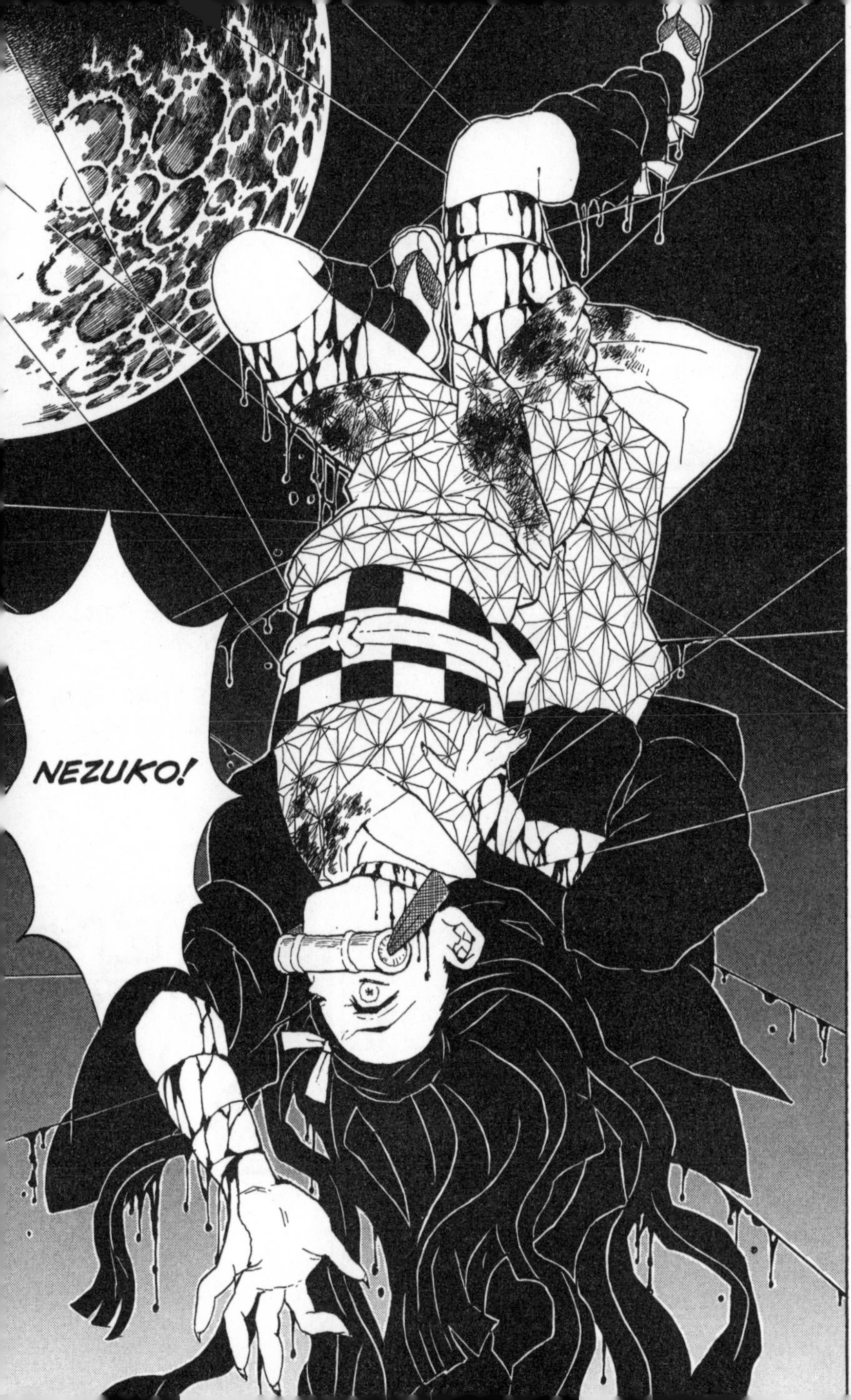
NEZUKO!

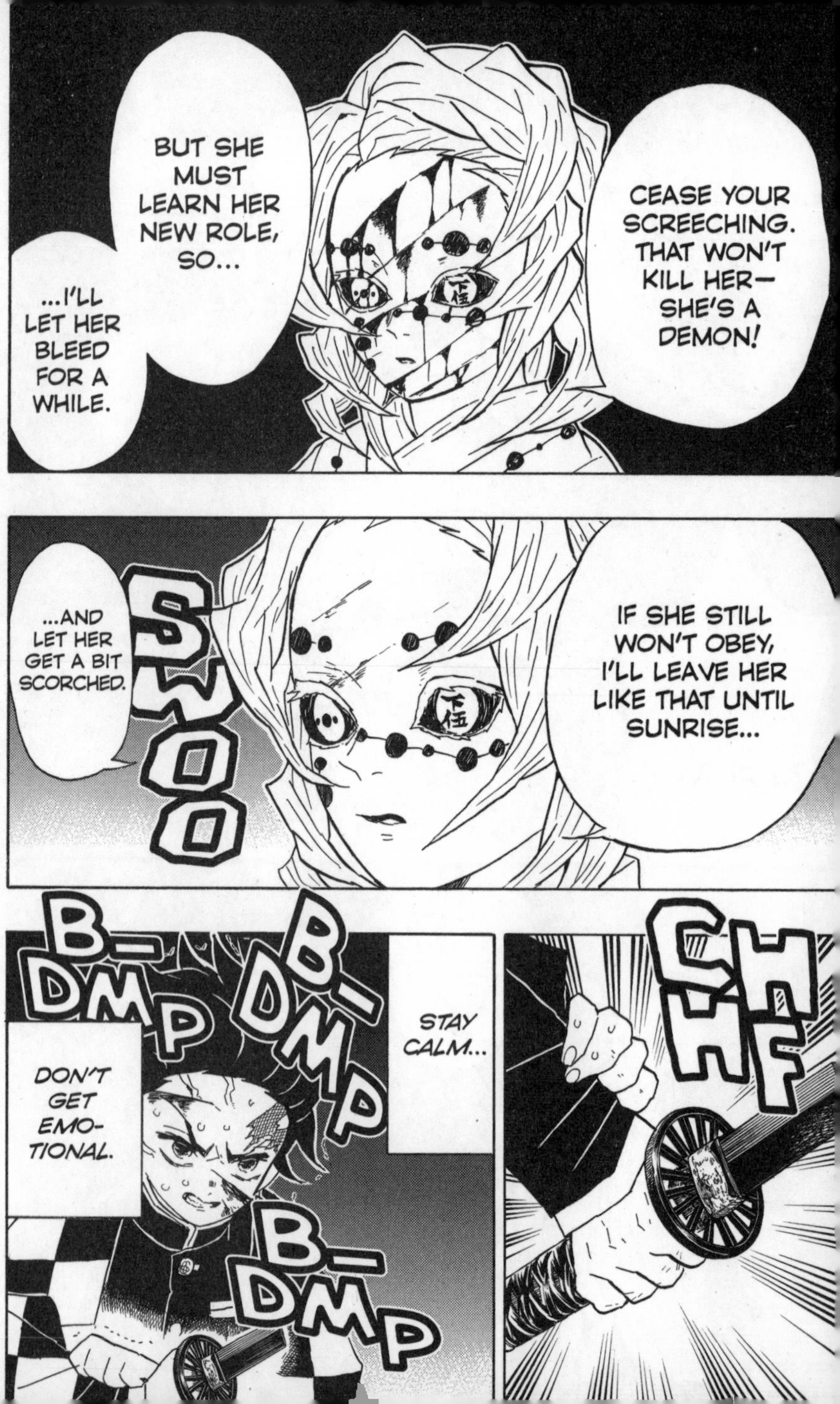
CEASE YOUR SCREECHING. THAT WON'T KILL HER— SHE'S A DEMON!
BUT SHE MUST LEARN HER NEW ROLE, SO...
...I'LL LET HER BLEED FOR A WHILE.
IF SHE STILL WON'T OBEY, I'LL LEAVE HER LIKE THAT UNTIL SUNRISE...
SWOO
...AND LET HER GET A BIT SCORCHED.
CHHF
STAY CALM...
B-DMP
B-DMP
DON'T GET EMO-TIONAL.
B-DMP

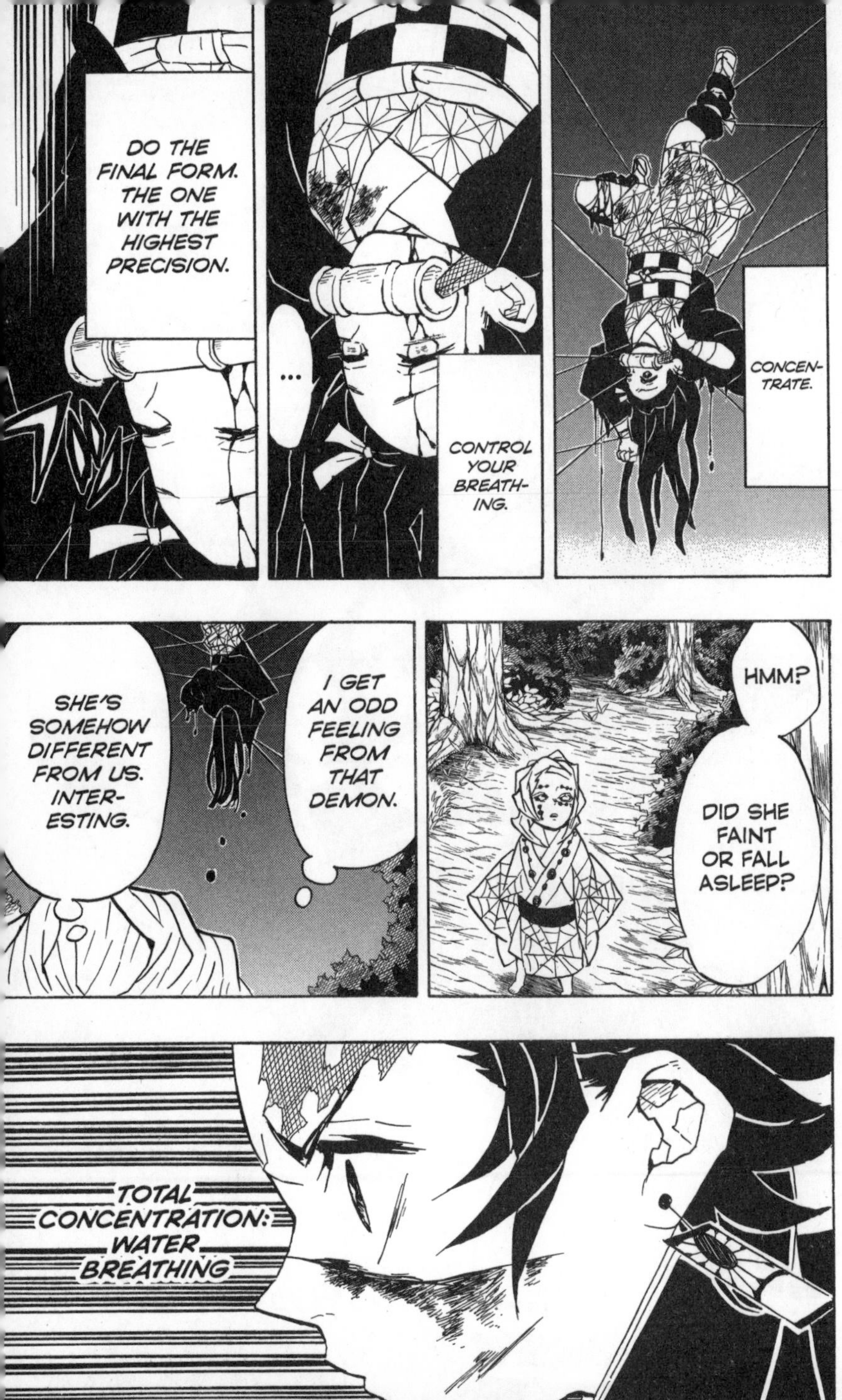
CONCEN-TRATE.
CONTROL YOUR BREATH-ING.
...
DO THE FINAL FORM. THE ONE WITH THE HIGHEST PRECISION.
HMM?
DID SHE FAINT OR FALL ASLEEP?
I GET AN ODD FEELING FROM THAT DEMON.
SHE'S SOMEHOW DIFFERENT FROM US. INTER-ESTING.
TOTAL CONCENTRATION: WATER BREATHING

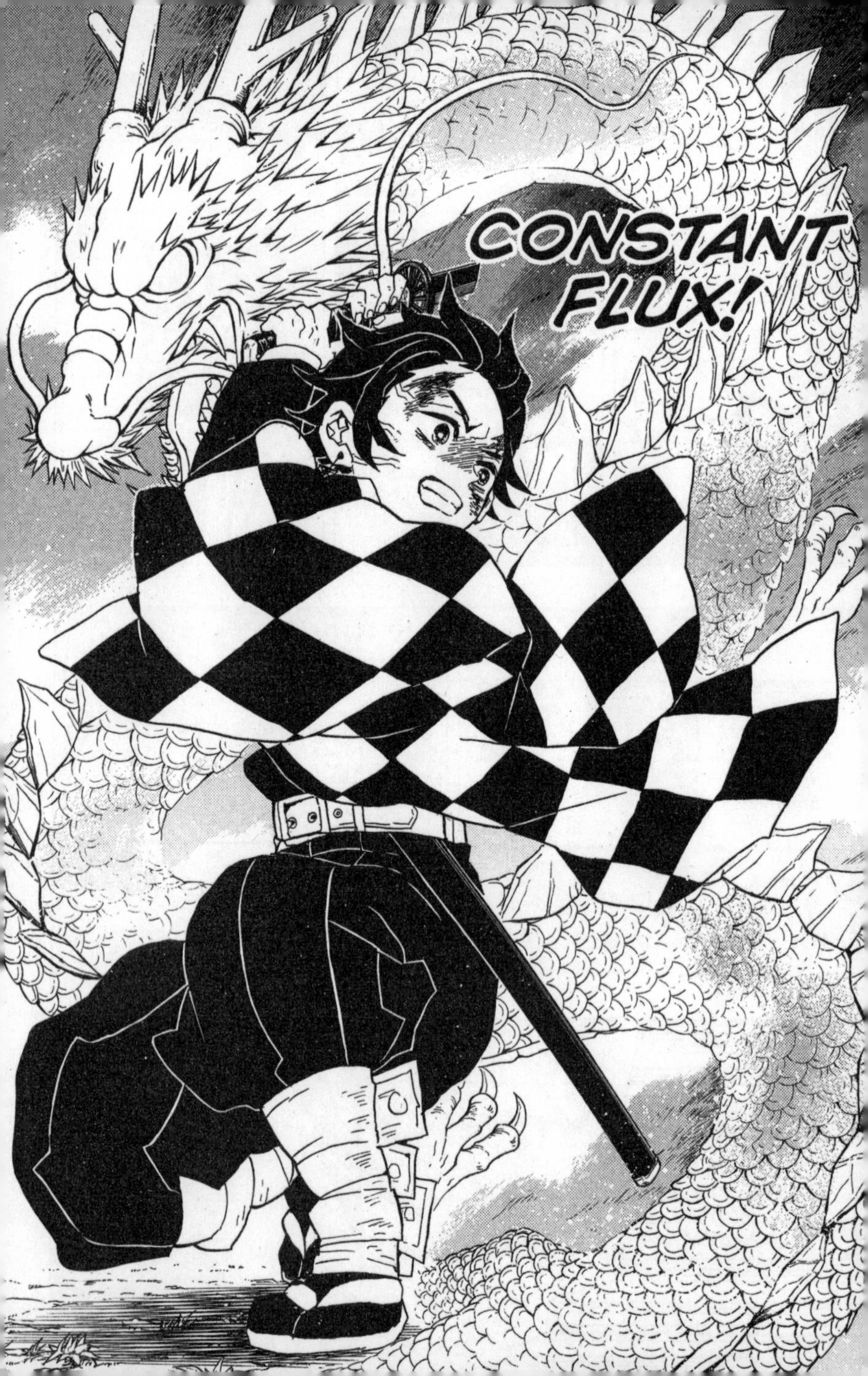
CONSTANT FLUX!

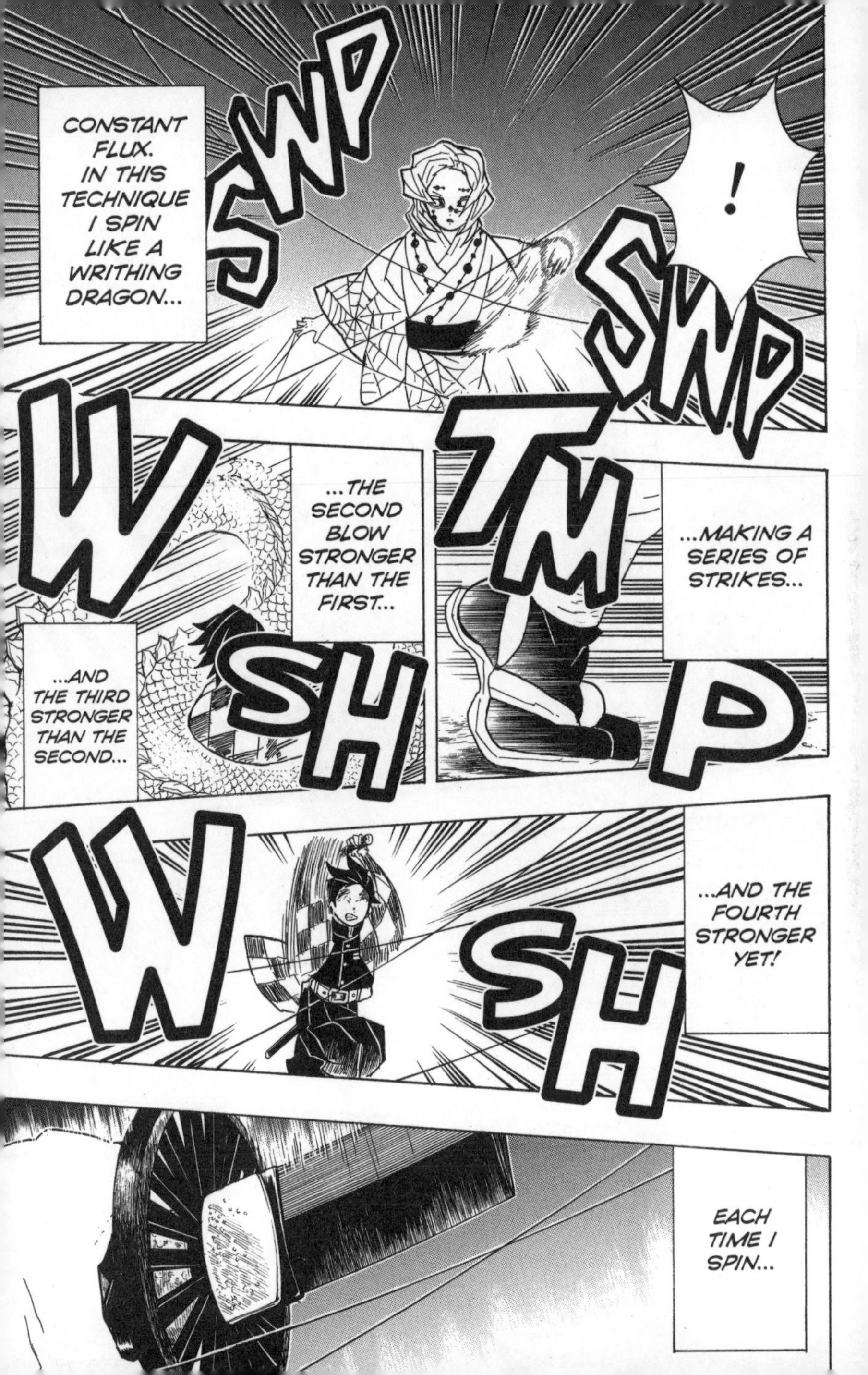
!
SWP
SWP
CONSTANT FLUX. IN THIS TECHNIQUE I SPIN LIKE A WRITHING DRAGON...
...MAKING A SERIES OF STRIKES...
TM
P
...THE SECOND BLOW STRONGER THAN THE FIRST...
W
SH
...AND THE THIRD STRONGER THAN THE SECOND...
...AND THE FOURTH STRONGER YET!
SH
W
EACH TIME I SPIN...

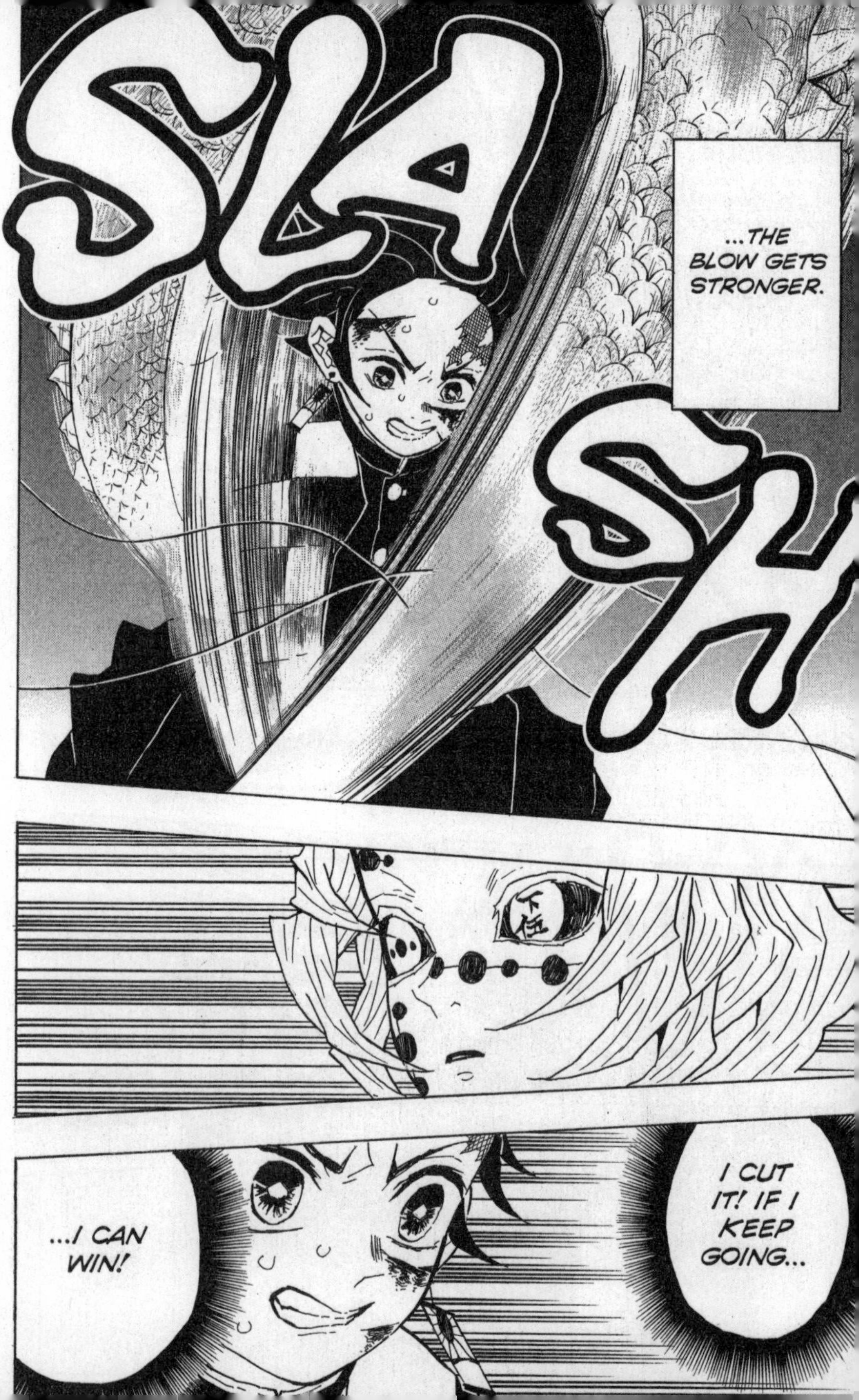
...THE BLOW GETS STRONGER.
SLA
SH
I CUT IT! IF I KEEP GOING...
...I CAN WIN!

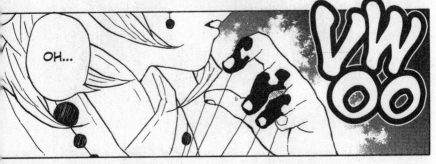

OH...

VWOO

DID YOU THINK THAT WAS THE STRONGEST THREAD I COULD MAKE?

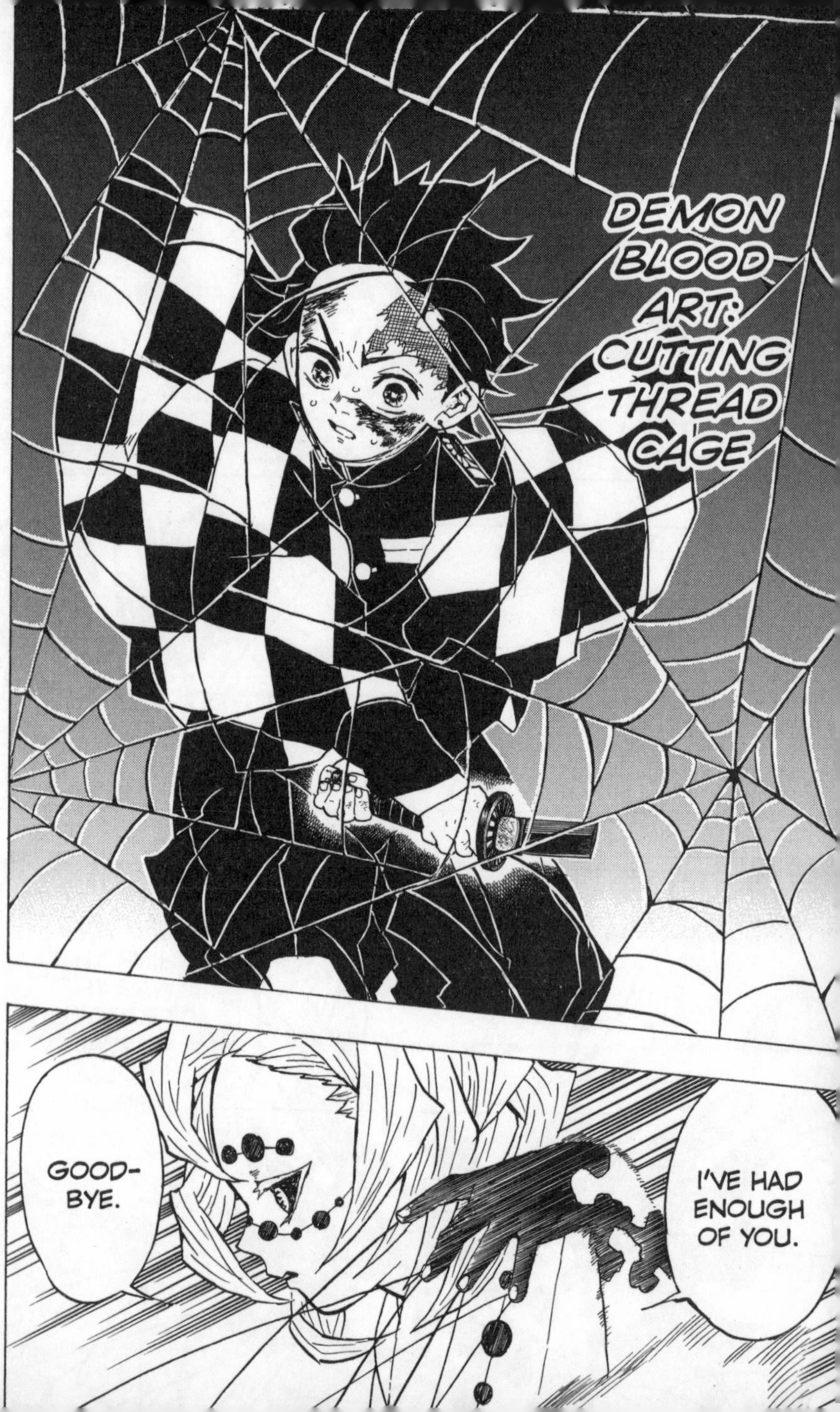
DEMON BLOOD ART: CUTTING THREAD CAGE
I'VE HAD ENOUGH OF YOU.
GOOD-BYE.

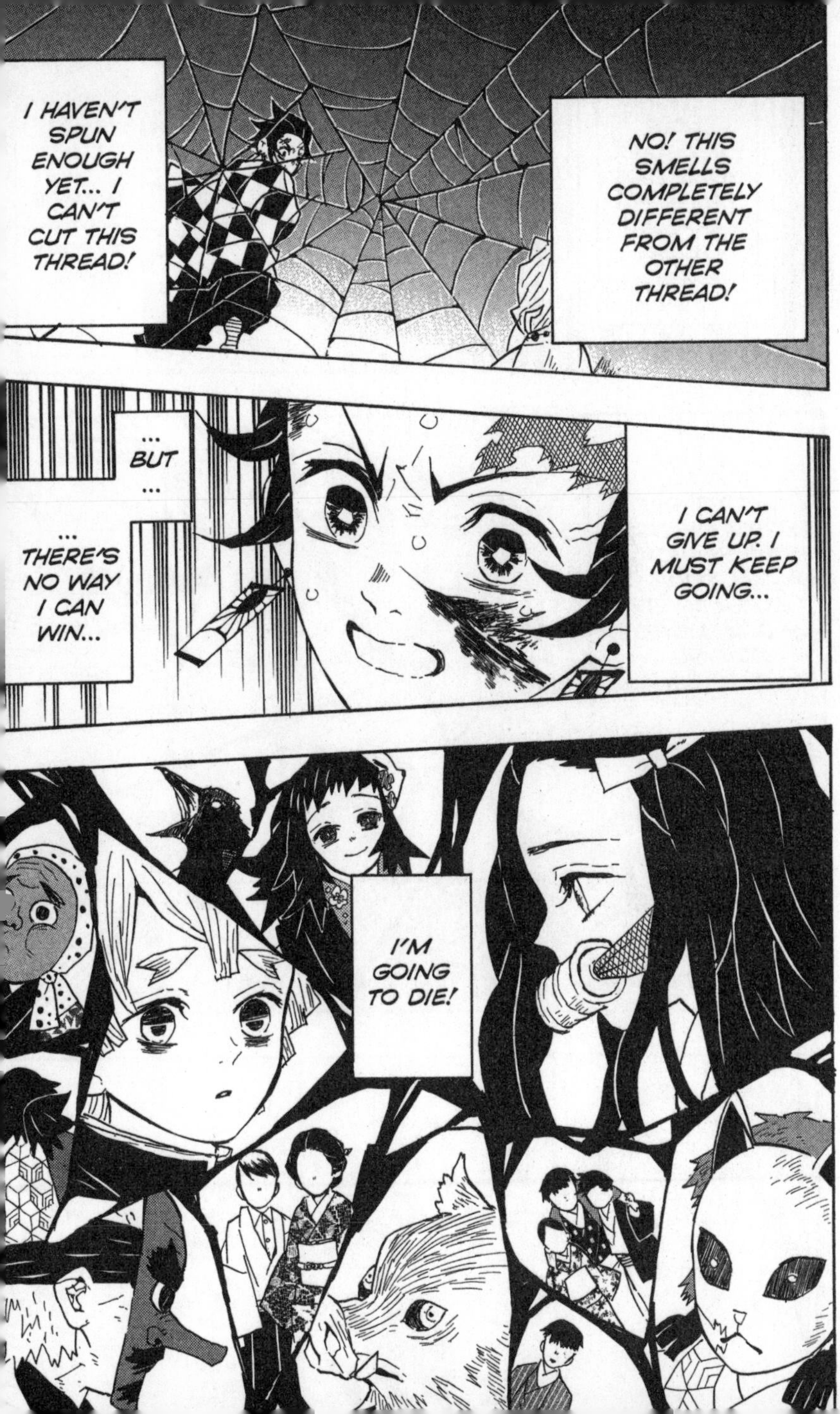
NO! THIS SMELLS COMPLETELY DIFFERENT FROM THE OTHER THREAD!
I HAVEN'T SPUN ENOUGH YET... I CAN'T CUT THIS THREAD!
I CAN'T GIVE UP. I MUST KEEP GOING...
... BUT ...
... THERE'S NO WAY I CAN WIN...
I'M GOING TO DIE!

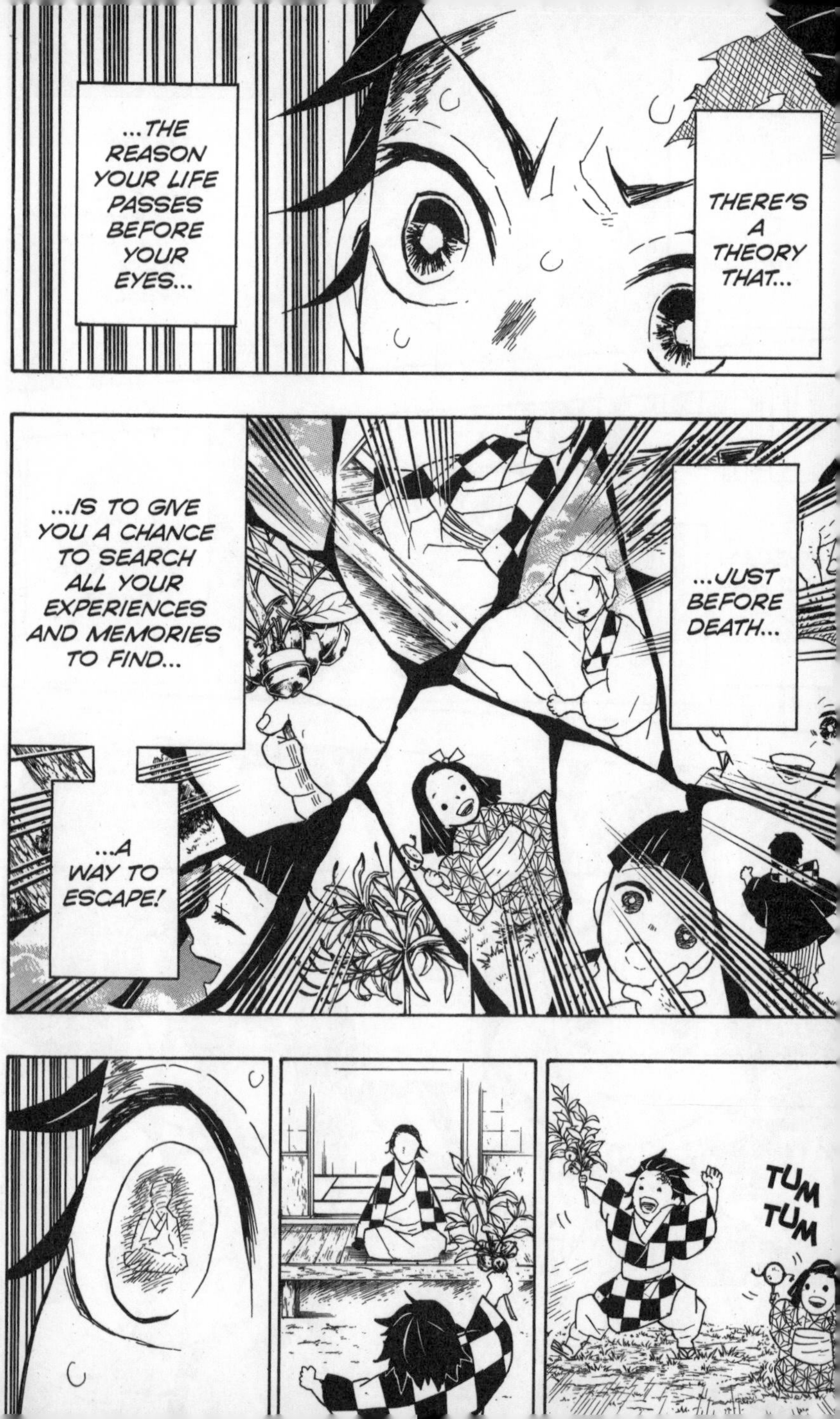
THERE'S A THEORY THAT...
...THE REASON YOUR LIFE PASSES BEFORE YOUR EYES...
...JUST BEFORE DEATH...
...IS TO GIVE YOU A CHANCE TO SEARCH ALL YOUR EXPERIENCES AND MEMORIES TO FIND...
...A WAY TO ESCAPE!
TUM TUM

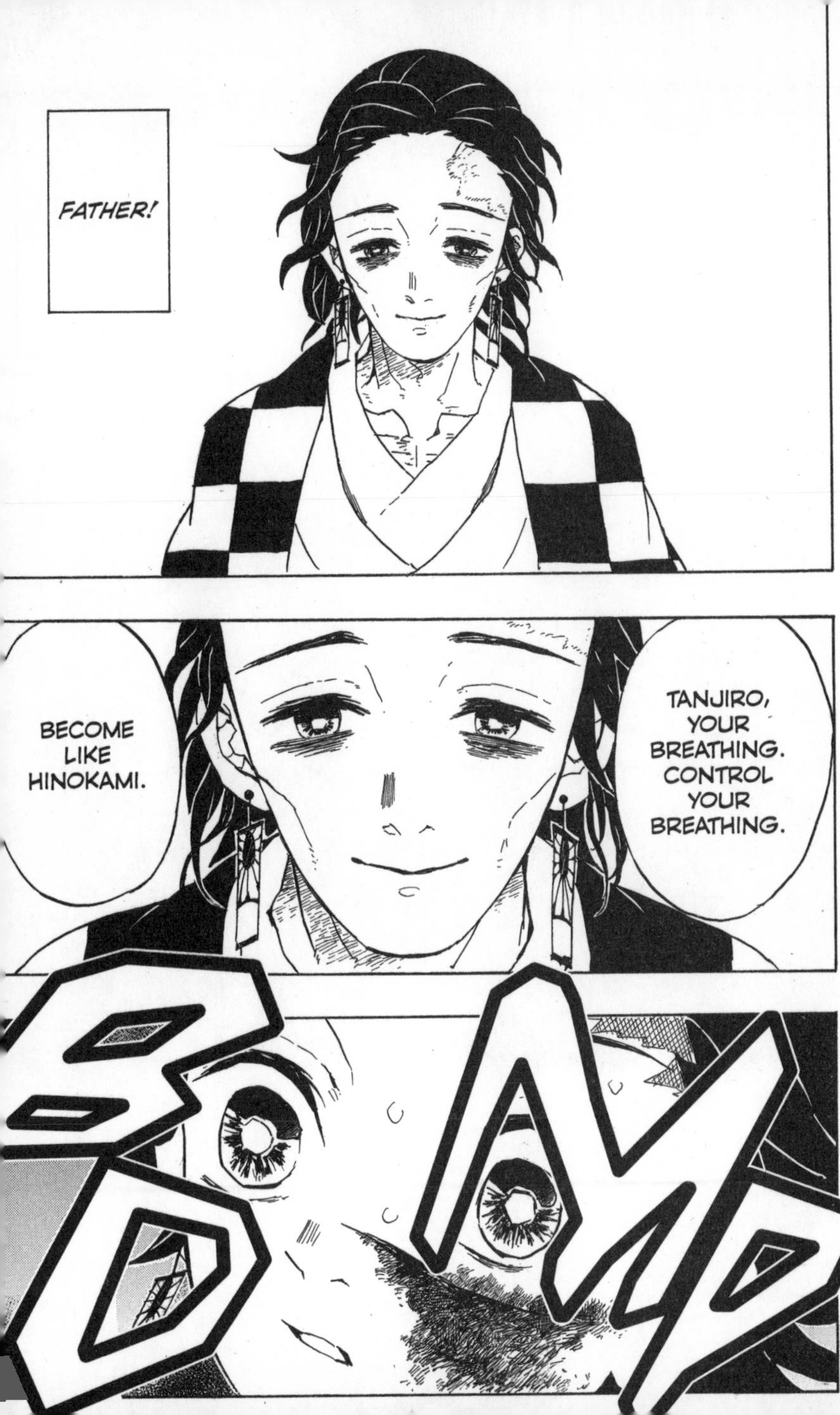
FATHER!
TANJIRO, YOUR BREATHING. CONTROL YOUR BREATHING.
BECOME LIKE HINOKAMI.

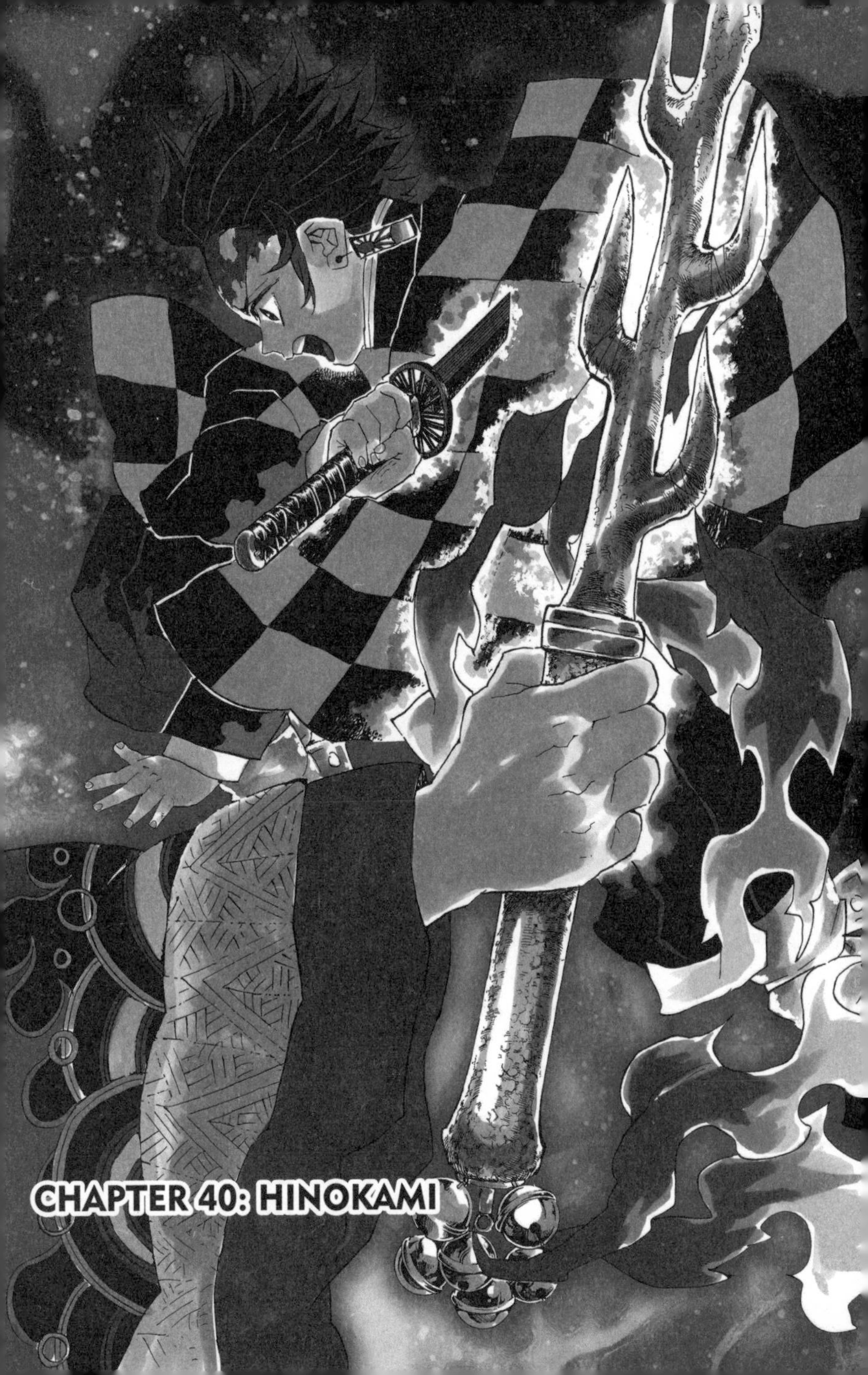
CHAPTER 40: HINOKAMI

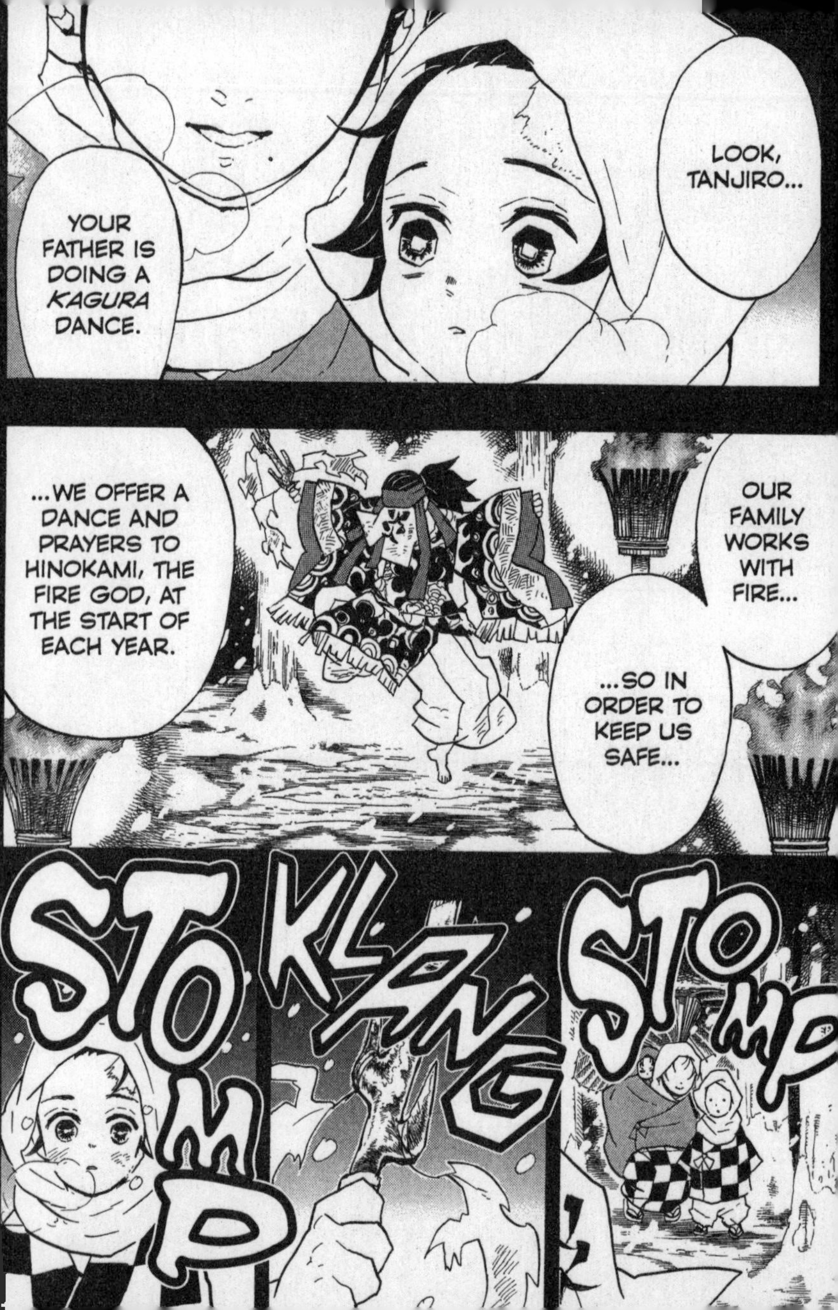
LOOK, TANJIRO...
YOUR FATHER IS DOING A *KAGURA* DANCE.
OUR FAMILY WORKS WITH FIRE...
...SO IN ORDER TO KEEP US SAFE...
...WE OFFER A DANCE AND PRAYERS TO HINOKAMI, THE FIRE GOD, AT THE START OF EACH YEAR.
STOMP
KLANG
STOMP

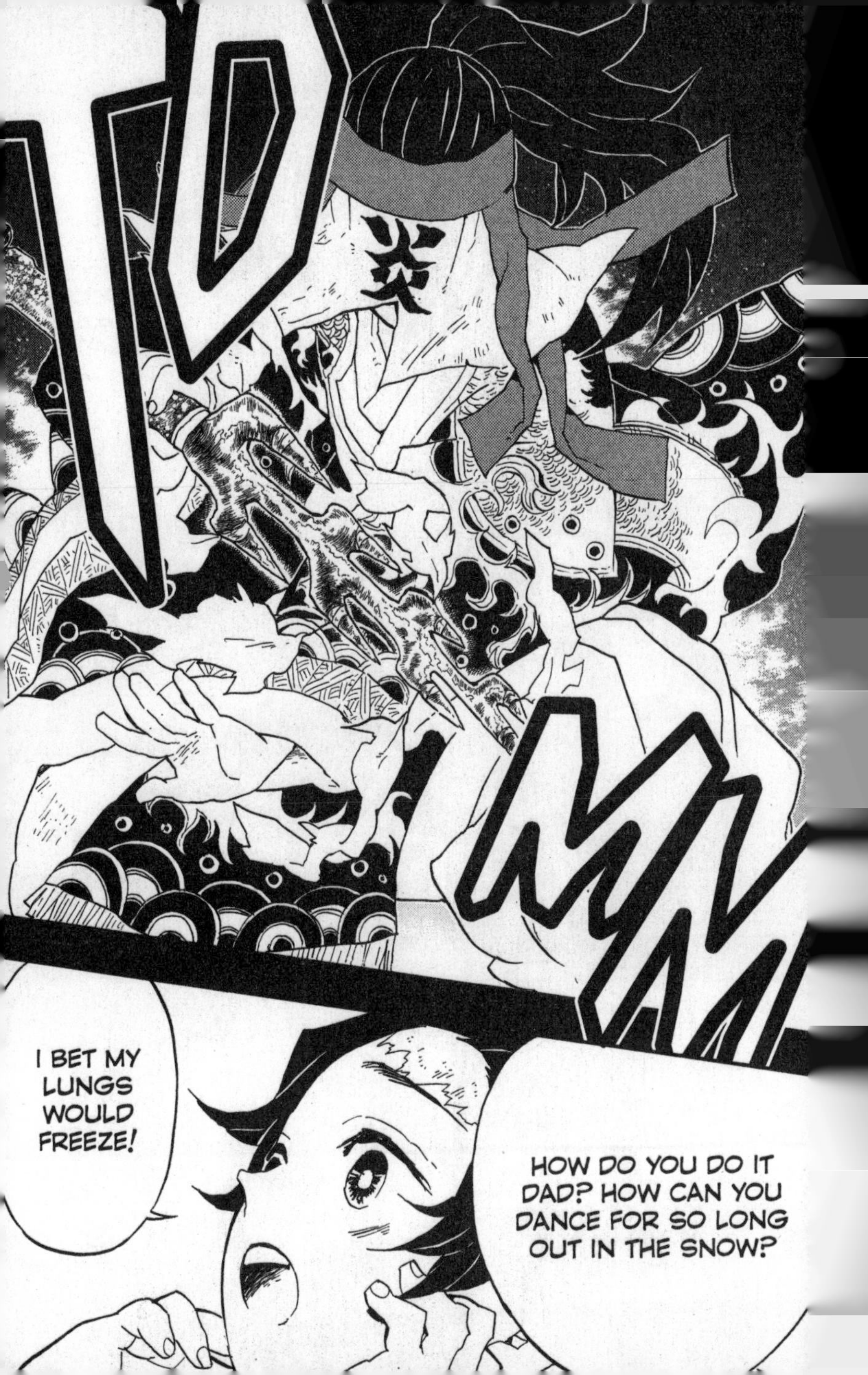
炎
HOW DO YOU DO IT DAD? HOW CAN YOU DANCE FOR SO LONG OUT IN THE SNOW?
I BET MY LUNGS WOULD FREEZE!

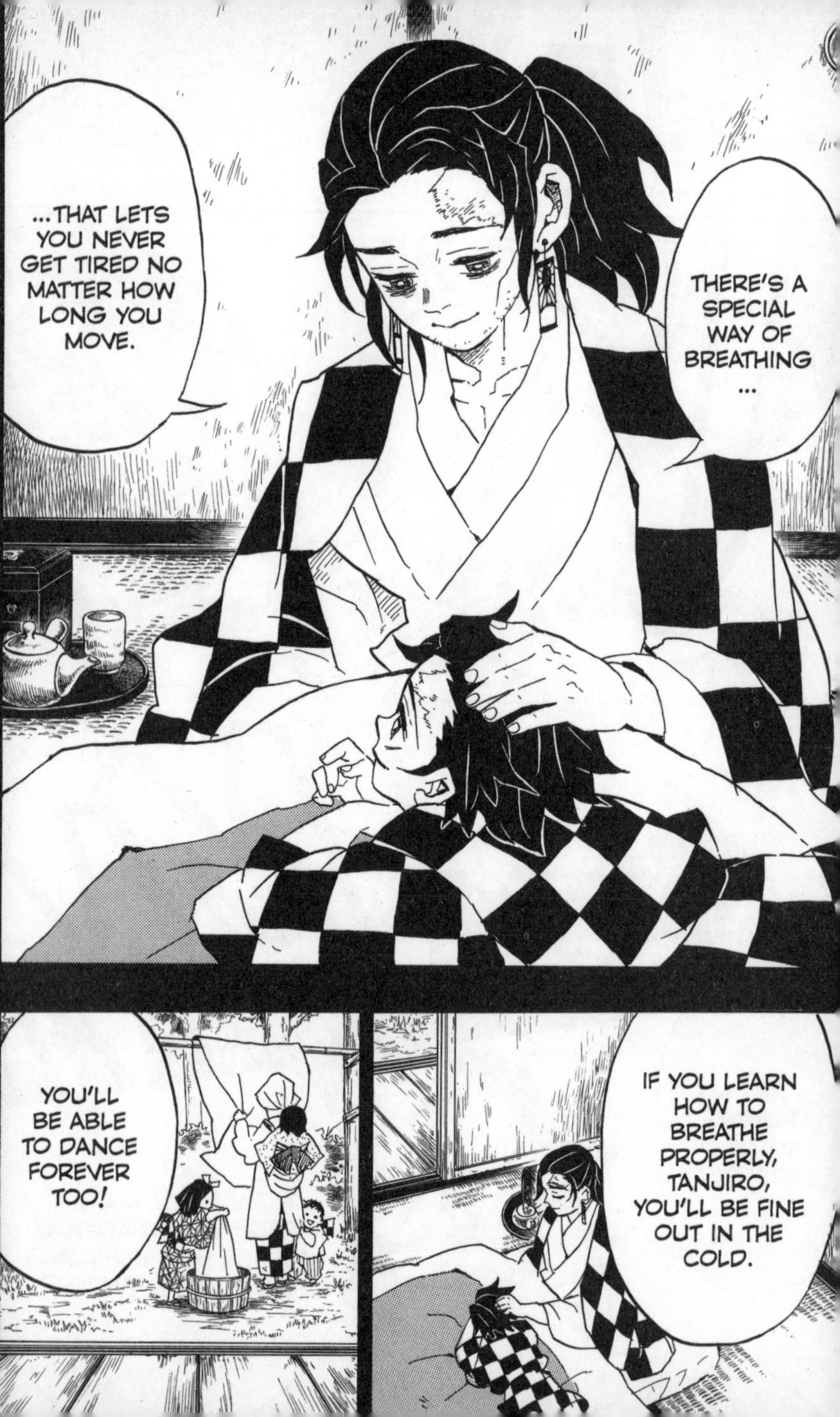
THERE'S A SPECIAL WAY OF BREATHING ...
...THAT LETS YOU NEVER GET TIRED NO MATTER HOW LONG YOU MOVE.
IF YOU LEARN HOW TO BREATHE PROPERLY, TANJIRO, YOU'LL BE FINE OUT IN THE COLD.
YOU'LL BE ABLE TO DANCE FOREVER TOO!

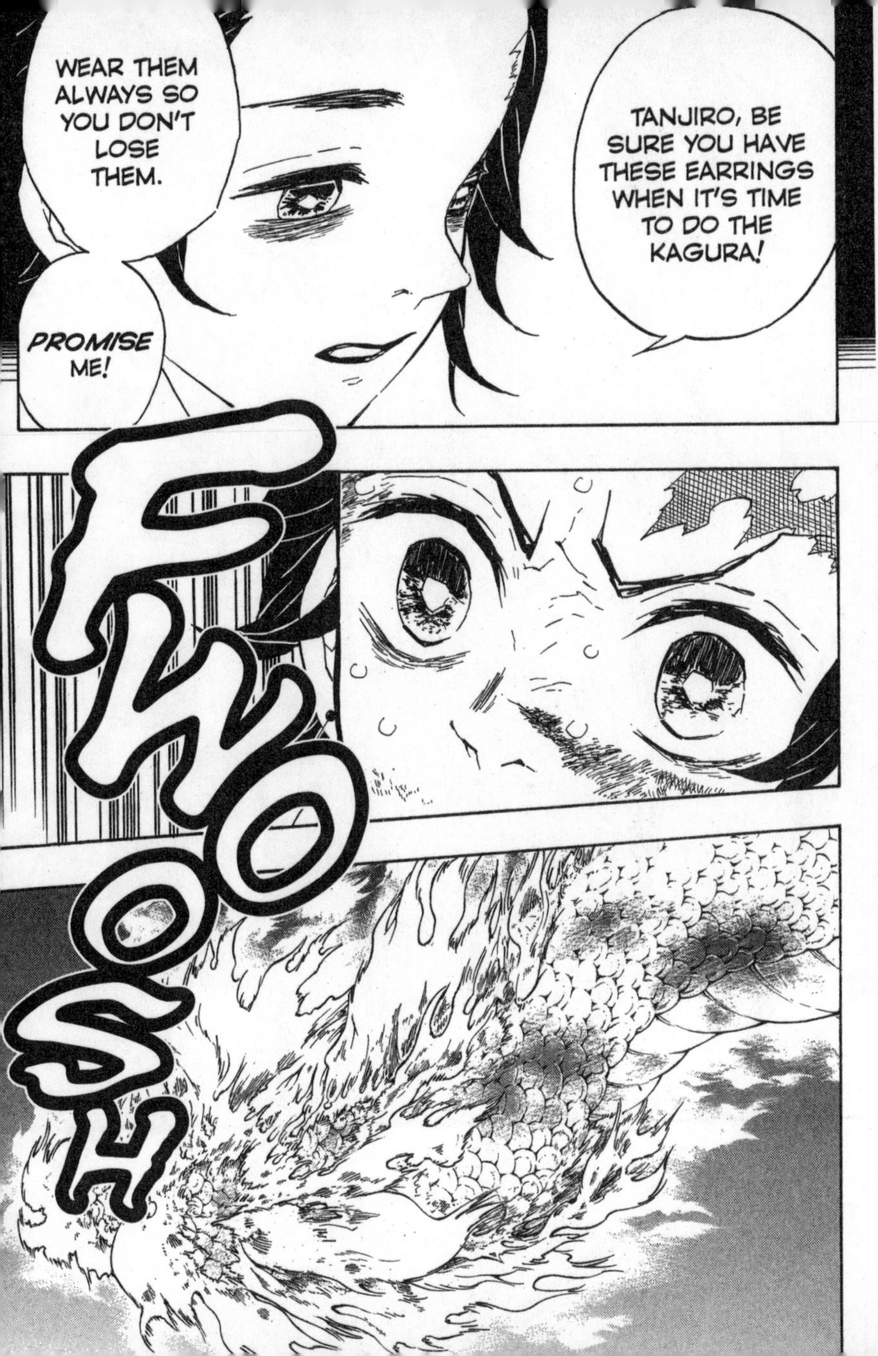
TANJIRO, BE SURE YOU HAVE THESE EARRINGS WHEN IT'S TIME TO DO THE KAGURA!
WEAR THEM ALWAYS SO YOU DON'T LOSE THEM.
PROMISE ME!
WHOOSH

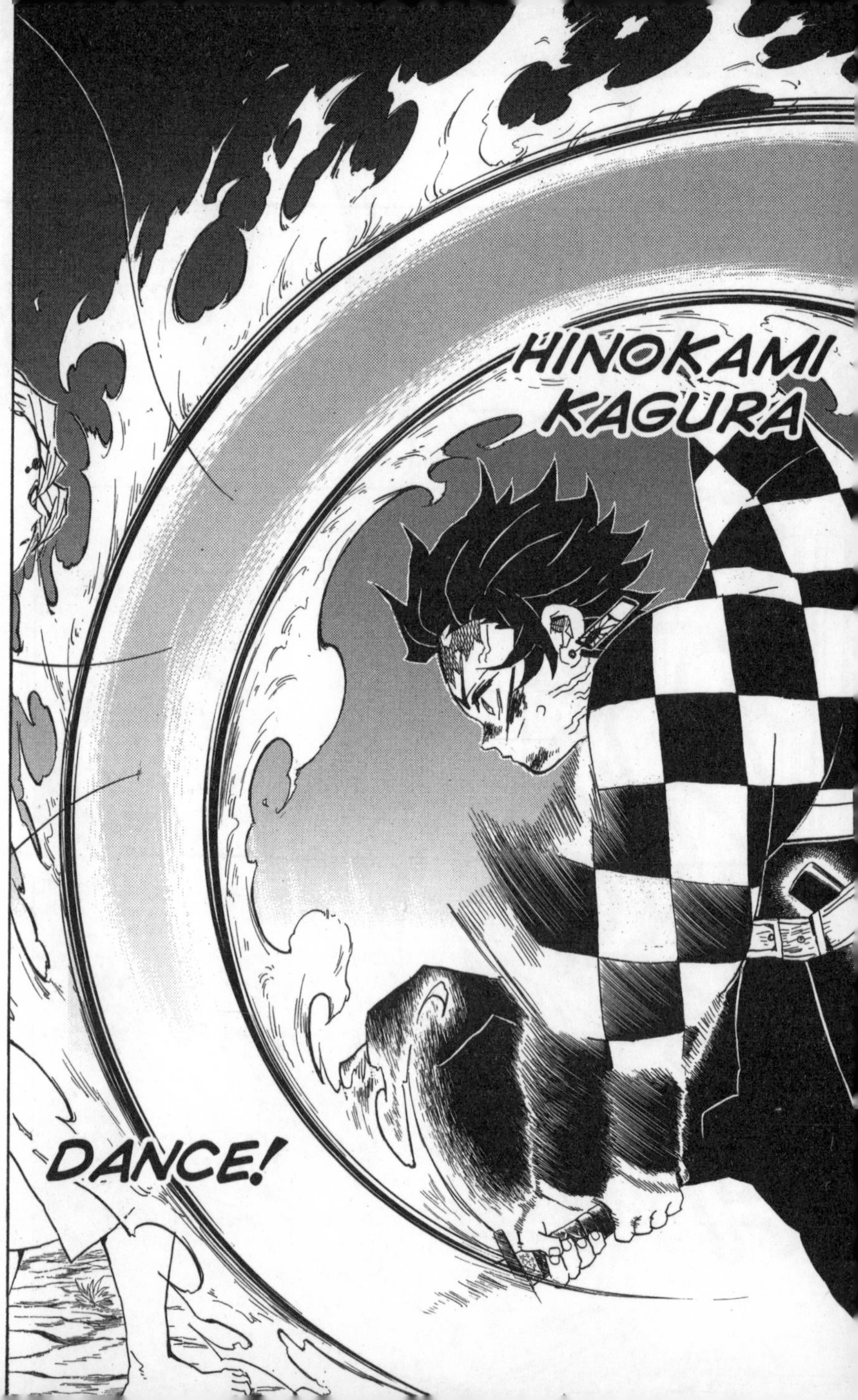
HINOKAMI KAGURA
DANCE!

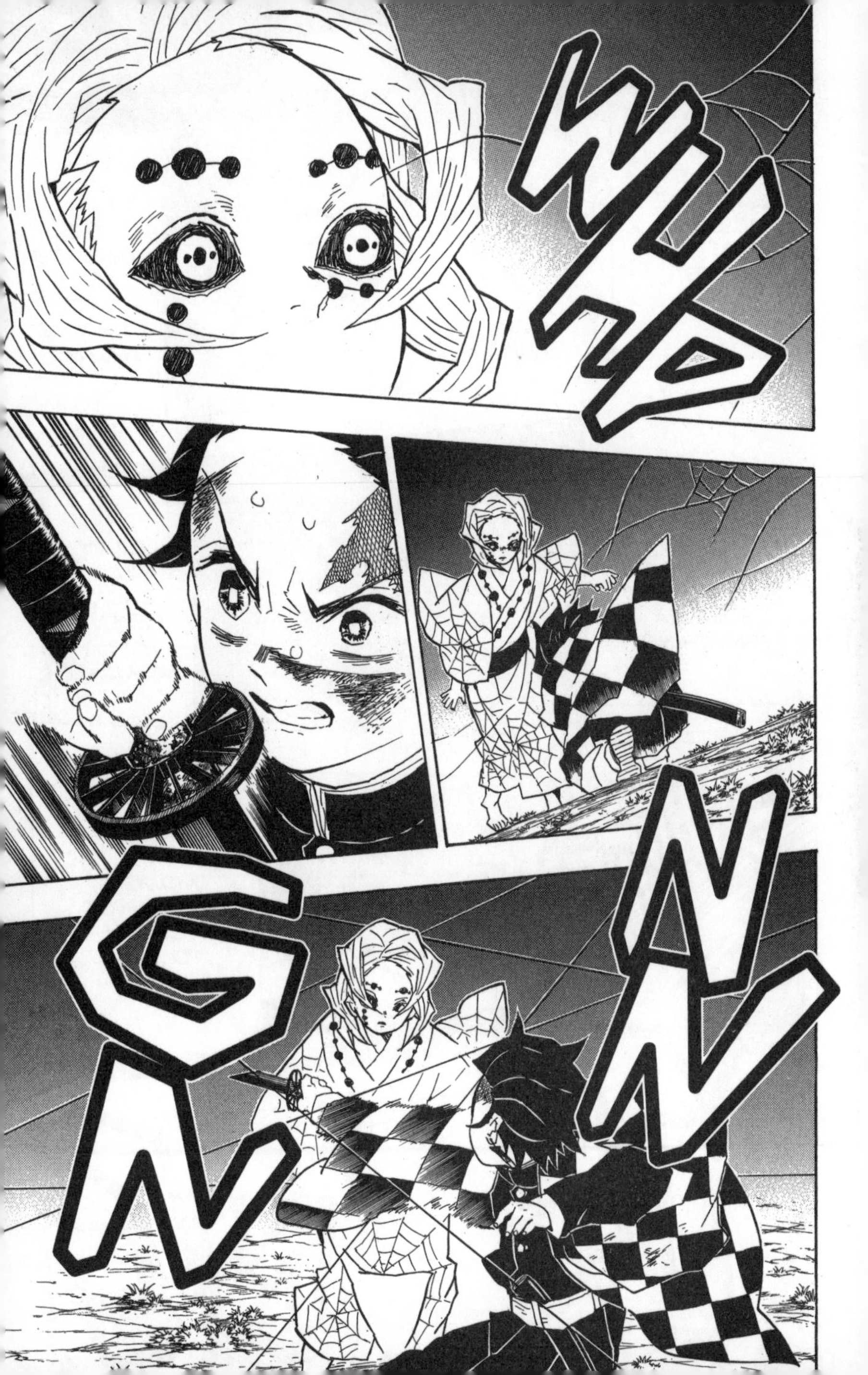
WHIP
GNNN

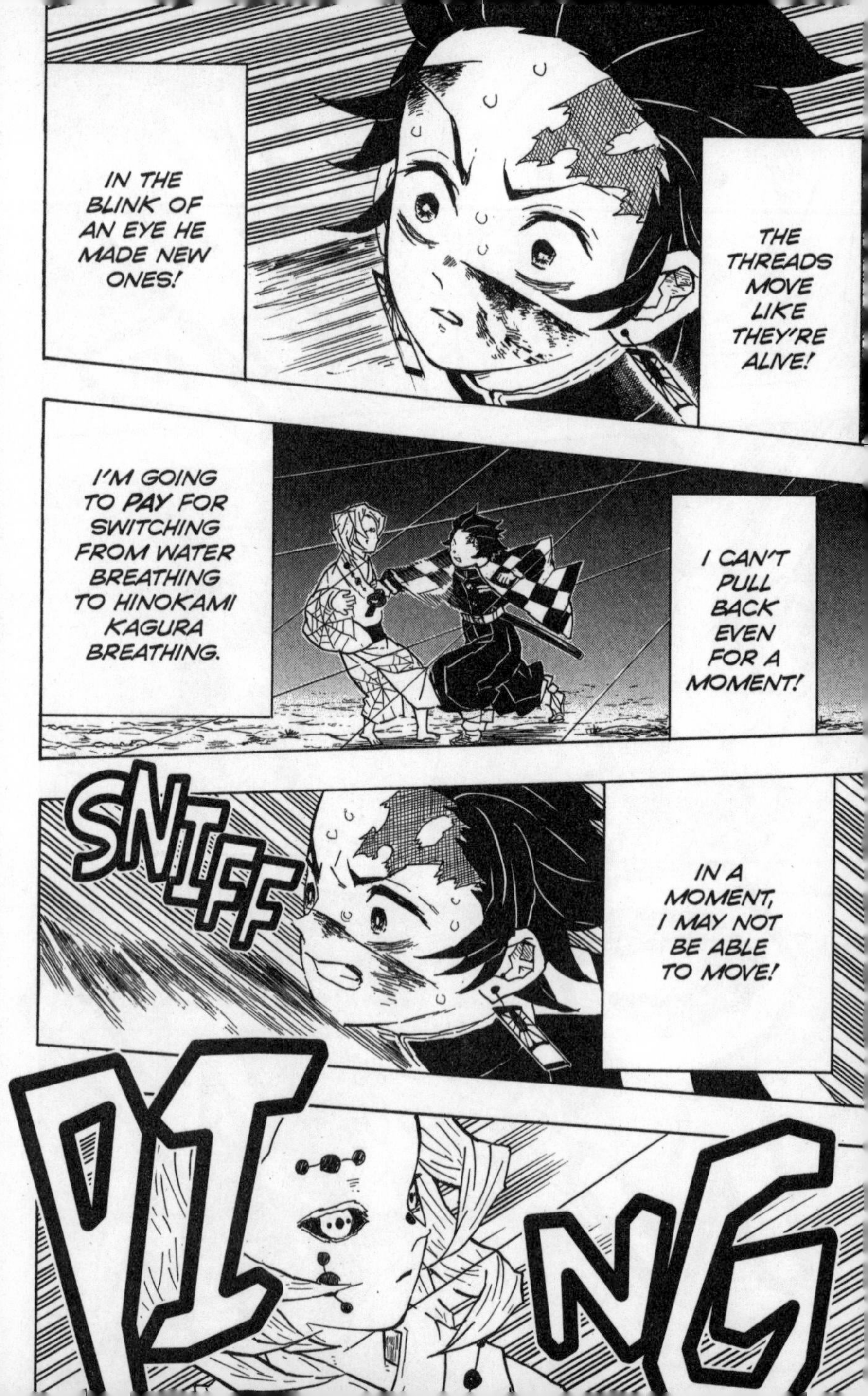
THE THREADS MOVE LIKE THEY'RE ALIVE!
IN THE BLINK OF AN EYE HE MADE NEW ONES!
I CAN'T PULL BACK EVEN FOR A MOMENT!
I'M GOING TO PAY FOR SWITCHING FROM WATER BREATHING TO HINOKAMI KAGURA BREATHING.
IN A MOMENT, I MAY NOT BE ABLE TO MOVE!
SNIFF
PING

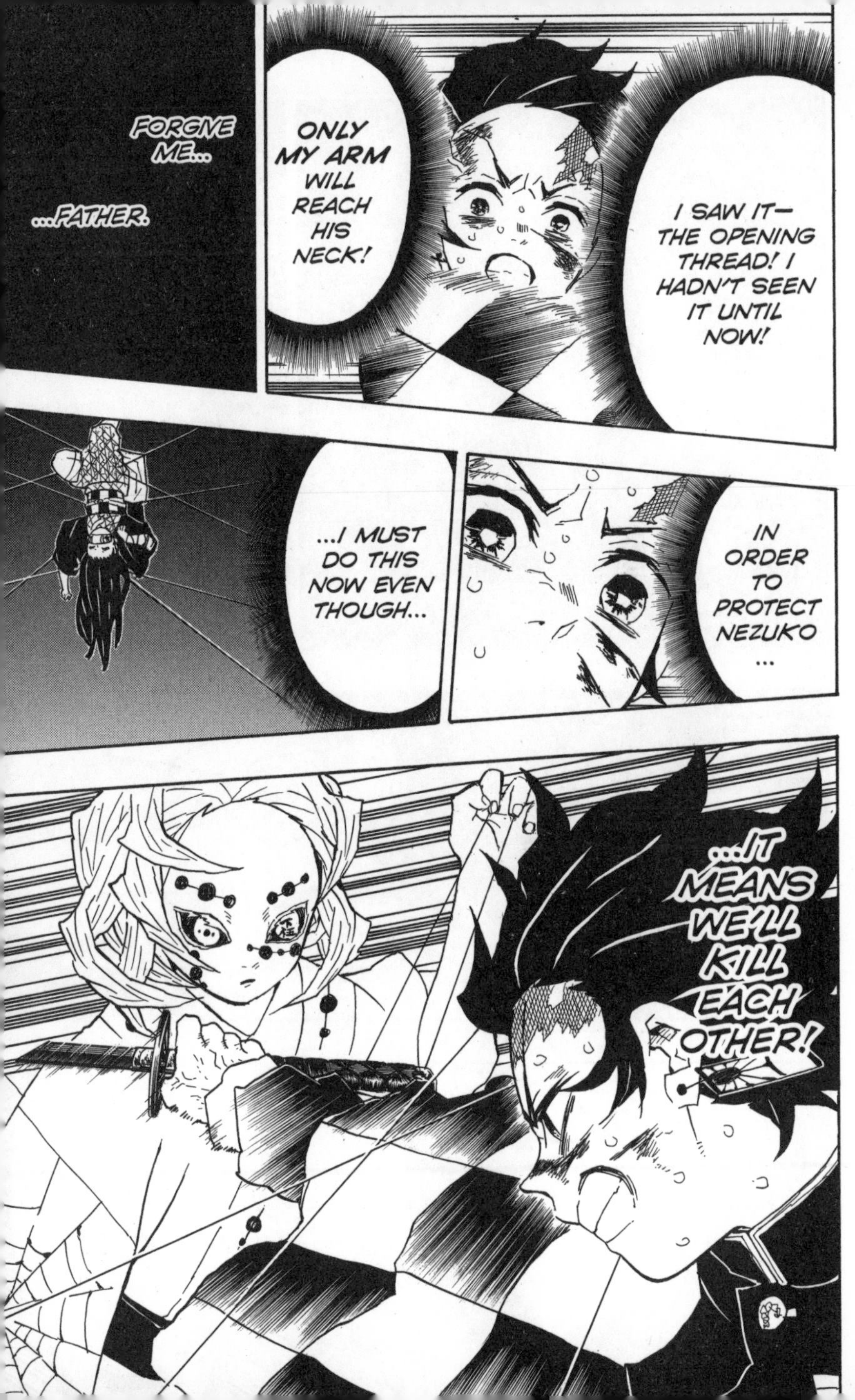
I SAW IT— THE OPENING THREAD! I HADN'T SEEN IT UNTIL NOW!
ONLY MY ARM WILL REACH HIS NECK!
FORGIVE ME...
...FATHER.
IN ORDER TO PROTECT NEZUKO ...
...I MUST DO THIS NOW EVEN THOUGH...
...IT MEANS WE'LL KILL EACH OTHER!

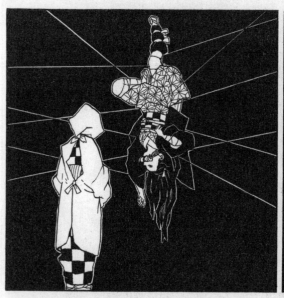
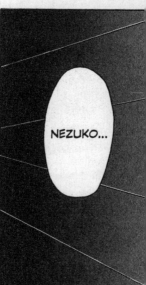

NEZUKO...

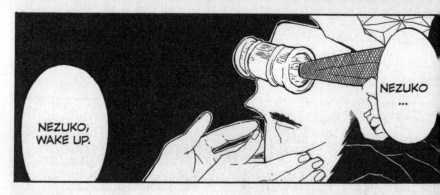

NEZUKO, WAKE UP.

NEZUKO...

TRY HARD.

THE WAY YOU *ARE* NOW, YOU CAN *DO* THIS.

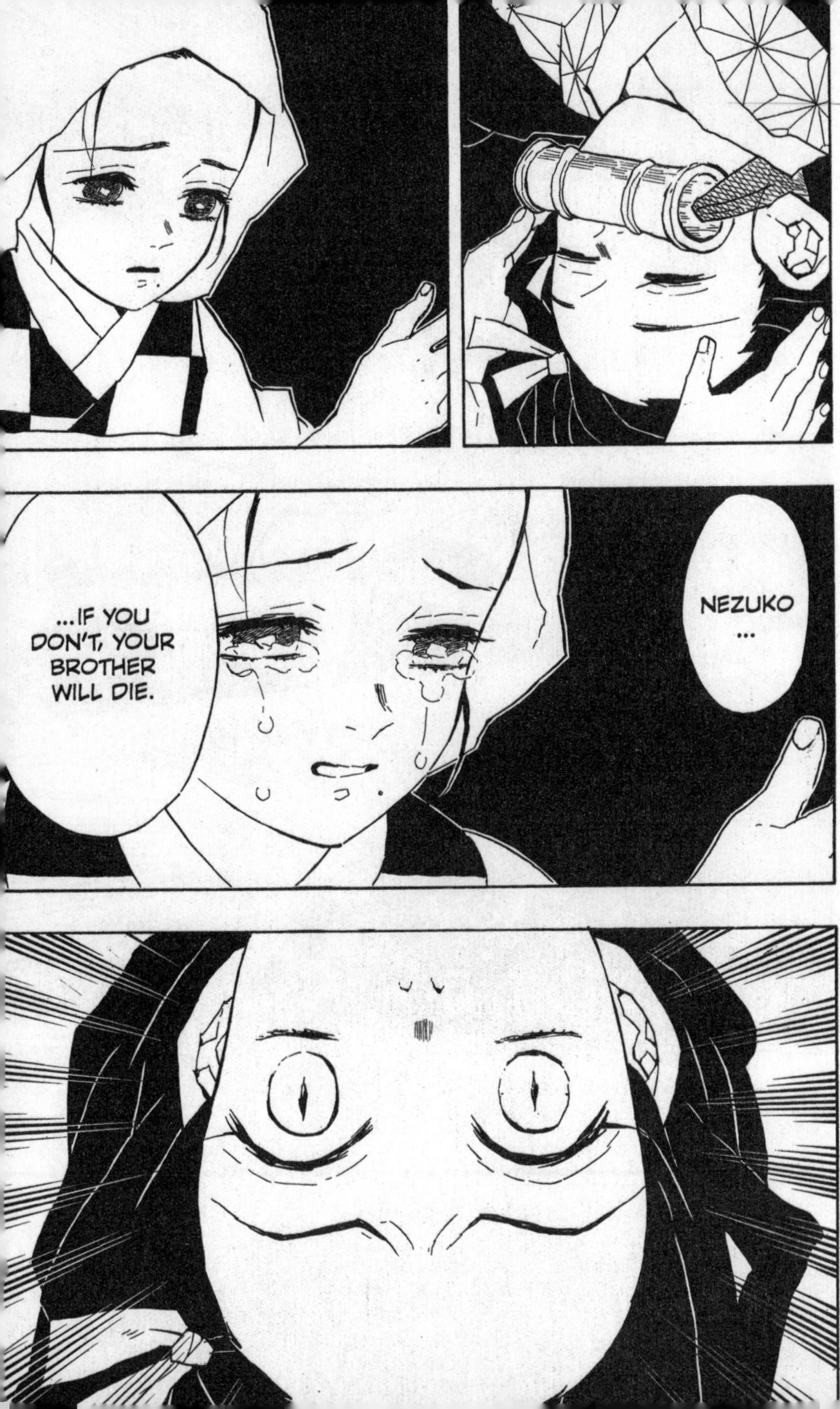
NEZUKO ...
...IF YOU DON'T, YOUR BROTHER WILL DIE.

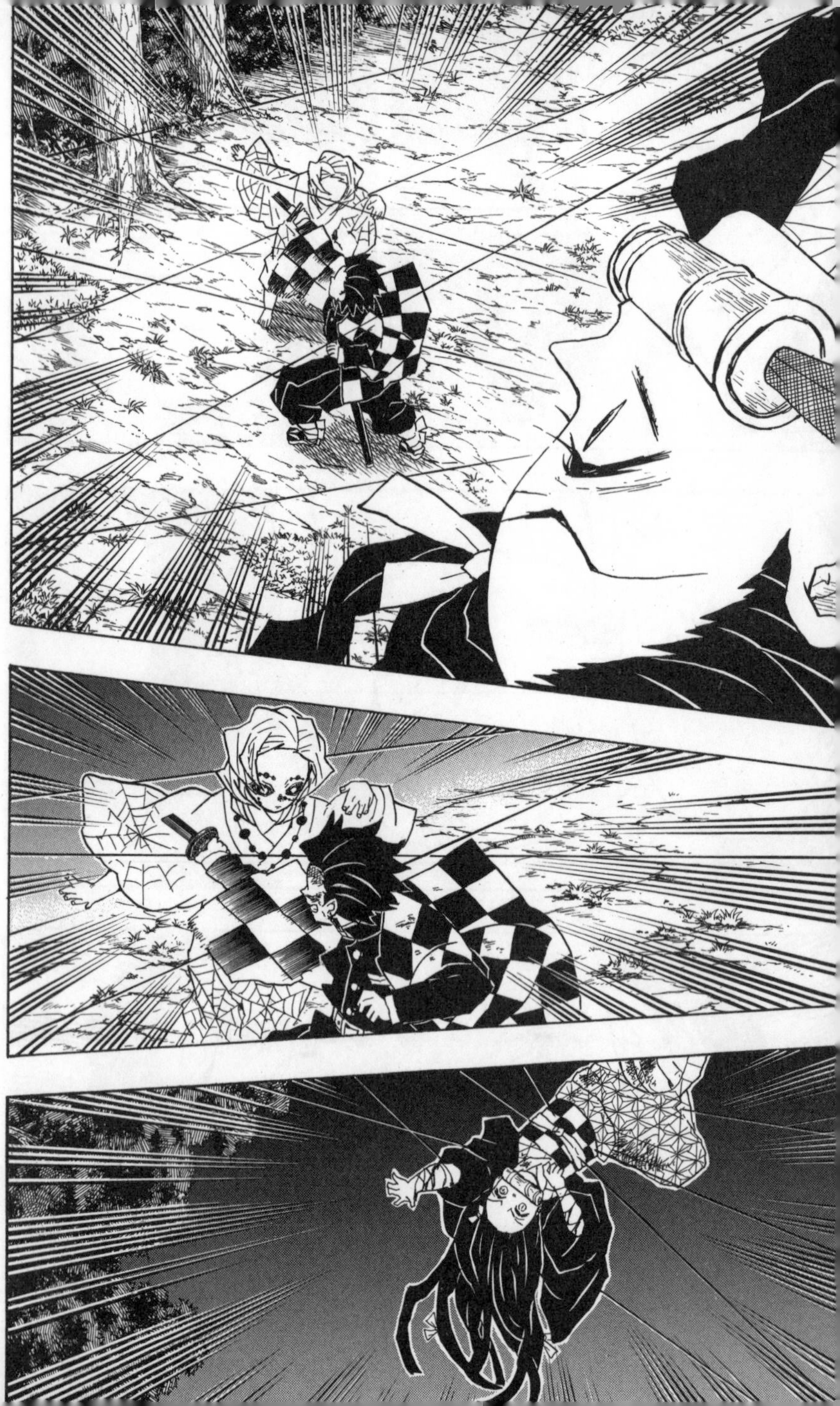

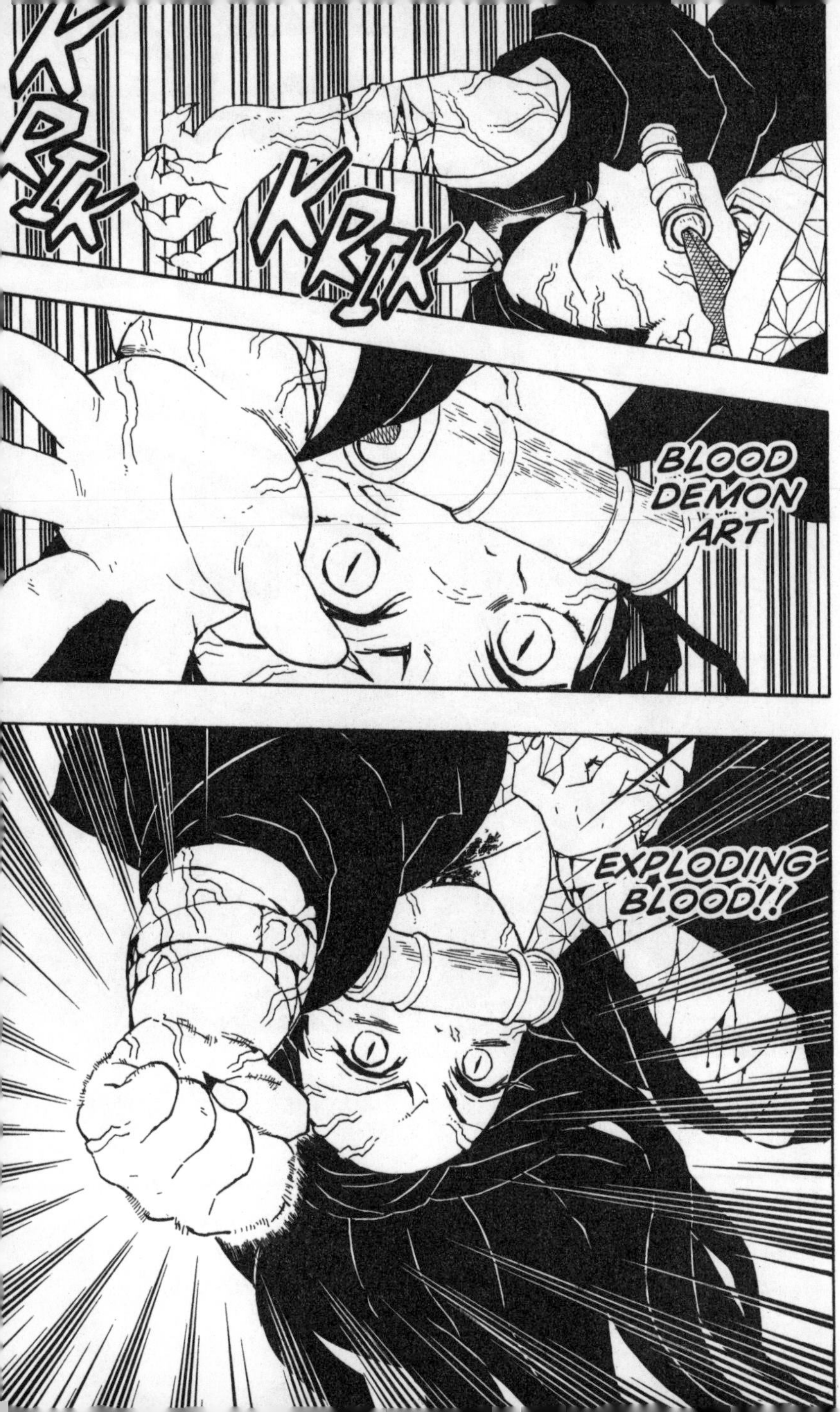
KRIK
KRIK
BLOOD DEMON ART
EXPLODING BLOOD!!

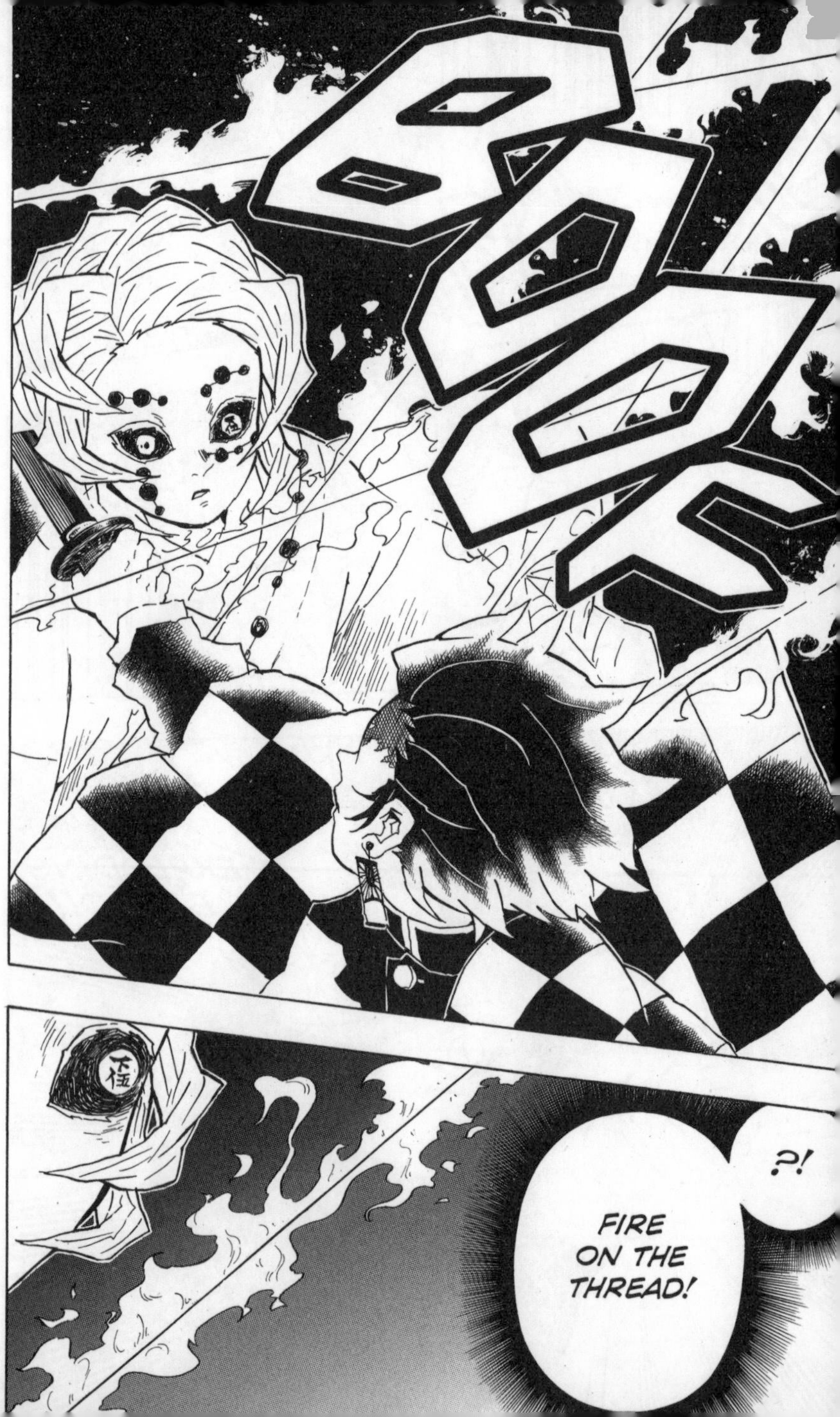
?!
FIRE ON THE THREAD!

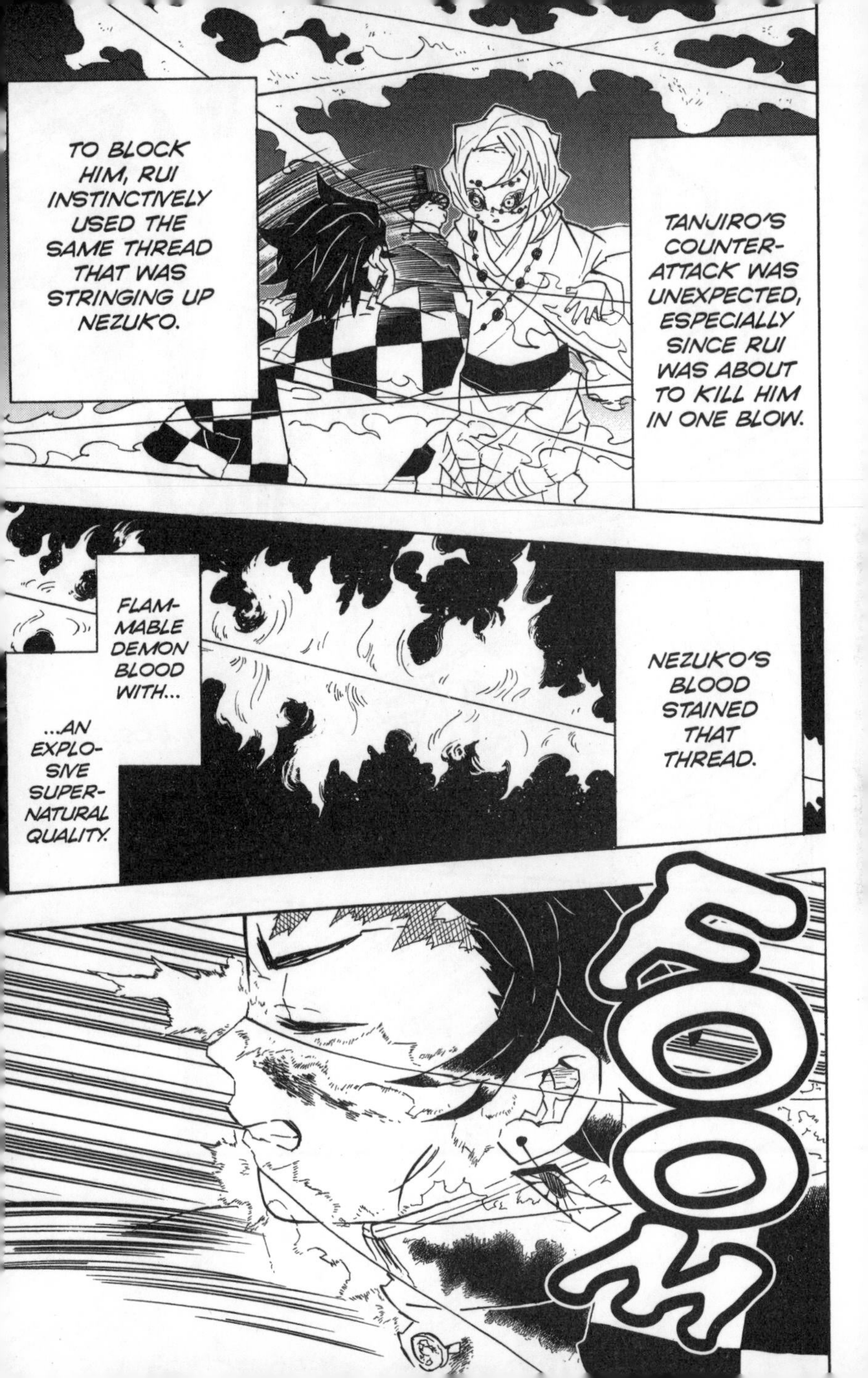
TANJIRO'S COUNTER-ATTACK WAS UNEXPECTED, ESPECIALLY SINCE RUI WAS ABOUT TO KILL HIM IN ONE BLOW.
TO BLOCK HIM, RUI INSTINCTIVELY USED THE SAME THREAD THAT WAS STRINGING UP NEZUKO.
NEZUKO'S BLOOD STAINED THAT THREAD.
FLAM-MABLE DEMON BLOOD WITH...
...AN EXPLO-SIVE SUPER-NATURAL QUALITY.

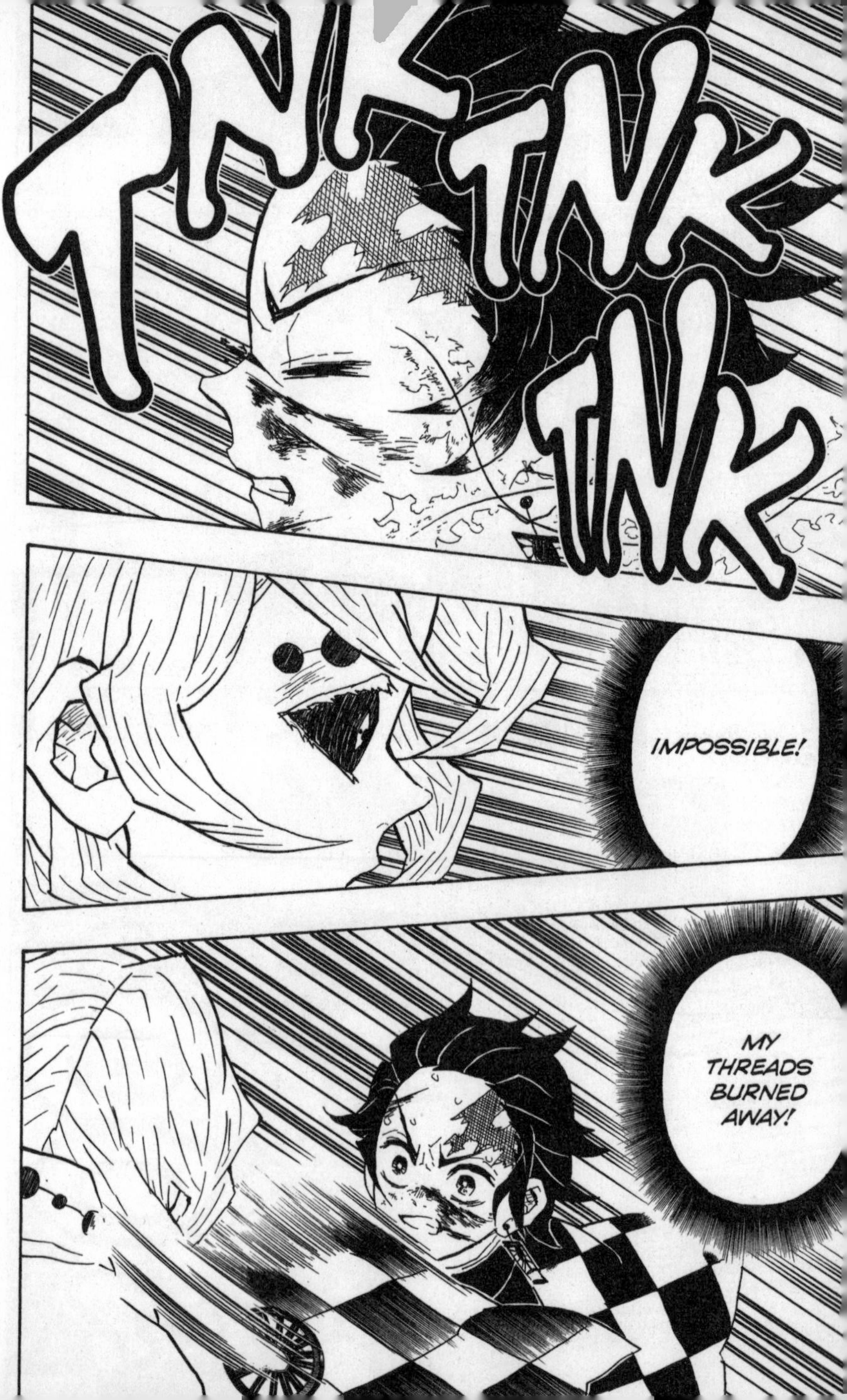
TNK TNK TNK
IMPOSSIBLE!
MY THREADS BURNED AWAY!

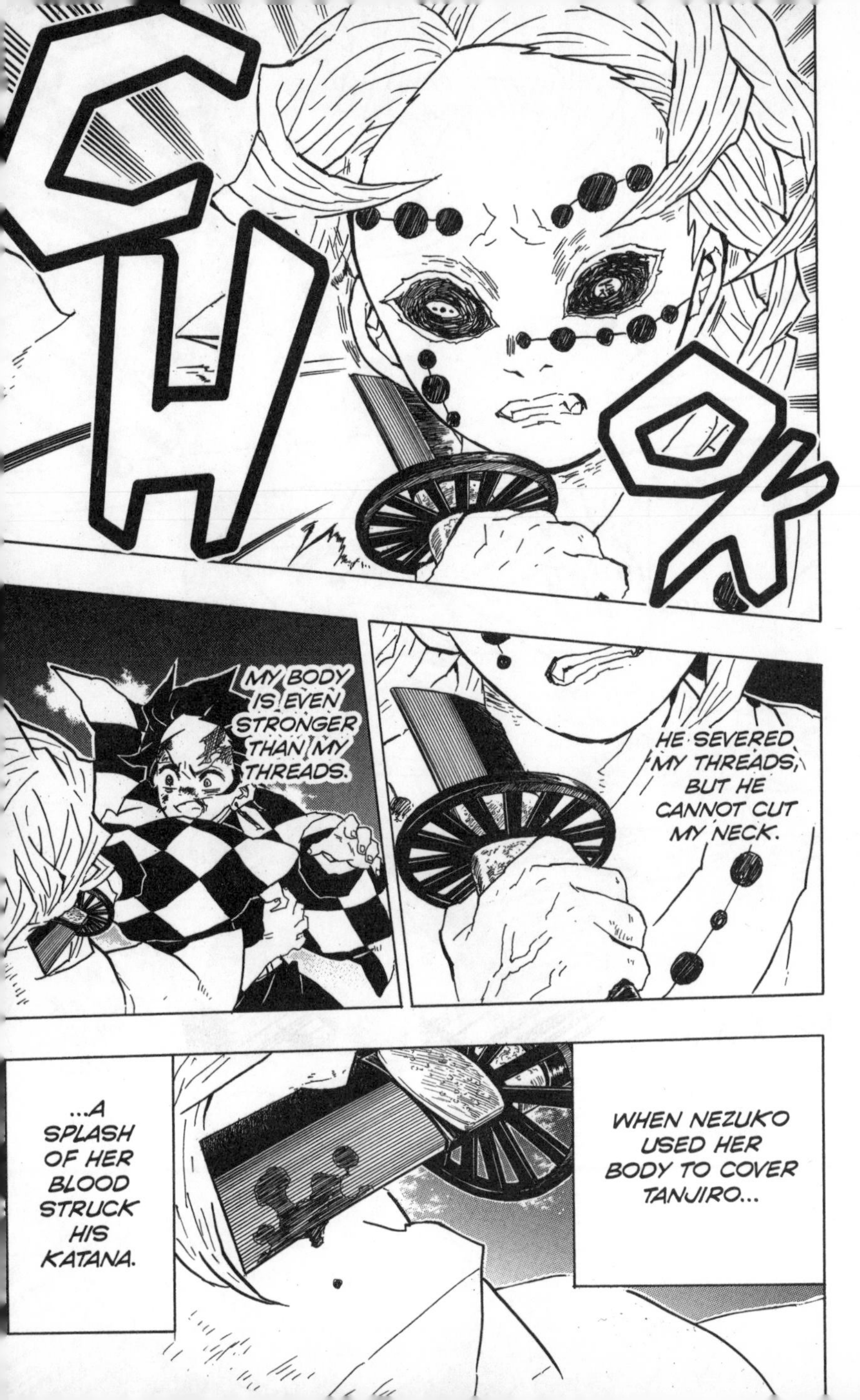
CHOK
HE SEVERED MY THREADS, BUT HE CANNOT CUT MY NECK.
MY BODY IS EVEN STRONGER THAN MY THREADS.
WHEN NEZUKO USED HER BODY TO COVER TANJIRO...
...A SPLASH OF HER BLOOD STRUCK HIS KATANA.

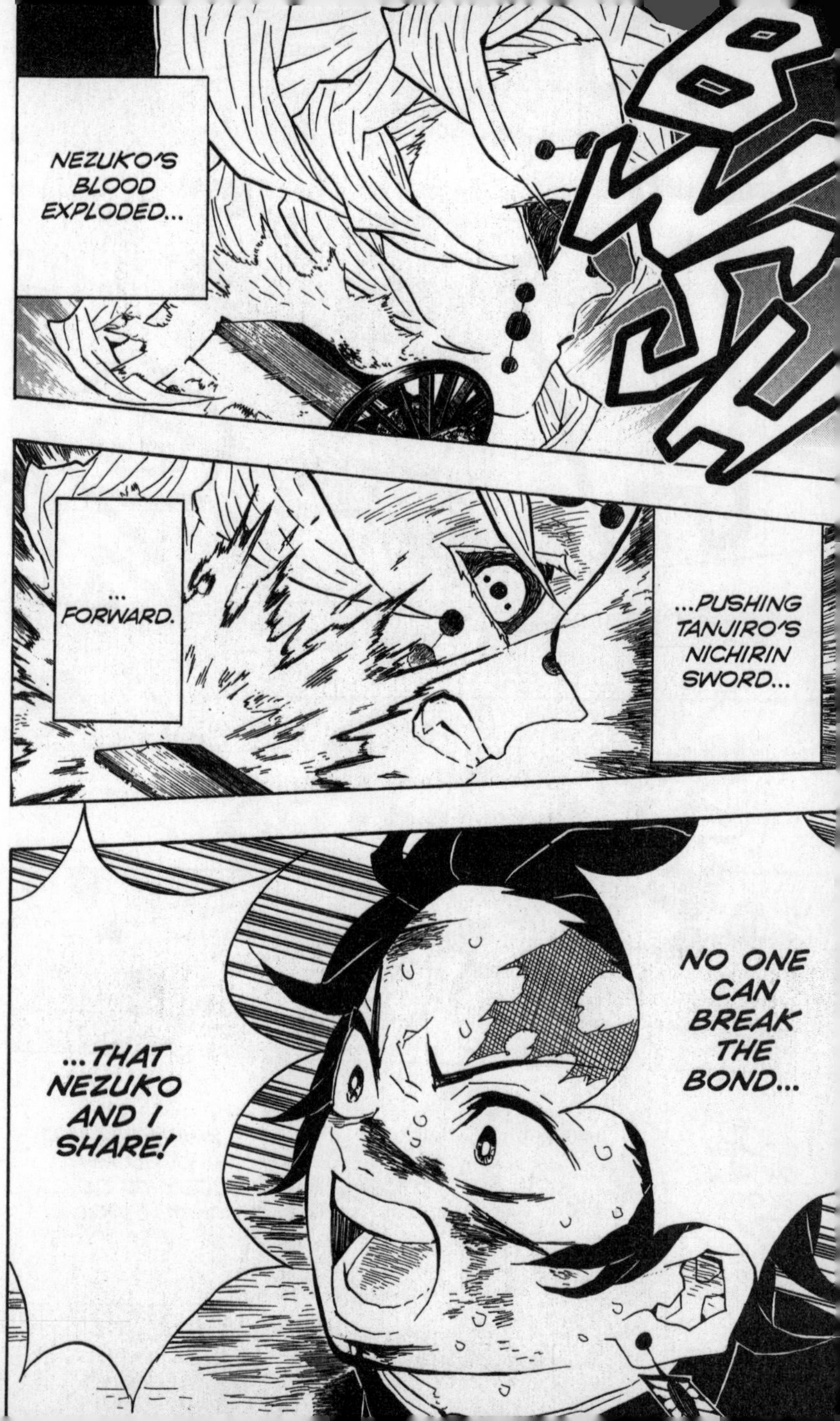
NEZUKO'S BLOOD EXPLODED...
...PUSHING TANJIRO'S NICHIRIN SWORD...
...FORWARD.
NO ONE CAN BREAK THE BOND...
...THAT NEZUKO AND I SHARE!

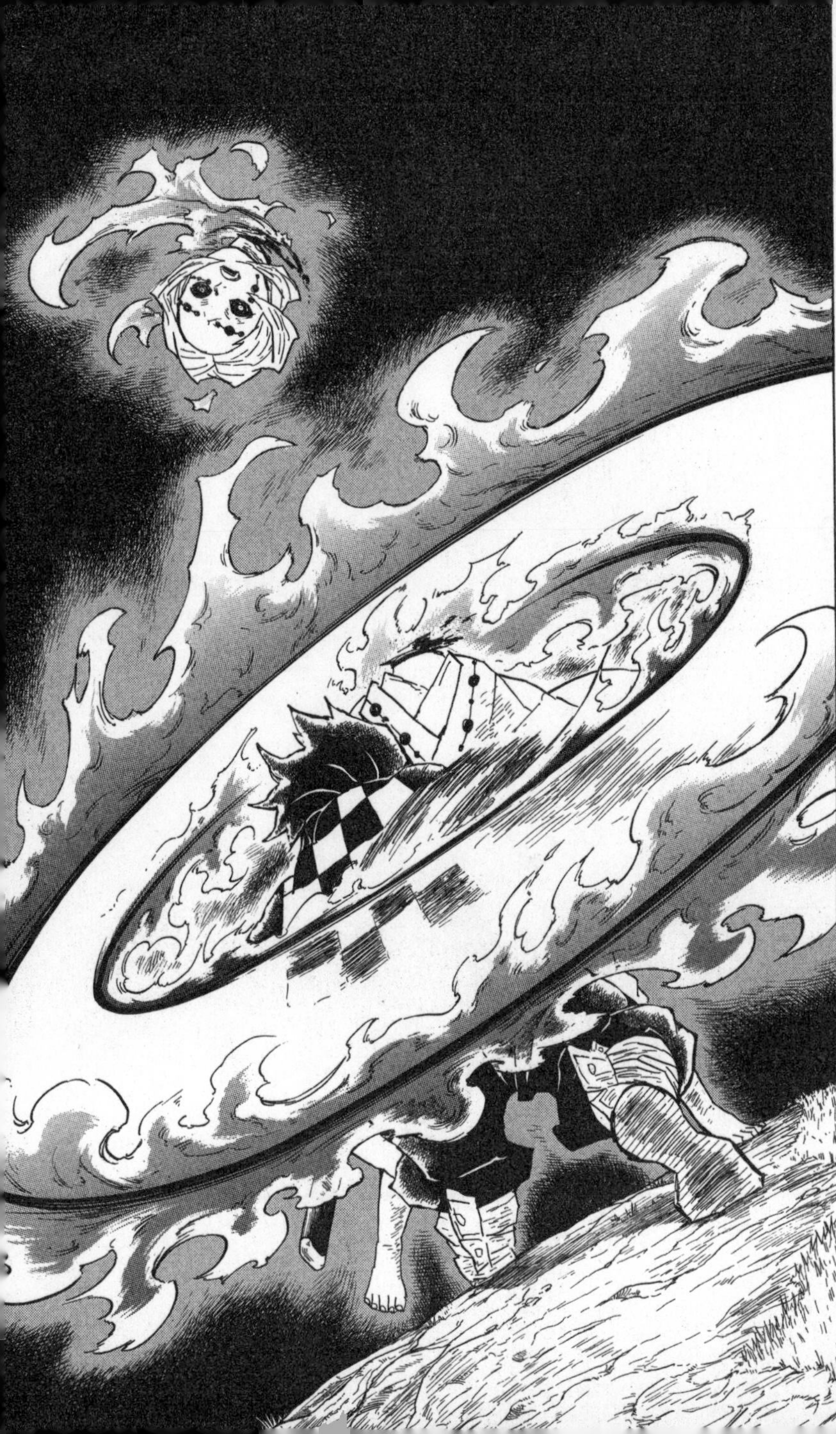

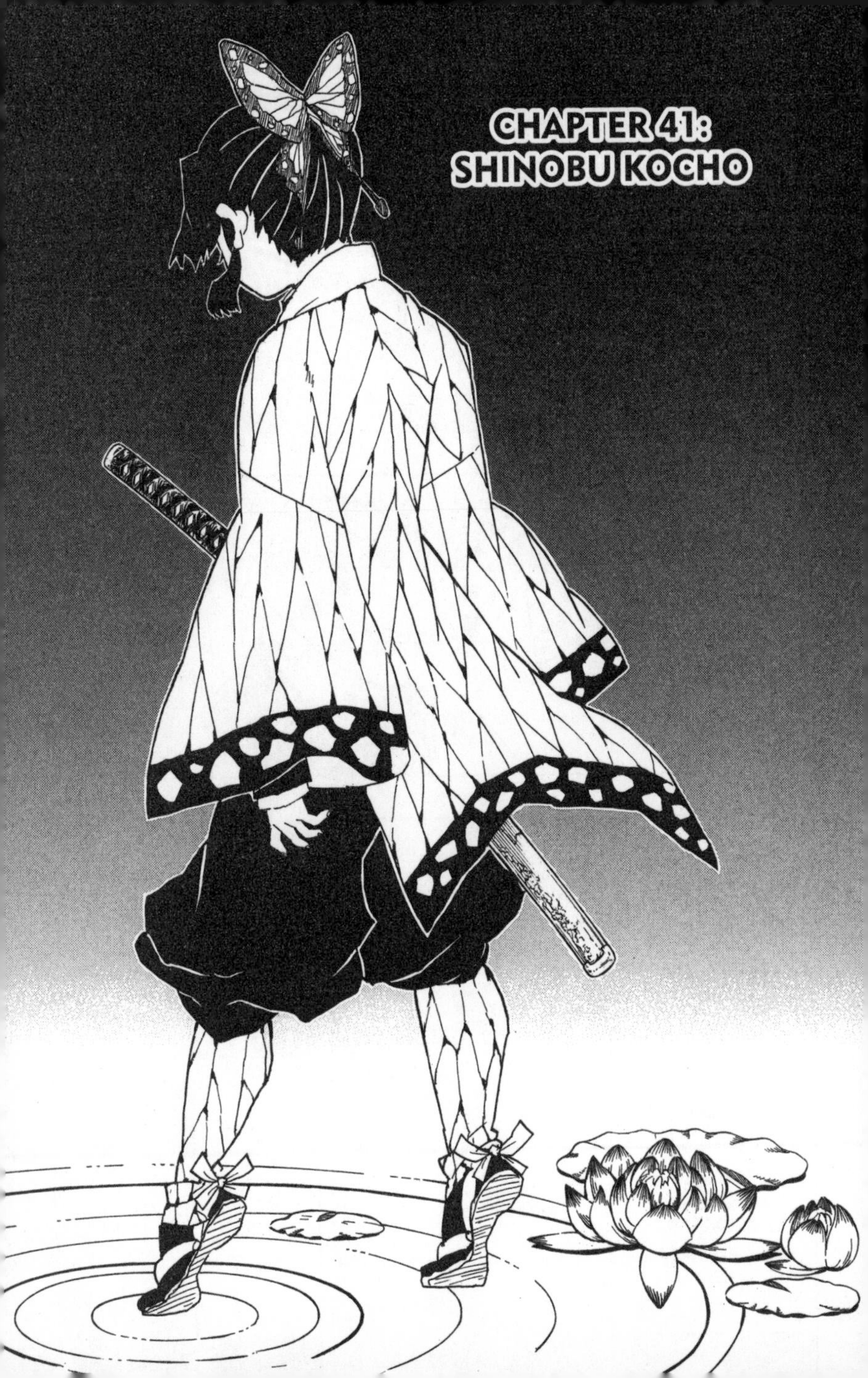
CHAPTER 41:
SHINOBU KOCHO

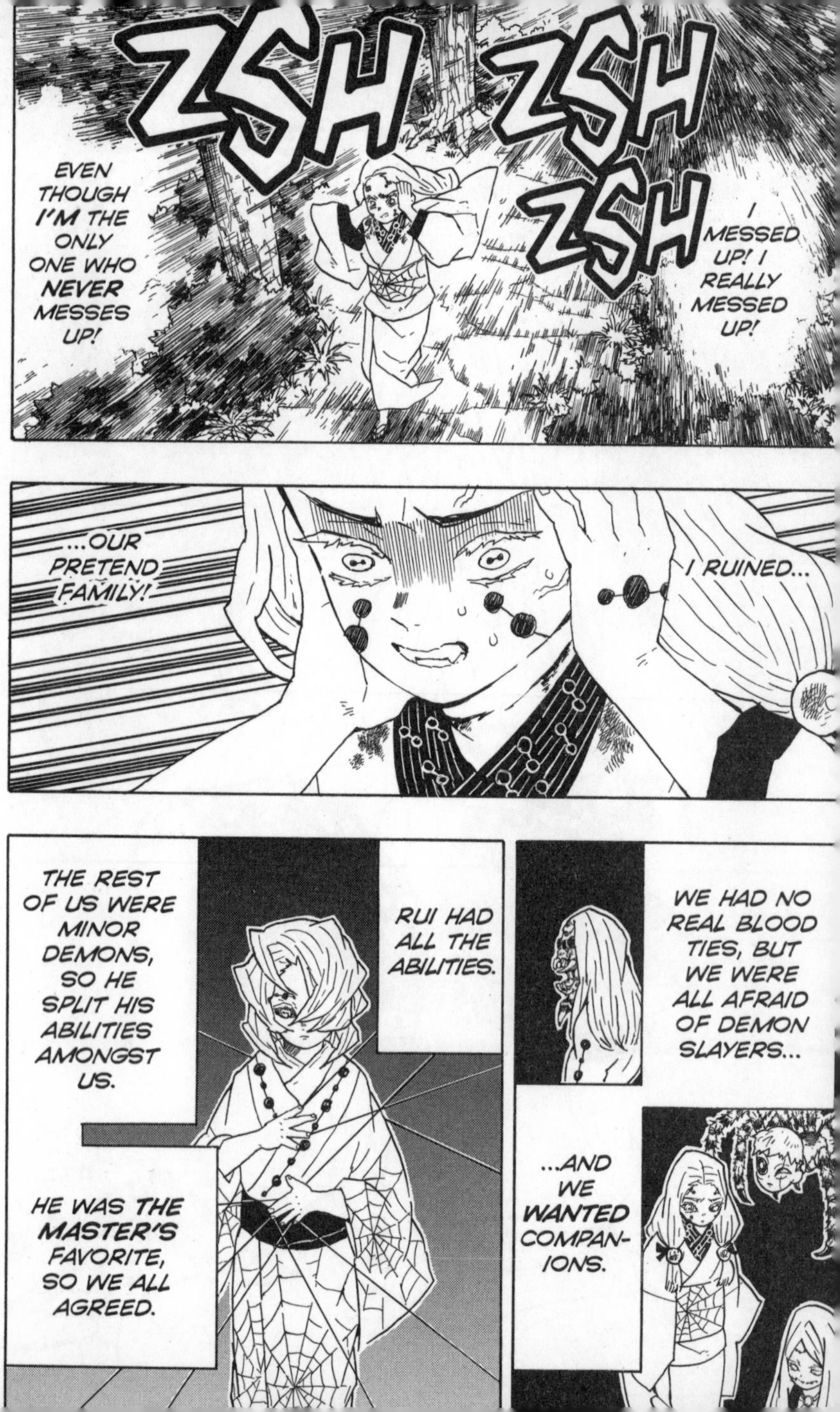
ZSH ZSH ZSH
I MESSED UP! I REALLY MESSED UP!
EVEN THOUGH I'M THE ONLY ONE WHO NEVER MESSES UP!
I RUINED...
...OUR PRETEND FAMILY!
WE HAD NO REAL BLOOD TIES, BUT WE WERE ALL AFRAID OF DEMON SLAYERS...
...AND WE WANTED COMPANIONS.
RUI HAD ALL THE ABILITIES.
THE REST OF US WERE MINOR DEMONS, SO HE SPLIT HIS ABILITIES AMONGST US.
HE WAS THE MASTER'S FAVORITE, SO WE ALL AGREED.

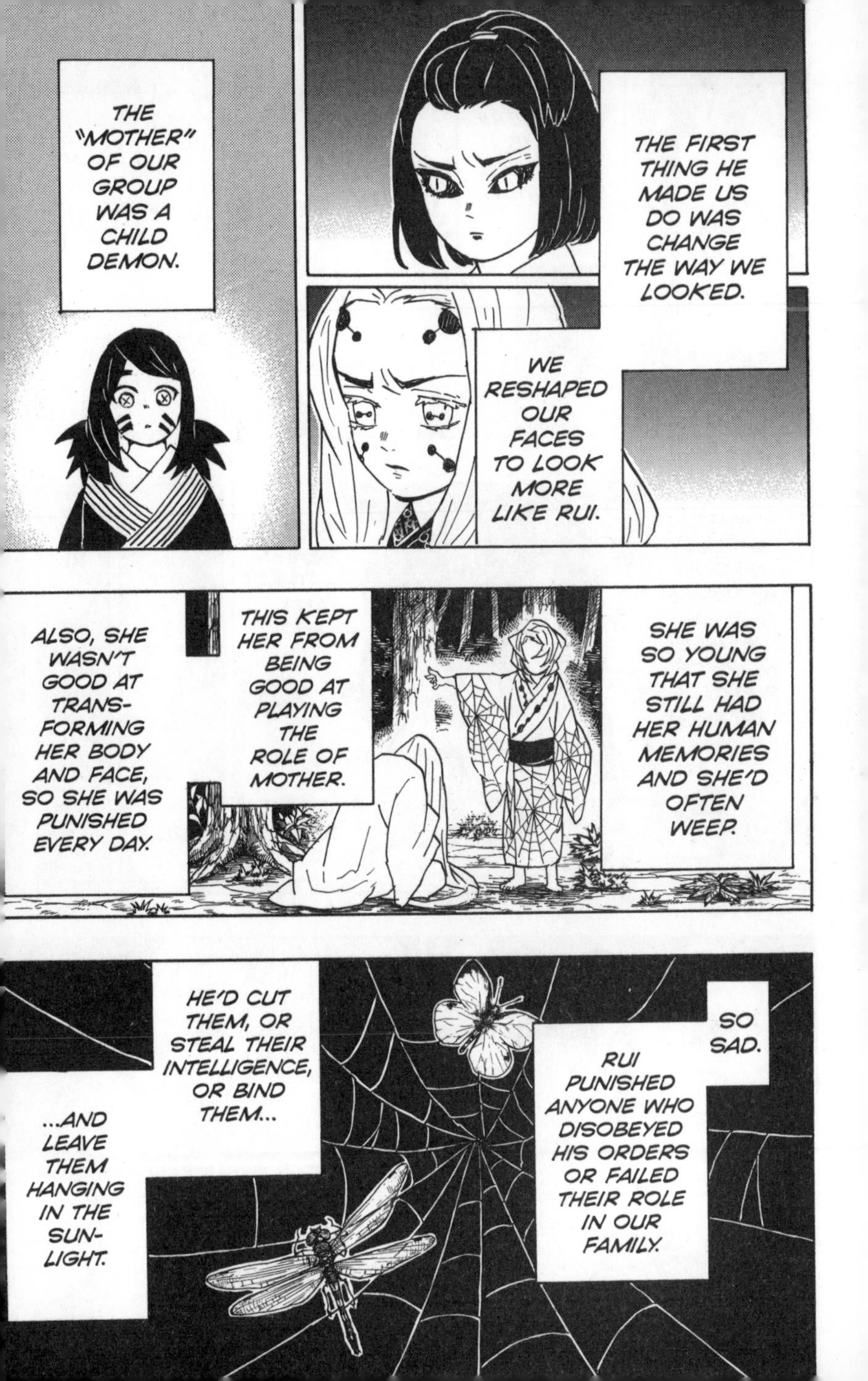
THE FIRST THING HE MADE US DO WAS CHANGE THE WAY WE LOOKED.
WE RESHAPED OUR FACES TO LOOK MORE LIKE RUI.
THE "MOTHER" OF OUR GROUP WAS A CHILD DEMON.
SHE WAS SO YOUNG THAT SHE STILL HAD HER HUMAN MEMORIES AND SHE'D OFTEN WEEP.
THIS KEPT HER FROM BEING GOOD AT PLAYING THE ROLE OF MOTHER.
ALSO, SHE WASN'T GOOD AT TRANS-FORMING HER BODY AND FACE, SO SHE WAS PUNISHED EVERY DAY.
SO SAD.
RUI PUNISHED ANYONE WHO DISOBEYED HIS ORDERS OR FAILED THEIR ROLE IN OUR FAMILY.
HE'D CUT THEM, OR STEAL THEIR INTELLIGENCE, OR BIND THEM...
...AND LEAVE THEM HANGING IN THE SUN-LIGHT.

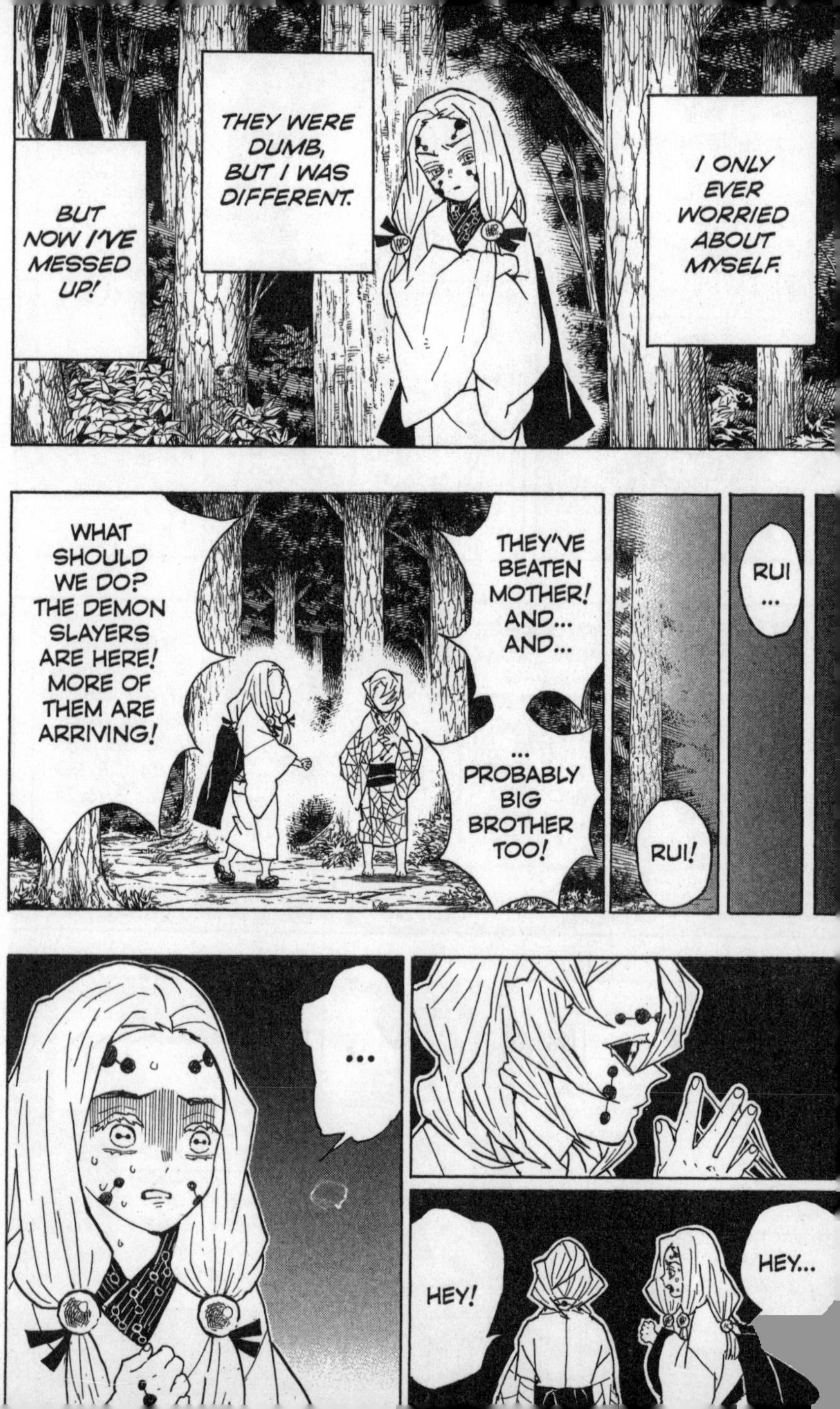
I ONLY EVER WORRIED ABOUT MYSELF.
THEY WERE DUMB, BUT I WAS DIFFERENT.
BUT NOW I'VE MESSED UP!
RUI ...
RUI!
THEY'VE BEATEN MOTHER! AND... AND...
... PROBABLY BIG BROTHER TOO!
WHAT SHOULD WE DO? THE DEMON SLAYERS ARE HERE! MORE OF THEM ARE ARRIVING!
HEY...
HEY!
...

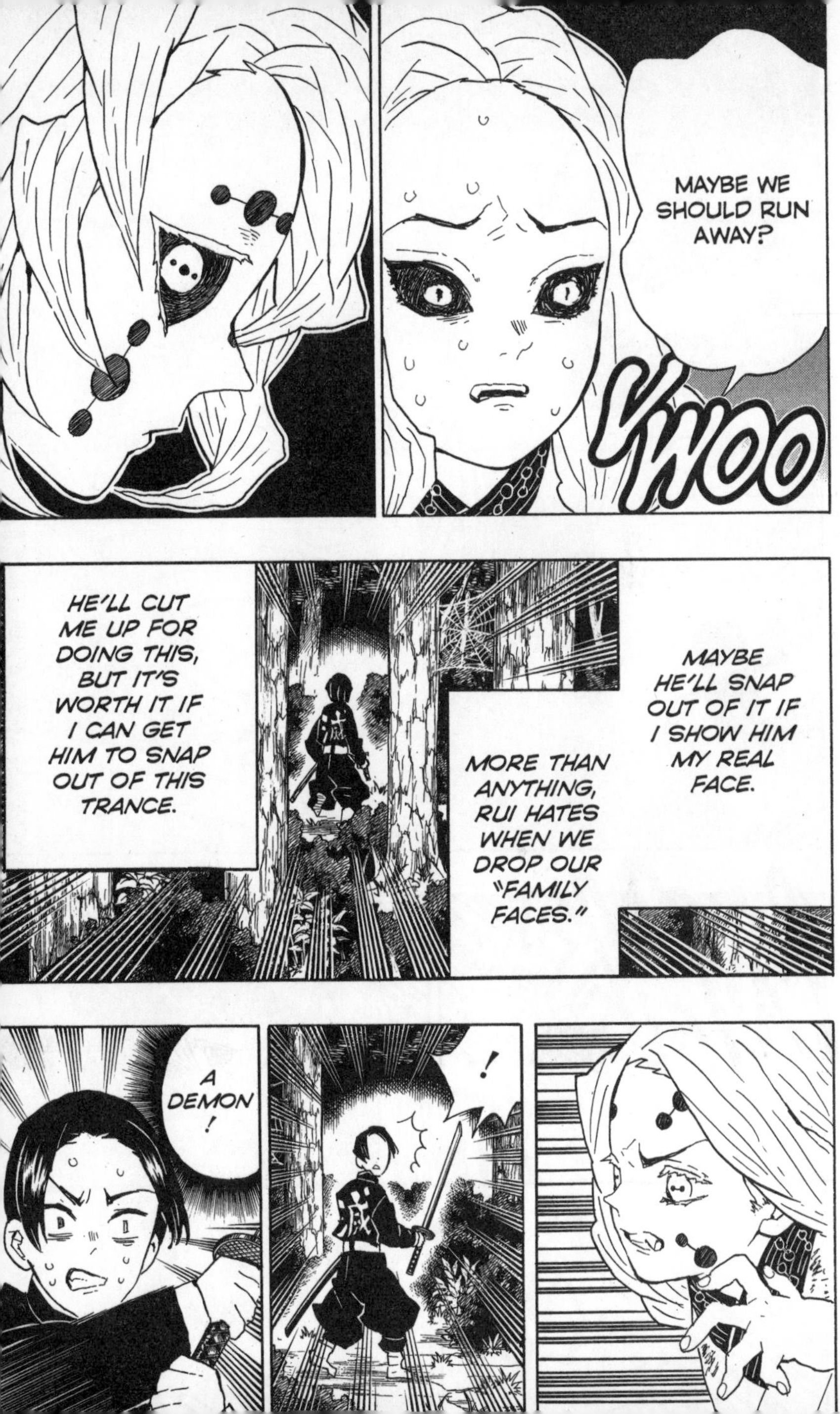
MAYBE WE SHOULD RUN AWAY?
VWOO
MAYBE HE'LL SNAP OUT OF IT IF I SHOW HIM MY REAL FACE.
MORE THAN ANYTHING, RUI HATES WHEN WE DROP OUR "FAMILY FACES."
HE'LL CUT ME UP FOR DOING THIS, BUT IT'S WORTH IT IF I CAN GET HIM TO SNAP OUT OF THIS TRANCE.
!
A DEMON!

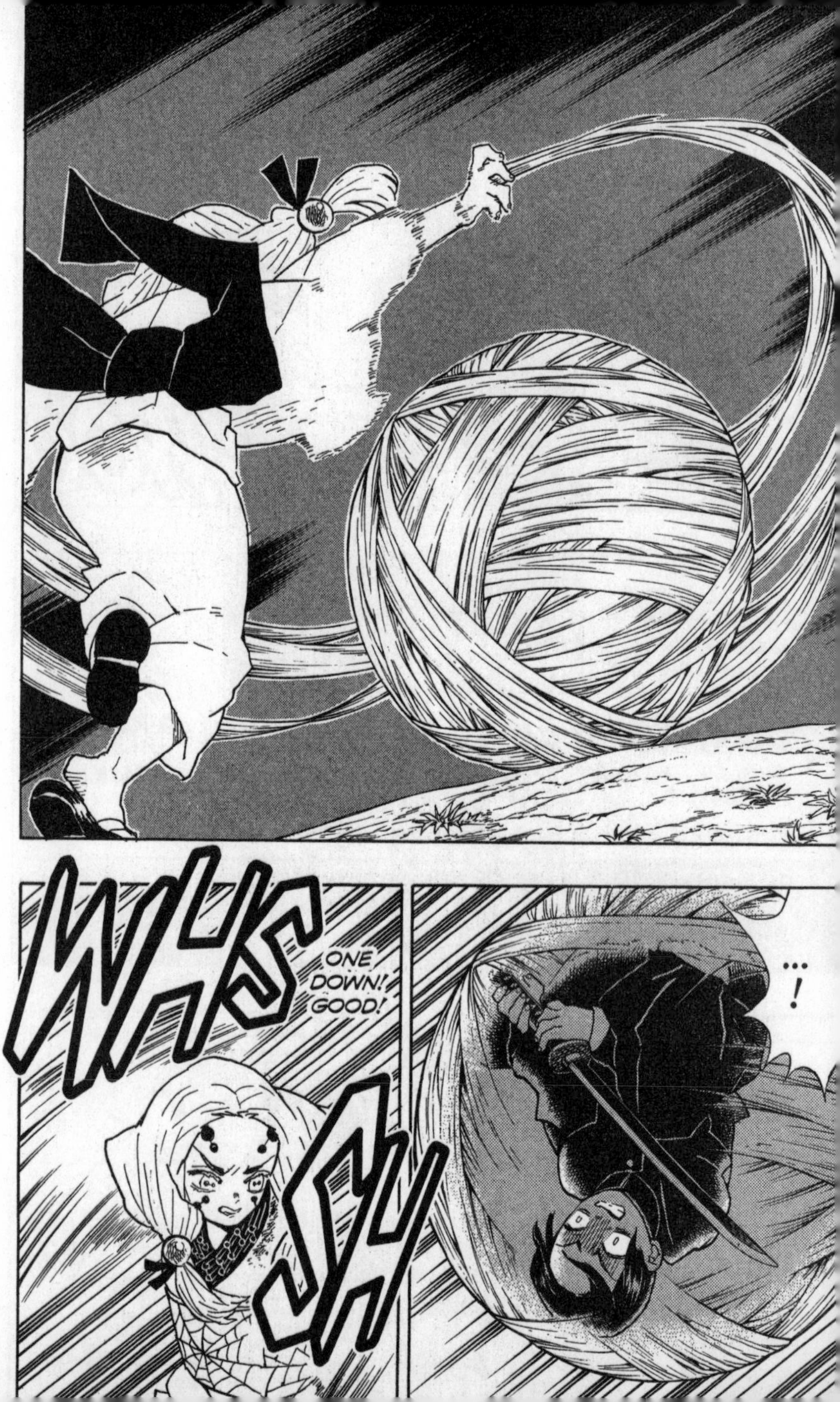
...!
ONE DOWN! GOOD!
WHS
SH

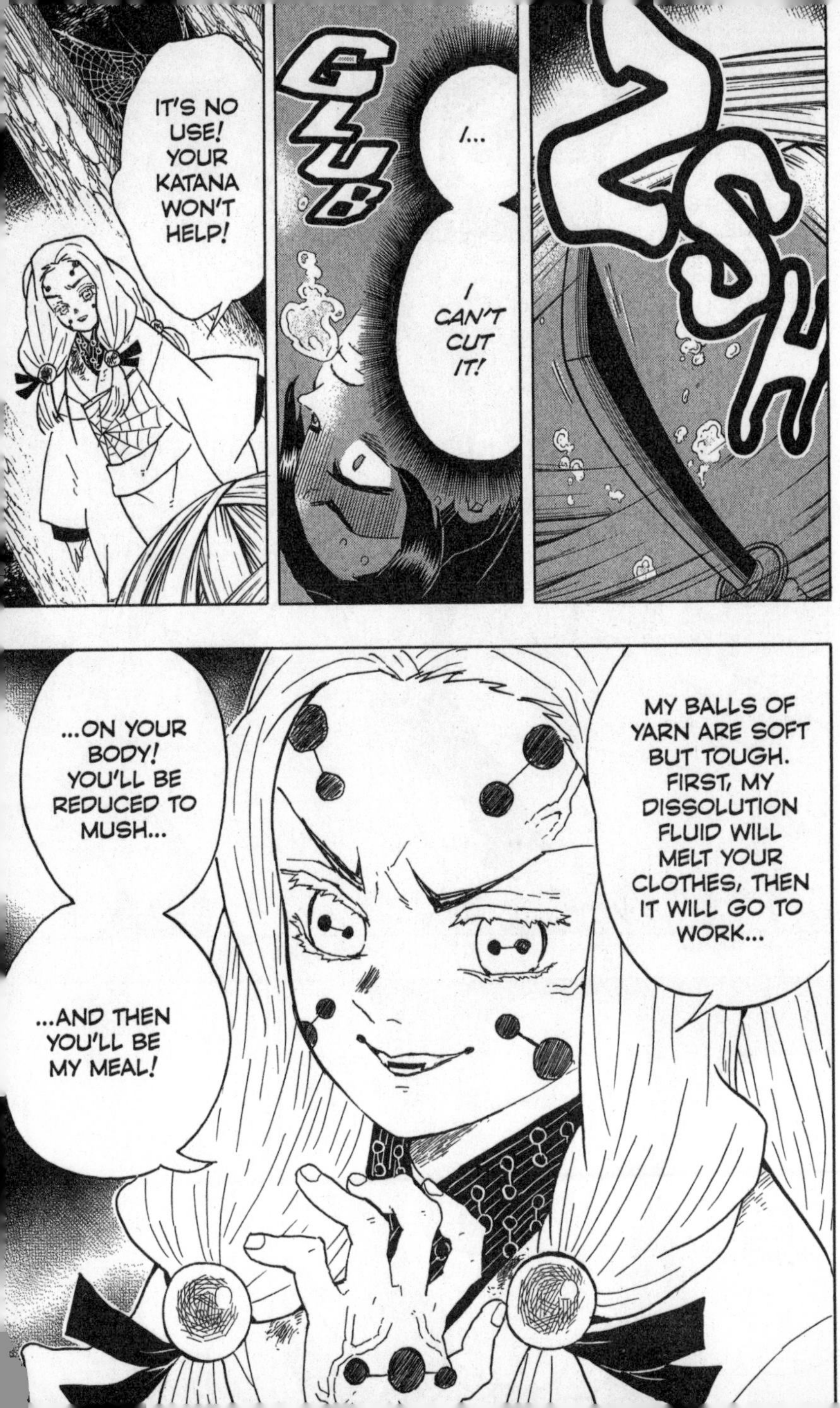
GLUB
I...
I CAN'T CUT IT!
IT'S NO USE! YOUR KATANA WON'T HELP!
MY BALLS OF YARN ARE SOFT BUT TOUGH. FIRST, MY DISSOLUTION FLUID WILL MELT YOUR CLOTHES, THEN IT WILL GO TO WORK...
...ON YOUR BODY! YOU'LL BE REDUCED TO MUSH...
...AND THEN YOU'LL BE MY MEAL!

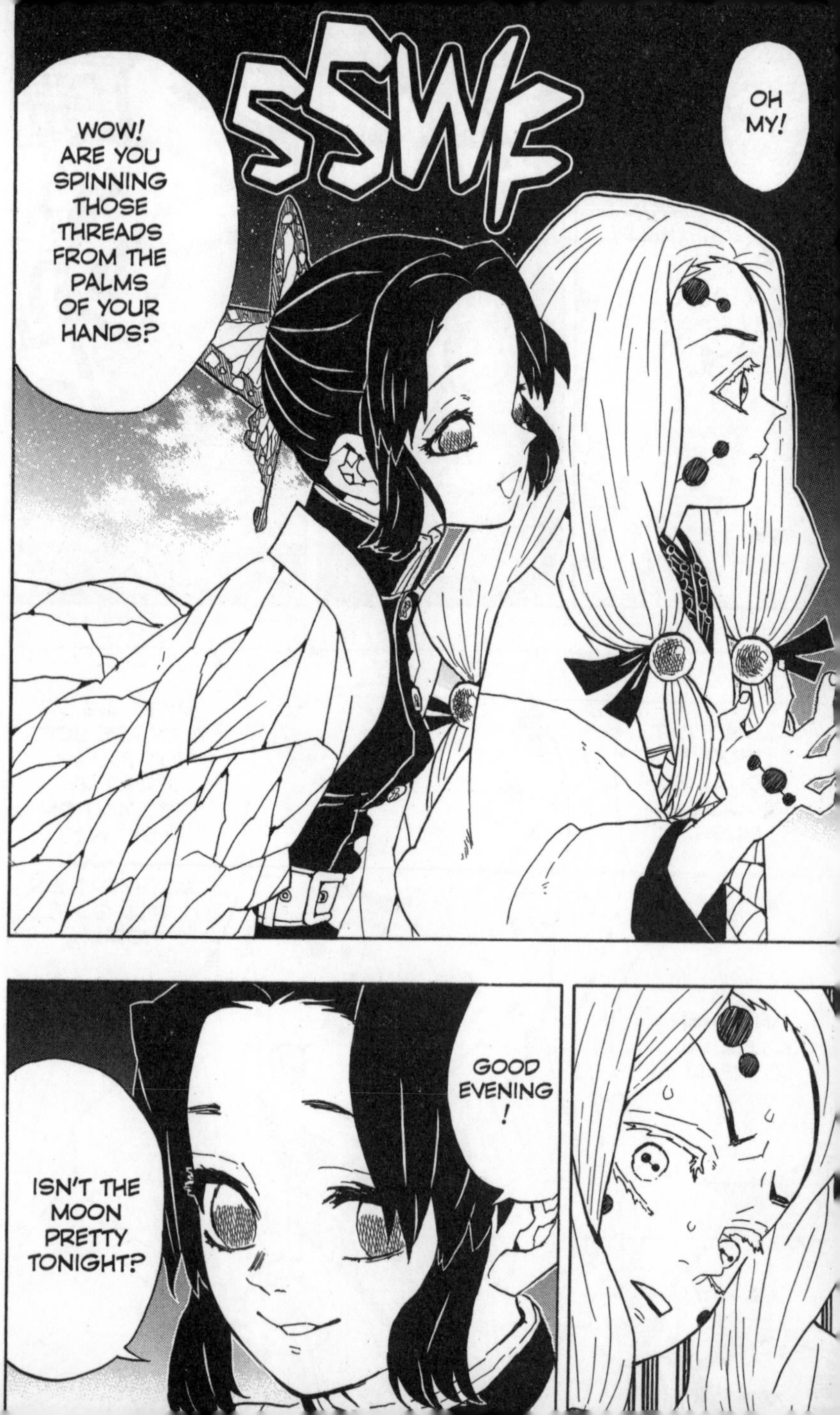
OH MY!
SSWF
WOW! ARE YOU SPINNING THOSE THREADS FROM THE PALMS OF YOUR HANDS?
GOOD EVENING!
ISN'T THE MOON PRETTY TONIGHT?

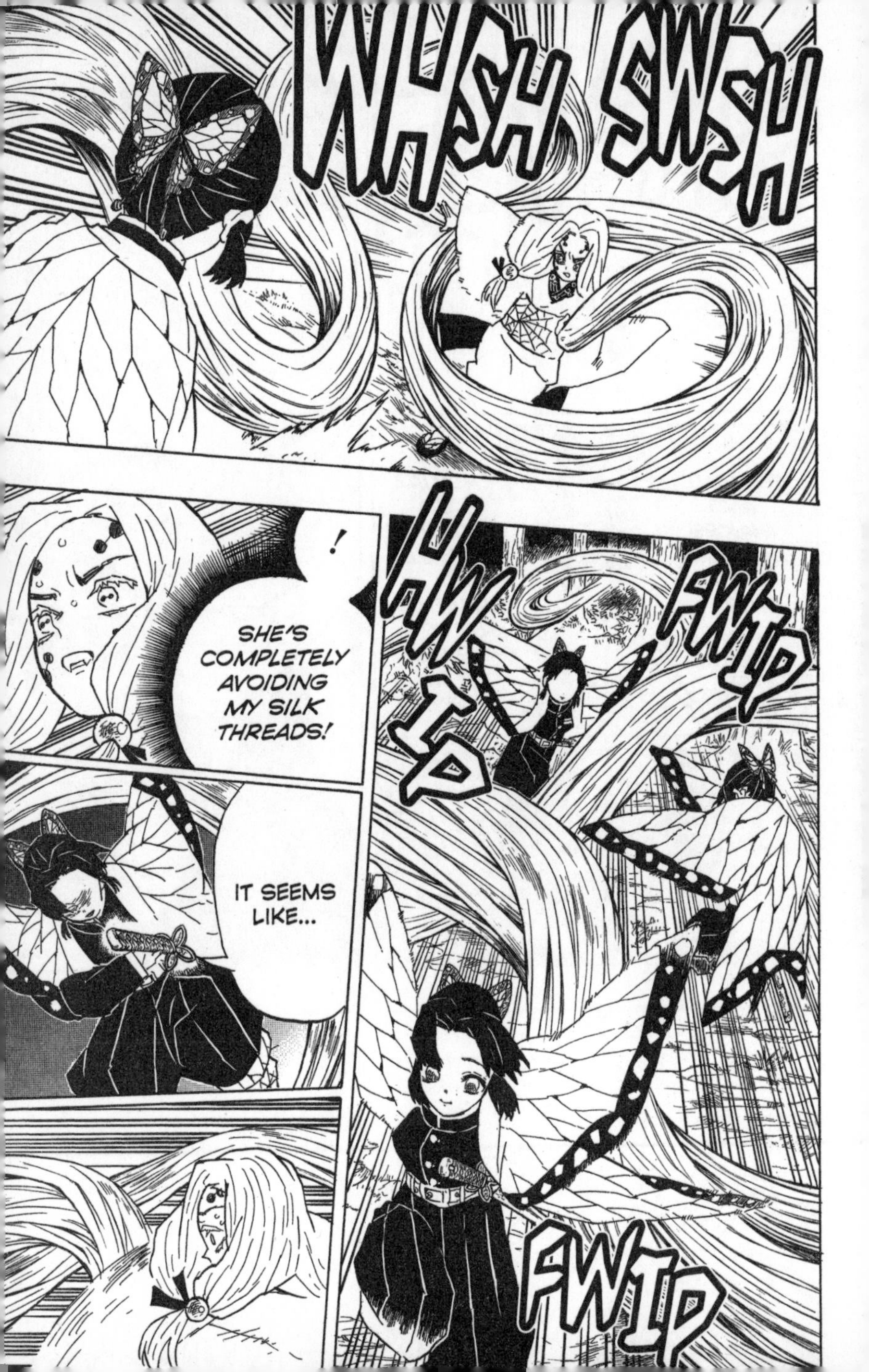
WHSH SWSH
FWIP
HWIP
FWIP
!
SHE'S COMPLETELY AVOIDING MY SILK THREADS!
IT SEEMS LIKE...

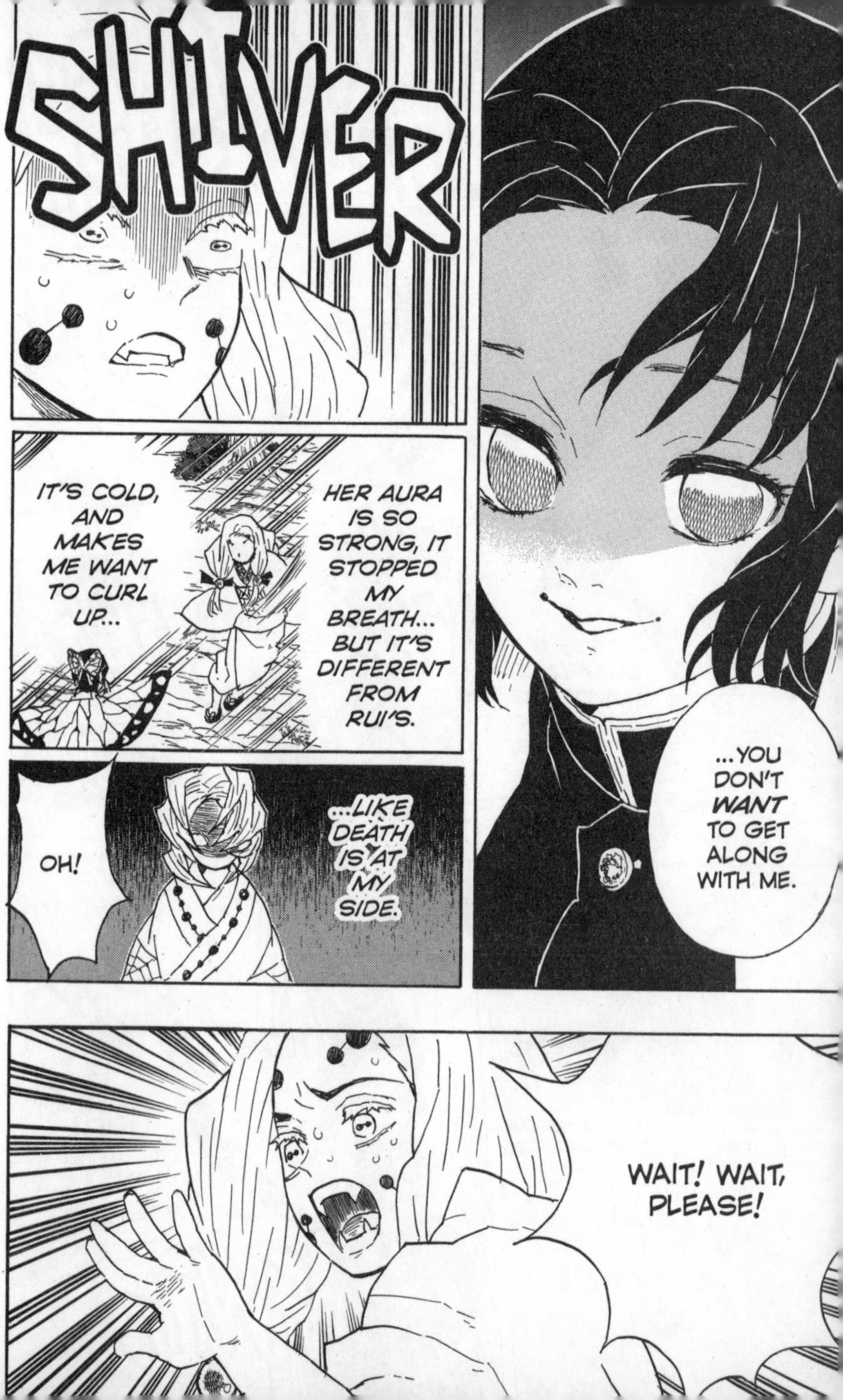
...YOU DON'T *WANT* TO GET ALONG WITH ME.
SHIVER
HER AURA IS SO STRONG, IT STOPPED MY BREATH... BUT IT'S DIFFERENT FROM RUI'S.
IT'S COLD, AND MAKES ME WANT TO CURL UP...
...LIKE DEATH IS AT MY SIDE.
OH!
WAIT! WAIT, PLEASE!

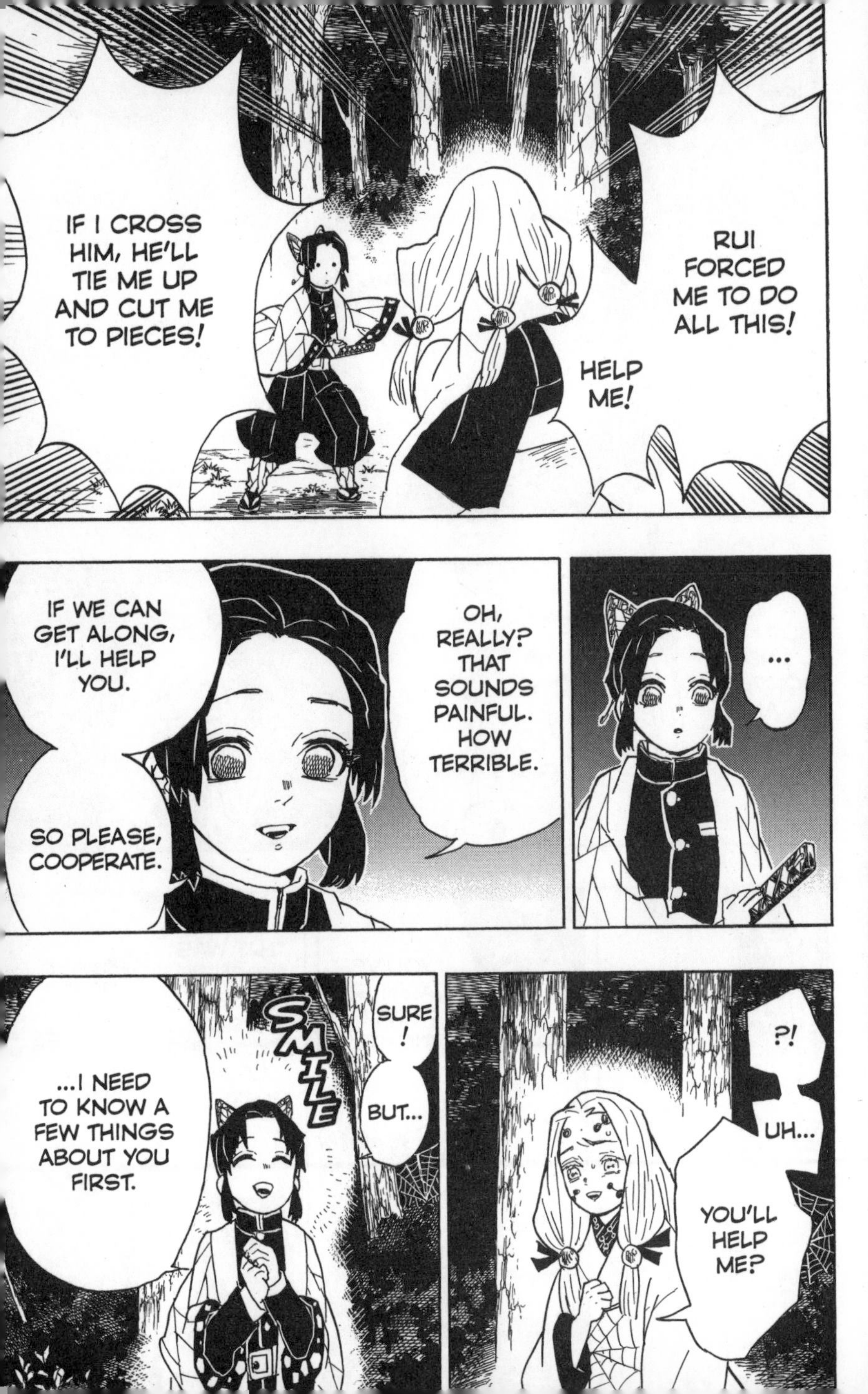
RUI FORCED ME TO DO ALL THIS!
HELP ME!
IF I CROSS HIM, HE'LL TIE ME UP AND CUT ME TO PIECES!
...
OH, REALLY? THAT SOUNDS PAINFUL. HOW TERRIBLE.
IF WE CAN GET ALONG, I'LL HELP YOU.
SO PLEASE, COOPERATE.
?!
UH...
YOU'LL HELP ME?
SURE!
SMILE
BUT...
...I NEED TO KNOW A FEW THINGS ABOUT YOU FIRST.

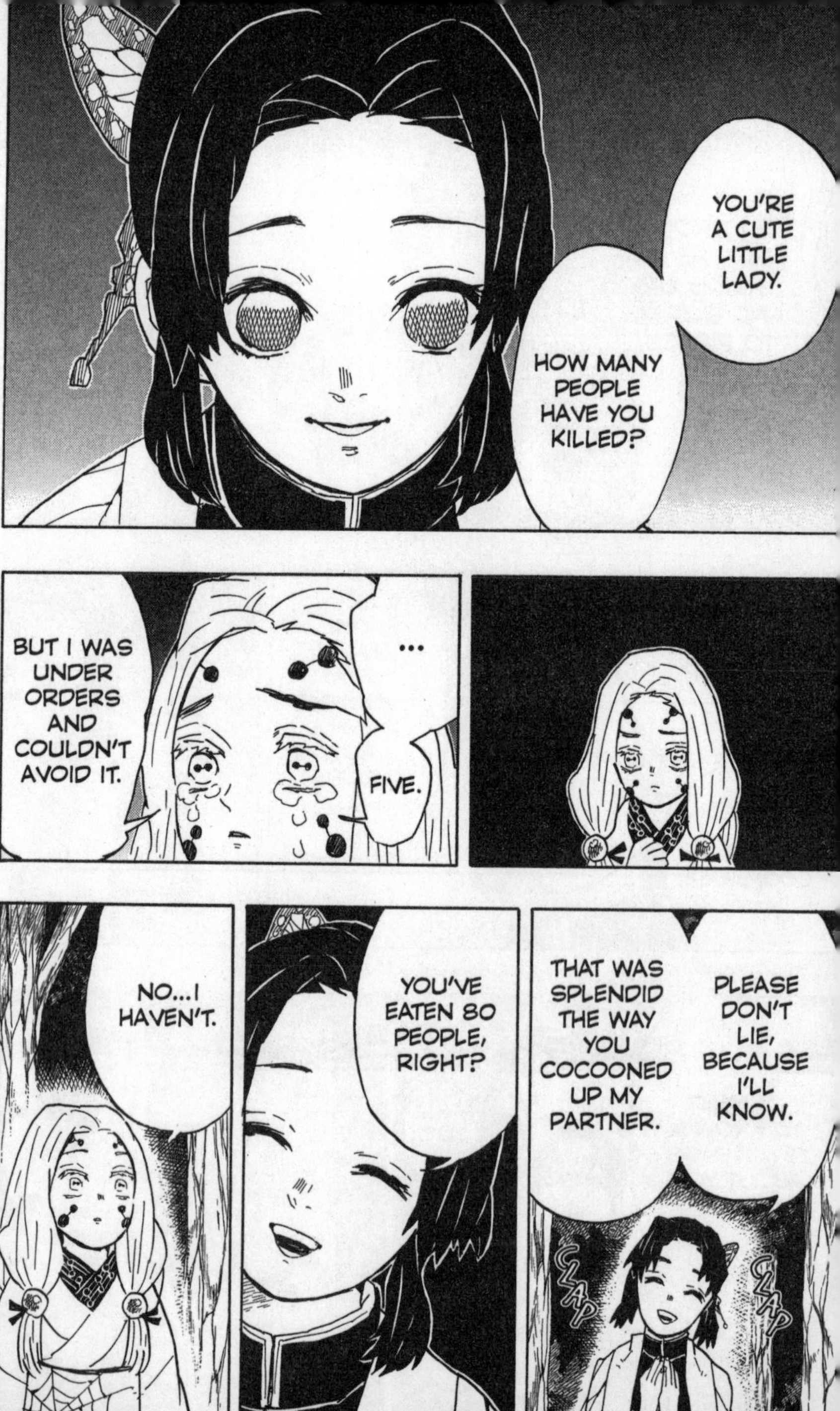
YOU'RE A CUTE LITTLE LADY.
HOW MANY PEOPLE HAVE YOU KILLED?
...
FIVE.
BUT I WAS UNDER ORDERS AND COULDN'T AVOID IT.
PLEASE DON'T LIE, BECAUSE I'LL KNOW.
THAT WAS SPLENDID THE WAY YOU COCOONED UP MY PARTNER.
CLAP
CLAP
YOU'VE EATEN 80 PEOPLE, RIGHT?
NO...I HAVEN'T.

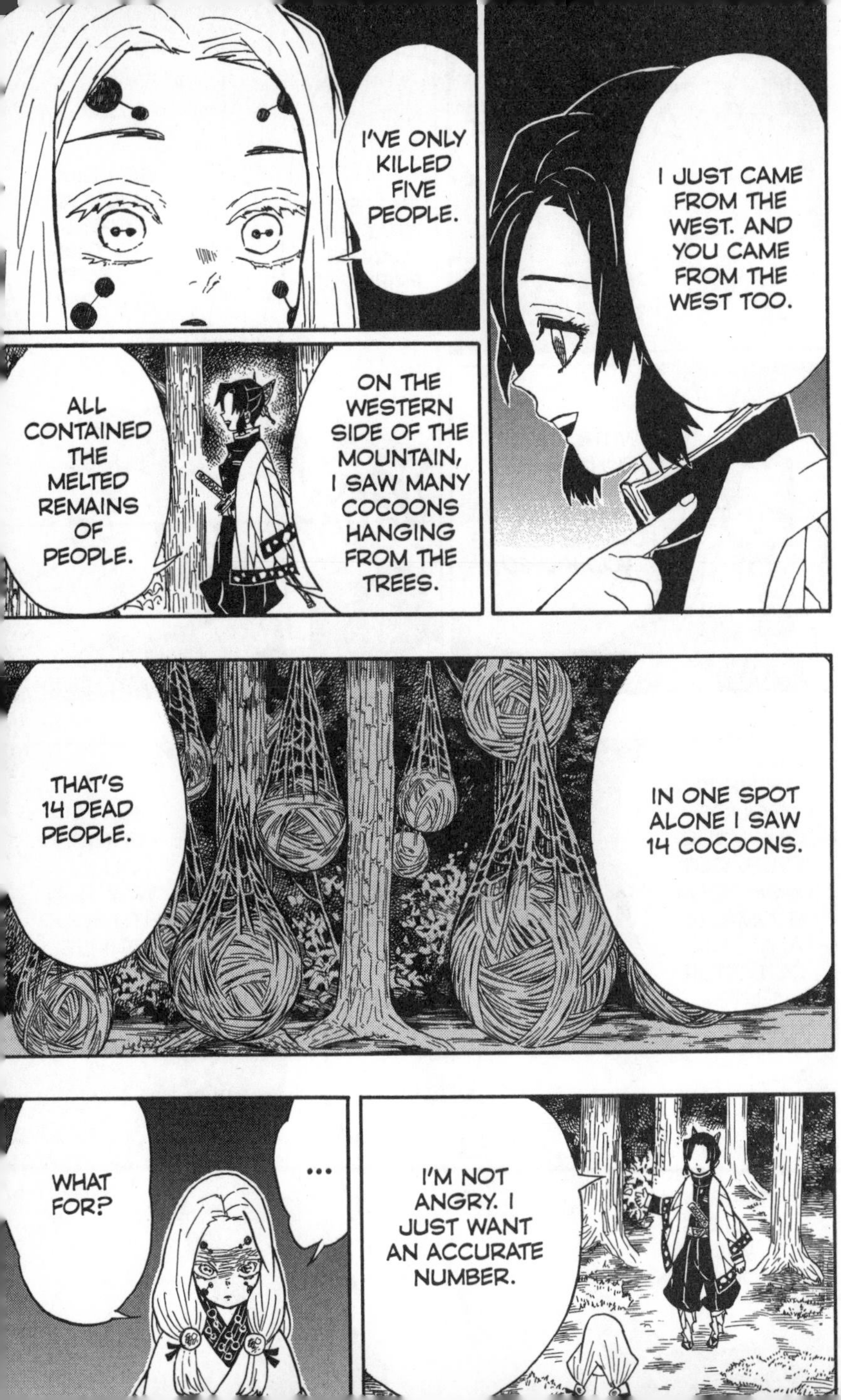
I'VE ONLY KILLED FIVE PEOPLE.
I JUST CAME FROM THE WEST. AND YOU CAME FROM THE WEST TOO.
ON THE WESTERN SIDE OF THE MOUNTAIN, I SAW MANY COCOONS HANGING FROM THE TREES.
ALL CONTAINED THE MELTED REMAINS OF PEOPLE.
IN ONE SPOT ALONE I SAW 14 COCOONS.
THAT'S 14 DEAD PEOPLE.
I'M NOT ANGRY. I JUST WANT AN ACCURATE NUMBER.
...
WHAT FOR?

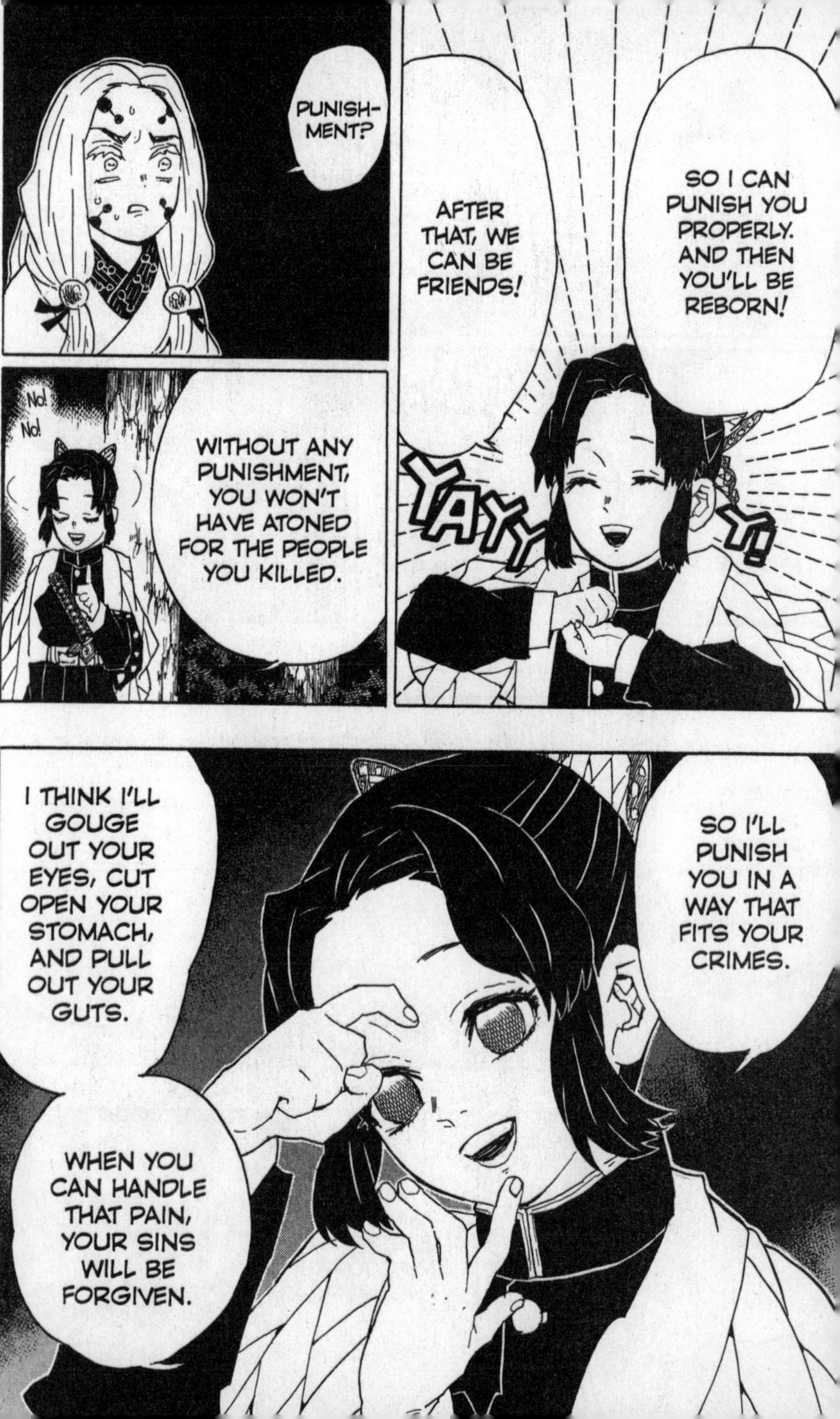
SO I CAN PUNISH YOU PROPERLY. AND THEN YOU'LL BE REBORN!
AFTER THAT, WE CAN BE FRIENDS!
YAYYY!
PUNISH-MENT?
No! No!
WITHOUT ANY PUNISHMENT, YOU WON'T HAVE ATONED FOR THE PEOPLE YOU KILLED.
SO I'LL PUNISH YOU IN A WAY THAT FITS YOUR CRIMES.
I THINK I'LL GOUGE OUT YOUR EYES, CUT OPEN YOUR STOMACH, AND PULL OUT YOUR GUTS.
WHEN YOU CAN HANDLE THAT PAIN, YOUR SINS WILL BE FORGIVEN.

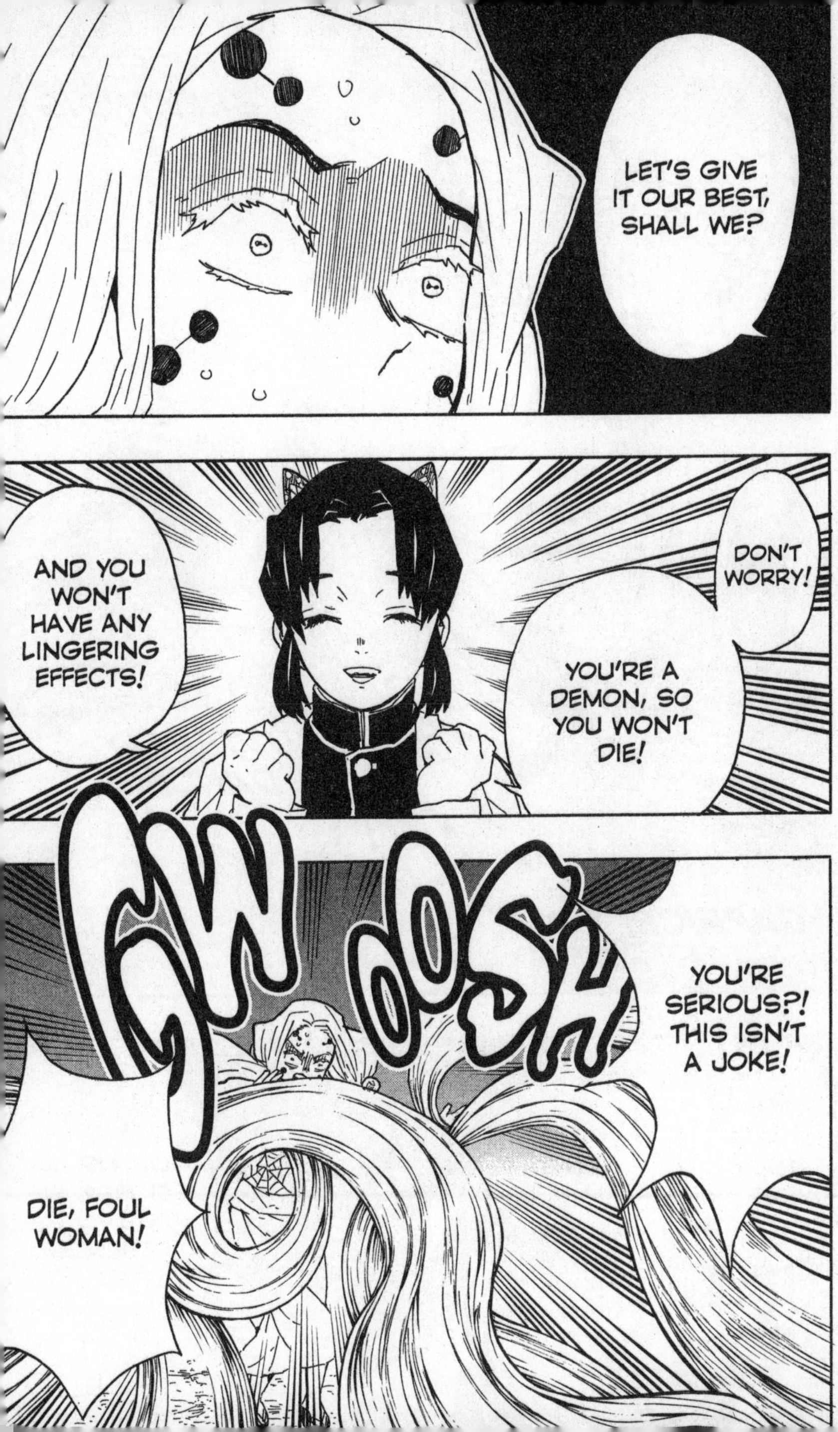
LET'S GIVE IT OUR BEST, SHALL WE?
DON'T WORRY!
YOU'RE A DEMON, SO YOU WON'T DIE!
AND YOU WON'T HAVE ANY LINGERING EFFECTS!
FWOOSH
YOU'RE SERIOUS?! THIS ISN'T A JOKE!
DIE, FOUL WOMAN!

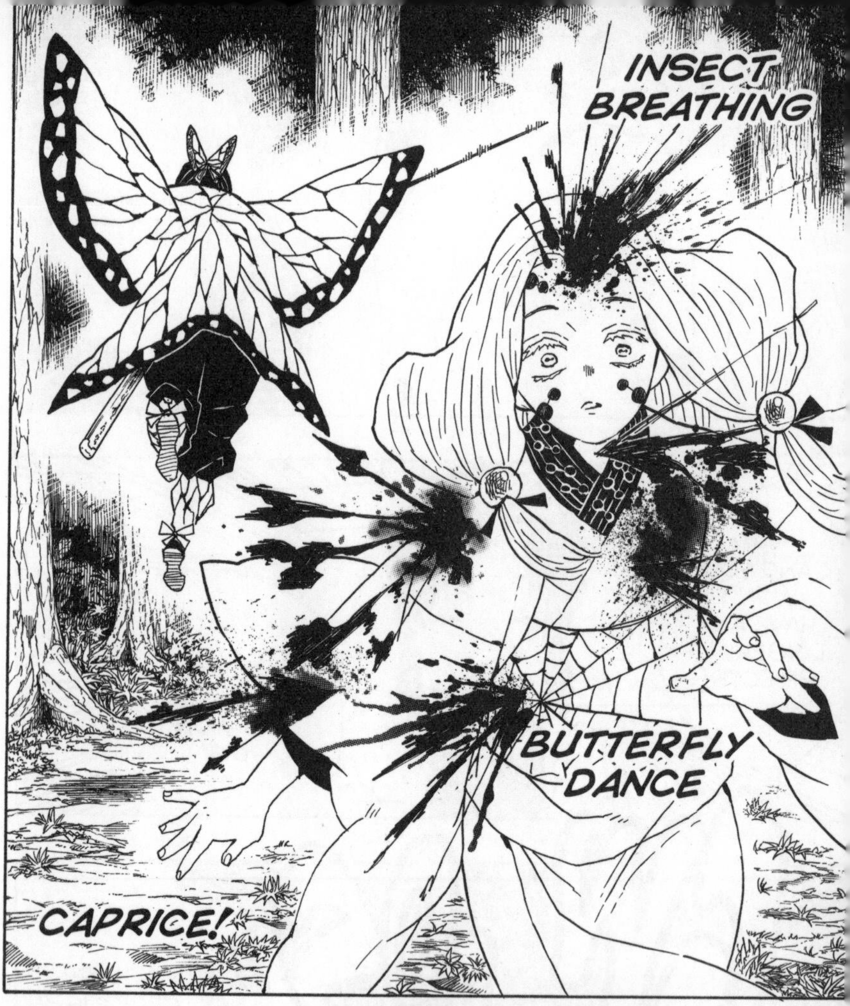
INSECT BREATHING
BUTTERFLY DANCE
CAPRICE!
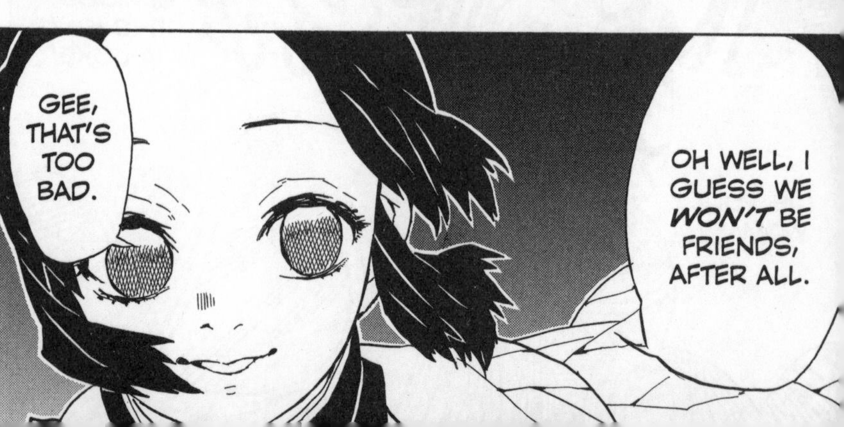
OH WELL, I GUESS WE *WON'T* BE FRIENDS, AFTER ALL.
GEE, THAT'S TOO BAD.

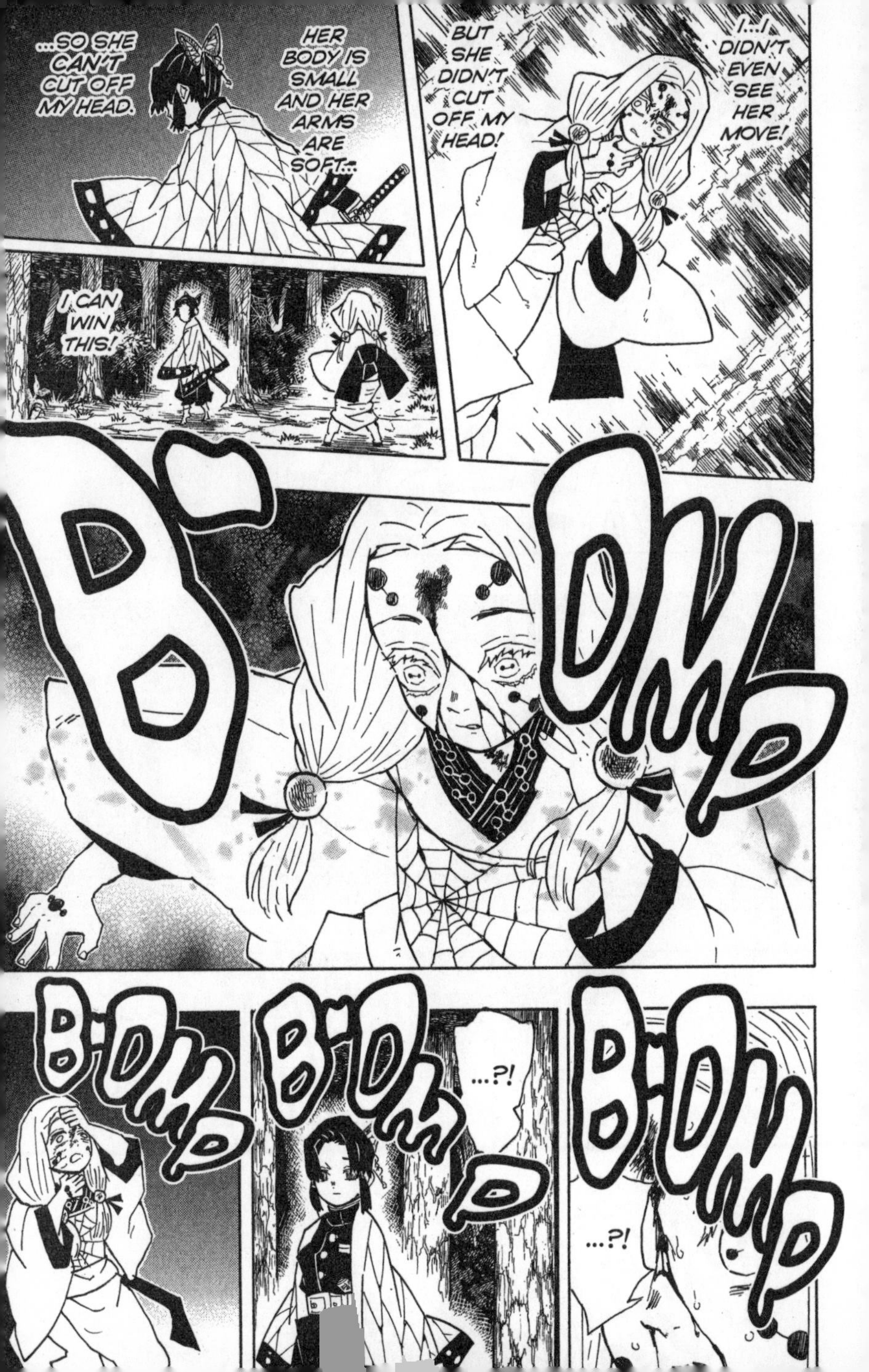
I...I DIDN'T EVEN SEE HER MOVE!
BUT SHE DIDN'T CUT OFF MY HEAD!
HER BODY IS SMALL AND HER ARMS ARE SOFT...
...SO SHE CAN'T CUT OFF MY HEAD.
I CAN WIN THIS!
B-DOMP
B-DOMP
...?!
B-DOMP
...?!
B-DOMP

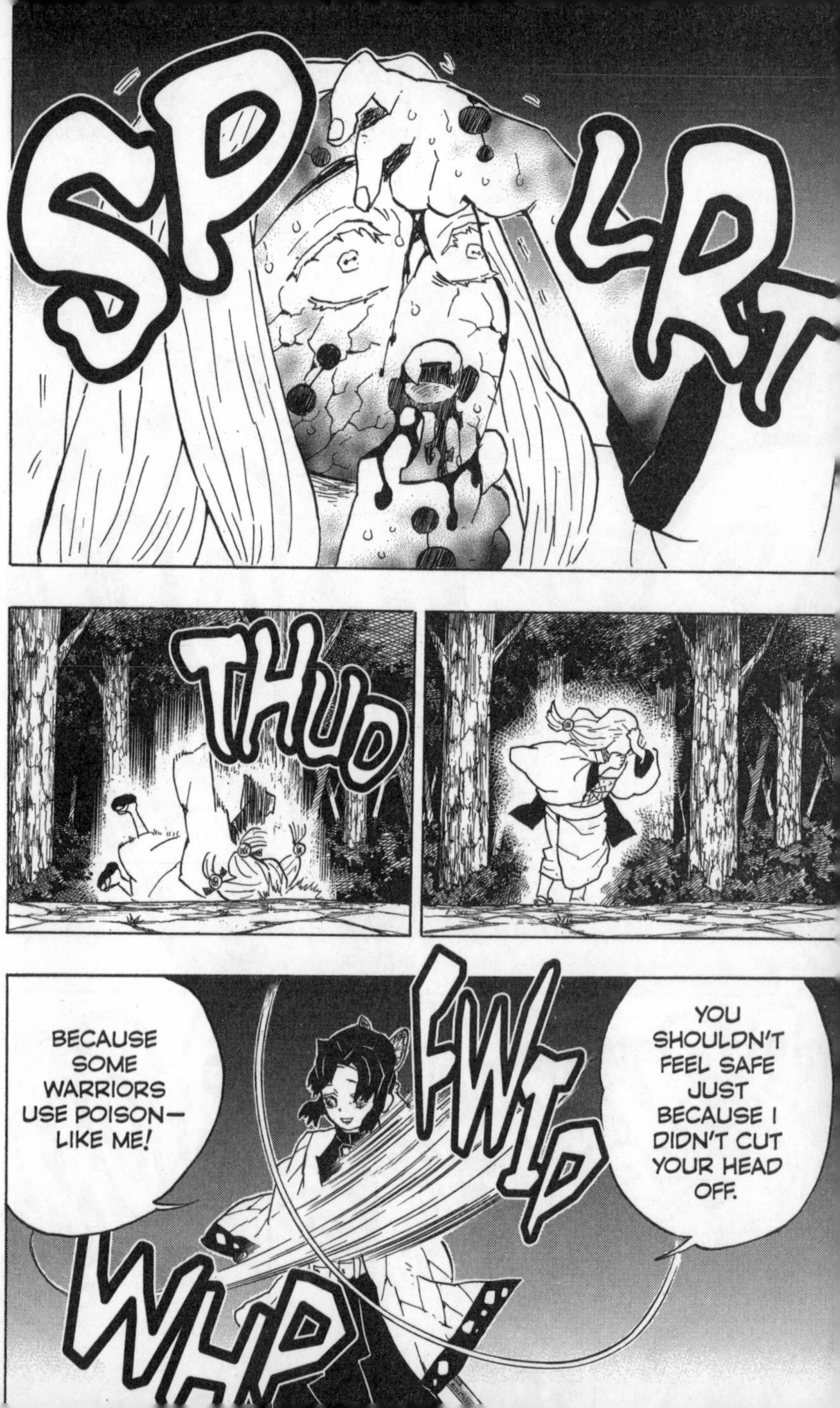
SPLRT
THUD
YOU SHOULDN'T FEEL SAFE JUST BECAUSE I DIDN'T CUT YOUR HEAD OFF.
FWIP
BECAUSE SOME WARRIORS USE POISON— LIKE ME!

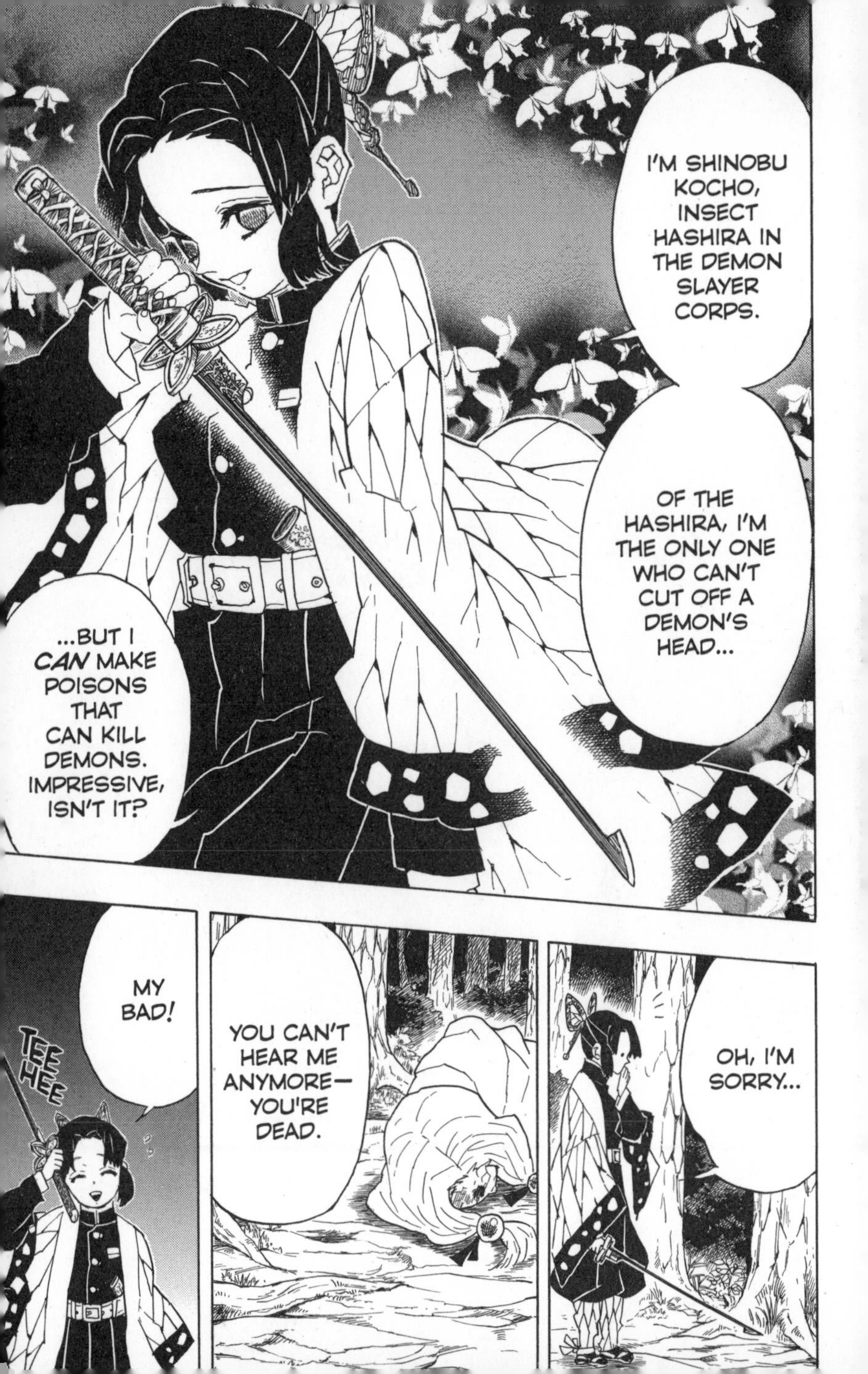
I'M SHINOBU KOCHO, INSECT HASHIRA IN THE DEMON SLAYER CORPS.
OF THE HASHIRA, I'M THE ONLY ONE WHO CAN'T CUT OFF A DEMON'S HEAD...
...BUT I *CAN* MAKE POISONS THAT CAN KILL DEMONS. IMPRESSIVE, ISN'T IT?
OH, I'M SORRY...
YOU CAN'T HEAR ME ANYMORE—YOU'RE DEAD.
MY BAD!
TEE HEE

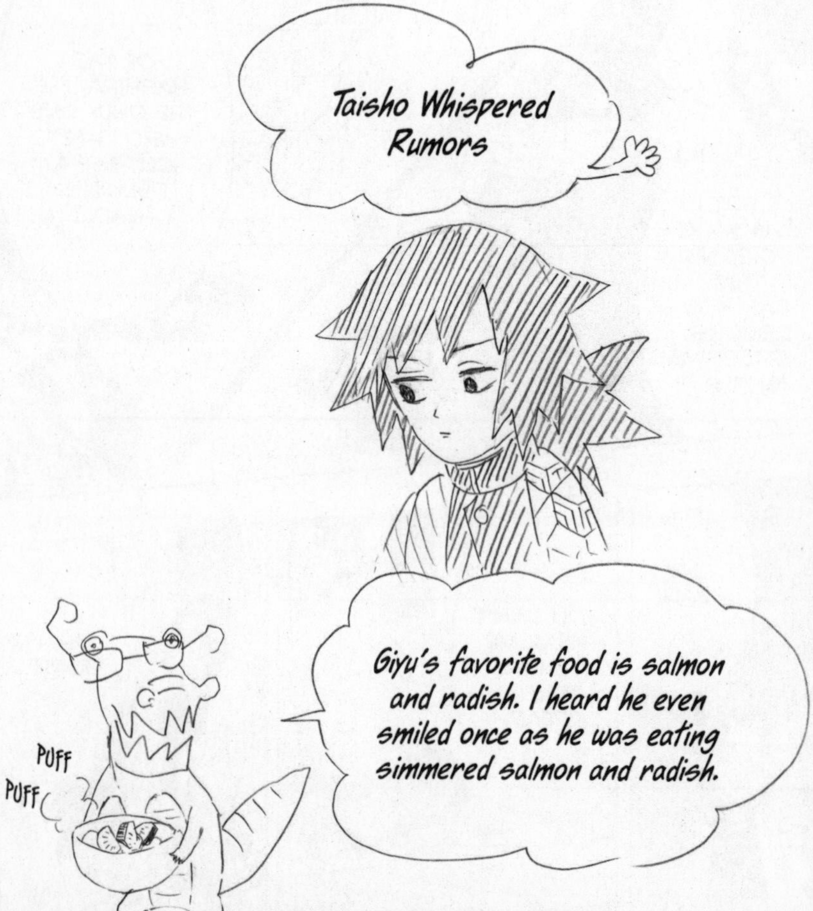
Taisho Whispered Rumors
Giyu's favorite food is salmon and radish. I heard he even smiled once as he was eating simmered salmon and radish.
PUFF PUFF

CHAPTER 42: BEHIND

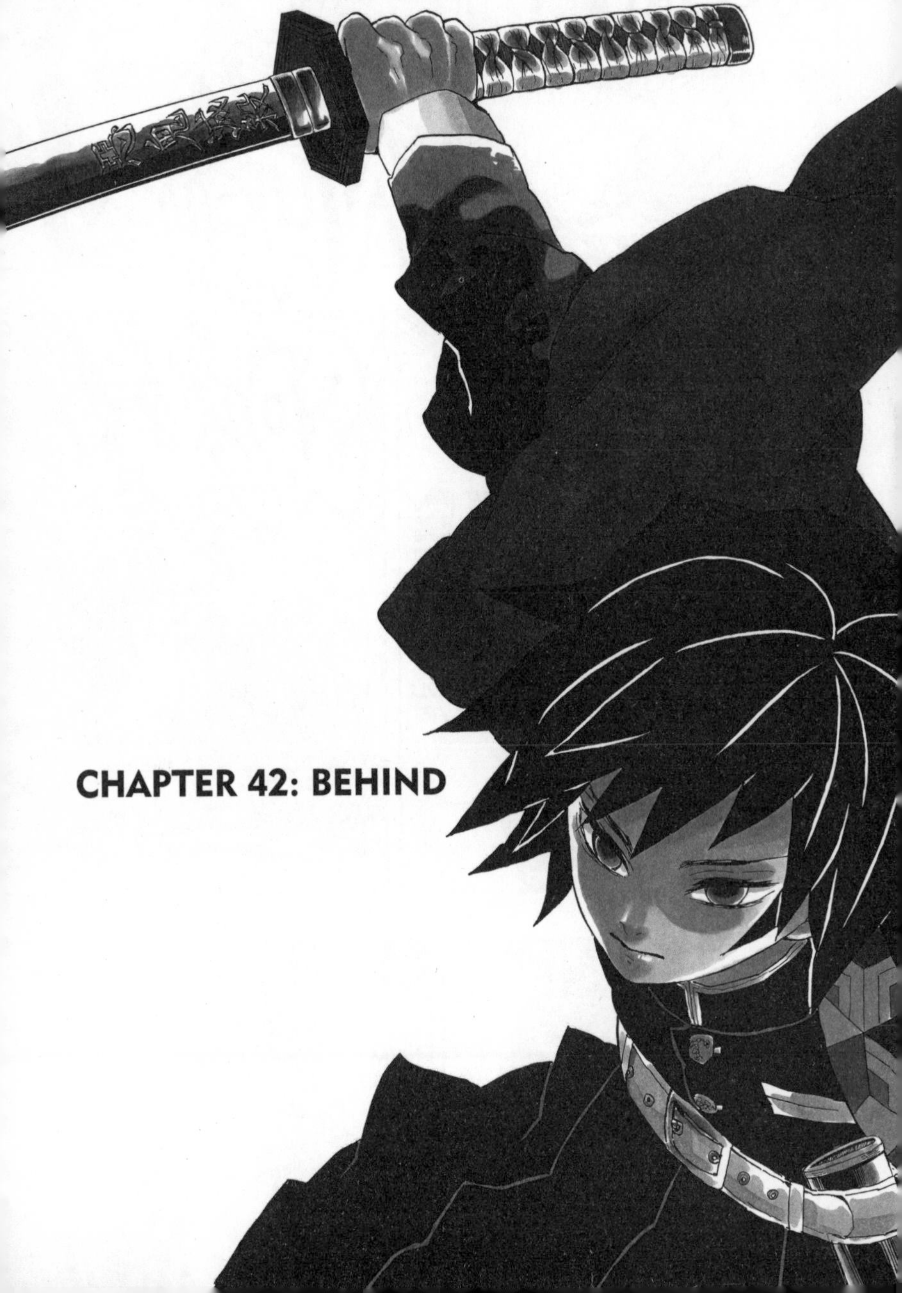

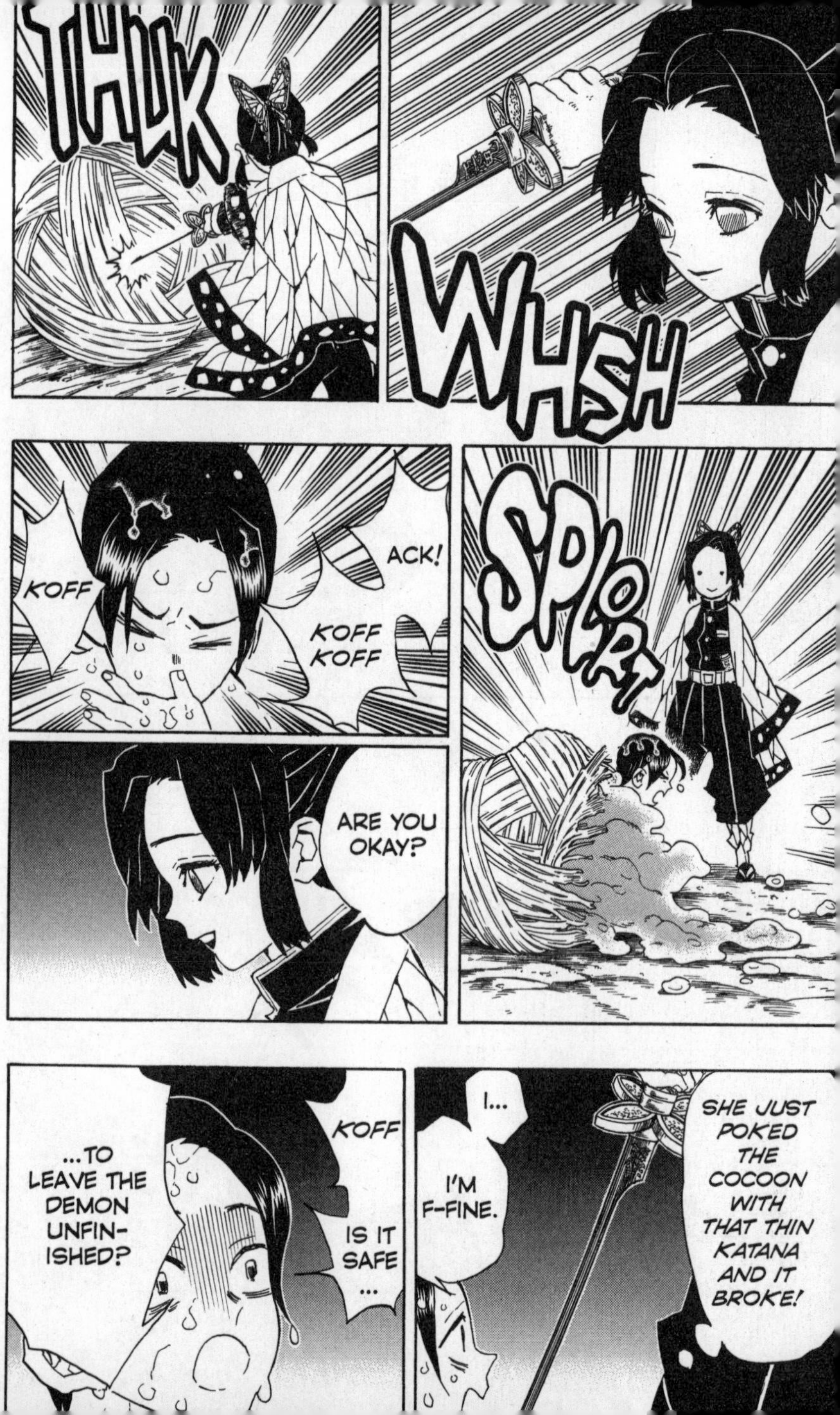
WHSH
THUK
SPLORT
ACK!
KOFF KOFF
KOFF
ARE YOU OKAY?
SHE JUST POKED THE COCOON WITH THAT THIN KATANA AND IT BROKE!
I...
I'M F-FINE.
KOFF
IS IT SAFE ...
...TO LEAVE THE DEMON UNFINISHED?

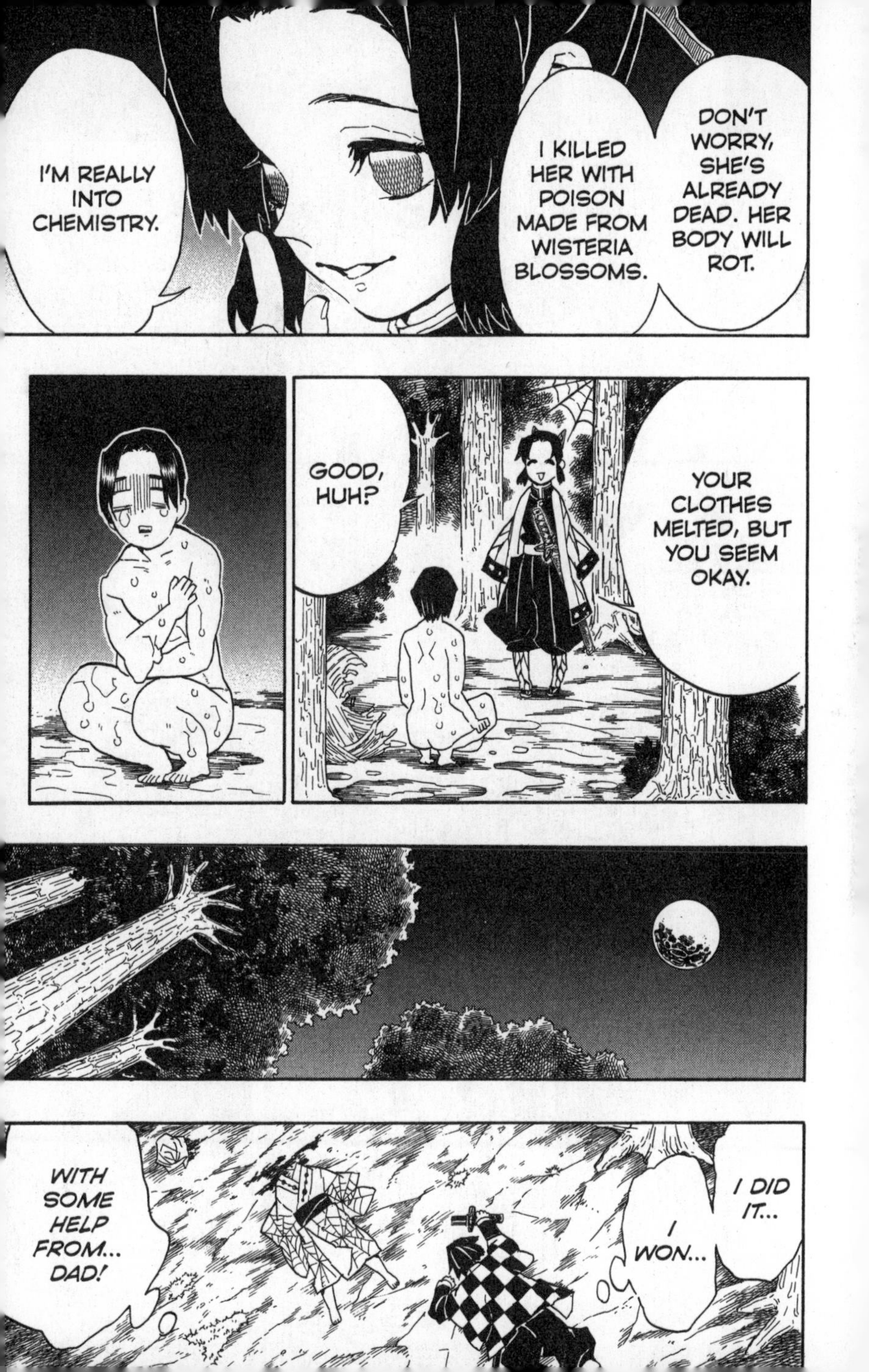
DON'T WORRY, SHE'S ALREADY DEAD. HER BODY WILL ROT.
I KILLED HER WITH POISON MADE FROM WISTERIA BLOSSOMS.
I'M REALLY INTO CHEMISTRY.
YOUR CLOTHES MELTED, BUT YOU SEEM OKAY.
GOOD, HUH?
I DID IT...
I WON...
WITH SOME HELP FROM... DAD!

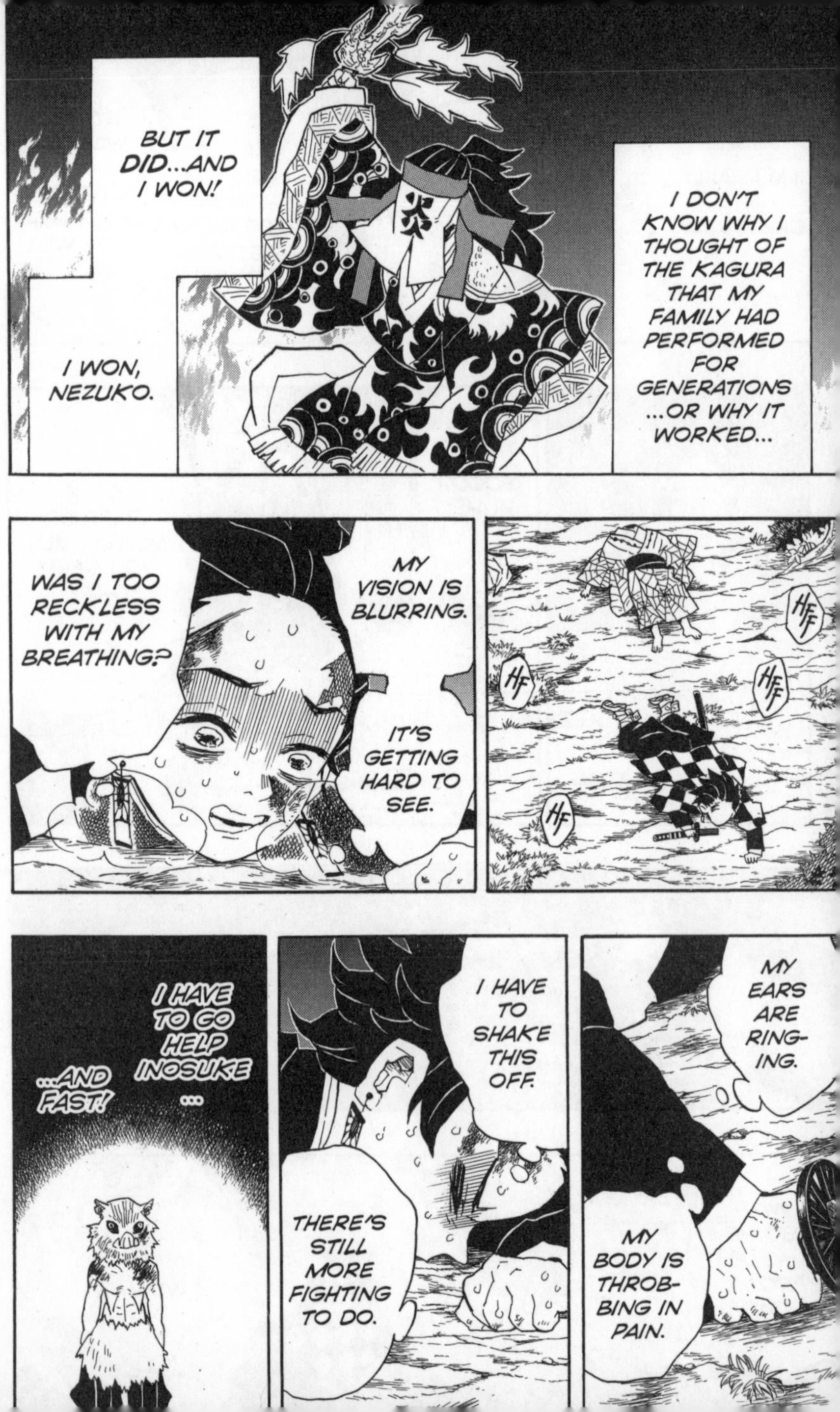
I DON'T KNOW WHY I THOUGHT OF THE KAGURA THAT MY FAMILY HAD PERFORMED FOR GENERATIONS ...OR WHY IT WORKED...
BUT IT DID...AND I WON!
I WON, NEZUKO.
HFF
HF
HFF
HF
MY VISION IS BLURRING.
WAS I TOO RECKLESS WITH MY BREATHING?
IT'S GETTING HARD TO SEE.
MY EARS ARE RING-ING.
MY BODY IS THROB-BING IN PAIN.
I HAVE TO SHAKE THIS OFF.
THERE'S STILL MORE FIGHTING TO DO.
I HAVE TO GO HELP INOSUKE ...
...AND FAST!

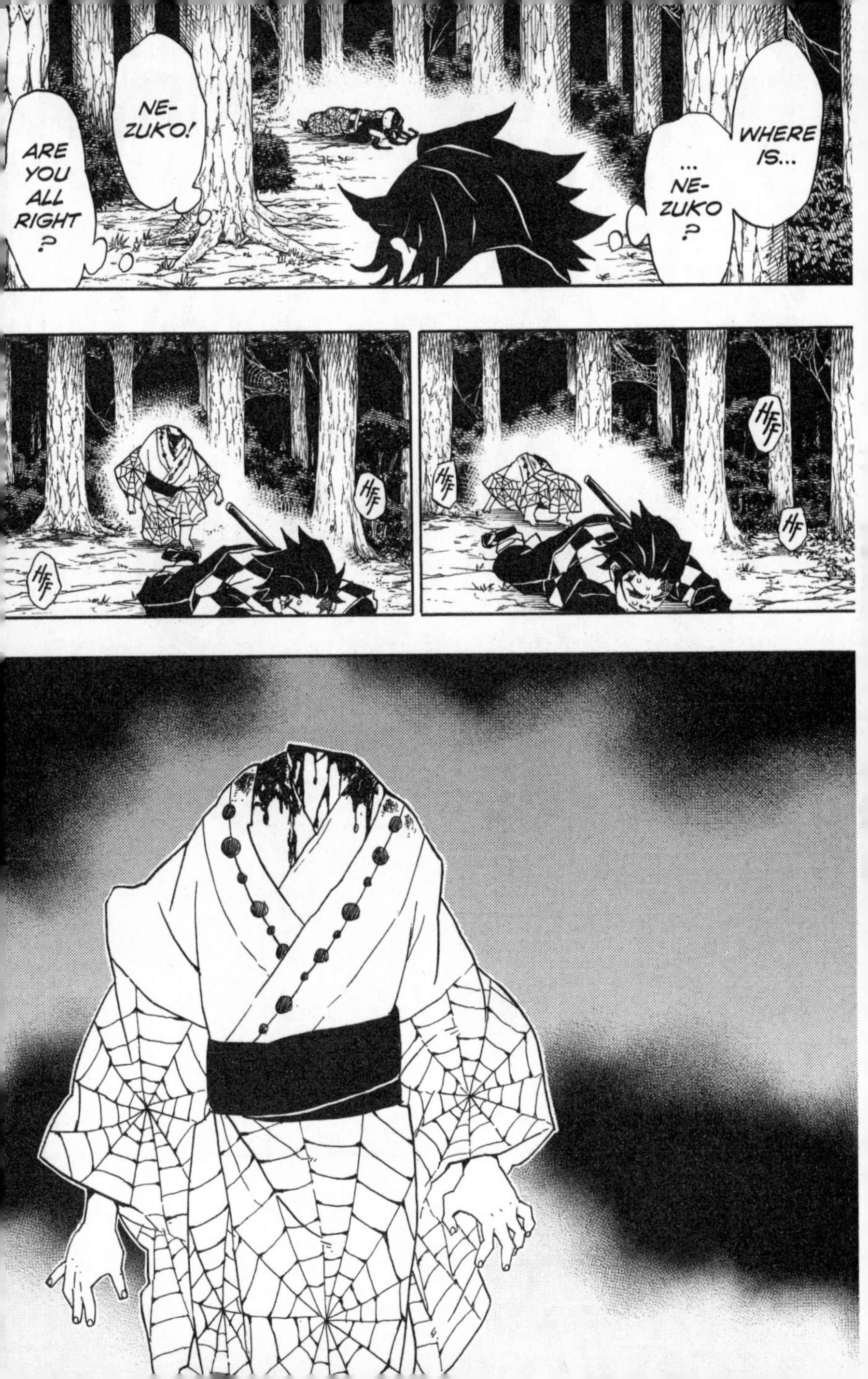
WHERE IS...
...NE-ZUKO?
NE-ZUKO!
ARE YOU ALL RIGHT?
HFF
HF
HFF
HFF
HFF

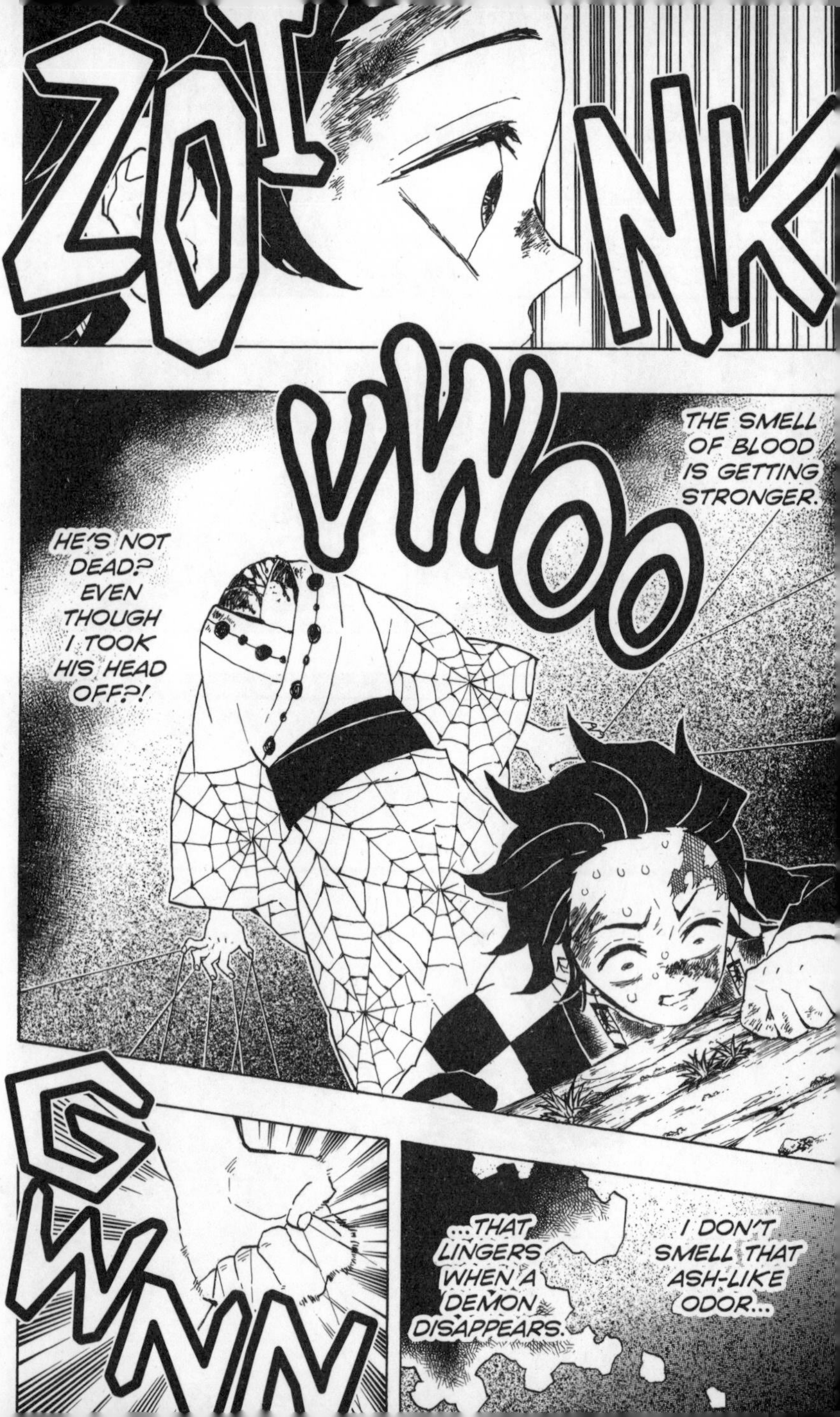
ZOINK
VWOO
THE SMELL OF BLOOD IS GETTING STRONGER.
HE'S NOT DEAD? EVEN THOUGH I TOOK HIS HEAD OFF?!
I DON'T SMELL THAT ASH-LIKE ODOR...
...THAT LINGERS WHEN A DEMON DISAPPEARS.
GWNN

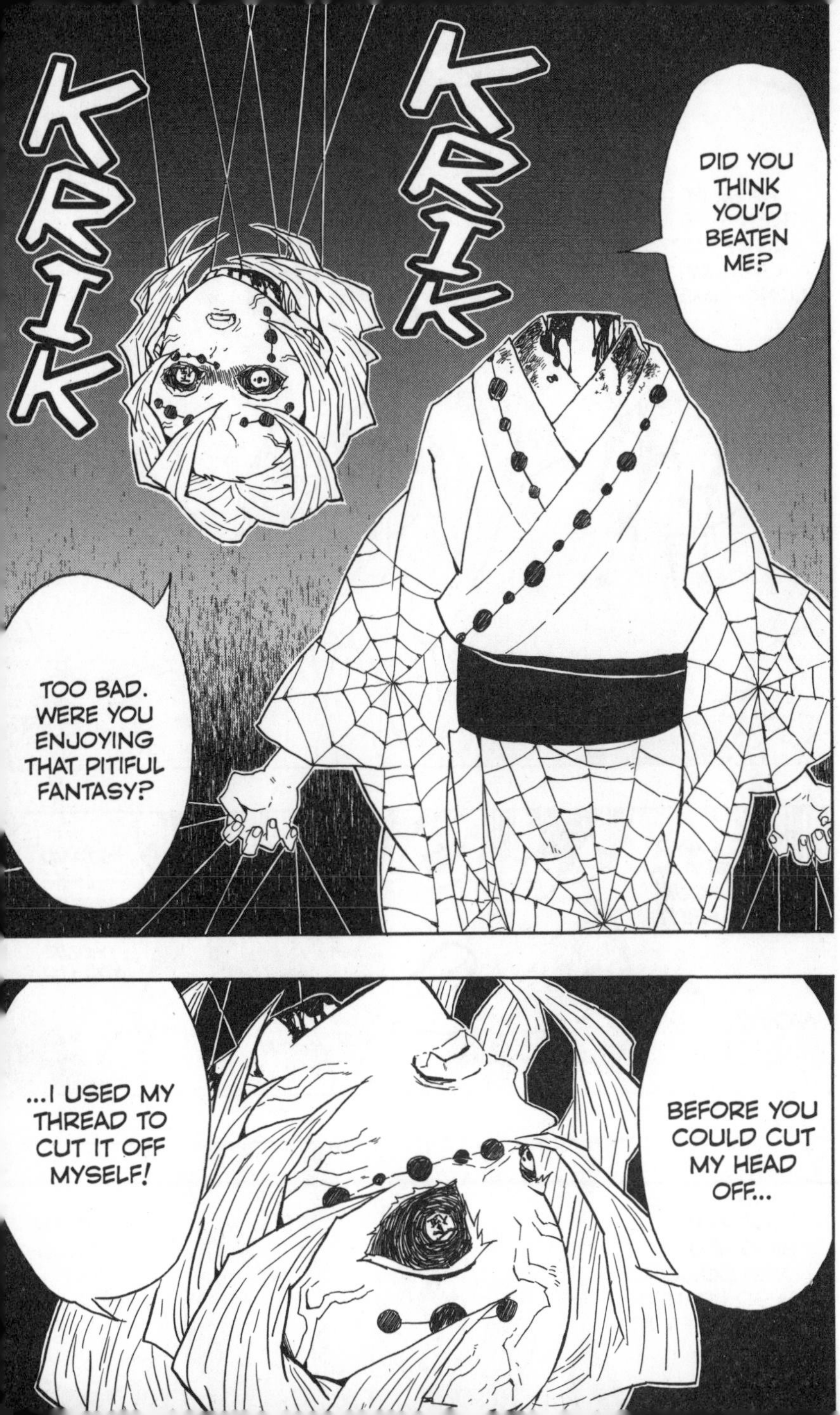
DID YOU THINK YOU'D BEATEN ME?
KRIK
KRIK
TOO BAD. WERE YOU ENJOYING THAT PITIFUL FANTASY?
BEFORE YOU COULD CUT MY HEAD OFF...
...I USED MY THREAD TO CUT IT OFF MYSELF!

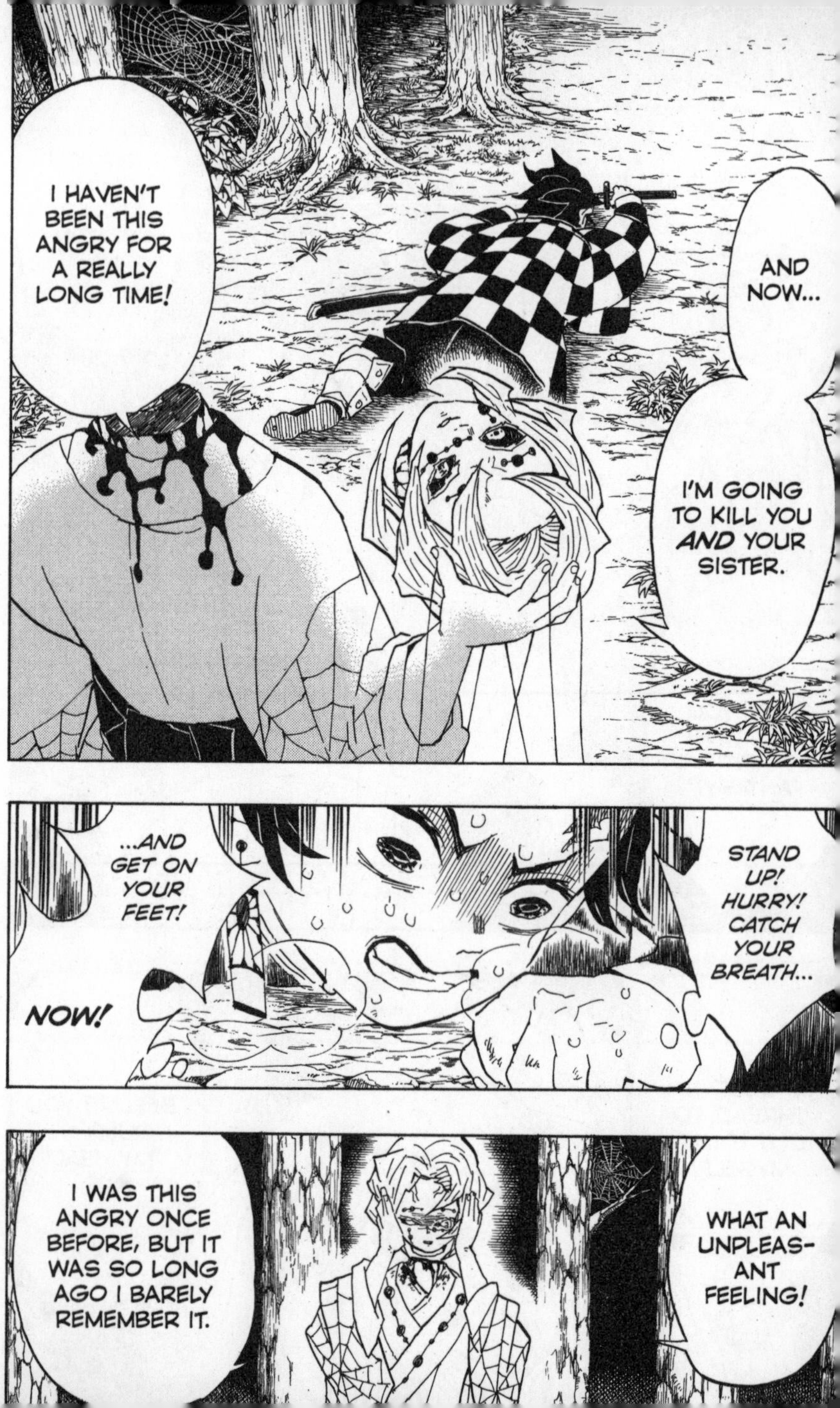
AND NOW...
I'M GOING TO KILL YOU *AND* YOUR SISTER.
I HAVEN'T BEEN THIS ANGRY FOR A REALLY LONG TIME!
STAND UP! HURRY! CATCH YOUR BREATH...
...AND GET ON YOUR FEET!
NOW!
WHAT AN UNPLEAS-ANT FEELING!
I WAS THIS ANGRY ONCE BEFORE, BUT IT WAS SO LONG AGO I BARELY REMEMBER IT.

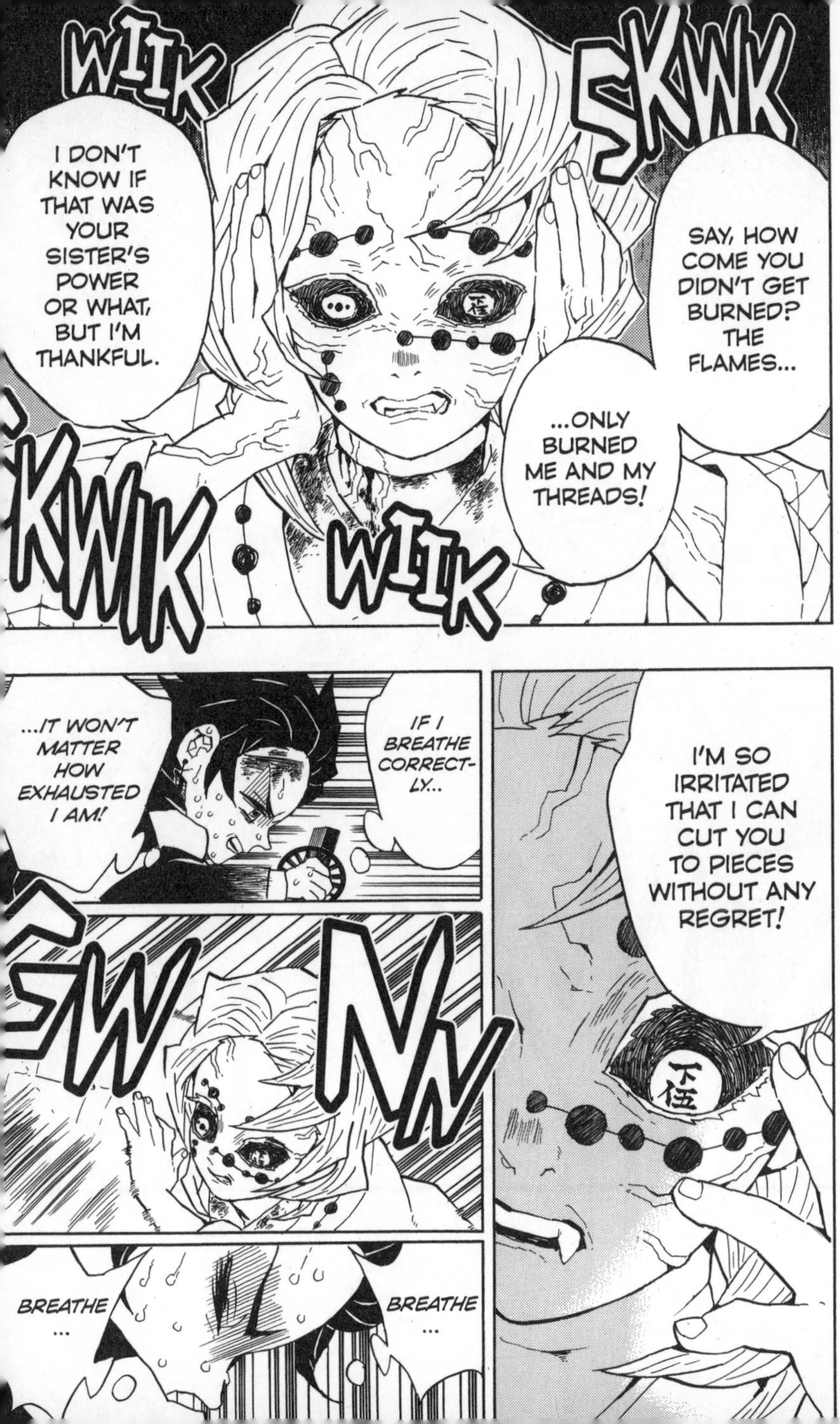
SKWK
SAY, HOW COME YOU DIDN'T GET BURNED? THE FLAMES...
...ONLY BURNED ME AND MY THREADS!
WIIK
I DON'T KNOW IF THAT WAS YOUR SISTER'S POWER OR WHAT, BUT I'M THANKFUL.
WIIK
SKWK
I'M SO IRRITATED THAT I CAN CUT YOU TO PIECES WITHOUT ANY REGRET!
IF I BREATHE CORRECTLY...
...IT WON'T MATTER HOW EXHAUSTED I AM!
SWNN
BREATHE...
BREATHE...

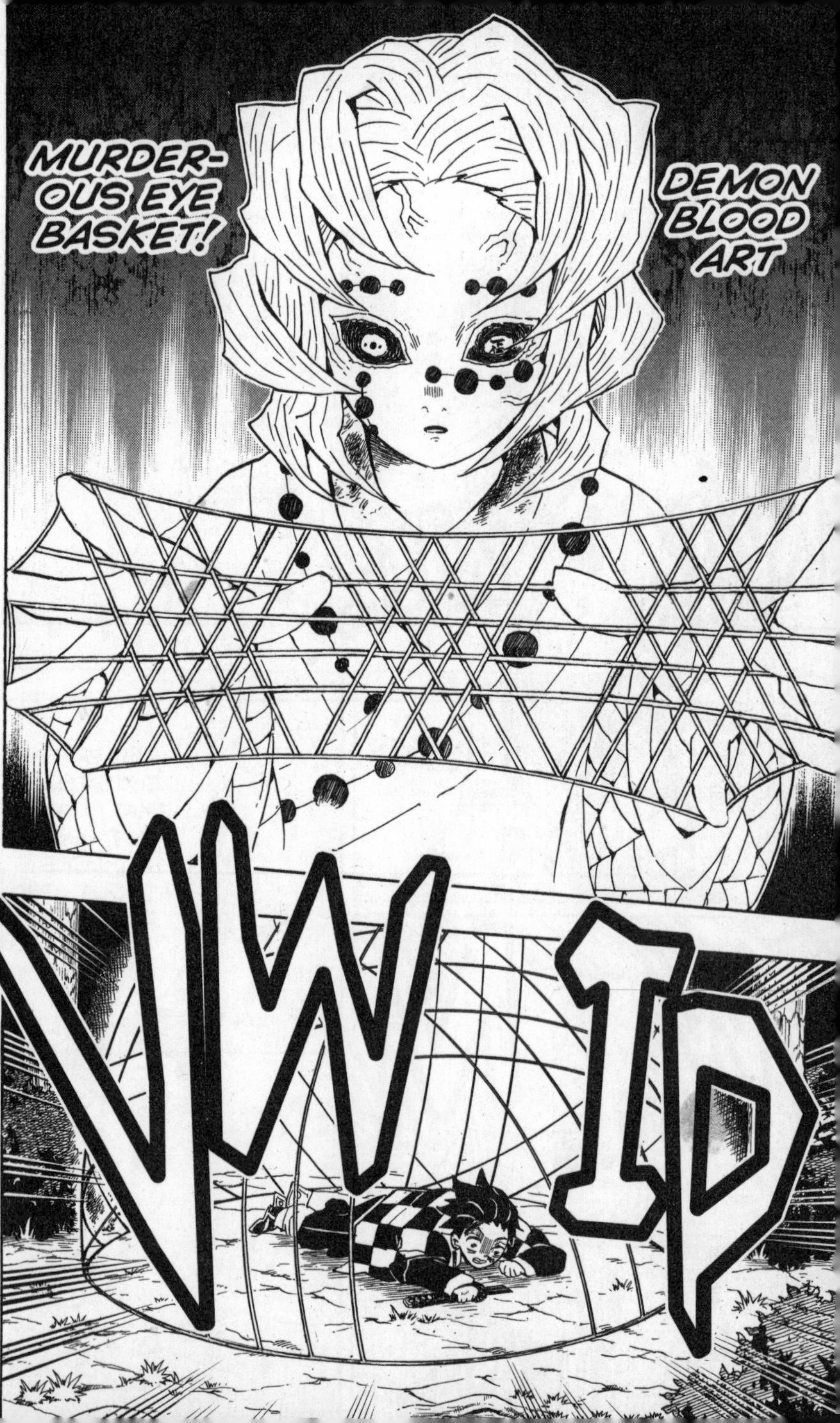
DEMON BLOOD ART
MURDER-OUS EYE BASKET!
VWIP

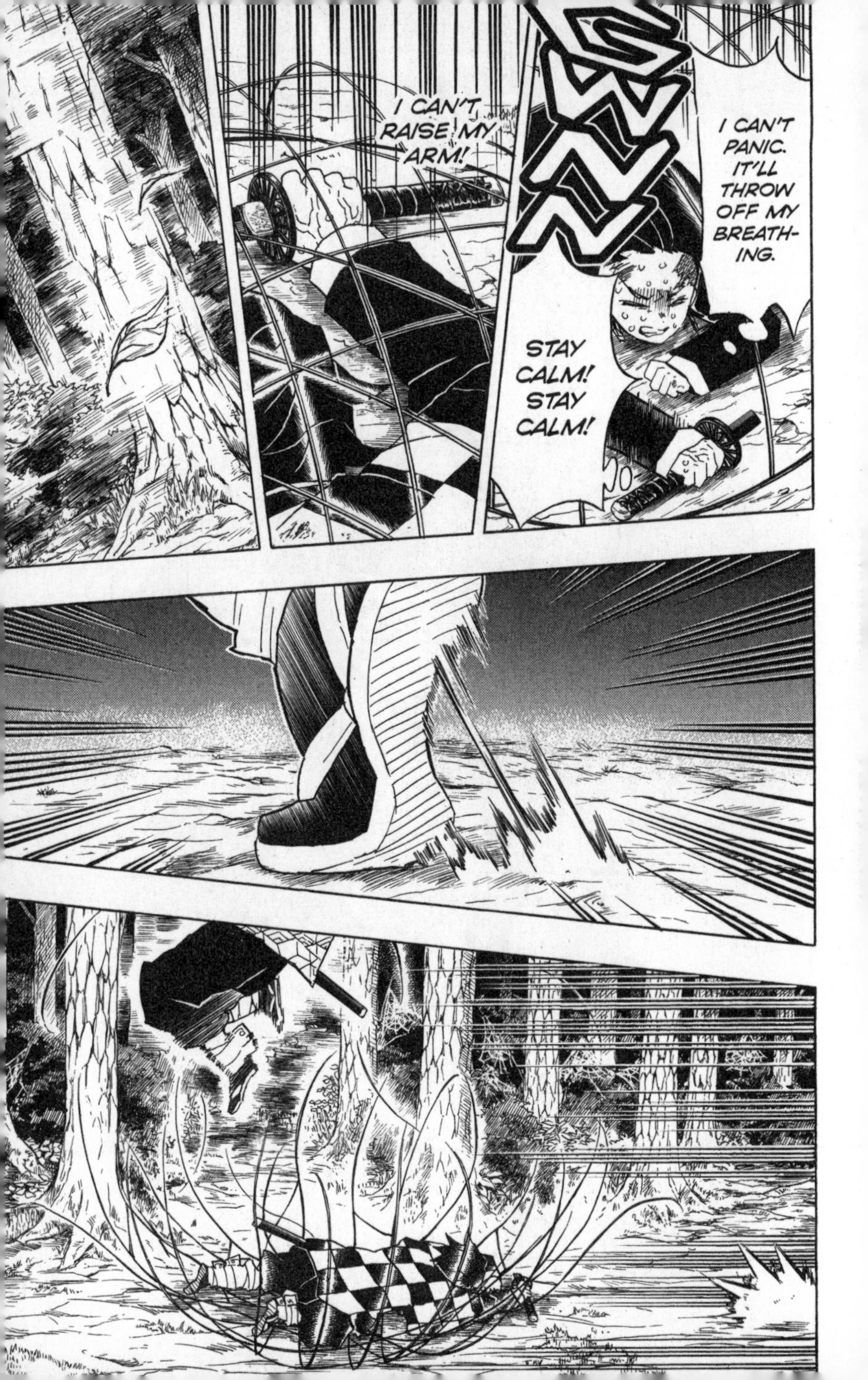
I CAN'T PANIC. IT'LL THROW OFF MY BREATHING.
STAY CALM! STAY CALM!
I CAN'T RAISE MY ARM!

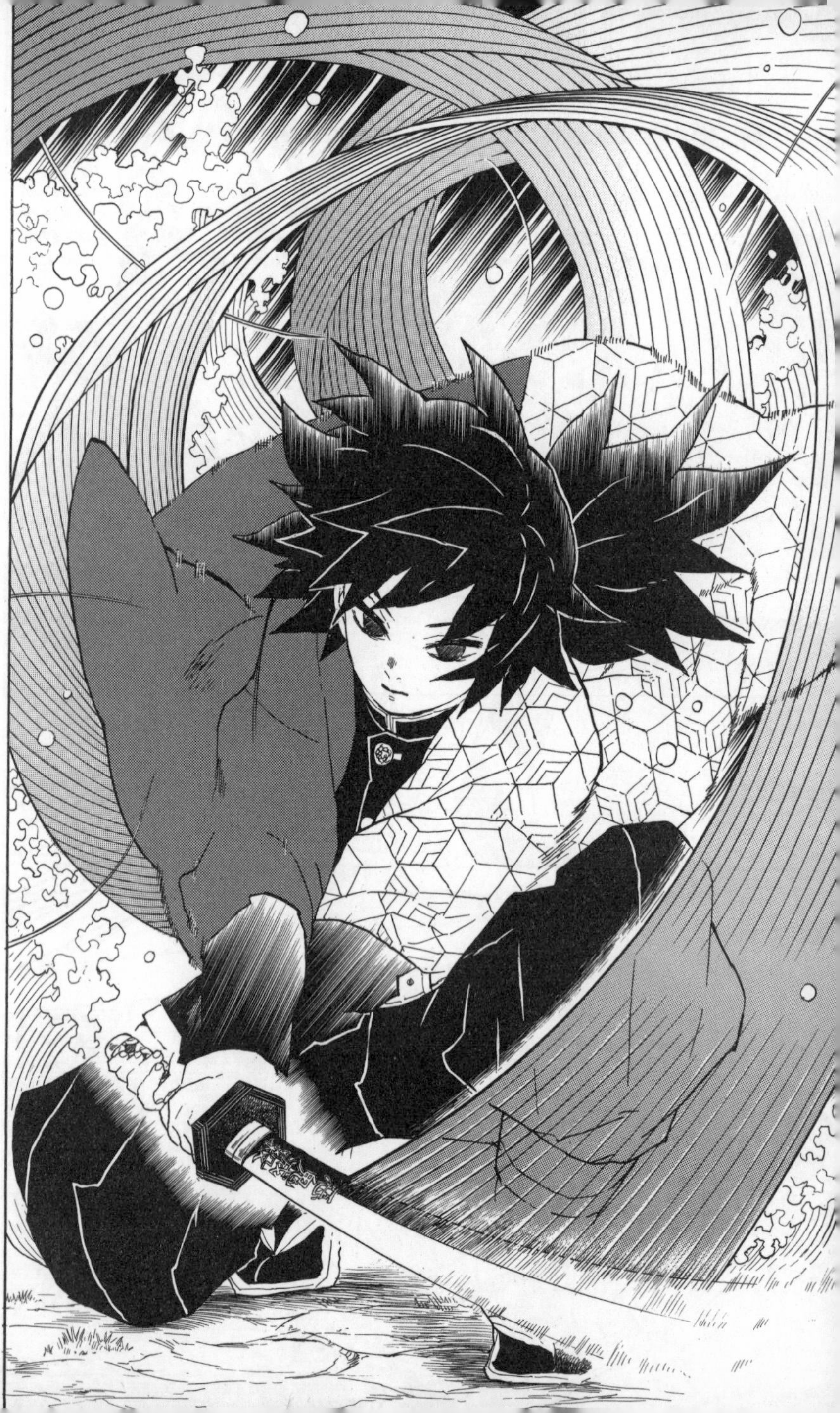

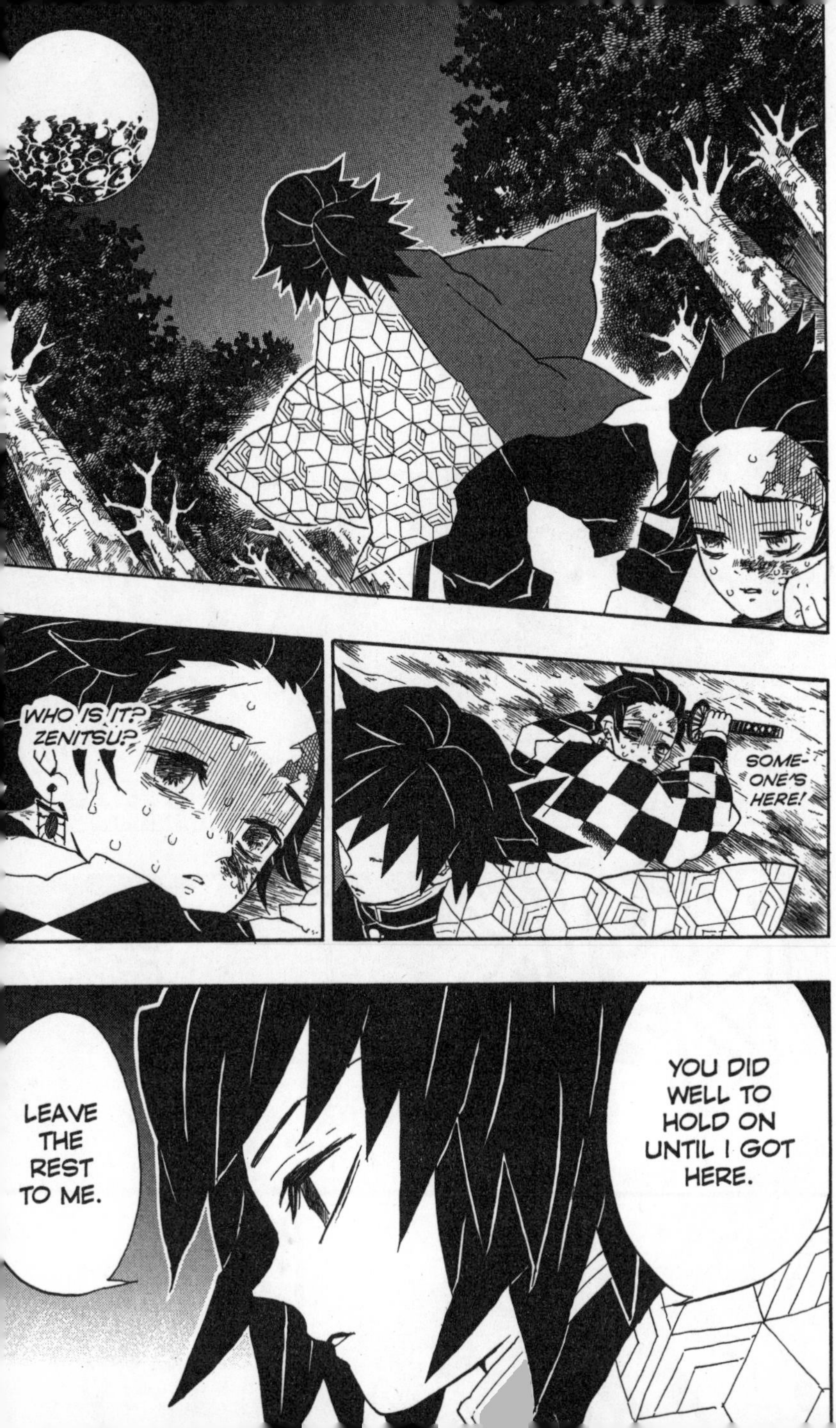
SOME-ONE'S HERE!
WHO IS IT? ZENITSU?
YOU DID WELL TO HOLD ON UNTIL I GOT HERE.
LEAVE THE REST TO ME.

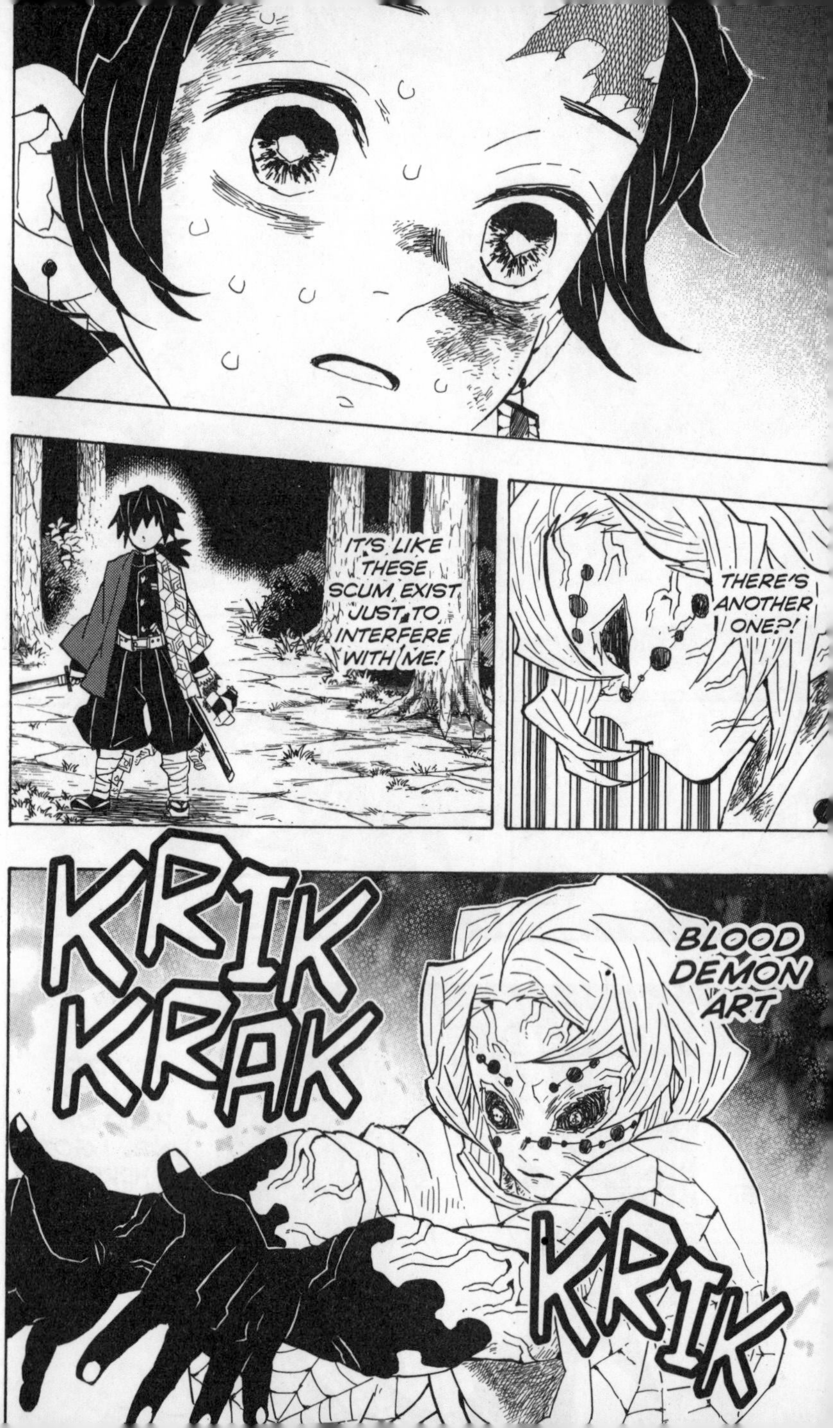
THERE'S ANOTHER ONE?!
IT'S LIKE THESE SCUM EXIST JUST TO INTERFERE WITH ME!
BLOOD DEMON ART
KRIK KRAK
KRIK

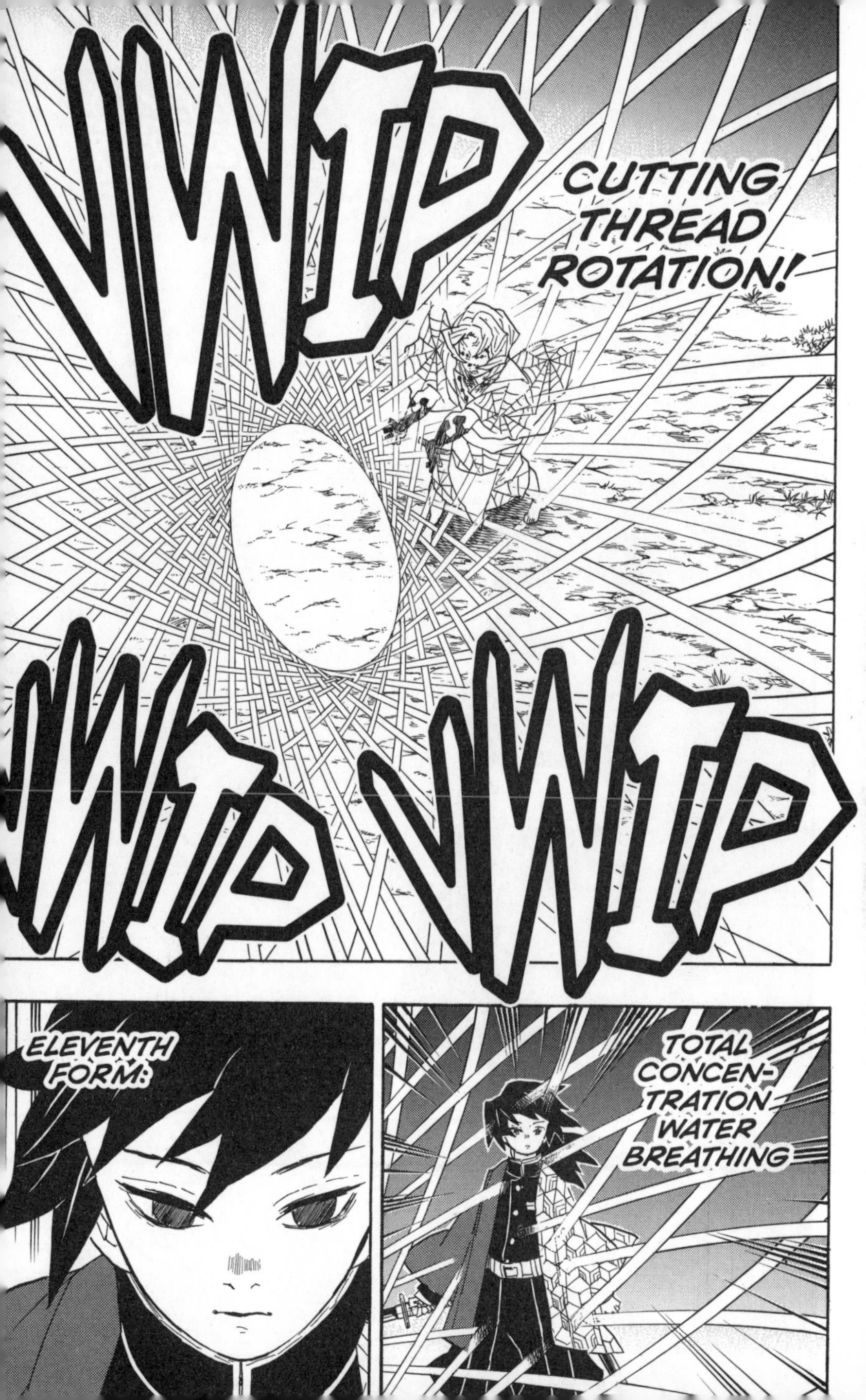
VWIP
CUTTING THREAD ROTATION!
WIP VWIP
TOTAL CONCEN-TRATION WATER BREATHING
ELEVENTH FORM:

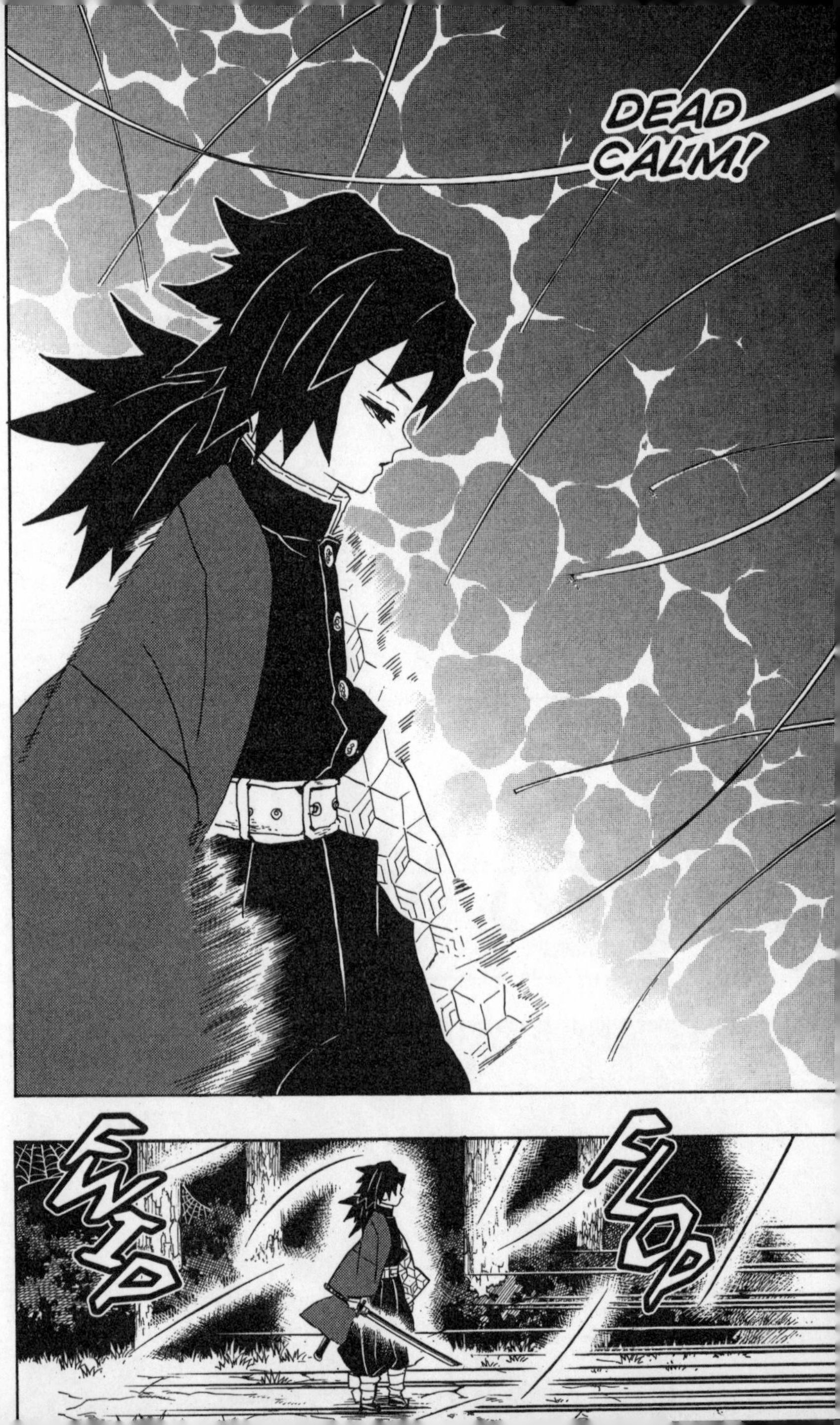
DEAD CALM!
FLOP
FWIP

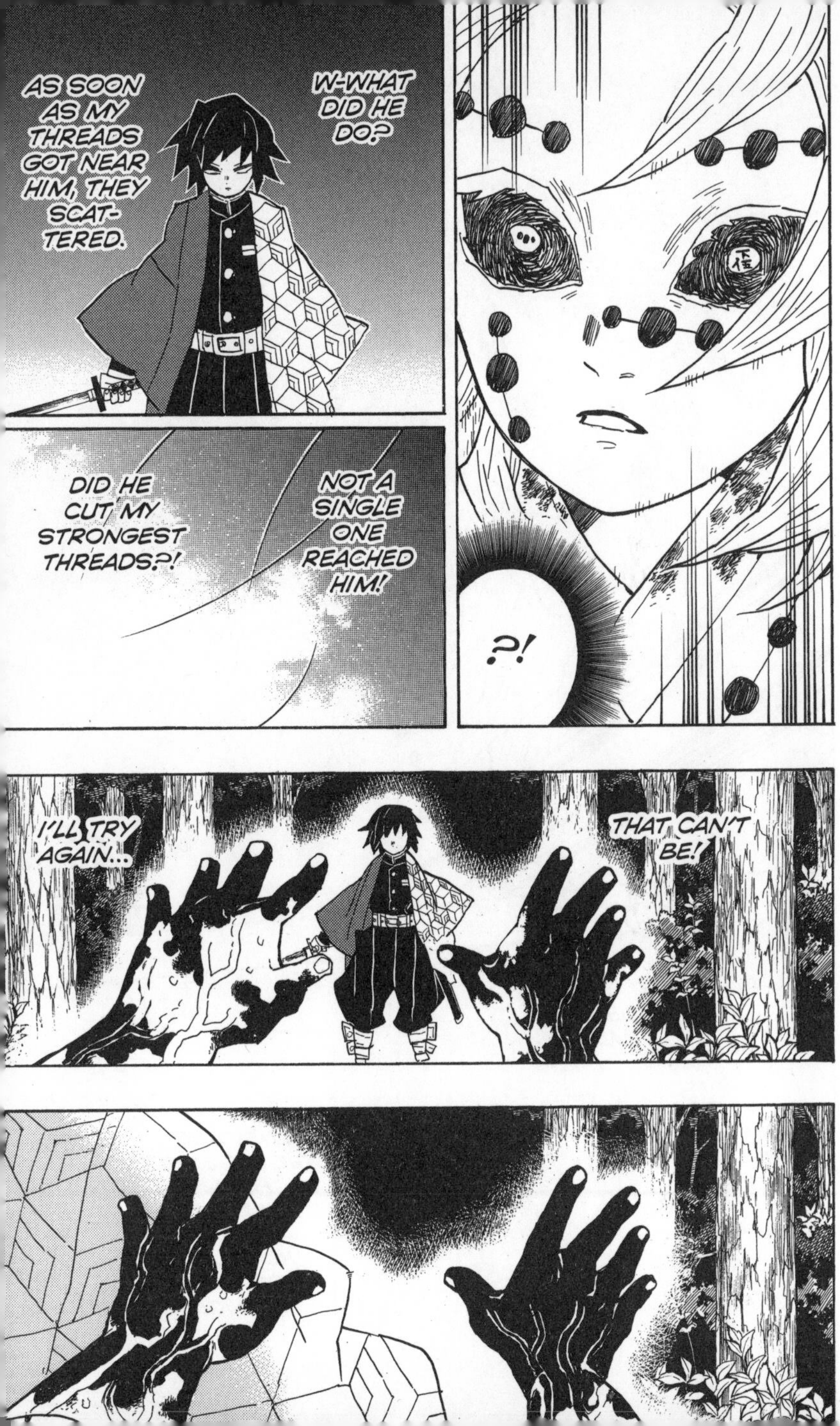
?!
W-WHAT DID HE DO?
AS SOON AS MY THREADS GOT NEAR HIM, THEY SCAT-TERED.
NOT A SINGLE ONE REACHED HIM!
DID HE CUT MY STRONGEST THREADS?!
THAT CAN'T BE!
I'LL TRY AGAIN...

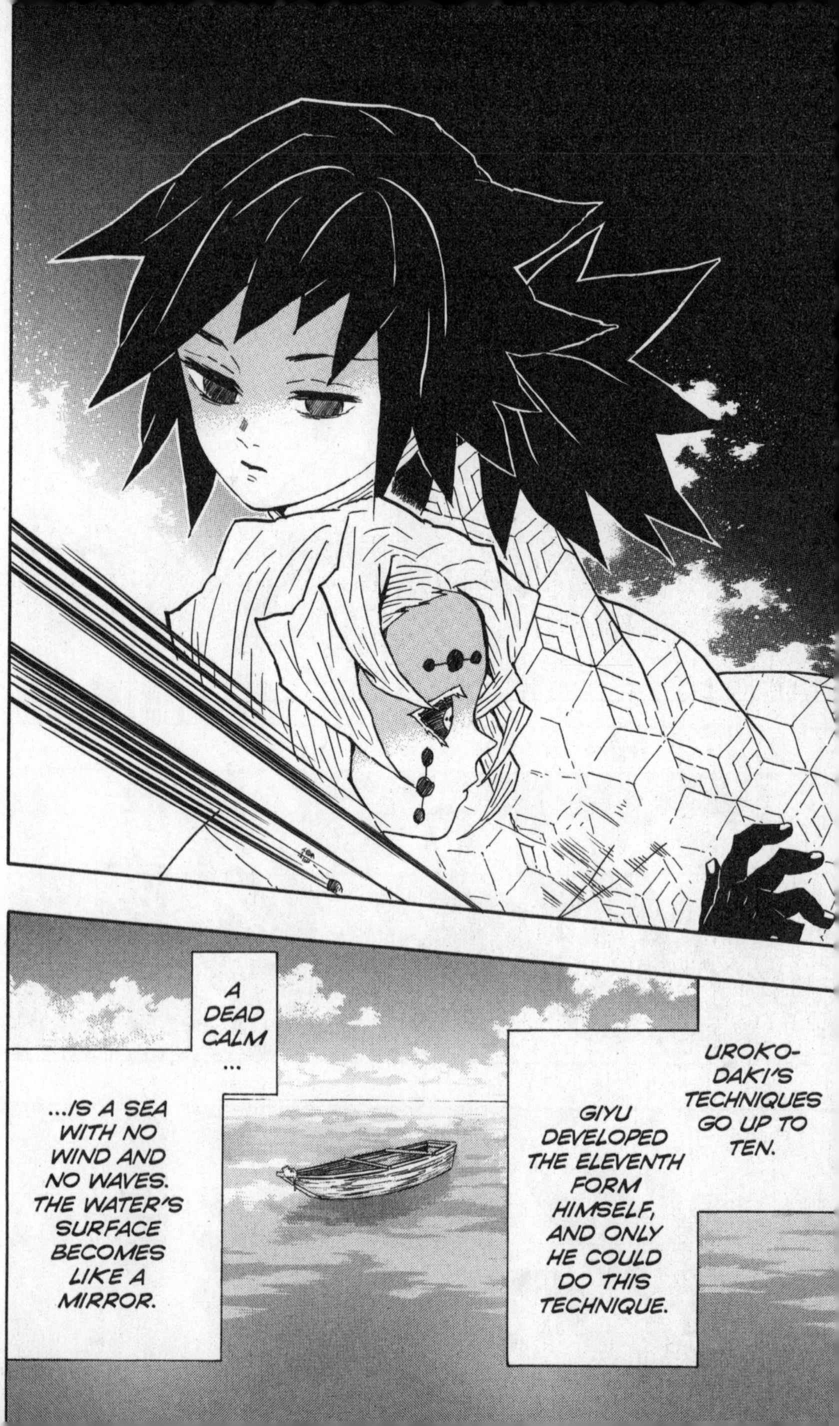
UROKO-DAKI'S TECHNIQUES GO UP TO TEN.
GIYU DEVELOPED THE ELEVENTH FORM HIMSELF, AND ONLY HE COULD DO THIS TECHNIQUE.
A DEAD CALM ...
...IS A SEA WITH NO WIND AND NO WAVES. THE WATER'S SURFACE BECOMES LIKE A MIRROR.

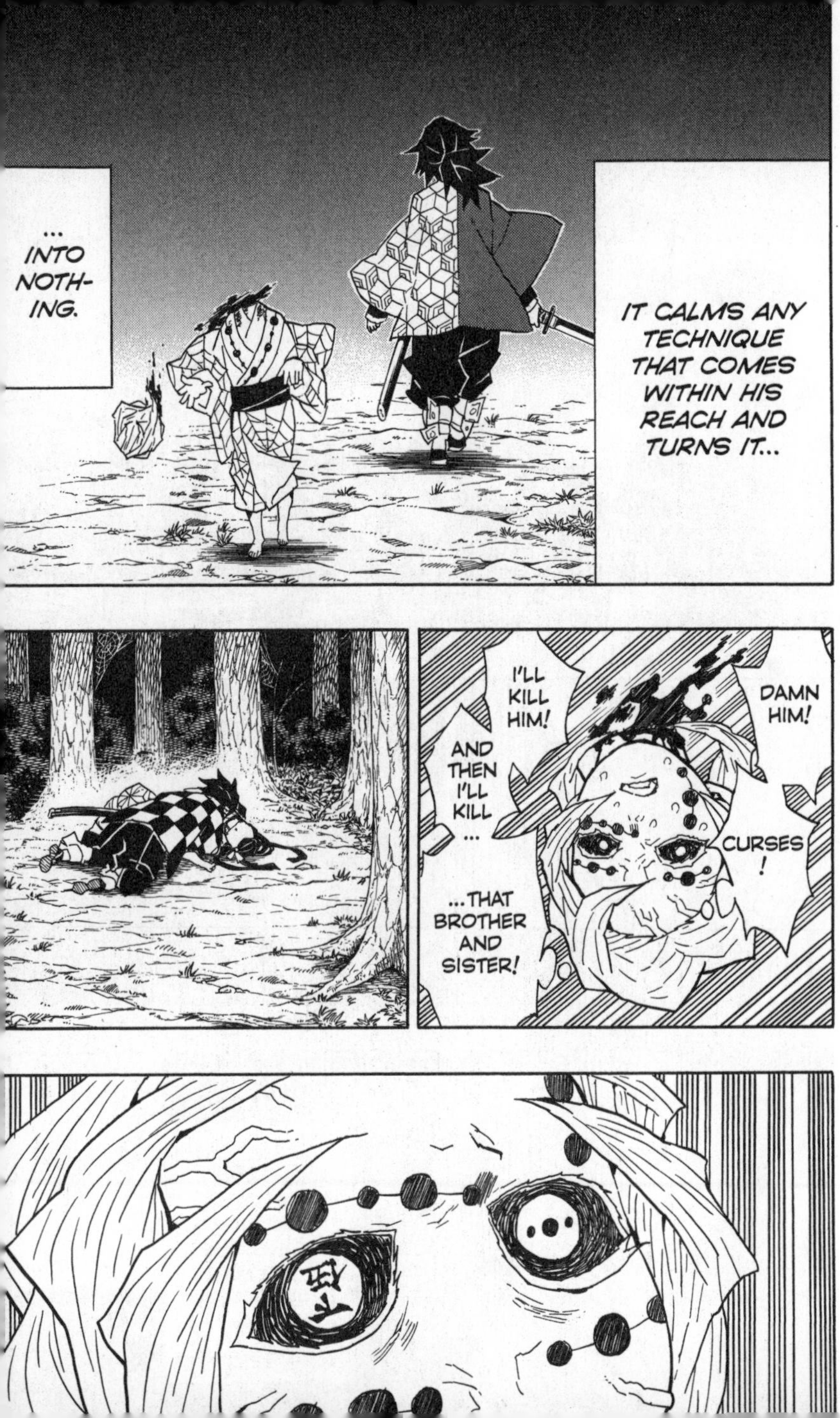
IT CALMS ANY TECHNIQUE THAT COMES WITHIN HIS REACH AND TURNS IT...
... INTO NOTH-ING.
DAMN HIM!
CURSES!
I'LL KILL HIM!
AND THEN I'LL KILL ...
...THAT BROTHER AND SISTER!

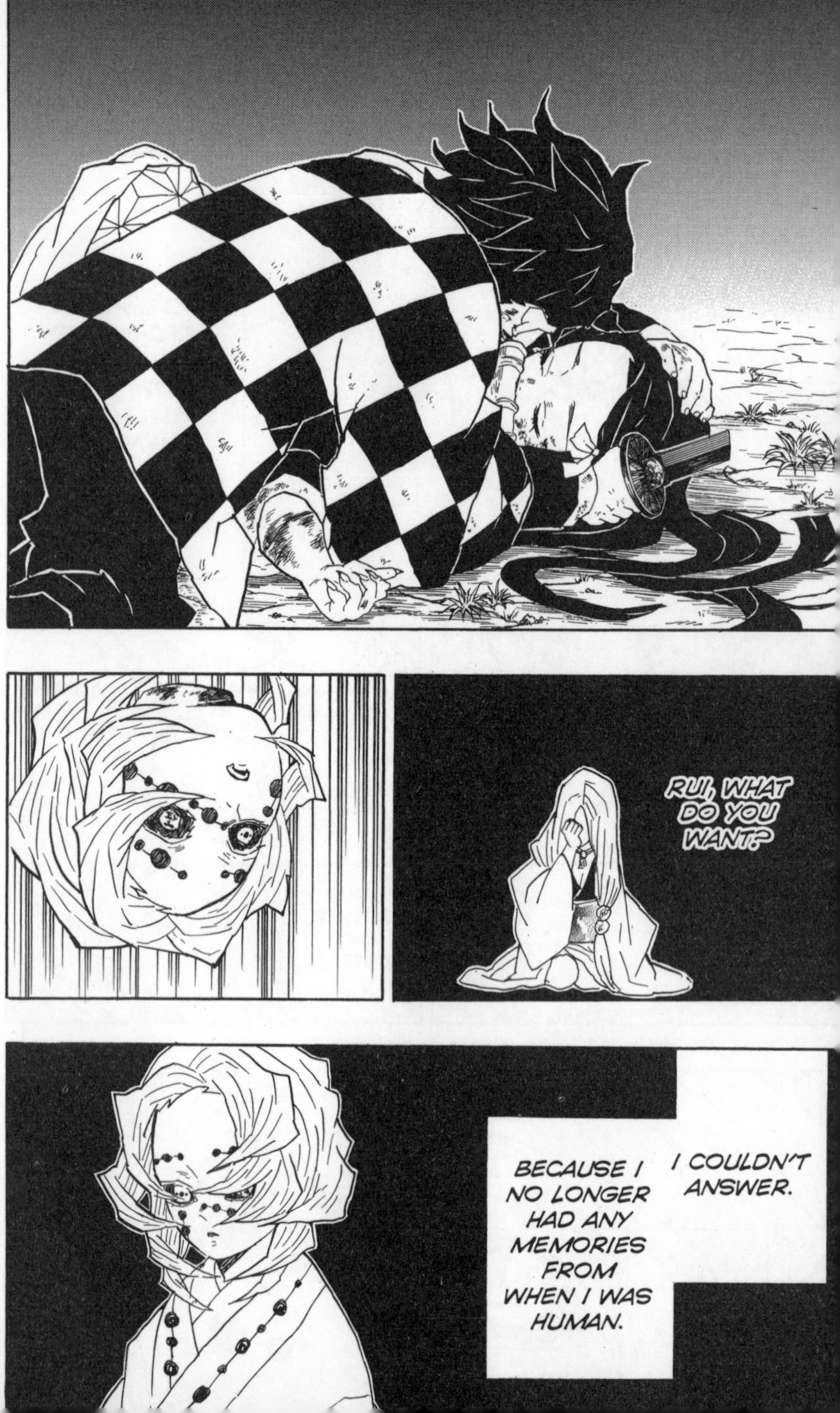
RUI, WHAT DO YOU WANT?
I COULDN'T ANSWER.
BECAUSE I NO LONGER HAD ANY MEMORIES FROM WHEN I WAS HUMAN.

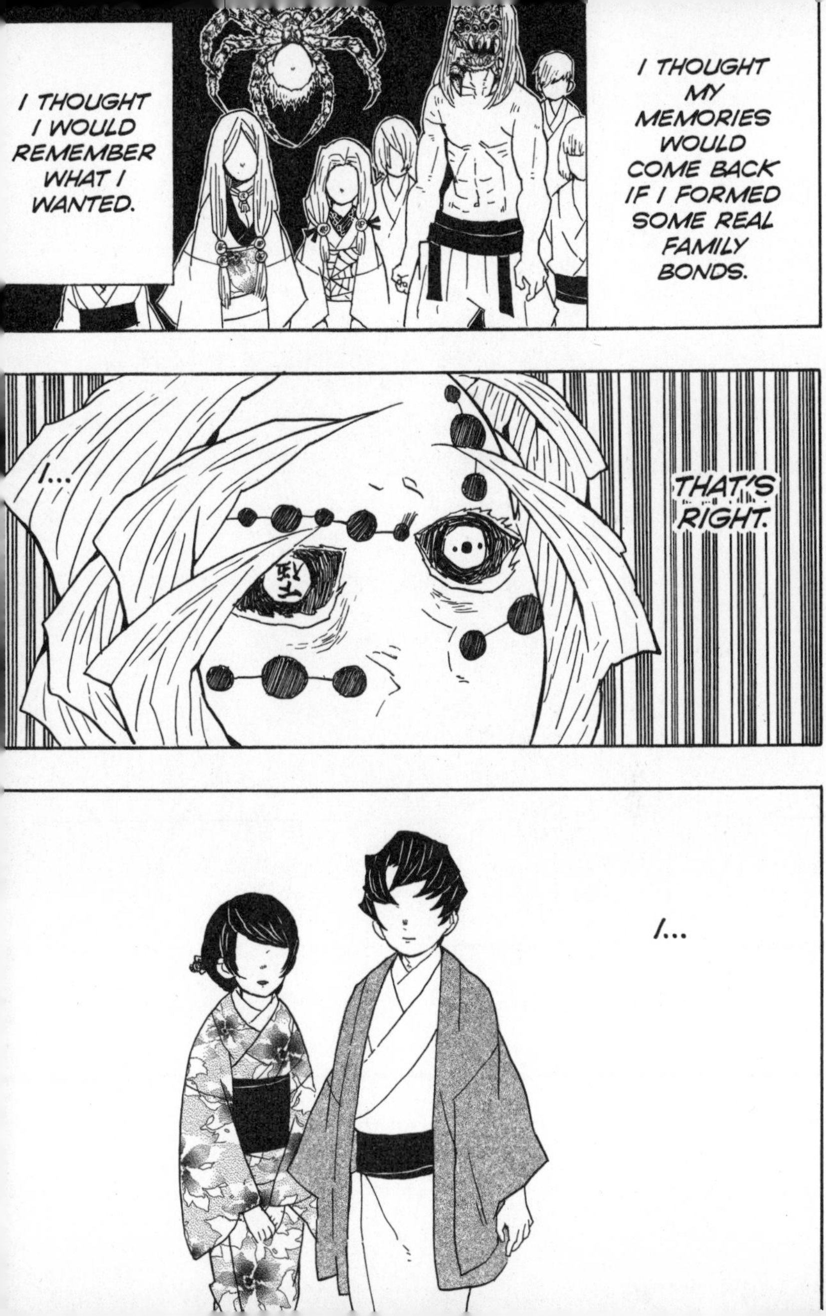
I THOUGHT MY MEMORIES WOULD COME BACK IF I FORMED SOME REAL FAMILY BONDS.
I THOUGHT I WOULD REMEMBER WHAT I WANTED.
THAT'S RIGHT.
I...
I...

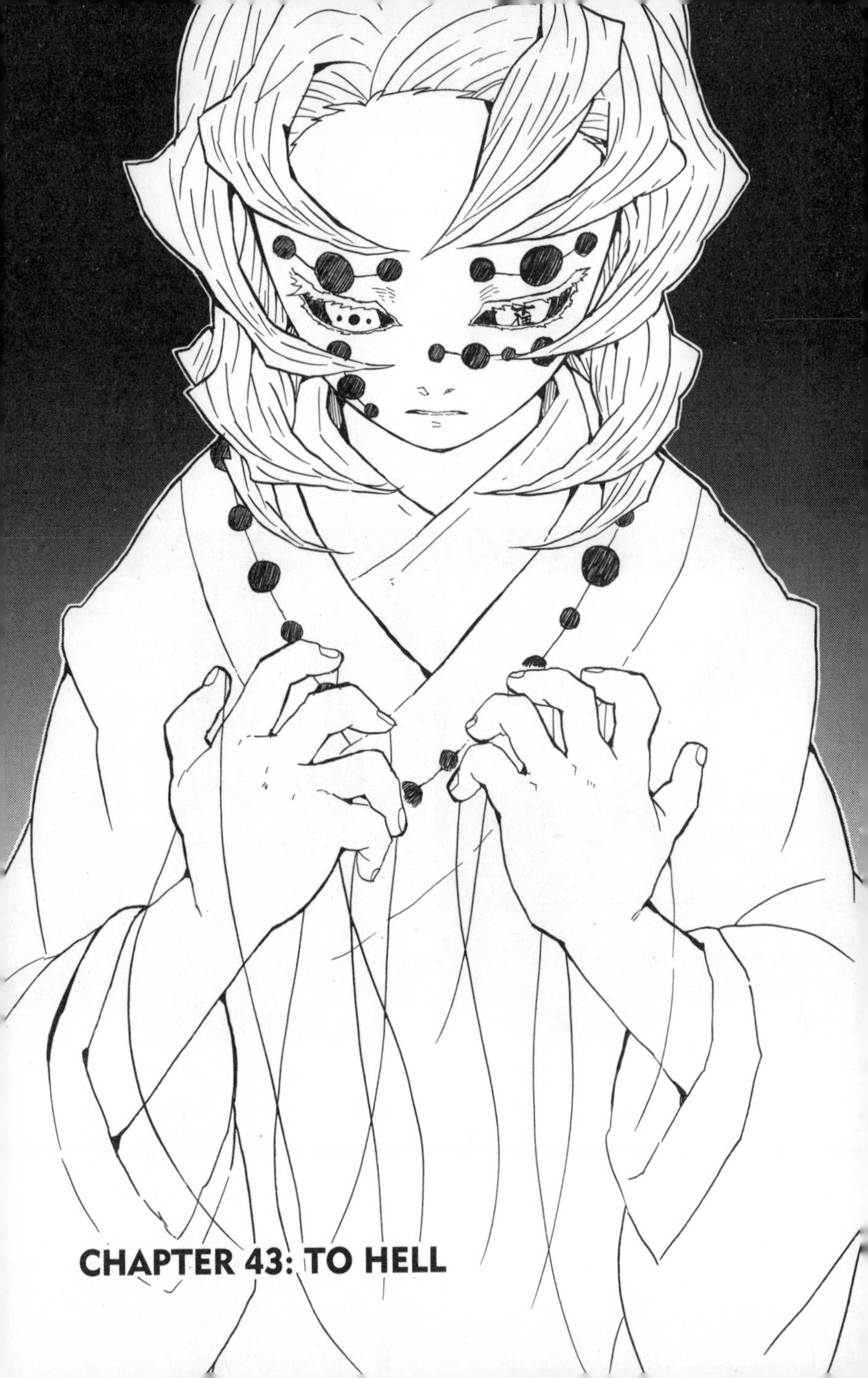

CHAPTER 43: TO HELL

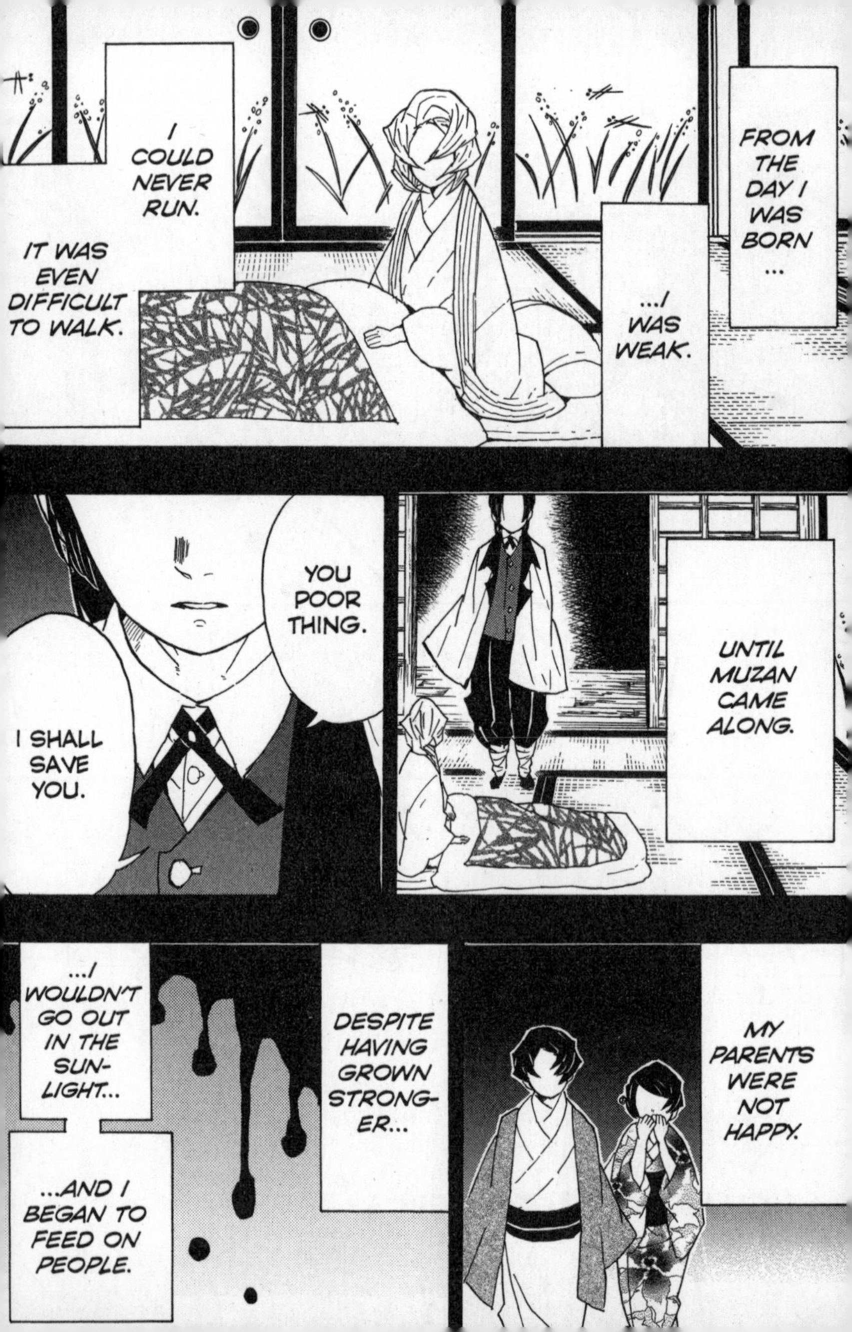
FROM THE DAY I WAS BORN...
...I WAS WEAK.
I COULD NEVER RUN.
IT WAS EVEN DIFFICULT TO WALK.
UNTIL MUZAN CAME ALONG.
YOU POOR THING.
I SHALL SAVE YOU.
MY PARENTS WERE NOT HAPPY.
DESPITE HAVING GROWN STRONGER...
...I WOULDN'T GO OUT IN THE SUN-LIGHT...
...AND I BEGAN TO FEED ON PEOPLE.

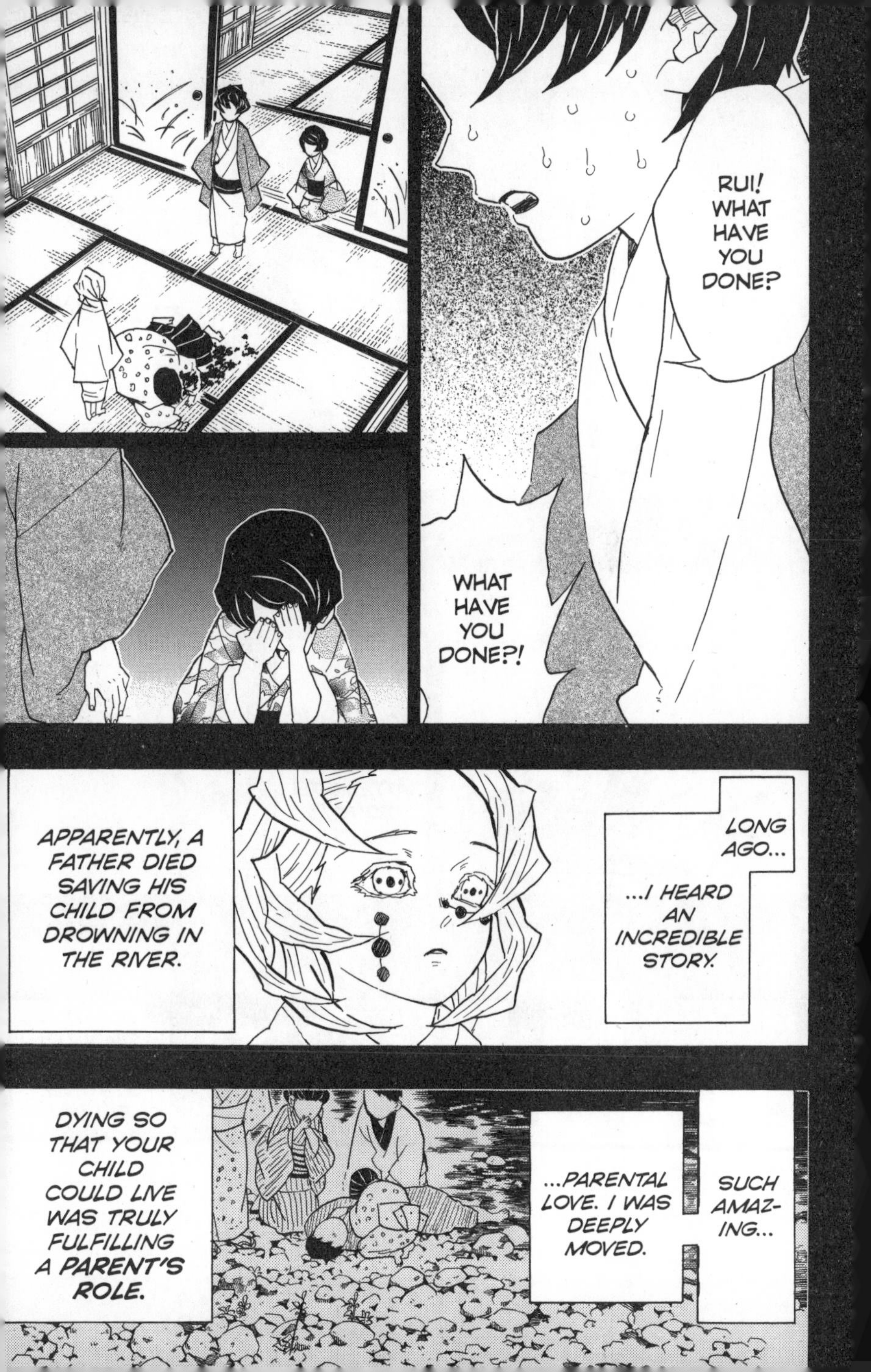
RUI! WHAT HAVE YOU DONE?
WHAT HAVE YOU DONE?!
LONG AGO...
...I HEARD AN INCREDIBLE STORY.
APPARENTLY, A FATHER DIED SAVING HIS CHILD FROM DROWNING IN THE RIVER.
SUCH AMAZ-ING...
...PARENTAL LOVE. I WAS DEEPLY MOVED.
DYING SO THAT YOUR CHILD COULD LIVE WAS TRULY FULFILLING A PARENT'S ROLE.

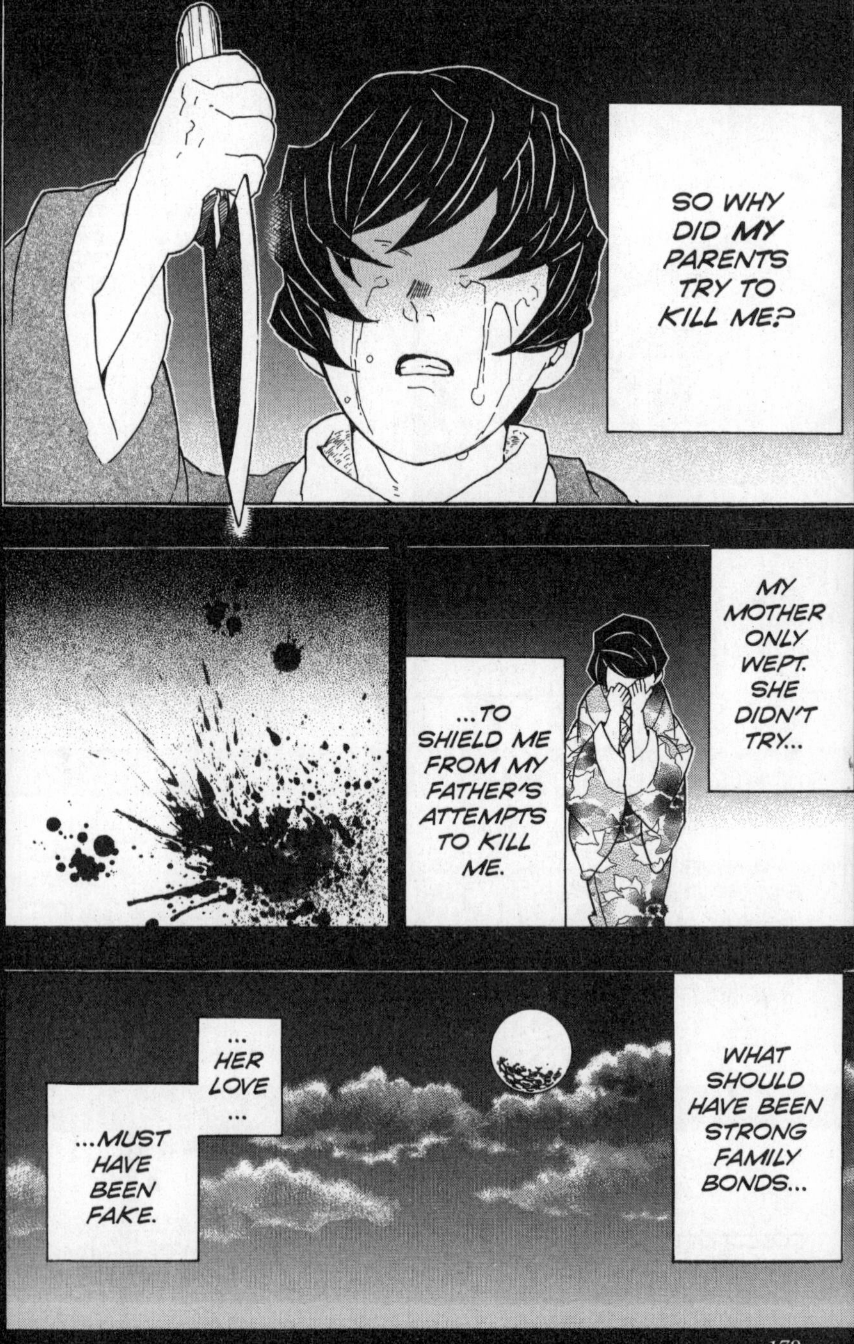
SO WHY DID MY PARENTS TRY TO KILL ME?
MY MOTHER ONLY WEPT. SHE DIDN'T TRY...
...TO SHIELD ME FROM MY FATHER'S ATTEMPTS TO KILL ME.
WHAT SHOULD HAVE BEEN STRONG FAMILY BONDS...
... HER LOVE ...
...MUST HAVE BEEN FAKE.

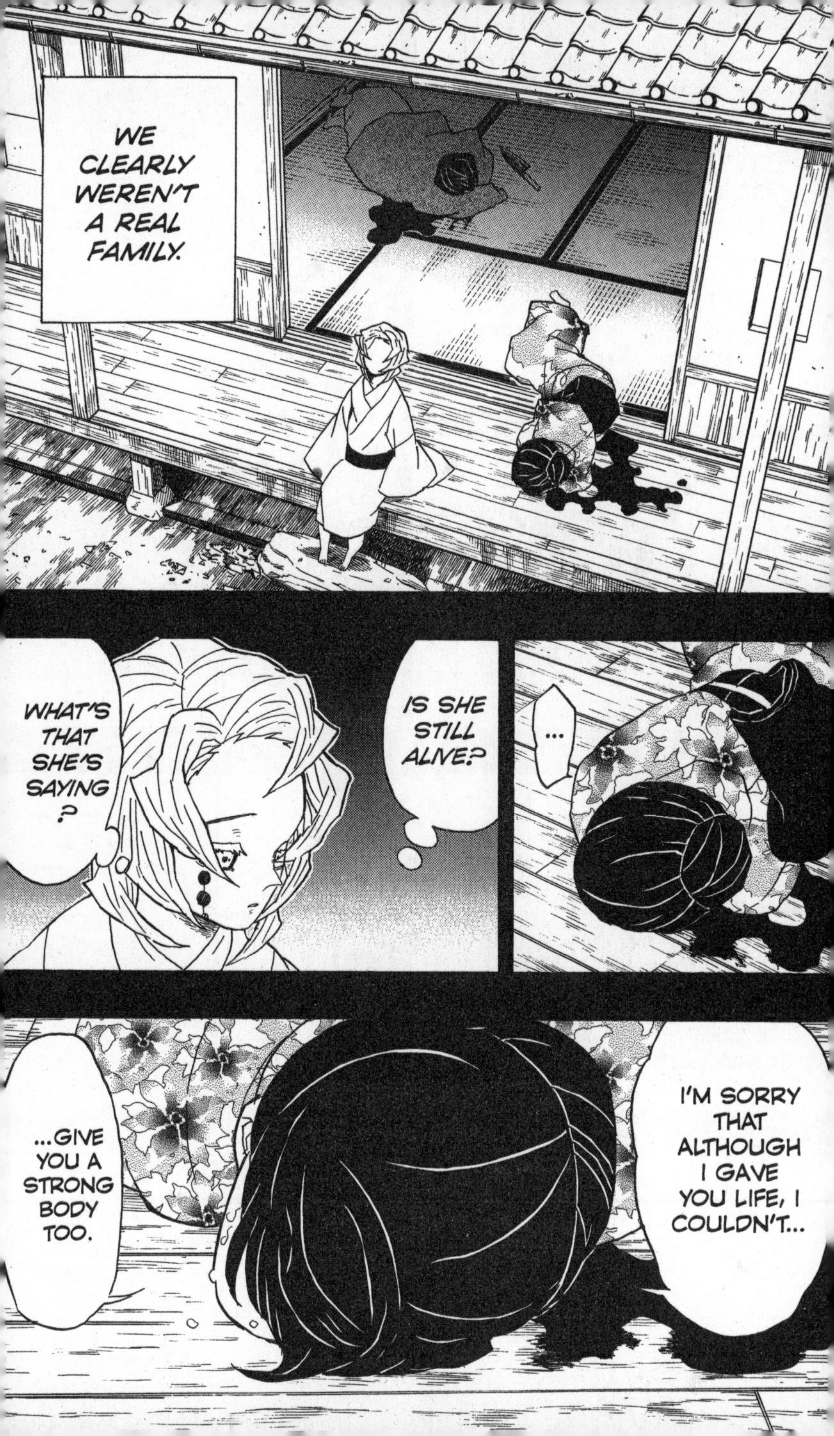
WE CLEARLY WEREN'T A REAL FAMILY.
...
IS SHE STILL ALIVE?
WHAT'S THAT SHE'S SAYING?
I'M SORRY THAT ALTHOUGH I GAVE YOU LIFE, I COULDN'T...
...GIVE YOU A STRONG BODY TOO.

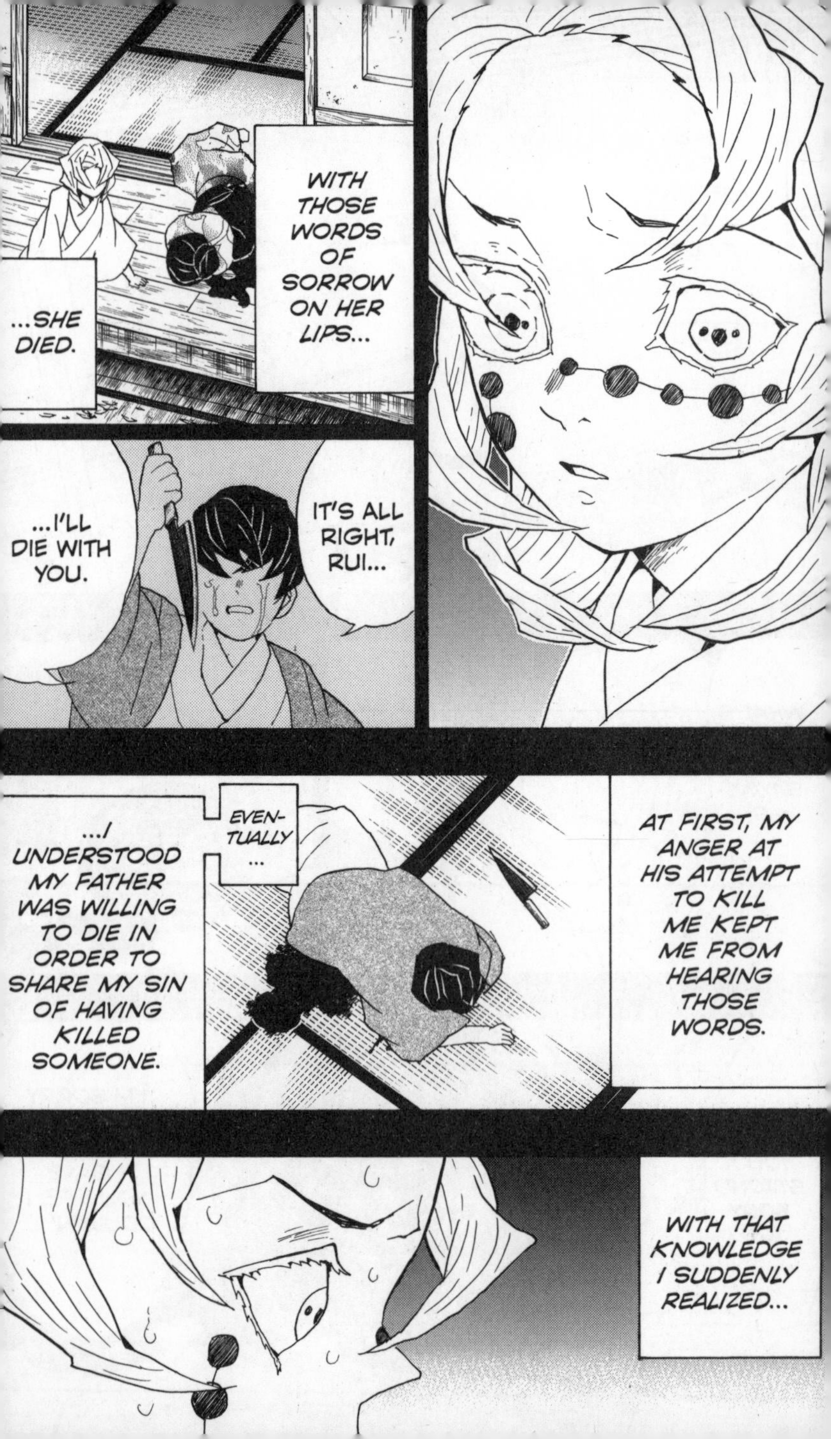
WITH THOSE WORDS OF SORROW ON HER LIPS...
...SHE DIED.
IT'S ALL RIGHT, RUI...
...I'LL DIE WITH YOU.
AT FIRST, MY ANGER AT HIS ATTEMPT TO KILL ME KEPT ME FROM HEARING THOSE WORDS.
EVEN-TUALLY...
...I UNDERSTOOD MY FATHER WAS WILLING TO DIE IN ORDER TO SHARE MY SIN OF HAVING KILLED SOMEONE.
WITH THAT KNOWLEDGE I SUDDENLY REALIZED...

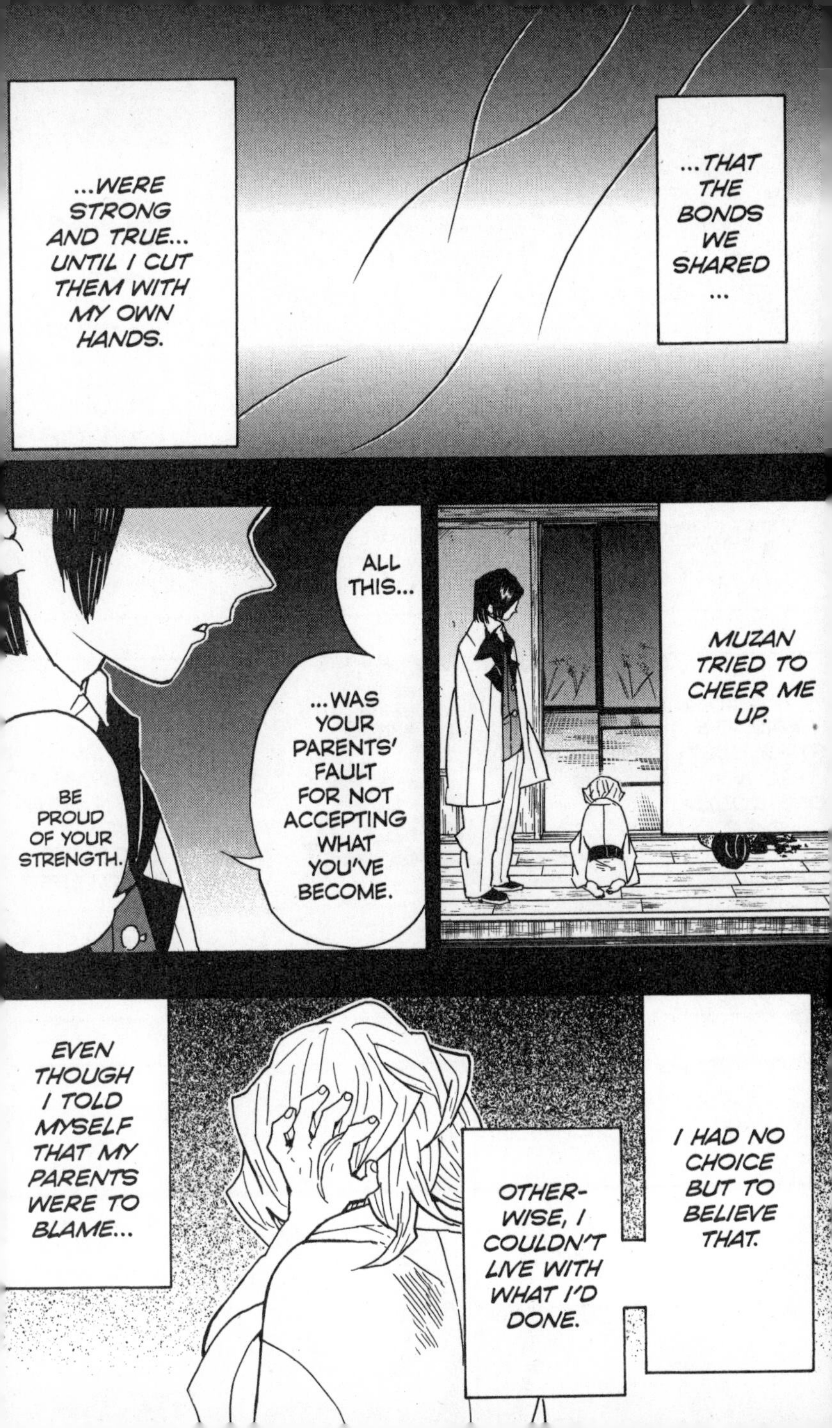
...THAT THE BONDS WE SHARED ...
...WERE STRONG AND TRUE... UNTIL I CUT THEM WITH MY OWN HANDS.
MUZAN TRIED TO CHEER ME UP.
ALL THIS...
...WAS YOUR PARENTS' FAULT FOR NOT ACCEPTING WHAT YOU'VE BECOME.
BE PROUD OF YOUR STRENGTH.
I HAD NO CHOICE BUT TO BELIEVE THAT.
OTHER-WISE, I COULDN'T LIVE WITH WHAT I'D DONE.
EVEN THOUGH I TOLD MYSELF THAT MY PARENTS WERE TO BLAME...

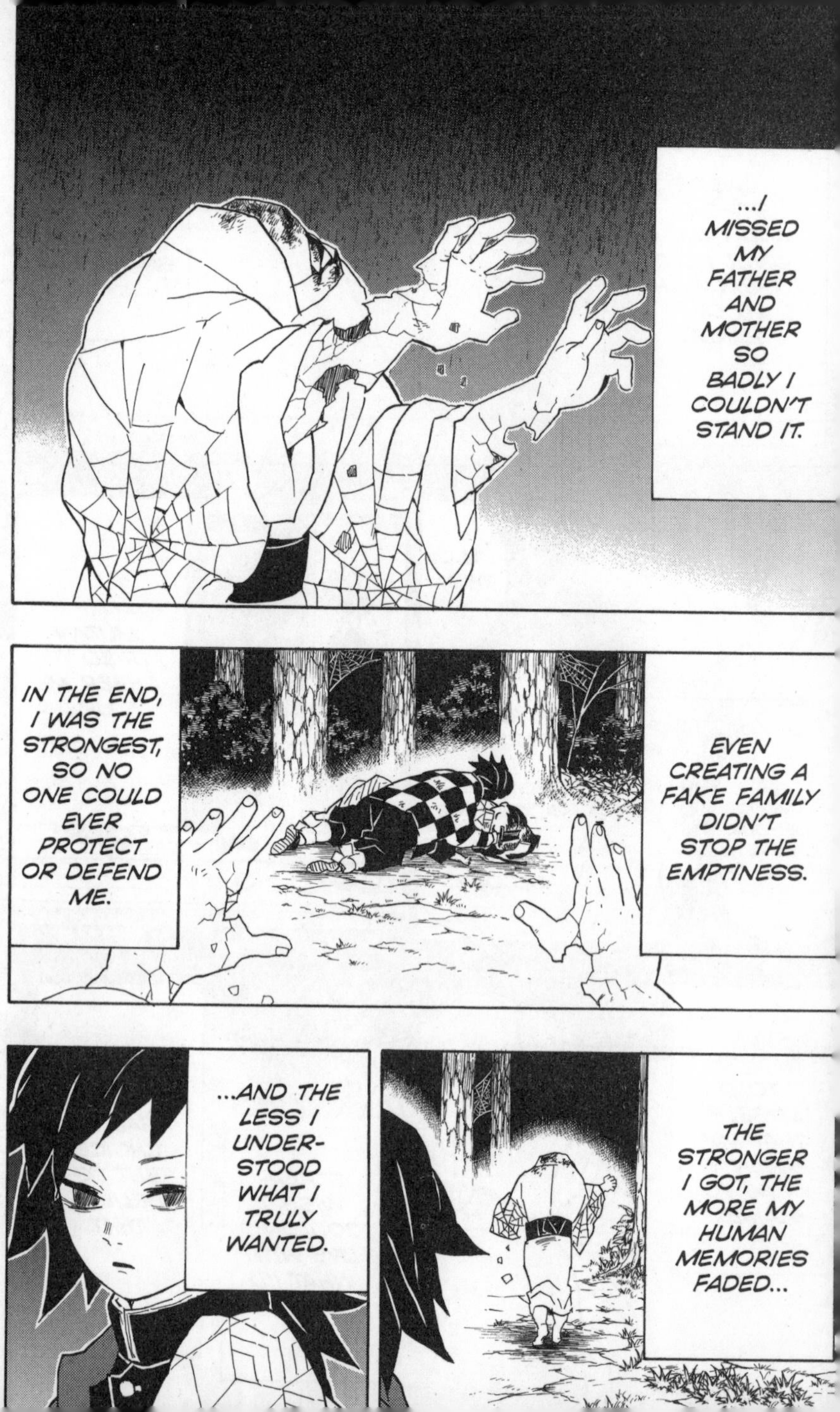
...I MISSED MY FATHER AND MOTHER SO BADLY I COULDN'T STAND IT.
EVEN CREATING A FAKE FAMILY DIDN'T STOP THE EMPTINESS.
IN THE END, I WAS THE STRONGEST, SO NO ONE COULD EVER PROTECT OR DEFEND ME.
THE STRONGER I GOT, THE MORE MY HUMAN MEMORIES FADED...
...AND THE LESS I UNDER-STOOD WHAT I TRULY WANTED.

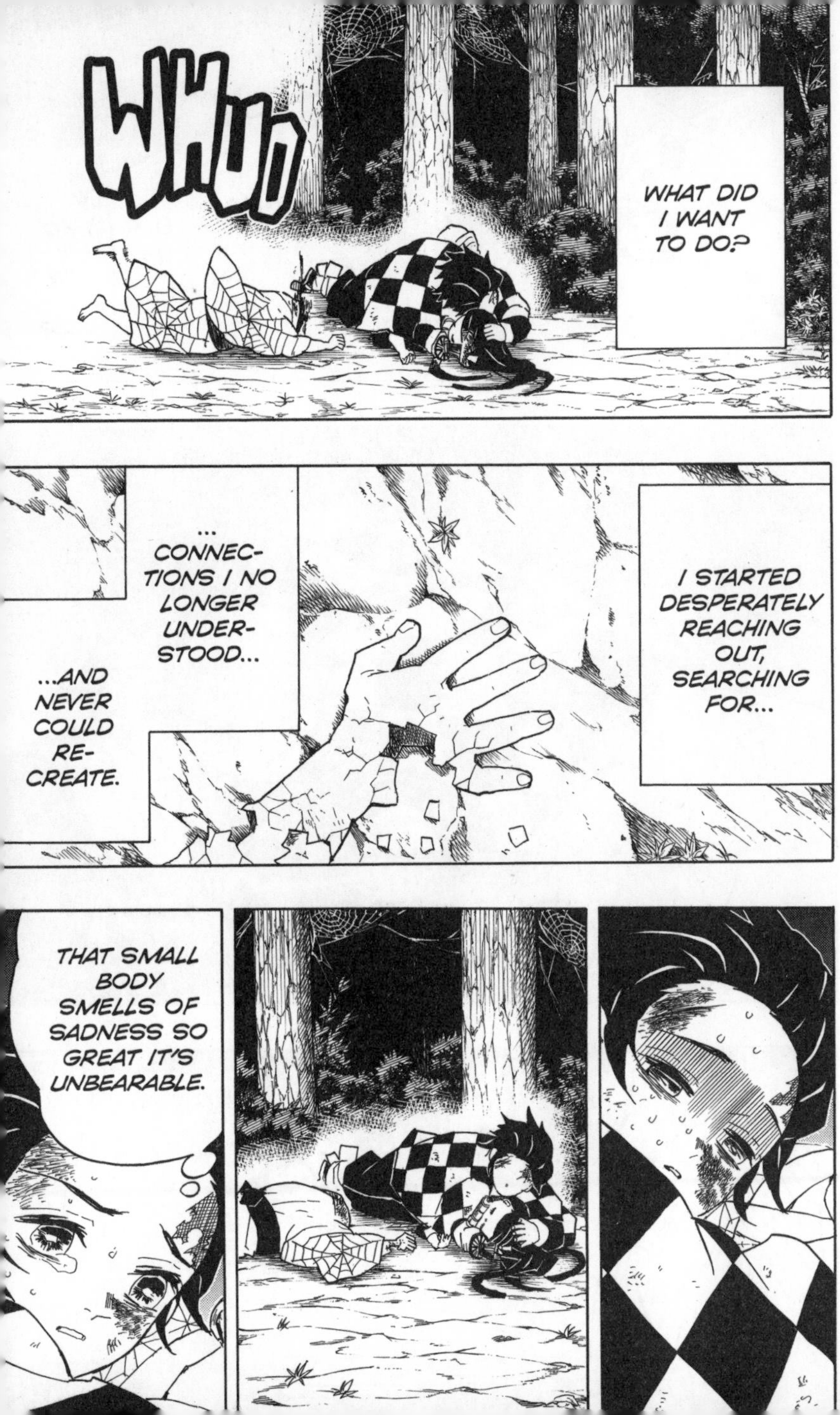
WHAT DID I WANT TO DO?
WHUD
I STARTED DESPERATELY REACHING OUT, SEARCHING FOR...
... CONNECTIONS I NO LONGER UNDERSTOOD...
...AND NEVER COULD RE-CREATE.
THAT SMALL BODY SMELLS OF SADNESS SO GREAT IT'S UNBEARABLE.

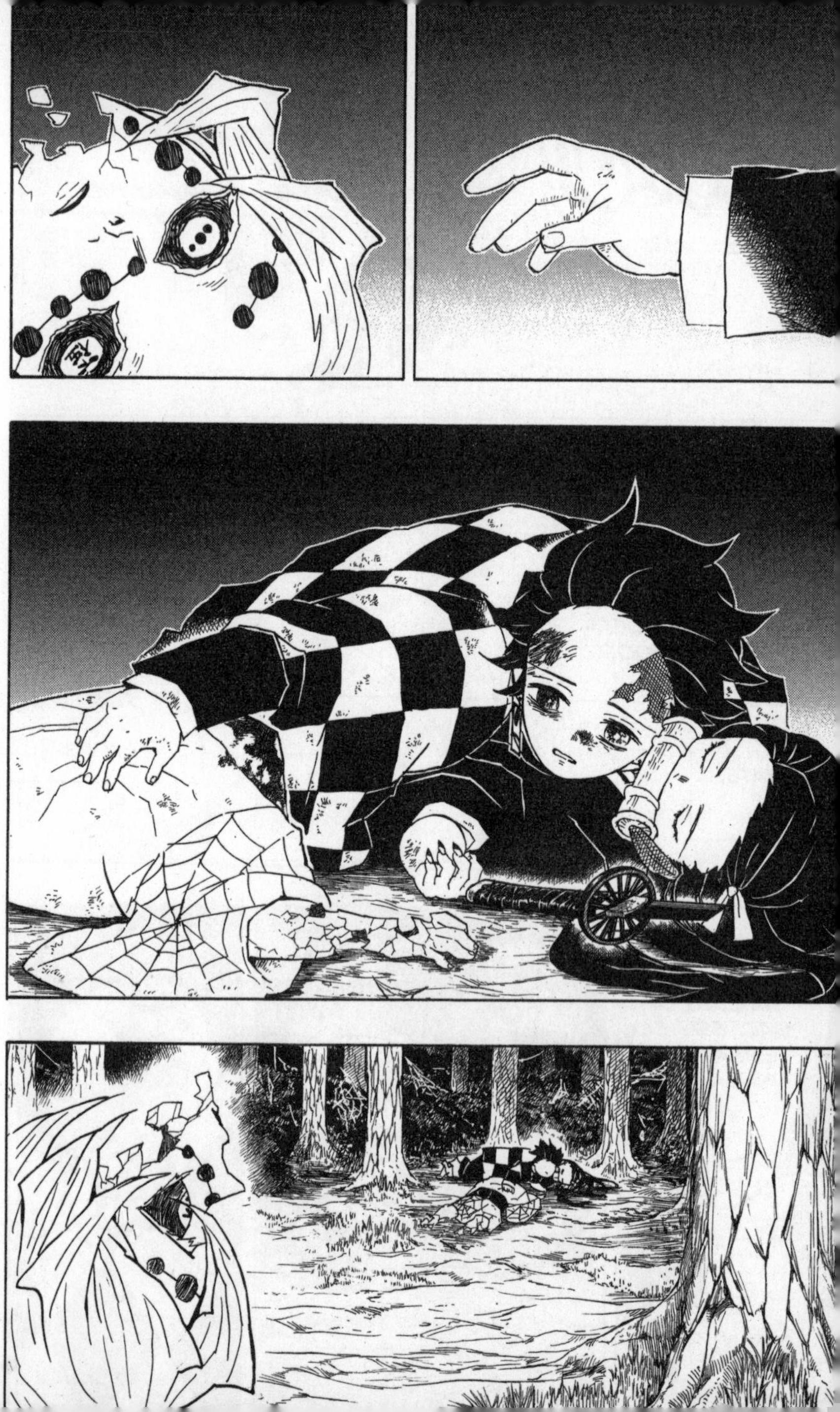

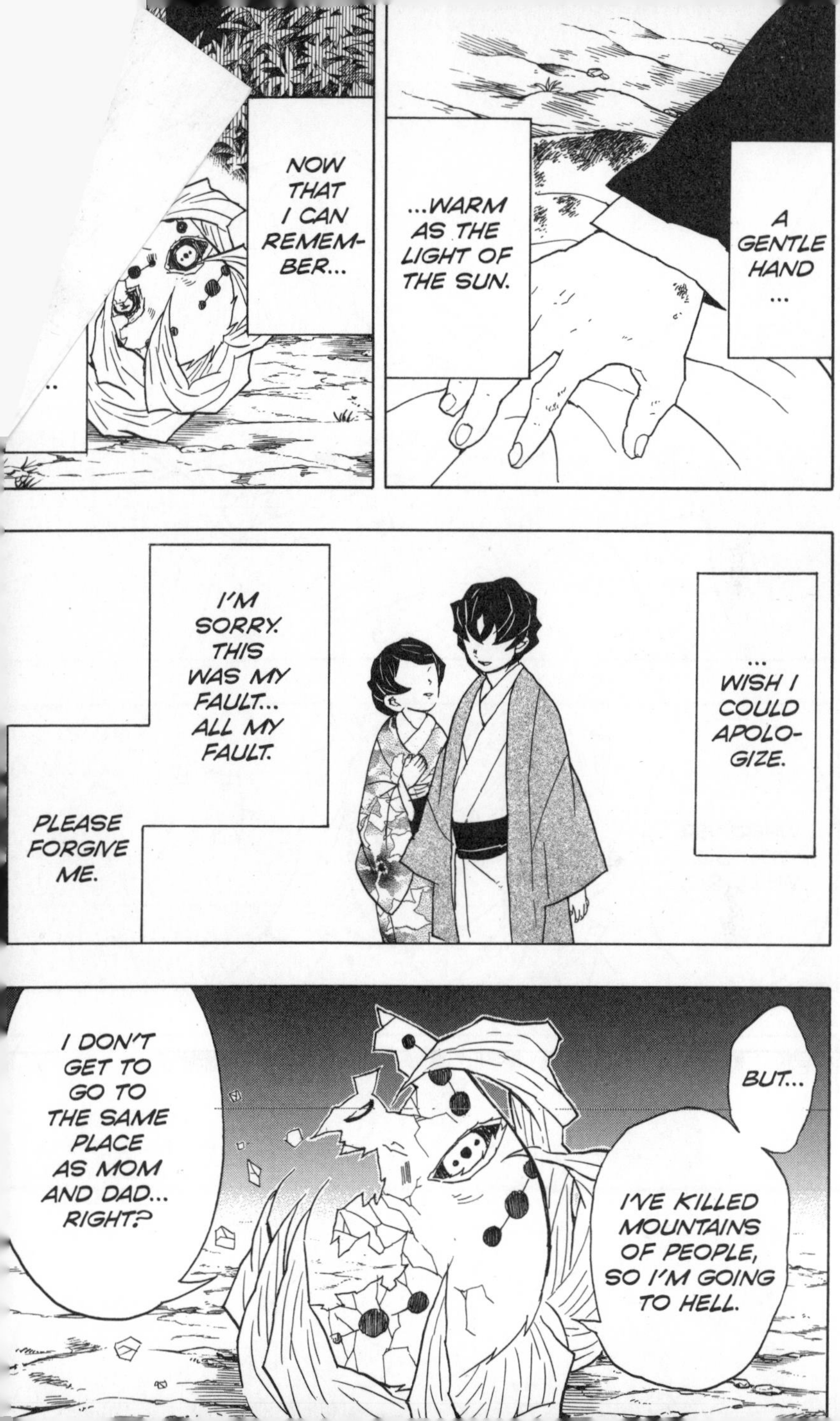
A GENTLE HAND ...
...WARM AS THE LIGHT OF THE SUN.
NOW THAT I CAN REMEMBER...
...
... WISH I COULD APOLOGIZE.
I'M SORRY. THIS WAS MY FAULT... ALL MY FAULT.
PLEASE FORGIVE ME.
BUT...
I'VE KILLED MOUNTAINS OF PEOPLE, SO I'M GOING TO HELL.
I DON'T GET TO GO TO THE SAME PLACE AS MOM AND DAD... RIGHT?

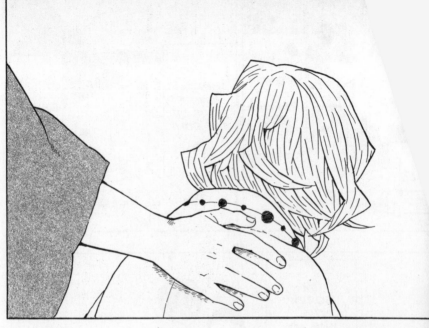

WHEREVER
YOU GO,
WE'LL GO.

WE'RE YOUR
PARENTS. WE'LL
EVEN GO WITH
YOU TO HELL.

I'M SORRY!

THIS IS ALL MY FAULT!

SO VERY SORRY ...!

FWOOM

I'M SORRY, I'M SO SORRY!

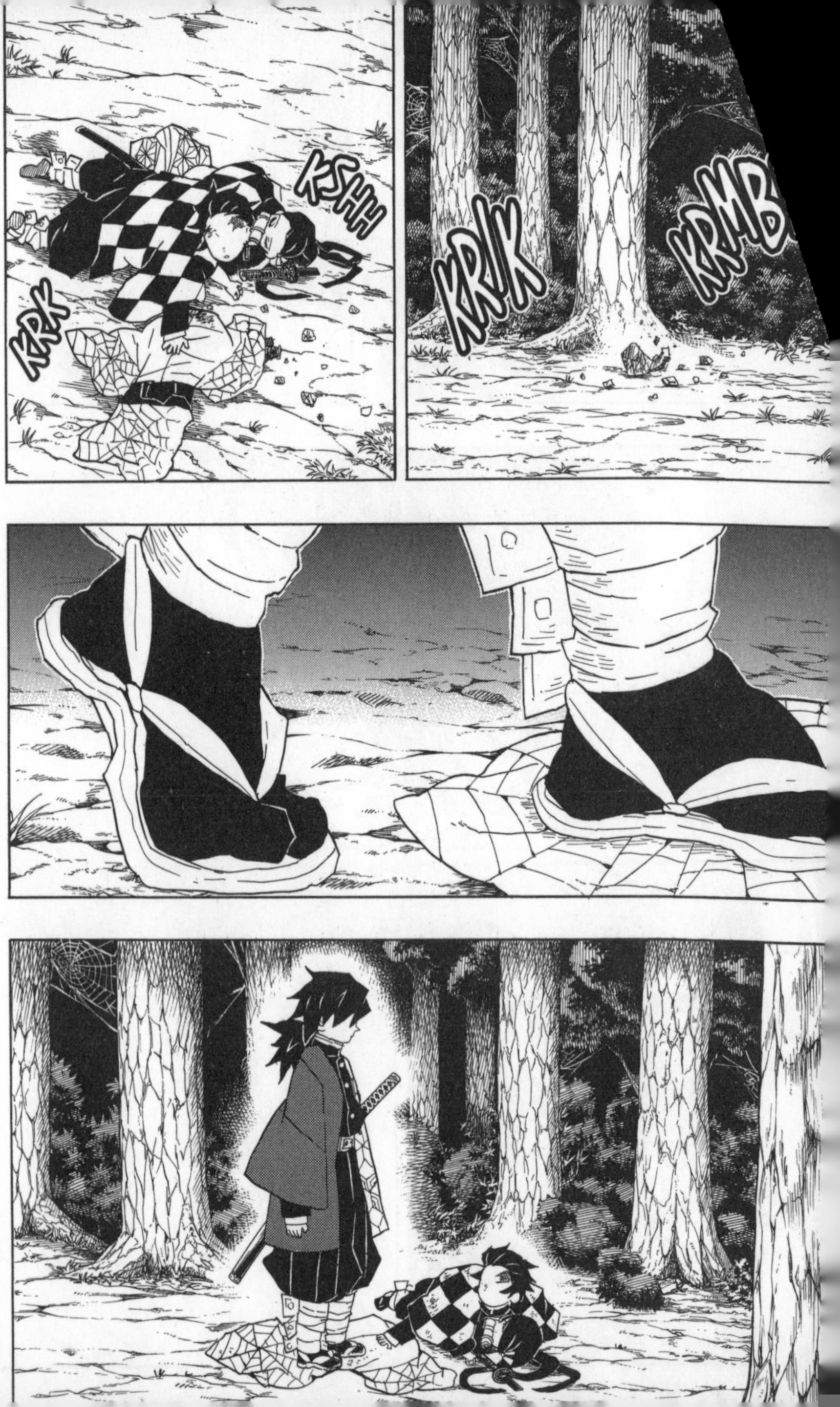
KRMB
KRIK
KSHH
KRK

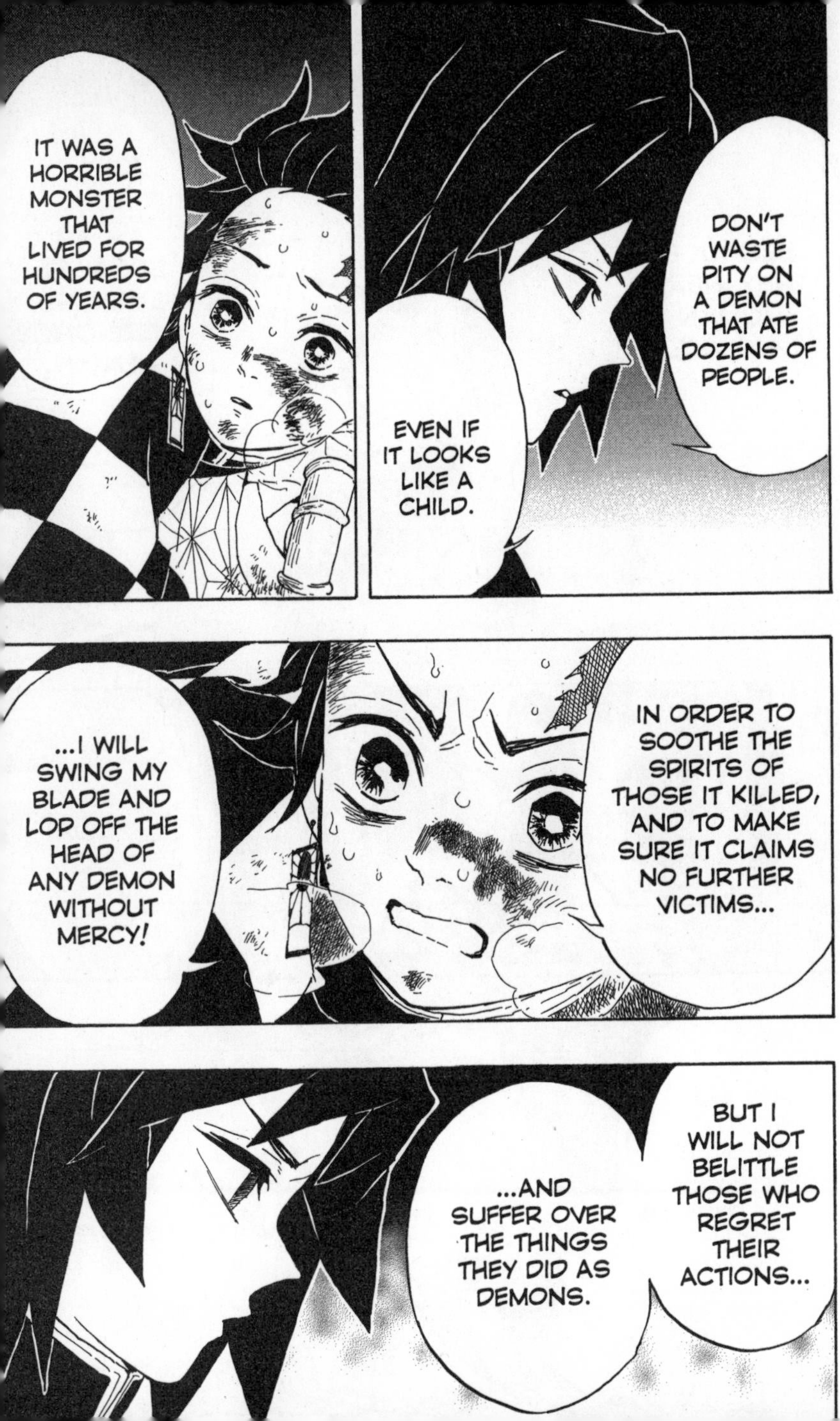
DON'T WASTE PITY ON A DEMON THAT ATE DOZENS OF PEOPLE.
EVEN IF IT LOOKS LIKE A CHILD.
IT WAS A HORRIBLE MONSTER THAT LIVED FOR HUNDREDS OF YEARS.
IN ORDER TO SOOTHE THE SPIRITS OF THOSE IT KILLED, AND TO MAKE SURE IT CLAIMS NO FURTHER VICTIMS...
...I WILL SWING MY BLADE AND LOP OFF THE HEAD OF ANY DEMON WITHOUT MERCY!
BUT I WILL NOT BELITTLE THOSE WHO REGRET THEIR ACTIONS...
...AND SUFFER OVER THE THINGS THEY DID AS DEMONS.

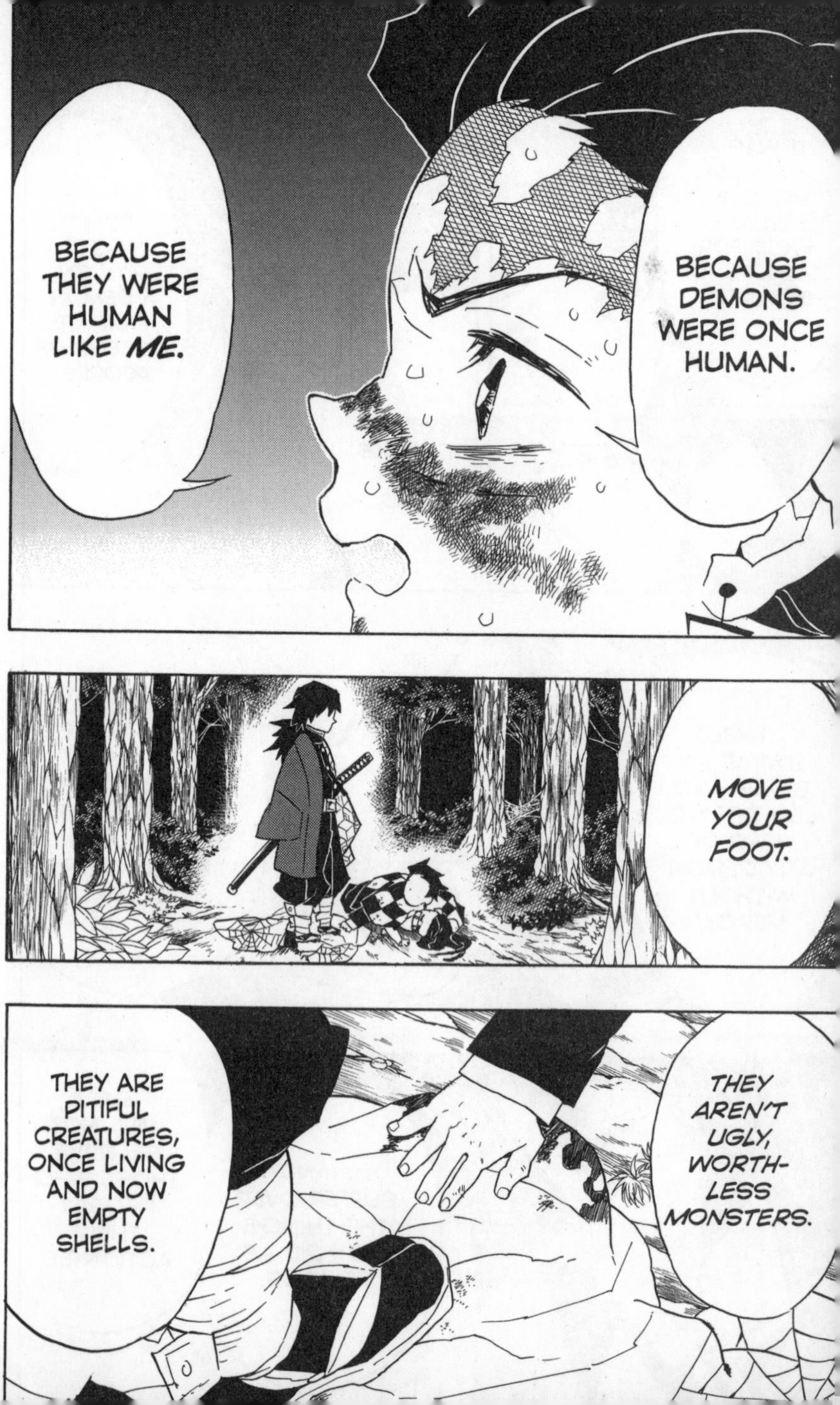
BECAUSE DEMONS WERE ONCE HUMAN.
BECAUSE THEY WERE HUMAN LIKE *ME*.
MOVE YOUR FOOT.
THEY AREN'T UGLY, WORTH-LESS MONSTERS.
THEY ARE PITIFUL CREATURES, ONCE LIVING AND NOW EMPTY SHELLS.

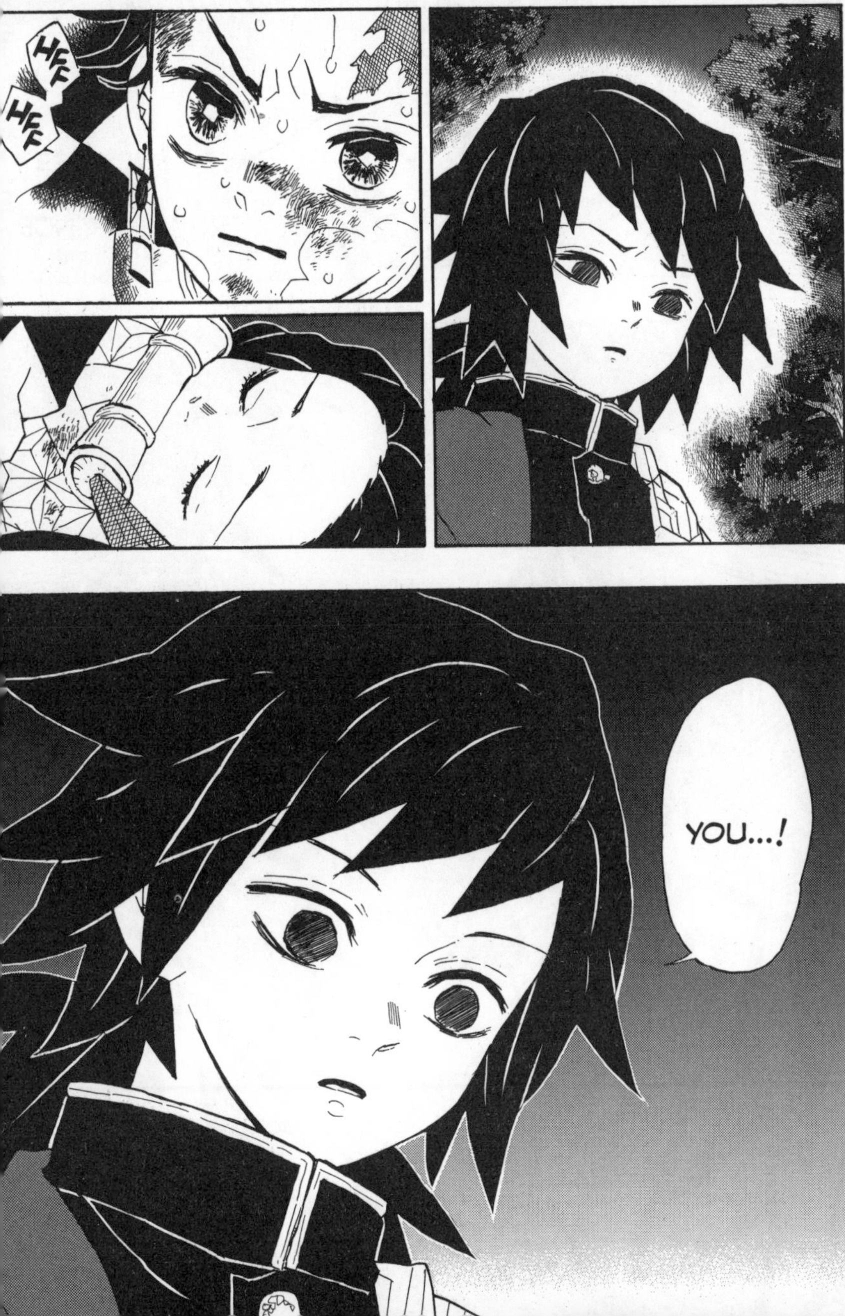
HFF
HFF
YOU...!

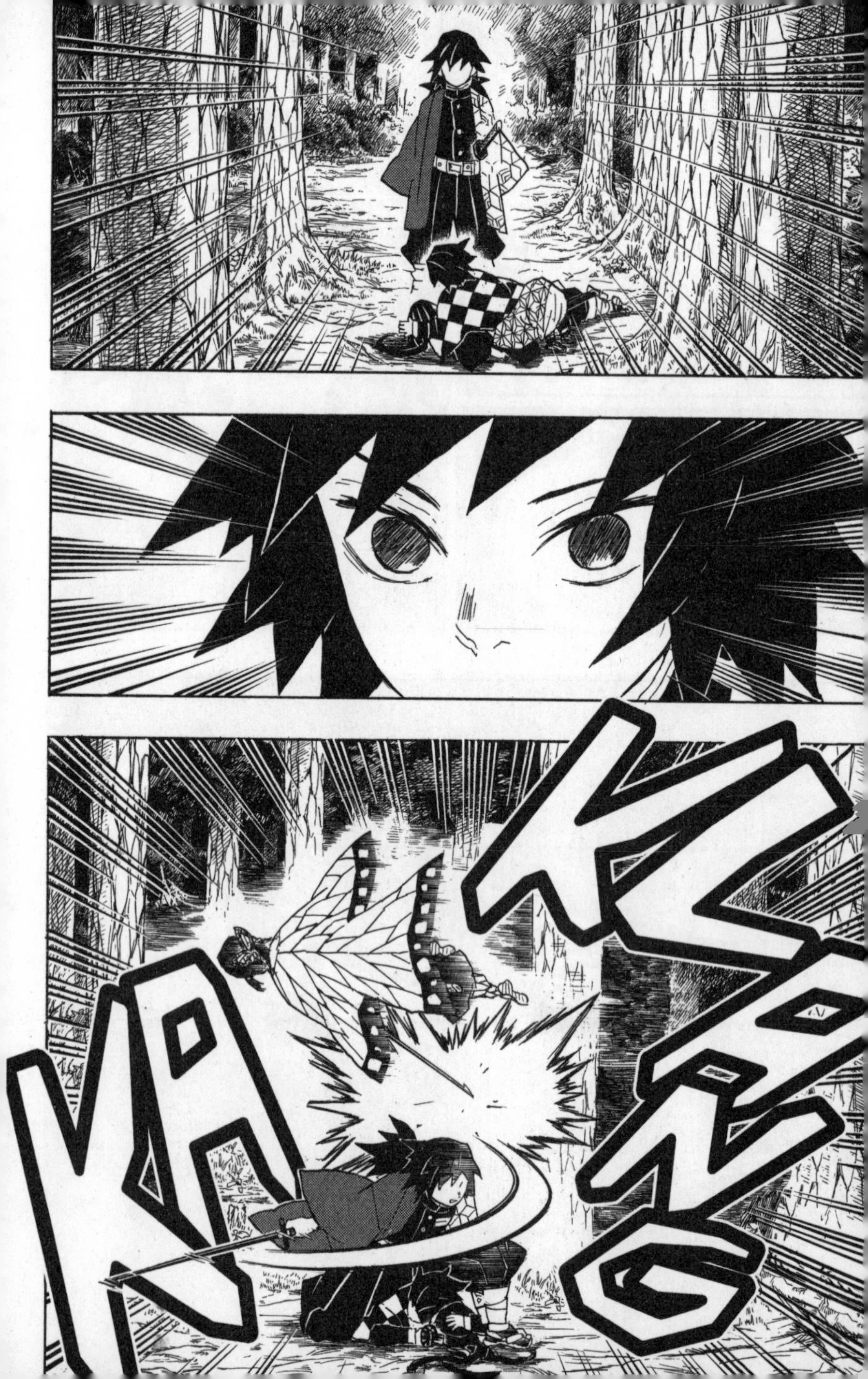
KLANG

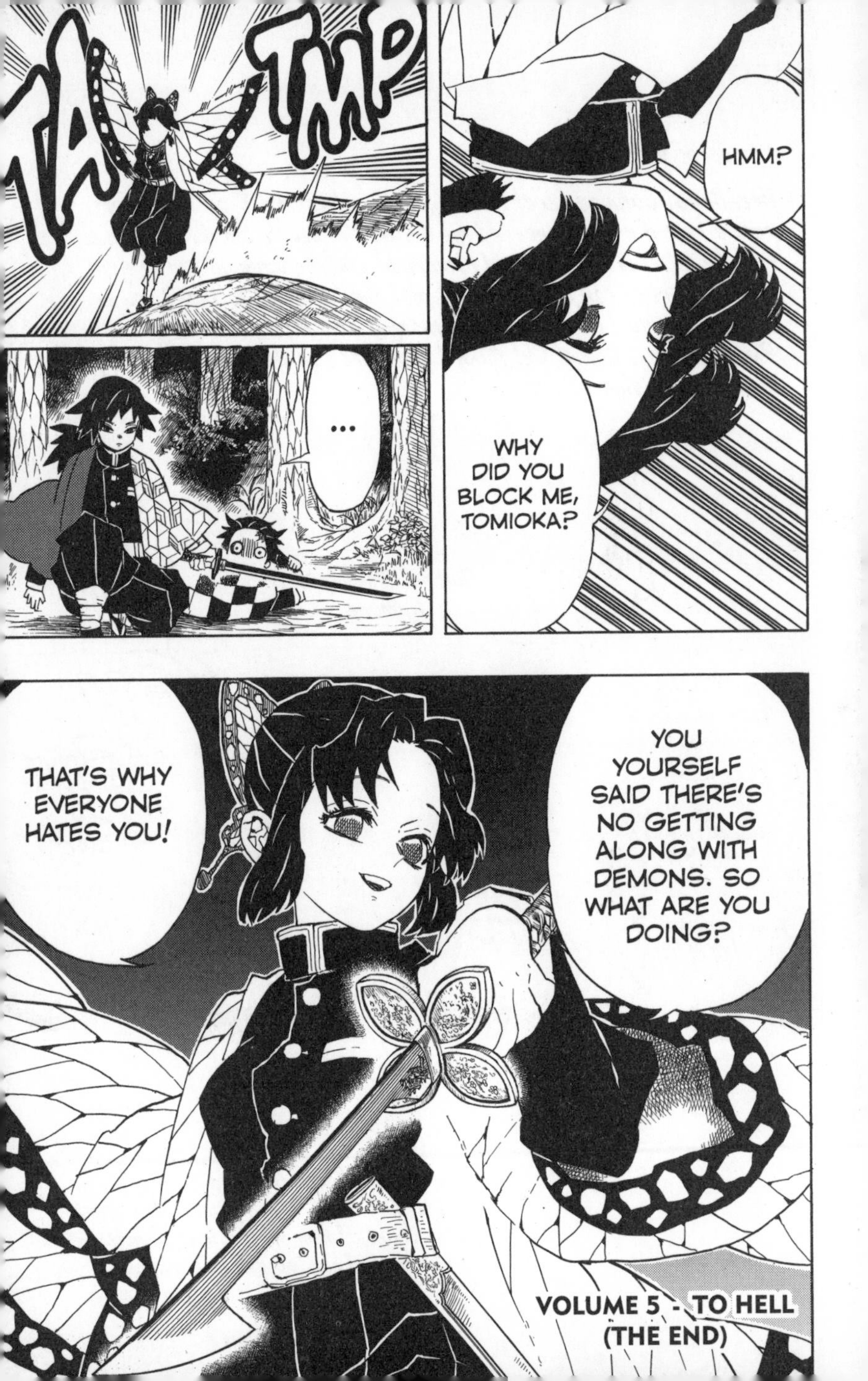
HMM?
WHY DID YOU BLOCK ME, TOMIOKA?
TMP
TA
...
YOU YOURSELF SAID THERE'S NO GETTING ALONG WITH DEMONS. SO WHAT ARE YOU DOING?
THAT'S WHY EVERYONE HATES YOU!
VOLUME 5 - TO HELL (THE END)

Words of Gratitude

Greetings! Gotouge here! I managed to get volume 5 out! Lots of people helped me and cheered me on, so I'm deeply thankful. Thanks for the letters, snacks, and handmade stuffed animals you've sent me. I'm sorry I can't reply individually. The best way to thank you is to work as hard as I can on the manga, so I hope you'll forgive me. Please stick with me! Oh! Also, I apologize for there not being many bonus pages this volume.

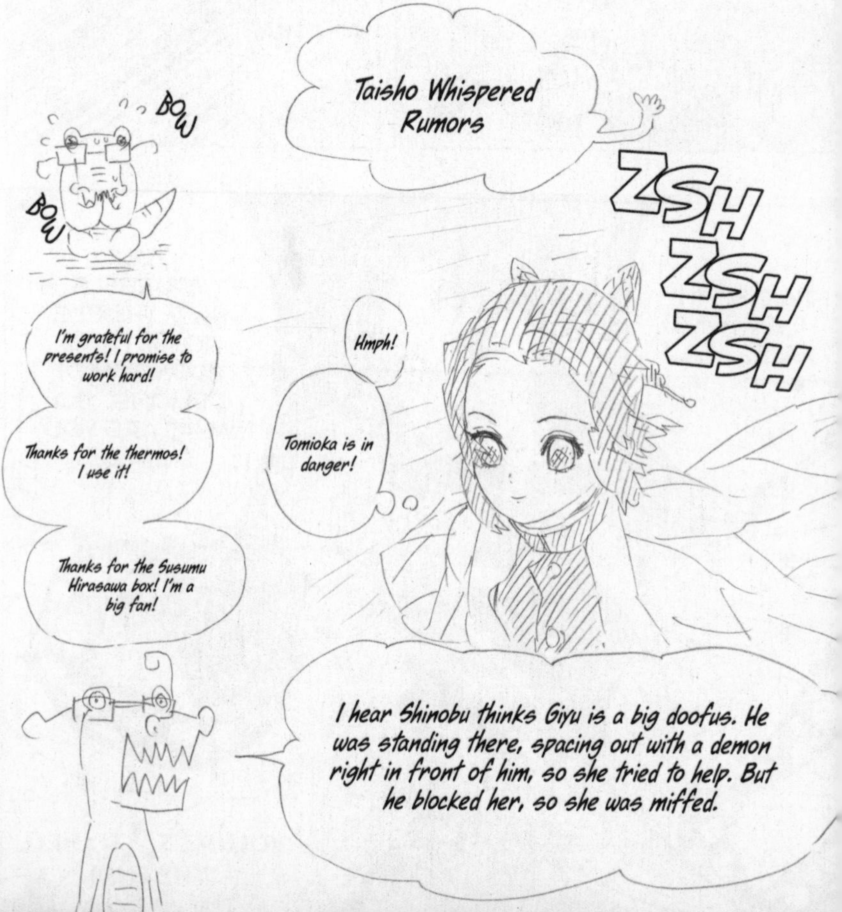
Taisho Whispered Rumors
ZSH ZSH ZSH
Hmph!
Tomioka is in danger!
BOW BOW
I'm grateful for the presents! I promise to work hard!
Thanks for the thermos! I use it!
Thanks for the Susumu Hirasawa box! I'm a big fan!
I hear Shinobu thinks Giyu is a big doofus. He was standing there, spacing out with a demon right in front of him, so she tried to help. But he blocked her, so she was miffed.

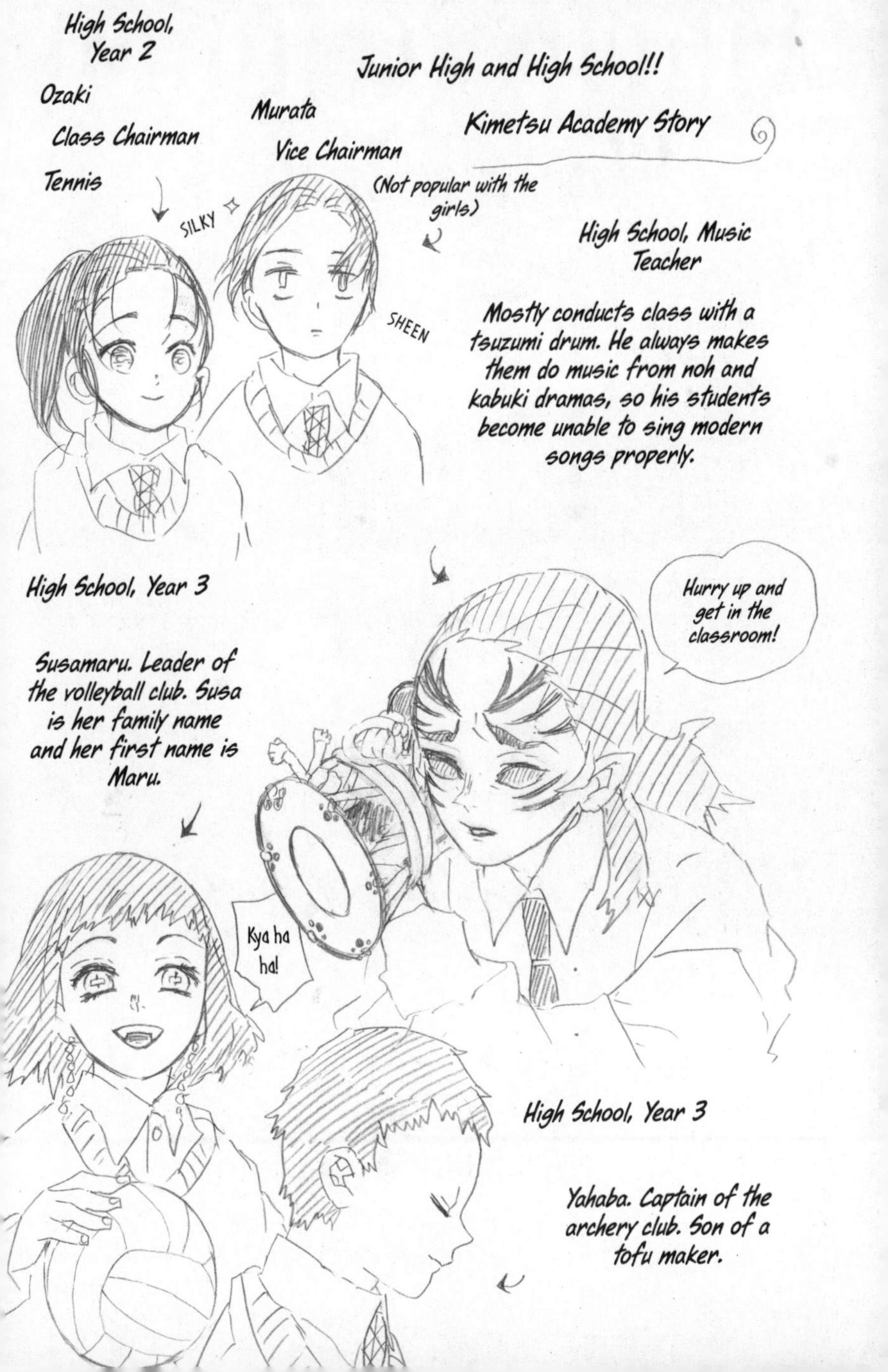

Junior High and High School!!
Kimetsu Academy Story
High School, Music Teacher
Mostly conducts class with a tsuzumi drum. He always makes them do music from noh and kabuki dramas, so his students become unable to sing modern songs properly.
Hurry up and get in the classroom!
Murata
Vice Chairman
(Not popular with the girls)
SHEEN
SILKY
High School, Year 2
Ozaki
Class Chairman
Tennis
High School, Year 3
Yahaba. Captain of the archery club. Son of a tofu maker.
Kya ha ha!
High School, Year 3
Susamaru. Leader of the volleyball club. Susa is her family name and her first name is Maru.

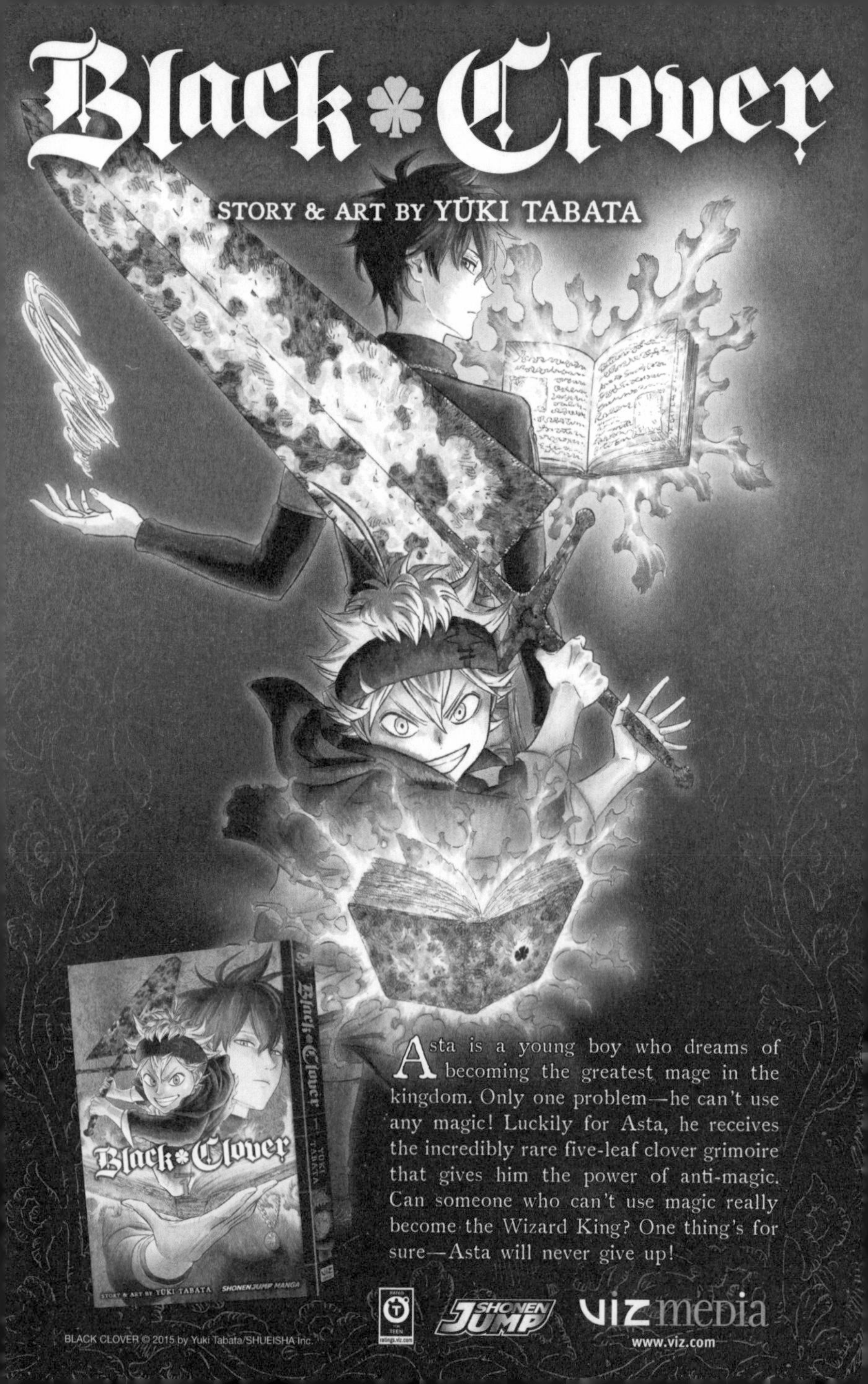
Black Clover
STORY & ART BY YŪKI TABATA
Asta is a young boy who dreams of becoming the greatest mage in the kingdom. Only one problem—he can't use any magic! Luckily for Asta, he receives the incredibly rare five-leaf clover grimoire that gives him the power of anti-magic. Can someone who can't use magic really become the Wizard King? One thing's for sure—Asta will never give up!
Black Clover
STORY & ART BY YŪKI TABATA
SHONEN JUMP MANGA
BLACK CLOVER © 2015 by Yuki Tabata/SHUEISHA Inc.
TEEN
ratings.viz.com
SHONEN JUMP
VIZ media
www.viz.com

YOU'RE READING THE
WRONG WAY!

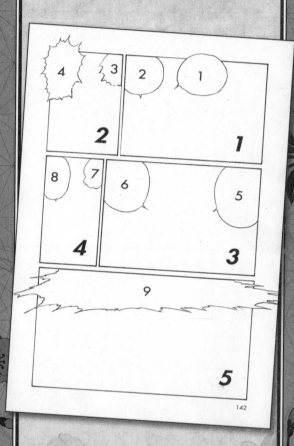

DEMON SLAYER: KIMETSU NO YAIBA
reads from right to left, starting in the
upper-right corner. Japanese is read from
right to left, meaning that action, sound
effects and word-balloon order are completely reversed from English order.